CREATIVE AND
MENTAL GROWTH

THE MACMILLAN COMPANY
NEW YORK · CHICAGO
DALLAS · ATLANTA · SAN FRANCISCO
LONDON · MANILA

IN CANADA
BRETT-MACMILLAN LTD.
GALT, ONTARIO

creative and
mental growth

3rd edition

Viktor Lowenfeld
professor of art education
the pennsylvania state university

The Macmillan Company · New York

PREFACE TO FIRST EDITION

THIS BOOK IS WRITTEN FOR ART TEACHERS—TEACHERS WHO TEACH ART, teachers and kindergarten teachers, and all who want not only to appreciate the creative production of children merely from an aesthetic viewpoint but would like to look behind the doors to see the sources from which their creative activity springs. It is written for those who want to understand the mental and emotional development of children. The idealistic concept of the child as an innate artist who has simply to get material and nothing else in order to create has done as much harm to art education as the neglect of the child's creative impulse. Books that are written from an idealistic view discourage teachers who are unable to produce the same easy and "beautiful" responses described by the writers of such books. Much of the literature in art education deals with results achieved under ideal conditions rather than with the outcomes which may be reasonably expected in the average classroom. These books are usually written by successful intuitive educators, who have the power to bring out what is in the child. They are apt to create a feeling of inferiority in teachers who do not possess this special gift and who therefore feel discouraged by the discrepancy between the results achieved in their own classroom and what is reported in these books.

Some subjects require an individual approach in teaching. The aversion shown by some educators to suggesting *any* teaching method in such fields has brought progressive art education to a point where it relies almost completely upon the mere intuitive approach, which the teacher either has or has not. Most books on art education today deal with ideal classroom situations and do not face the reality of schools with large classes and limited use of materials. The effect of such books is to provide an excuse for not using art at all rather than to use it with "insufficient" means.

It also seems to me of little use to emphasize—as has been frequently done—that the working process is of greater importance than the final outcome, without analyzing the reasons behind this opinion. Strangely enough, we see the same educators who stress this important viewpoint showing illustrations that are selected from the mere aesthetic viewpoint, thereby laying stress on the effect of the final product. "What should we do if the child does not draw large, with big motions in his uninhibited straightforwardness, as we have read the child is supposed to do?" "My children, even if I give them a large sheet of paper, draw only small." Such questions and many similar ones were asked by discouraged teachers who had read books on art education that neither presented methods nor gave an insight into the connection between the child's creative activity and his general development.

In this book an attempt has been made to show how the child's general growth is tied up with his creative development and vice versa. Creative expression is as differentiated as are individuals. This is as clearly evident in the minds of artists as it is in the minds of educators and psychologists. However, the child's creative expression during specific stages in his mental and emotional growth can only be understood and appreciated if the general causal interdependence between creation and growth is understood.

Since such an investigation necessarily cannot deal only with the analysis of individual expressions but must also be concerned with general findings, much of the discussion on the quality of the single child's work has been sacrificed to questions of general importance. Only through the understanding of these basic questions will the teacher arrive at the proper stimulation of the child during the different developmental stages. This book is an outcome of the study of many thousands of creative works over a period of more than twenty years. It tries to introduce methods which are results of the child's needs, and are therefore flexible. It attempts to give any teacher, not only art teachers, an understanding of the psychology necessary for the understanding of the child's creative production.

It is the conviction of the author that all teachers who desire to learn and understand the child's needs, thinking, and emotions should use creative expression as one of the richest sources of teaching method. In the same way that the kindergarten teacher should see the connection between the achievement of motor coordination in the child's creative work and motor coordination that is necessary for proper eating, the high-school teacher should know of the changing imaginative activity of a pre-adolescent child and an adolescent youth, an activity that commences as an unconscious approach and evolves into controlled critical awareness. For the art teacher, in particular, this book tries, by avoiding any rigid statements or methods, to present the psychological background and understanding necessary for a correct art stimulation suited to the different age levels. An attempt has been made to apply this psychological background to the practical teaching situation. Thus the connection among technique, topic, and material has been stressed and analyzed in both its emotional and mental aspects.

On the elementary-education levels, the meaning of the final product is treated in a subordinated way according to its nature. The discussion of methods of approach and the general effect of art education upon the mental growth of the child is primarily the problem during this important initial period. The reason why so many children lose their creative abilities when they approach adolescence has been discussed and analyzed. The kind of stimulation is shown that may prevent the child from stopping his creativity. During adolescence, skills become increasingly important, and the creative approach changes from an unconscious creation to one done with critical awareness. That is why it has been found necessary to include a discussion of the various techniques and their functions, as well as an analysis of the meaning of line, shape, form, color and unity.

An analysis of extreme cases usually results in a greater clarification of our common problems. For this purpose a chapter on "The Art of the Handicapped" has been included. In this chapter an attempt has been made to show the close interdependence between creative activity and mental status in extreme cases. Also the adjustive effect of art has been demonstrated by means of case histories.

In this book an attempt has been made to show methods of approach in art education based upon psychological relationships between creation and creator on the different age levels. Since these relationships cannot be bound by strict rules, the methods must necessarily be flexible. It is, however, the author's belief that as long as art is taught merely intuitively, art education is either the special province of a few privileged educators or a source of failure for the general classroom teacher.

The author owes his indebtedness to Mr. Victor E. D'Amico, director of the Educational Project of The Museum of Modern Art, New York, for providing him with a wealth of illustrative material. He is especially grateful to Miss Dorothy Knowles, secretary of the Educational Project and art educator in her own realm, for her assistance in explaining the sources and data of the illustrative material placed at the author's disposal by Mr. D'Amico. Acknowledgments are due to Dr. Marion R. Trabue, dean of the School of Education, the Pennsylvania State College, for his continued interest in the book and his encouragement, and to Dr. Willis E. Pratt, head of the Department of Education, who kindly helped to select the title of this book. Most especially is he grateful to Dr. A. Eason Monroe, director of the Reading Clinic of the Pennsylvania State College, who kindly undertook the task of putting the content into more readable English.

Viktor Lowenfeld

PREFACE TO SECOND EDITION

THE FIRST EDITION OF THIS BOOK WAS WRITTEN BECAUSE OF THE LONG-felt desire to share with others my feelings and experiences in teaching and my experiments in art. It was born out of the urge to make this world a better world to live in. Having experienced the devastating effect of rigid dogmatism and disrespect for individual differences, I know that force does not solve problems and that the basis for human relationships is usually created in the homes and kindergartens. I feel strongly that without the imposed discipline common in German family lives and schools the acceptance of totalitarianism would have been impossible. Without it, this world might have been saved from the most devastating of wars.

We are again in the midst of a world confusion. In times of such crises matters of evaluation become easily confused. What may be of value under normal conditions may become obscured under conditions of emergency. Spiritual and moral values change in times of stress. It is with this in mind that I asked The Macmillan Company to consider a new edition. I gratefully acknowledge the excellent cooperation I received. The new material, especially that on the evaluation of child growth through art, and the necessary experimentation for arriving at it, was completed long ago with the exception of some experimentation in "scribbling." For it the scribblings of 220 children were correlated with their personality characteristics obtained from case study reports.

I want to use this occasion to thank deeply the students, teachers, and audiences everywhere for their excellent cooperation and warm response, for their untiring willingness to study with me the creative and mental growth of our children. Greatly encouraged and overwhelmed by this response of the teachers in the United States and abroad to the first edition,

I felt the necessity for including important additions in a new edition of *Creative and Mental Growth.* In the second edition an attempt is made to lay a foundation for an evaluation of growth by means of creative products. It is made to give every classroom teacher an understanding of the intimate relationship between growth and creative expression. It should help to clarify the important aspect of integrative experiences in art, and should provide the teacher with a "tool" to evaluate creative products in terms of child growth. Perhaps now more than ever before it seems to me of prime significance to safeguard the free growth of our children, "to give every child a fair chance for a healthy personality." [1] This, to my feeling, is the only way to build a firm foundation for a better future. While I believe strongly in intuitive approaches in the classroom, evaluation cannot and must not depend on mere intuition.

It is with a humble feeling and the hope that the new material may help our children and youth to grow freely and creatively, to identify themselves with their own experiences and also with the needs of their neighbors and thus provide for better relationships in our society, that I present this new edition for consideration.

Viktor Lowenfeld

[1] Theme of the Midcentury White House Conference on Children and Youth, Washington, 1950.

PREFACE TO THIRD EDITION

THIS NEW AND THIRD EDITION HAS GROWN OUT OF THE AUTHOR'S
extensive contact with teachers throughout the nation and his desire to
include in the book new knowledge and the results of new experiments
and to apply them to teaching. New material has been added, mainly to the
part which deals with adolescent art, which was somewhat neglected in
the last revision. Some sections for the elementary level also have been
added and rewritten for greater clarity. On this level one of the most vital
questions deals with the effect of stereotypes, as found in coloring and
workbooks, on the creativeness of children. New experiments have been
included in an attempt to replace mere opinion with facts. The vital question of "grading" has been placed in a new chapter. Student teachers
almost everywhere go out with an idealistic concept of "self discipline";
later, in their classrooms, they find out that it does not always work.
It appeared important to include a chapter on the role of discipline.

I hope that new meaning has been added to the problem of Adolescent
Art. The understanding of the nature of visual and nonvisual art expression has received new confirmations by an entirely independent study
by W. Grey Walter, reported in this edition. While I have emphasized
again and again that visual and nonvisual forms of art expression lie on a
continuum, and that "most individuals fall between the extremes, with
a preference toward one or the other," and with overlappings of both,
distorted reference to the mere existence of pure types has been made by
some teachers and writers.

It appeared important to deal not only with the nature of adolescent
needs in terms of art expression but also of subject matter. An entirely
new outlook has been attempted in revising and reorganizing a course of

study for secondary schools. It is not meant to be used in its totality; it is thought that parts of it can be used, separated from the rest.

Finally the author feels the necessity of a positive approach to art therapy which clearly delineates the specific contribution of art education to this important field.

It is with a deep and sincere feeling of gratitude to all teachers and to my students that I offer this third edition, in the hope that it will be used flexibly and with the thought that nothing can replace the intuitive quality of a good teacher who places sensitivity to problems above knowledge and aesthetic experience above rules and who is continuously conscious of the importance of the individual child.

Viktor Lowenfeld

TABLE OF CONTENTS

CREATIVE AND
MENTAL GROWTH

CHAPTER I THE MEANING OF
ART FOR
EDUCATION

A T THE OUTSET OF A DISCUSSION ON THE MEANING OF ART FOR EDUCA-
tion, the fact should be clear in our minds that it is education in all its
mental, emotional, and spiritual implications which is largely responsible
for attitudes and actions, scientific achievements, as well as the inability
to get along in this world, and last but not least, for the five millions
of mental and emotional ills of this nation. Psychologists say that there
are only two forces which can be responsible for behavior: heredity and
environment. Yet we know from experimentation that the best seed will
not grow in a dry soil while the poorest seed, when it is well cared
for, may grow in a rich soil. It is then environment, or education in the
broadest sense, which is the main force responsible for our actions. If we
lead a rich life it is education which has sensitized us for it; if we live in a
spirit of cooperation, it is education which has in early years recognized
the need for it and thus planted the seed in us; if we live in peace with ourselves, it is education which recognized spiritual harmony as one of the
greatest contributors to life; if we, however, live in discord with ourselves,
it is also education which has neglected to emphasize emotional growth, the
ability to adjust to new situations, and thus help us solve our difficulties in

1

life; if we are dull toward all the riches which life offers, it is also education which did not develop in us the sensitivity and the spiritual responsiveness which is essential for its appreciation; if we live a selfish life it is also education which has neglected to teach one of the most essential points for cooperation, the ability to identify with the needs of others; and if we do not regard the individual as the most precious good of a democratic society, regardless of race, color or creed, education has failed in one of its most basic aspects. While education, in particular elementary education, has made tremendous progress during the last few years in shifting from a subject-matter-centered to a child-centered institution we are, as it seems, just at the beginning of a new era.

In our present educational system still everything points toward learning, which in most instances means acquiring knowledge. Yet we know too well that knowledge if it cannot be used by a free mind will neither be of benefit to the individual, nor will it be of help to society. Our one-sided education with the emphasis on knowledge has neglected those attributes of growth which are responsible for the development of the individual's sensibilities, for his spiritual life, as well as for his ability to live cooperatively in a society. The growing number of emotional and mental illnesses in this nation, the largest in any nation, as well as our inability to accept human beings first of all as human beings regardless of nationality, religion, race, creed, or color, is a frightening sign and vividly points out that education so far has failed in one of its most significant aims. While our high achievements in specialized fields, particularly in the sciences, have improved our material standards of living, they have also diverted us from those values which are responsible for our emotional and spiritual needs. They have introduced a false set of values which neglect the most inner needs of an individual. In a well-balanced educational system, in which the development of the *whole* individual is stressed, his thinking, feeling, and perceiving must be equally developed in order that the potential creative abilities of each individual can unfold. Art education, introduced in the early years of childhood may well mean the difference between a flexible, creative human being and one who, in spite of all learning, will not be able to apply it and will remain an individual who lacks inner resources and has difficulty in his relationship to the environment. Because perceiving, thinking, and feeling are equally stressed in any creative process, art may well be the necessary balance for the child's intellect and his emotions.

METHODS OF APPROACH

It should be stressed in the beginning that there is no single approach
to freeing children or adults in their creative potentialities, or to making
them more sensitive toward themselves and their environment. However, it
can be said that whatever a teacher does in stimulating creativeness greatly
depends on three factors: (1) his own personality, of which his own
creativeness, his degree of sensitivity, and flexible relationships to environment are an important part; (2) his ability to put himself into the place
of others, and (3) his understanding and knowledge of the needs of those
whom he is teaching. It is quite impossible to say that any one approach—
may it be given the best sounding name—is good for all. At one time it
may be better to have the children divided in groups working on group
projects, at another simultaneously with different materials in one classroom, or individually on the same motivation. This all depends on individual needs. Every sensitive teacher feels when his group is keyed up to
one experience through which his whole group has just gone. At that time
it would not only be quite out of place but superficial to divide the group
into smaller groups and "motivate" them to work with different materials.
Let us be clear that our task is to help individuals in their identification
with their own selves and stimulate creativeness with whatever methods it
can most effectively be done. For the same reason it would be quite ineffec-
tive or even frustrating to use group approaches if the individual either
feels the group is interfering with his own individual mode of expression
or if he cannot conceive of group work, if he is not ready for it. It must
always be kept in mind that the child's needs change and that the teacher
must adjust to these changing needs.

I have often been asked whether children are not restricted in their
creativeness when the teacher is using classroom motivations, that is,
when the whole group is motivated simultaneously by one experience. We
have clearly to differentiate between content or subject matter and mode
of expression. As long as the child has the freedom to use his *own* mode
of expression, his creativeness remains free. On the contrary, it has experimentally been proven that a motivation is not always most effective when
given individually. Every teacher knows how a classroom motivation can
become "contagious," getting hold of all children, much as a football
game with a large attendance. The best game with poor attendance may
be little exciting. Indeed, it has been established that the same motivations

may have different effects under different circumstances and treatment.[1] The teaching situation as well as the need of the children should always be the decisive factor in choosing the method of approach, for it is the effect which the creative process has on the child and not the final product which is of decisive significance.

EFFECT OF THE CREATIVE PROCESS

Recent experimentations in finding attributes which are responsible for *general* creativeness in individuals have revealed that they are the same attributes as found in any creative art process. Vice versa, it can then be said that creative art processes stimulate creativeness in general.[2] This very important fact shows vividly the significance of art education in a democratic society. It is here that the philosophy in Art Education distinctly differs from the so-called Fine Arts. Whereas the emphasis in art education is on the effect which creative processes have on individuals, the sensitivity derived from aesthetic experiences, it is the aesthetic product which is of importance in the Fine Arts. It is needless to say that, with the improved creativeness of an individual, his greater sensitivity toward experiences, and his increased ability to integrate them, the quality of his aesthetic product will grow. A one-room school teacher in one of my classes identified so closely with the mural she painted that it became very difficult for her to part with it. She identified herself with each of her children, whom she so meaningfully depicted in her naïve manner. For her the mural was as significant as the Sistine Chapel may have been for Michelangelo. It is this relative significance which is decisive for growth and thus for art education. It should then be clearly stated that in art education art is used only

---

[1] McVitty, L. F., "An Experimental Study on Various Methods in Art Motivations." Unpublished doctoral dissertation, The Pennsylvania State University, 1954.

[2] Dr. J. P. Guilford [3] and his staff at the University of Southern California have been working under a Naval grant on a factor analytical study to find out the criteria of creativity which significantly differentiate between creative and less creative people. This investigation is based on subjects belonging to the exact and applied sciences. In an entirely independent study, Dr. W. Lambert Brittain [4] did extensive research in finding criteria of creativity which significantly differentiate between highly creative people in the visual arts and those who were less or not creative. The significant factor of the two entirely independent studies, with entirely different experimental groups, testing the same phenomena, but for different purposes, is that they arrived at almost exactly the same criteria of creativity. A study by Dr. Kenneth Beittel conclusively revealed that the two tests significantly correlate. Thus, it appears that, according to the data available and under the conditions tested, creativity regardless of where it is applied, has common attributes.

[3] Guilford, J. P., "Creativity," *American Psychologist,* 1950, 9, pp. 444–454.

[4] Brittain, W. Lambert, "Can Creativity be Measured," Research Yearbook, National Art Education Assoc., 1956; and an unpublished doctoral dissertation, The Pennsylvania State University, 1952.

as a means to an end and not as an end in itself. It is the aim of art education to use the creative process to make people more creative regardless of
where this creativeness will be applied. If Johnny grows up and through
his aesthetic experiences has become a more creative person who will apply
it to his living and to his profession, one of the main aims of art education
will have been fulfilled.

In order to understand the effect of the creative process on the child,
and how the various components of growth are part and parcel of it, let
us try actually to find out what goes on in Johnny's mind while he is busy
creating, in this case, a painting. It is needless to say that neither quality
nor intensity of the creative process depends on the material used.

First of all, when he begins he must think of "something." Often this
"something" seems to us insignificant. For the child, however, it always
means a confrontation with his own self, with his own experience. Some
children cannot think of "something" because they either lack sensitive
relationships to meaningful experiences or their minds are blocked and go
around in circles. If they lack sensitive experiences, they need to be motivated. If their minds are blocked and move around in stereotypes, *their
frame of reference needs to be extended.*

THE IMPORTANT PRINCIPLE OF EXTENDING
THE FRAME OF REFERENCE

The extension of the frame of reference constitutes one of the most
important principles in art education, or indeed, in education in general.
To extend the frame of reference implies that we have always to start on
the level of the individual and have to extend the child's thinking, feeling
and perceiving on *his* level and the stage of *his* development. If, for instance, Mary scribbles small in a corner of her paper, it would be useless to
tell her to scribble larger, or to cover the whole paper. Such suggestions
would not enhance in her the freedom necessary for larger motions, nor
would it permit her to discover the meaningfulness of the paper which
is at her disposal. For that her frame of reference for motions needs to be
enlarged; that is, the scribbling motion has to be extended to a more
meaningful motion, the area on the paper to other more meaningful areas.
In this case one could ask Mary, "Have you been in a skating rink?"—
"Suppose you have the whole space for yourself, would you only skate in
the corner?"—"Show me how you would skate."—"Suppose the sheet of
paper is your skating rink. Let's skate with our crayon on it." One motion
has been referred to another more meaningful motion and has thus

achieved greater significance. One area has been related to another area in relationship to an experience more meaningful to the child than obviously scribbling has been. This extension of the frame of reference has sensitized the child both to his own motions as well as to the meaningfulness of the drawing area. Obviously only meaningful experiences will be effective.

"My child only draws airplanes"—"My child only draws guns," etc. These are remarks which we continually hear, both from parents and teachers. "Don't draw these silly guns!" would obviously not contribute to the child's greater flexibility and understanding of his environment. On the contrary, it may for the moment deprive him of his need for security which he obviously found in such repetitive statements. To repeat the same thing over and over merely expresses the child's inability to adjust to new situations. For him his stereotype repetition constitutes an escape, which he always uses whenever he cannot face a new situation. This is also true for children who go into a tantrum, which also represents an escape mechanism, which the child introduces whenever he is unable to adjust to a new situation. Mary may be peacefully playing with her doll, when you suddenly interrupt her and tell her that her time is over and that she has to go to bed. Because Mary cannot adjust quickly to the new situation she may escape into a tantrum. There is nothing easier than to condition her gradually to what will come and thus prevent such a quick and drastic adjustment. "Mary, will your doll soon go to sleep? You know that soon you will have to go to bed, too." This can be repeated, depending on the adjustability of the child, until the "final step" no longer will represent a decisive change. In art education such conditioning to a new situation often constitutes an important part of the motivation, especially for the extension of the child's frame of reference. If Johnny draws airplanes only, the important fact is to make the airplane *meaningful,* to make it "alive," by extending the child's frame of reference. Again we have to start on the level of the child. If the child drew all airplanes alike, it would already be a discovery for the child to distinguish between big and small planes. "Where does your plane fly?"—"High above ground or low?"—"Does it fly through clouds?"—"Where does it land?"—"Where do people get out?" To make the plane and its environment meaningful to the child presumes that the teacher also has to identify with the child's needs in particular in his relations and feelings for airplanes. In this way he has extended the frame of reference from the child's stereotype meaningless airplane-symbol to an expression of a meaningful variety of airplanes; from a meaningless background area to a meaningful space which has become part of the child's experience. It is needless to say that diverting the child from his problem by making him do different things in different materials will not help him. It has been proven that diversion may only add to his frustration. If he is "fixed" on airplanes their meaningfulness, however, can also be improved by an extension to another material, that is, from drawing to three-dimensional form. The new and fresh approach in new materials may often break down old established stereotypes.

Fortunately most of our children are free and not bound up with stereotypes. Johnny, for instance, *can* think of something, because he has experienced something. As he "thinks" of it, his thoughts concentrate on the experience to be painted. His thought process, the ability to think for himself and concentrate on something, becomes stimulated. This initial intellectual process is an important part in creative activities. It is self-evident that he will include only those things which he knows and which are important to him. Important to him, however, are only those things to which he has established some more or less sensitive relationship. Thus his emotional relationship will be an important part in his creative process. Let us say that Johnny wants to paint "how he plays with other children in the yard." For Johnny, the apple tree in the yard may have big buds because he was watching them grow. He includes the buds in his painting because they are important to him. They are part of his knowledge, his observation, and his experience. Bob was using the tree only for climbing; buds had no meaning and were therefore not included in his painting. Johnny was interested in Mary's dress. He likes Mary. His painting indicates more details on Mary than elsewhere. He paints Mary much larger than anything else, because she is important to him. His painting, like that of all children, is not an objective representation. On the contrary, it expresses his likes and dislikes, his emotional relationships to his own world and the world which surrounds him. It also expresses not only what he knows, but also what he feels, sees, and touches, if he has become sensitively aware of it.

In order to understand this fully, let us go back to our own experiences. We, too, can only recall things to the extent to which either our knowledge or our individual emotional relationships permit us. Let us think, for instance, of a traffic light. We all know that it consists of three different colored lights. Our knowledge has registered that. We will, however, not be so sure with regard to the location of the colors if we have not become sensitized to them. Is the green light on top, or the red? Only the degree of intensity with which we have observed it, will be responsible for our recalling it. Once we have become sensitized toward this particular location by conscious observation, that is, by seeing in detail, we shall incorporate this newly gained relationship into our permanent understanding. Such more sensitive relationships can, however, be fostered by experience which we have with things. If we, for instance, were color-blind, we would have to depend on the location of the lights, and would very soon have to become aware of the red light on the top. If we had to install the lights, we too would by necessity have to become aware of their location. But also emotional experience with things will intensify our relationships to environment. It is not the same whether we experience the vastness of the sea with an underlying feeling of loneliness, all by ourselves, or accompanied by the noise of countless people happily splashing in the oncoming waves. Needless to say, the more sensitive relationships we establish toward experiences in general, the richer is our life, for what is true about the traffic light is also true about flowers, trees, textures, colors, and all that surrounds us.

Johnny, therefore, has given us an intimate understanding, through his painting, of the type of relationships which he has established to the things he represented. Of course, as he grows, these relationships change. He will know more about things, and his emotional interest will also shift. The greater the variety in his paintings, the more flexible will he be in his relationships and vice versa. *It must, however, be remembered that it is one of the most important tasks of the teacher continually to encourage and motivate sensitive, rich, and flexible relationships.*

As Johnny continues to paint his backyard scene, he adds things according to the significance they have to him. Perhaps the swings on the apple tree come first to his mind. He loves to swing on them. But there is Bob. Johnny does not like him because he always teases him. So, according to his likes and dislikes in color and placement, he gives expression to his dislike for Bob in his painting. Johnny is weaker than Bob; he can never show his dislike directly, but in his painting he can. He feels better afterwards, just as we feel better after we have talked about a disagreeable thing with a good friend. It bothers us to keep things all to ourselves, to have them "eat into us."

It is needless to say that everything that Johnny does and to which he is exposed has some influence upon him. If he in his creative work continually attempts to relate all his experiences, such as thinking, feeling, perceiving (seeing, touching, and so on), to one another, it must also have a unifying effect on his personality. This has been established experimentally, at least by implication.[5]

As Johnny goes on to paint his back yard picture, he includes Rowdy, his dog, and also Dad, who fixes the fence. Rowdy is digging a hole in the

[5] See page 37.

lawn. Johnny is quite aware that this may spoil the lawn, and Dad does not like it. Dad fixes the fence; Johnny could not draw Dad without putting himself into his place while fixing the fence. This makes him better understand Dad. He even thinks how Dad lifts the heavy hammer to drive the post into the ground. Dad must be strong. It is one of the important attributes of any creative process that we become more sensitive to things with which we are dealing. If Johnny thinks of his environment more sensitively, he has been taught to do one of the most important things that we need in the world today—*to become more sensitive to the needs of others*. This is one of the most vital prerequisites for a cooperative attitude. In putting himself into the place of Dad in his picture, Johnny has just experienced this vital need.

Johnny not only becomes more sensitive to the things he paints, he also develops a great sensitivity to the materials he uses. He learns by experience that the lines of a crayon are different if he puts different pressure on it, that he can use the broad side of the crayon, that water color merges easily and produces beautiful mixtures—all this he learns by trial and error, and soon incorporates it into his painting. To discover and explore *what different art materials can do,* "to learn their behavior" is one of the important trends which the child develops through creative activities. Johnny even learns to predict their behavior; he knows exactly how much he can bend wood, what he can do with wire, what colors to mix in order to get the one he wants. He has become *so sensitive* to the reactions of paint that he uses great skills in handling them. This development of skill which is only a result of the urge for expression is also a vital part of the creative process.

When Johnny began to paint his back yard picture, he had to decide where to put the tree, the swings, the fence, Mary, Dad, Rowdy, and Bob. Thus, he had to "organize" all these things meaningfully. What he knew of the tree, the swing, Mary, the fence, and Dad, and Bob, had to be related to how he felt about these things, and this had to be related to the location of the things on the paper. He also gave some definite color and shape to the objects which he painted. He had to invent and explore his forms in relationship to the material he used. It is needless to say that all this organization takes place in the child subconsciously. But it all belongs to Johnny's personality, and is part and parcel of the creative process and the resulting aesthetic product, for aesthetic growth consists of the growth from a chaotic to a harmonious organization of expression in which feeling, perceiving, and thinking are completely integrated.

Virginia, for instance, cannot express herself as flexibly as Johnny. She is tense and has developed a certain emotional inflexibility. She cannot meet new situations, as Johnny does. Her mind does not adjust as easily to her environment and therefore she has established a certain sameness of reactions. She always draws the same kinds of patterns. Her mind is fixed on one thing—and this she keeps repeating. This repetition gives her a certain security. She knows she can repeat it again and again. She also knows that she does not need to meet new situations when she draws. It is a false security into which she escapes whenever she cannot do justice to a situation.

Johnny through his continued art motivations could adjust flexibly to any situation which he was facing. During the creative process he not only used his intellect in finding out about the tree, the swing, the fence, Rowdy, Dad, and the other things, but he gave expression to his emotional relationships to Mary, his dog, and even the tree, because he loved to climb it. He observed the buds, Mary's dress, and became more sensitive to his environment. He independently created his own forms and concepts. By putting himself in the place of others he learned the needs of others; by using his art material sensitively he actually learned to identify with its "behavior"; both are important parts of social growth. By organizing all his experiences into a creative product he integrated all these experiences into a total inseparable whole, the aesthetic product.

The great contribution of art education to our educational system and to our society is the emphasis on the individual and his *own* potential creative abilities, and above all the power of art to integrate harmoniously all the components of growth which are responsible for a well-balanced human being. As Johnny painted his back yard scene, he first had to become aware of what to include in it. This intellectual awareness of himself and his environment is an important part of intellectual growth. As he expressed his *likes* in Mary and his *dislikes* in Bob, his *affection* and *fears* for Rowdy, he documented his *emotional* relationship to his environment. But as he faces it he learns to *adjust* to it. Thus he engages in one of the most important aspects of *emotional growth.* He could never have depicted Dad, fixing the fence, without *putting himself in his place. To identify with the needs of others,* however, is one of the most important prerequisites for cooperation, for social growth. Johnny *observed* the buds, the trees, the texture of Mary's dress. He became sensitive to the differences in color in his painting. His perceptual growth has become stimulated by the creative process. Even physically he felt the urge to coordinate his hands with his vision. But it was through his aesthetic product that he showed his ability to organize harmoniously his thinking, feeling, and perceiving, and most of all he independently created his own concepts of himself and the world which surrounds him. He explored, investigated and experimented with his media of expression. Johnny is different from Virginia and so is his creative expression.

Because every creative process involves the *whole* child and not only a single segment of him, art education may well become the catalyst for a child-centered education in which the individual and his creative potentialities are placed above subject matter; in which his inner equilibrium may be considered as important as his scientific achievements.

For our children, however, art should become their friend to whom they turn with their joys and sorrows, their fears and frustrations, whenever words become inadequate. It is needless to say that through such experiences his art expression becomes "an integral part of the whole stream of his living." [6]

[6] Barkan, Manuel, *A Foundation for Art Education*. New York: The Ronald Press Company, 1955.

THE MEANING OF CREATIVE ACTIVITY IN ELEMENTARY EDUCATION

INTRODUCTION

IF CHILDREN DEVELOPED WITHOUT ANY INTERFERENCE FROM THE OUT-side world, no special stimulation for their creative work would be necessary. Every child would use his deeply rooted creative impulse without inhibition, confident in his own kind of expression. We find this creative confidence clearly demonstrated by those people who live in the remote sections of our country and who have not been inhibited by the influences of advertisements, funny books, and "education." Among these folk are found the most beautiful, natural, and clearest examples of children's art. What civilization has buried we must try to regain by recreating the natural base necessary for such free creation. Whenever we hear children say, "I can't draw that," we can be sure that some kind of interference has occurred in their lives. No Eskimo child would express such lack of confidence. These interferences might come from anywhere. To provide children with the kinds of stimulation necessary for their creative growth, it is important to examine some of the interferences that thwart such growth.

For the child, art is not the same as it is for the adult. Art for the child is merely a means of expression. Since the child's thinking is different from

12

that of the adult's, his expression must also be different. Out of this discrepancy between the adult's "taste" and the way in which a child expresses himself arises most of the difficulties and interferences in art teaching. I have seen and heard educators, intrigued by the beauty of children's drawings and paintings, asking for the "right" proportions and "good" color schemes. The child sees the world differently from the way he draws it. Precisely from our analysis of this discrepancy between the representation and the thing represented do we gain insight into the child's real experience. Therefore it is easy to understand that *any* correction by the teacher which refers to reality and not to the child's experience interferes greatly with the child's own expression. This interference starts perhaps when children scribble and eager parents expect to see something that fits their own adult conception. How ridiculous to overpower these little children's souls!

The seriousness of the problem of providing the appropriate stimulation every child needs for his work is illustrated by two typical case histories which follow:

The first is an example of the youngster who says, "I can't draw." The boy was completely incapable of (or better, inhibited from) producing any kind of picture. He did not want to draw a line. Under no circumstances could he be brought to use visual percepts. The child made a very nervous and unfree impression. His mother told me that he usually came home from school without speaking or telling anything of his experiences. He was very inhibited in his bodily movements. He had no friends at all.

Since nothing else availed, it occurred to me to try to distract his attention altogether from visual impressions, and I asked him to control his images by bodily feelings, which I emphasized by the choice of the topics. The stress was laid upon what the boy was doing and what he felt while doing it. The boy began to draw, and the more he drew, the more he drew out of proportion. He emphasized his experiences in proportions of value rather than in proportions of actual physical objects. At the same time, his mother reported that the boy had changed considerably, that he had begun to speak freely, that he was no longer shut in, that his nervousness had diminished, and that even his body movements were freer.

I investigated this case more closely and found that this child, the child of a teacher, had been influenced repeatedly to copy nature, to draw "beautifully" in correct proportions. Such an influence, which came in this case from the father, who wanted to see "good" and "nice" pictures and not the drawings of a child, had stifled the imagination of the child and diverted it into visual, rather than personal experiences. As the child learned that he could not draw as his father required (mothers usually have more instinct), he lost confidence in his creations and stopped his work. This loss of self-confidence inhibited the child as a whole. Encouraged to return to his own individual way of expression through the stimulation of his bodily feelings, the child found again his confidence in his own creations and his whole personality. What can we learn from this case? *Don't impose your own images on a child!* All modes of expression but the child's own are foreign to him. We should neither influence nor stimulate the child's imagination in any direction which is not appropriate to his thinking and perception. The child has his own world of experiences and expression.

The second case illustrates another way in which family influences upon art education may be unfortunate—the case of a brother and sister. The girl was very gifted; the boy just average. The girl, who was a very bright child, was always the favorite in the family; the boy was neglected. The girl drew very well. The boy, who could not draw as well as his sister, began to imitate her by taking over the same kind of representation his sister used in her drawings. He hoped this could be a way of getting the attention of his parents, as his sister got it with the same means. The boy became more and more bound up with a kind of representation that was not at all in accord with his own experience. It was as though he tried to speak a language that he was not able to understand. Whereas his sister was happy in creating new forms and thoughts, his anxiety to copy his sister prevented him from living his own life. So the child grew more and more sick mentally as well as emotionally. When he came home, he would throw himself on his bed and cry. His mother could not discover the reason. The child became extremely introverted. In this stage his mother brought the child to me. With my help, the boy returned to his former kind of expression and found again his own manner of representation, which I appreciated in the same way as I did that of his sister. Having found self-confidence in his own creations, the child grew happier, lost all the signs of disturbance, and was quite changed. The parents, very happy about this result (which required seven months to achieve) learned the correct way of showing their appreciation for both children.

What can we learn from this case? We see that through the efforts this boy made to compensate for his feelings of inferiority, he grew more and more fixed on a kind of representation that was not the expression of his own experiences. This fixation on strange expressions finally stopped the whole mental development of the child! Therefore, *never prefer one child's creative work over that of another!* Never give the work of one child as an example to another! *Never let a child copy anything!* This case exposes also the very devastating effect of the numerous color books which our children still get in school for the sake of "developing a sense of color," but which in reality inhibit their free creative development.

After this short introduction, the double function of art in the elementary-school classroom as self-expression and as a means of self-adjustment appears evident.

THE NATURE OF IMITATION

The difference in the meaning of imitation has created misunderstandings. Psychologists as well as educators agree that imitation is an important factor in learning. It is needless to say that one of the most important means of communication—language—is initially conceived by imitation. The importance of imitation as a means of learning, therefore, cannot be overlooked. Yet, if we would remain on the level of mere imitation, language would only become the repetition of words and man would go down to the level of a parrot, who repeats words without understanding their meaning or without any intent to express something. Imitation, when learning a language, is used with the aim to express oneself and to communicate with others. Indeed, *imitation in any learning situation is only used as a means to an end* and never as an end in itself. In using imitative means then, it is educationally important that teachers become aware of how imitation is used. As self-evident as this may appear, much confusion has been created by "methods" which promote "learning" in one direction but degrade the child to parrot-like imitation in the other. The child is not sliced into subject matters, but learns as a whole. What influences him in arithmetic may be seen in his art expression and vice versa. If the child becomes inhibited in one area it may be felt in the other.

THE EFFECT OF STEREOTYPED WORKBOOKS AND COLORING BOOKS ON CHILDREN

Certain workbooks commonly used in arithmetic and reading confront the child with the task of repeating the same concept again and again. "Add six birds to the three—how many do you have?" In promoting a "number concept" by using stereotypes the child may become inhibited creatively. In talking with me one of the authors of such a workbook defended his method by saying, "I am only interested in promoting better arithmetic—I don't know anything about art." My answer was that I am talking about the child and neither of art nor of arithmetic. The confusion lies between a subject-matter-centered and a child-centered method of teaching.

Research has experimentally proven that such imitative methods have a detrimental effect on the child's creativeness.[1] As one of the many examples, according to a commonly used arithmetic workbook, a child has to draw 76 repetitions of a stereotype of a rabbit, 88 of a bird, 62 of a kite, 80 of a balloon, 36 of a cat, etc. Such repetitions of concepts foreign to the child's own concept not only regiment the child into one type of representation, but deprive him of the expression of his own relationship to the representation. According to the experiments of Russell and Waugaman, 63 per cent of all children who had been motivated by experiences with birds lost their initially established sensitivity to them and changed their concepts to resemble the stereotype. (See Fig. 1a,b,c.) This is a devastating result of the influence of workbook methods. It is needless to say that such procedures are in complete disagreement with democratic methods of learning, for they completely neglect individual expression.

In order to understand the effect on children of coloring and workbooks which contain such repetitive stereotype forms, let us go through the process a child goes through while using them, and let us also find out the after-effect this process may have on our children.

Let us assume that the first picture the child has to fill in is that of a dog. As soon as the child is confronted with the task of following a predetermined outline, we have prevented him from solving his own relationships creatively. His relationship to a dog may be one of love, friendship, dislike, or fear. There is no opportunity for him to express his relationship and thus relieve himself of tensions of joy, hatred, or fear. There is no place in coloring books to express anxieties. There is not even a place for the individual differences of Johnny and Mary. In filling the outline drawings, they are regimented into the same type of activity, with no provision for their differences as individuals. Of course, some children, unaware of all these implications, and by nature somewhat lazy, enjoy coloring the dog; but as they color it with crayon they realize that they could never draw a dog as well as the one they are coloring. They may even be very proud when they are through with their activity. After all, they have colored the dog. Next time, in school or elsewhere, when one of these children is asked

[1] Russell, Irene, and Waugaman, Blanche, "A Study of the Effect of Workbook Copy Experiences on the Creative Concepts of Children." *Research Bulletin,* The Eastern Arts Assoc., Vol. 3, No. 1, 1952; Heilman, Horace, "The Effect of Workbook Stereotypes on the Creativeness of Children." Unpublished doctoral dissertation, The Pennsylvania State University, 1954.

a

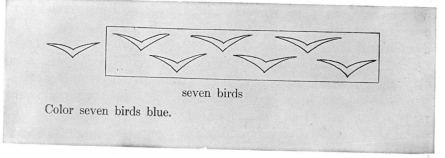

seven birds

Color seven birds blue.

b

c

Fig. 1. Effect of coloring books on a child's creative expression. (Courtesy Dr. Irene Russell, *Research Bulletin,* The Eastern Arts Association, Vol. 3, No. 1, 1952.)

a). A child's expression before he was exposed to coloring books.

b). Coloring book illustration which the child had to copy.

c). After copying from coloring books, the child lost his sensitivity, as shown in drawing.

to draw something, he remembers the dog in the coloring book. Realizing that he could not compete, he says, quite logically, "I can't draw."

I have heard many teachers or parents say, "But my children love coloring books." This is quite true. Children in general, however, do not discriminate between things good for them or things detrimental. That they love things is not always an indication that those things are good for them. Most children prefer sweets to vegetables, and without doubt would always prefer them. This, however, does not mean that we should adjust their diets to sweets. Children, once conditioned to over-protection, love it too. In fact, they become so dependent on it that they can no longer enjoy their freedom. In countless cases I have seen parents doing everything for their children—children who simply stretch out their leg and their shoe is laced, then turn around and their hair is combed—almost automatically like on the assembly line. These are the children who sit in the midst of their toys and don't know what to do with them, or go to camp and sit lonely in a corner while others enjoy their freedom and play.

A child, once conditioned to coloring books, will have difficulties in enjoying the freedom of creating. The dependency which such methods create is devastating. It has been revealed by experimentation and research that more than half of all children, once exposed to coloring books, lose their creativeness and their independence of expression, and become rigid and dependent.

Some teachers may still tell you that with the coloring books the child learns the discipline of staying within the lines of a given picture (area). It has also been proved by experiment that this is not true at all. More children color beyond the given boundaries in coloring books than in objects they draw themselves. If Johnny draws *his* dog, he has much more incentive to remain within *his* boundaries than if he colors a dog in a coloring book to which he has no relationship.

Thus it has been proved beyond any doubt that such imitative procedures as found in coloring and workbooks make the child dependent in his thinking (they do not give him the freedom to create what he wants); they make the child inflexible, because he has to follow what he has been given; they do not provide emotional relief, because they give the child no opportunity to express his own experience and thus acquire a release for his emotions; they do not even promote skills and discipline, because the child's urge for perfection grows out of his own desire for expression; and finally, they condition the child to adult concepts which he cannot produce alone, and which therefore frustrate his own creative ambitions.

Self-expression

The term "self-expression" has been misunderstood so often that I feel it necessary to clarify this term before using it. It would be wrong to think that self-expression means the expression of thoughts and ideas in general terms of content. This is the greatest mistake made in the use of this word. Thoughts and ideas can also be expressed imitatively. If one finds himself truly and originally occupied in any kind of medium, the outcome of this occupation and the mode of its expression are of decisive importance. What matters then is the mode of expression, not the content; not the "what" but the "how." That is why "scribbling" or, in another field of expression, "babbling," can be a means of self-expression as well as a potentially high form of creation. It can even happen that scribbling or babbling is a truer means of self-expression than a higher form of art, when the work of art moves from the sincere mode of expression to a form which is based upon the dependency on others, on imitation. In this connection it seems important to point out that the more primitive the stage of creative activity, the weaker the effect of such formal influences or interferences. The explanation of this fact seemingly lies in the nature of the more complex expression of art. Rarely can there be found a scribbling or babbling that is not a direct expression of an adequate mental and emotional state. However, more complex forms of art expression can be influenced easily by stronger personalities. This influence often grows to such an extent that complex forms of art, even in spite of technical perfection, lack completely the inner spirit or the adequate mental and emotional state of the "creator." They are, then, façades without substance, masks without life, condemned to die. However, this condemnation holds not only for the single art work, but also for the "creator," who cannot live because he cannot breathe with strange lungs. In the same way that a babbling child is unable to pronounce words correctly, even if urged to do so, a scribbling child if forced to draw "reality" can neither understand nor conceive what he is supposed to draw. Both would express themselves by strange means, which would not only inhibit them but would block their further development. This applies to all stages and all levels of creative activity. Such an education toward truth is one of the highest and deepest meanings of self-expression. This development toward freedom of expression, this great experience of individuals in finding themselves rests upon the knowledge of what truth is in art education. This knowledge cannot be achieved without a thorough study of what we can expect in modes of expression in the different age groups and on the different mental levels.

Self-adjustment

Any work that is forced upon a person creates tension and dissatisfaction. When the individual feels unable to perform a task, he becomes conscious of his own insufficiencies and develops lack of confidence, or even feelings of inferiority. All this, as we have seen in the Introduction, can happen if art education is applied improperly and if children are urged to do something not appropriate to their development, or even if their work is criticized in a way that is not adjusted to the level of the child's ability to understand.

For instance, when a scribbling child, whose control of body movements is not developed to the extent that he can correlate them with his visual experiences, is forced to represent something "real," he not only would be unable to perform a task which depends upon ability to achieve such correlation, but the child may also lose confidence in his own means of expression (scribbling). The child might even become aware of the fact that he does not represent anything real. A child who expresses the importance of an object by overemphasizing it—like the Egyptians who drew the king larger than the servants—would become confused by criticism based on our visual sense of proportion. The child not having another means to determine the importance of the object, would first become aware of the "inadequacy" of his expression, would then lose confidence in his own experiences, and would finally start to measure proportions rigidly until blocked in his further development. Inhibited by such a stimulation, the child would then stop expressing himself altogether. "I can't draw it" would be the known indication for such a discouragement.

However, if the child expresses himself adequately and freely by repeating his motions during scribbling with ever greater certainty, by expressing importance with his own adequate means, by feeling and expressing his space experience (contradicting that of adults), the satisfaction from such creative work documents itself in the profound feelings of a great achievement. And we all know how achievements create confidence. Since it is an established fact that nearly every emotional or mental disturbance is connected with a lack of self-confidence, it is easily understood that the proper stimulation of the child's creative abilities will be a safeguard against such disturbances.

Besides this natural adjustive effect, there is another way of using creative activity as a type of therapy. A special chapter deals with this approach for the abnormal individual. Here I would like to point out the principles in the use of creative ability as a therapy for merely retarded or maladjusted children, who can be found everywhere. Three points will be of especial interest. (1) How can such deficiencies be recognized? (2) What is their nature? (3) What means for adjustment can be used?

Two characteristics in particular make it possible to recognize deficiencies from children's drawings:

(1) If there is an abnormal discrepancy between chronological age and the development stage, which average periods of duration are given in our discussion, the existence of a mental retardation can be accepted as a certainty. For instance, if a child of seven years still scribbles, we can say that he is still concerned with the primitive experiences of mere kinesthetic feelings when he should feel the desire to represent something. The lower the mentality, the greater these discrepancies, and the greater will be the differences between chronological and mental age. Developmental stages in creative activity, however, always extend over a wide range in chronological age and in variety of forms of expression. Therefore, it is important to be flexible in the evaluation of creative products.

(2) If a child is emotionally blocked, his rigid repetitions demonstrate his inability to express experiences. In both cases, I have found that the stimulation of body experiences leads to an adjustment of these deficiencies in a rather short time, if the deficiencies are not too deeply rooted. As an example, I would like to discuss a case of an exceedingly shy girl who could approach her playmates only with great difficulty and who showed in her representations a great deal of such rigid repetitions. I asked this girl to catch a ball which I had thrown high into the air, and I said, "Who can catch it sooner, you or I?" This competitive stimulus aroused in her a greater insight into what she was doing. Then I asked her to draw this event. With repeated individual stimulation, she found such enjoyment in the newly gained correlation between her actions and her representations that she started to introduce all kinds of experiences as her own contribution. Thus she gained, through this constant correlation between herself and her drawings, a more conscious and free relationship to the world around her, which finally helped her completely to overcome her shyness. Although this analysis does not pretend to be scientific (such an analysis would require a more specific treatment of this special question beyond the limits of this textbook) the success which results from using this method of therapy makes it worth mentioning even in this very concise way. In the last chapter of this book questions of this kind are treated in more detail.

In summary, it seems important to point out the contrasting effects upon the child's development of creative activity as a means of self-expression and as a means of mere imitation.

Self-expression we have defined as the appropriate mode of expression according to the mental level of the child. Imitation, however, is expression according to adult, or at least foreign, levels. If the child expresses himself according to his own level, he becomes encouraged in his own independent thinking by expressing his own thoughts and ideas by *his own* means. The child who imitates becomes dependent in his thinking, since he relies for his thoughts and expressions upon others. The independent, thinking child will not only express whatever comes into his mind but will tackle any problem, emotional or mental, that he encounters in life. Thus his expression serves also as an emotional outlet.

Dependent thinking, however, restricts the child in his choice of subject matter as well as in his mode of expression. Since the imitative child cannot give expression to his own thoughts and emotions, his dependency leads directly to feelings of frustration. The child who uses creative activity as an emotional outlet will gain freedom and flexibility as a result of the release of unnecessary tensions. However, the child who feels frustrated develops inhibitions and, as a result, will feel restricted in his personality. The child who has developed freedom and flexibility in his expression will be able to face new situations without difficulties. Through his flexible approaches toward the expression of his own ideas, he will not only face new situations properly but will adjust himself to them easily. The inhibited and restricted child, accustomed to imitating rather than expressing himself creatively, will prefer to go along set patterns in life. He will not be able to adjust to new situations quickly but will rather try to lean upon others as the easiest way out. Since it is generally accepted that progress, success, and happiness in life depend greatly upon the ability to adjust to new situations, the importance of art education for personality growth and development can easily be recognized.

The diagram at the top of the facing page depicts clearly what has been said in the foregoing summary.

THE SIGNIFICANCE OF SELF-IDENTIFICATION THROUGH ART

The people who live in this world have to a great extent lost their ability to identify themselves with what they do and also with the needs of their neighbors. The reason for this increasing lack of ability for self-identifica-

Self-Expression	contrasted with	Imitation
Expression according to child's own level	————————	Expression according to strange level
Independent thinking	————————	Dependent thinking
Emotional outlet	————————	Frustration
Freedom and flexibility	————————	Inhibitions and restrictions
Easy adjustment to new situations	————————	Going along set patterns
Progress, success, happiness	————————	Leaning toward others, dependency, stiffness

tion may be found in certain trends in industry and also in education. Mass production apparently does not stimulate individual self-identification, and mass education seemingly does not contribute toward it either. Yet it is an established fact that self-identification with the things we do is essential for any well-balanced individual, and self-identification with the needs of our neighbors is one of the most important assumptions for cooperation. Thus, in our lives the ability for self-identification has become almost identical with the ability to live together in a peaceful society.

In education, the study of self-identification of the teacher with the needs of the child as well as that of the child with his own needs becomes a science—in the opinion of the author, one of the most important sciences today. On its promotion the very future of our youth may depend, for nothing less is at stake than the ability of our youths to live as well-balanced human beings cooperatively in their society. Almost all fields in the social sciences can be better understood through self-identification than through a mere study of facts. Self-identification in teaching becomes the vehicle for any effective motivation, for without identifying ourselves with the needs of the growing child we shall not be able to understand these needs.

No art expression is possible without self-identification with the experience expressed as well as with the medium by which it is expressed. This is one of the very intrinsic factors of creative expression. If we do not identify ourselves with these forces, art expression loses the very essence of its nature—its creativity.

The different trends in art education today depend entirely on the different emphasis used by educators in identifying themselves with the different forces determining creative processes. Some art educators identify themselves predominantly with aesthetic criteria, art media and their application, the elements of design and their organization; others identify themselves completely with the individual who produces. While the one group of educators concentrates on the organization of the creative product and its design values, the other identifies itself with the individual and his psychological needs only. In art education these trends must not be separated. They must be closely integrated, for it is the individual who uses his media and his form of expression according to his personal experiences. Since these experiences change with the growth of the individual, self-identification is a dynamic science. It embraces the understanding of *social, intellectual, emotional,* and *psychological* changes with the *creative needs* of the child.

In teaching

To identify oneself with the needs of the growing child is then imperative for any successful teaching. In art education it means that the teacher must know the child and his creative needs in order to understand him fully and also to motivate him effectively. This is not always easy. Two important attributes are essential for complying with this task.

(1) The teacher must be able to subordinate himself and his desires to the needs of the child.

(2) The teacher must make himself acquainted with the physical and psychological needs of the child.

For example, a teacher who sees a scribbling child must not only be able to identify himself with the needs of a child in this stage of development, but he must also be able to identify himself with the *particular* needs of this *individual* child. He, therefore, must completely subordinate his adult needs or desires to those of the child. In order to be able to identify himself with the general needs of a scribbling child he must make himself acquainted with the physiological as well as psychological characteristics of this developmental stage. Only then will he be able to identify himself with the particular needs of this individual child. Thus, it becomes essential that he study the needs of a scribbling child. If he discovers that the physical needs are of a purely kinesthetic origin, he will no longer motivate the child with visual imagery. He will then learn that an apple for this child is only something to eat, to smell or to hold, and *not to draw*. The child in this stage of development has no desire to relate visual imagery to his drawing activity. He enjoys solely the motions on the paper. To go even further with the self-identification, the teacher should realize that the motions the child is making are for the child different in size from the way they appear to him. Sizes always are proportionate to our own self. He will then remember that a table or the square in his town which appeared large in size to him when he was a child now appear to be much smaller. Sometimes, then, a big motion on a big sheet of paper means almost the same as "traveling" or "running" on the paper to the child. His physical needs of *motor activity*, therefore, must be recognized in order to be properly motivated. It might even become significant to know that the child during the beginning stages of scribbling usually does not focus continuously on the motions he produces. To identify ourselves with this sensation we would only have to scribble or draw with our eyes "blank"; that is, not focused at all, looking as it were into space. The teacher will understand then the *psychological* significance it has for the child when he discovers that there is a relationship between his motions and the lines on the paper. That he *can* repeat this performance is of great significance to him, because it gives him self-assurance and self-confidence that he *can master* a situation.

Once the teacher has been able to identify himself with the general needs of a scribbling child, he will be able to discover the specific needs of a particular individual. He may find out that this child lacks freedom in his motions because he has been continually discouraged or has not been given an opportunity to experience his freedom in his motor activity. Another child may appear particularly timid, fearful to use his material. He might have been punished for breaking crayons or "spoiling" or "wasting" paper. There are many more such individual needs to be discussed in the paragraph on "scribbling," which can only be understood if the general physical and psychological characteristics which are typical of this stage of development are understood.

Without the teacher subordinating his own self to the desires of the child and without knowing the child's general as well as specific physical and psychological needs, no proper self-identification is possible. Without it, the teacher will never reach the child with his motivations.

Self-identification of the child with his art experience

In spite of the teacher's fulfilling all the aforementioned prerequisites for an effective motivation, it may happen that the *child*, through improper influences, has difficulties in identifying himself with what *he* is doing.

Usually such children laugh about their own products or are continually unsatisfied with them. For these children the final product apparently is of greater significance than the working process. The child has lost connection with his own activity and only is eager to "please" others or himself. False criticism or too great an emphasis on the final product may easily produce such an attitude. The child unable to identify himself with his own experience has lost confidence in his own creative activity. To boost the child's confidence in his *drawing activity* would only increase the child's frustration. "Yes, you can draw," or "See how beautifully you have done it" would only direct the child's attention to his own inefficiency. *The final product is only the result of the precluding experience.* If the child cannot identify himself with the experience, the final product will necessarily show it.

It is, therefore, imperative that every child be able to face his own experience. If he cannot identify himself with it, the motivation in his *experience* must be boosted and not the drawing activity! Not, "You cannot draw picking flowers? Yes, you *can* draw it!" but, "You do not *know* how to pick flowers? Show me how you would pick them." *The child must first be able to identify himself with his own experience before he can be motivated to produce creatively,* or better, the urge for expression will only come through an intense experience.

From this it becomes clear that individual as well as classroom motivation must be presented in such a way that the individual child can identify himself with the given situation. Objective reports or illustrations are therefore unsuitable means for creating an inspiring atmosphere. The easier it is for the child to include himself in a given situation, the more readily will he identify himself with it.

Personality differences and different reactions toward experiences then count for the enormous variety in kind and intensity of self-identification. It is self-evident that vicarious experiences lend themselves just as well to creative motivations as experiences which the child actually has gone through. For both types of experiences, however, it is important that as great a variety of sensations, perceptions, and other experiences are activated as is possible. While it is apparent that the sensitive child will become sufficiently motivated through his own power of recalling sensations, it is in most cases necessary to confront the child with as great a number of experiences as possible in order that he may discover his own way of self-identification. For example, "sitting in a swing" will immediately bring to consciousness, in the sensitive child, all kinesthetic feelings of swinging back and forth, even the tickling sensation in his stomach; he will feel the texture of the rope in his hands, and he will experience the corresponding "up and down" of his motions with that of the horizon. All that and more will immediately be available for self-identification in the wide-awake child. However, a great number of children need to be faced with their experiences in order that they become strong enough for self-identification. This is still more true for experiences which are not directly drawn from the child's own life or are even vicarious. Since we do not know with which part or type of experience the individual child will identify himself a great variety of sensations, perceptions, and imagery should be included in a good motivation. If a child lacks confidence in his art expression, the cause usually lies in too weak or too diffuse an experience. Such an experience is not detailed enough for self-identification; its vagueness does not allow the child to grasp it and project himself into it. Therefore, if a child says, "I can't draw it," never be satisfied with such a general statement. It is imperative to find out which experience was too vague for self-identification. "What is it that you wanted to draw?" would be the proper investigation from the side of the teacher. If the child said, for example, "I want to draw skating," the teacher would know that most probably the child had difficulties in identifying himself with his experience. The proper stimulation then would be to draw from the child a detailed account of experiences in order that he identify himself with them. "You don't know how to skate?" "How is your body when skating?" "How are your legs—your arms?" "What do you wear?" "How does it feel?" etc., are questions which motivate the child in his ability to identify himself with his experiences. It is this self-identification with experiences which is one of the most vital assumptions for producing creatively.[2]

Self-identification with the art medium

Experimentation has been considered a most common principle in art education. "Give the child enough art material, and he will find his way of expression."

This attitude has done as much harm to the child as a meaningless restriction in the choice of art materials and techniques. While it is commonly agreed that experimentation which may be harmful to physical growth is dangerous, we do not apply the same caution when we deal with the child's mental or emotional growth. For instance, we would never expose an infant to an unselected variety of foods in order to find out what

[2] McVitty, L. F., "An Experimental Study on Various Methods in Art Motivations." Unpublished doctoral dissertation, The Pennsylvania State University, 1954.

is best for him. The child's ability to discriminate between "right" and "wrong," between materials which help him in his urge for expression and those which inhibit him is not developed, especially in early childhood. Yet psychologists agree that most of the influences which affect the child's mental or emotional growth occur during this decisive period. It is therefore important to investigate more closely the attributes which art media must have to promote self-identification of the child with his experiences.

Before discussing these attributes it seems imperative to clarify an existing confusion between what is commonly called "technique" and "procedure."

Technique and procedure

A technique is the individual use of materials as a means of expression. Thus the same material may be used for different techniques, depending on the different ways by which it is used to express something. One child may use crayons only linearly; the other may use the same material with the broadside. The one child may express himself by means of outlines; the other may require filled-in spaces to satisfy his needs. Thus a technique develops according to the individual's own needs. It is highly individual. *A technique, therefore, cannot be explained or taught.* Each child must develop his *own* technique. What can be explained is a procedure. A procedure consists of the different steps in the *general* principles in using a material. There are, for instance, general principles in making an etching. These principles refer to the preparation of the plate, the acid used for etching, the control of the process of etching, printing process, etc. These procedures can be explained. They lead the individual to a possible development of an individual application to *his* technique. It is needless to say that a technique in etching cannot be developed unless the individual has an intimate understanding of the procedures and that a procedure such as etching would not only be too complex for children, but would make them overconscious of the working process.

From what has been said it becomes apparent that any technique or material used with children must fit their special need for expression, because only then will the child be able to identify himself with the medium he uses. A technique, therefore, which does not help the child to express his particular desires is not a good one. Since the child's desires for and needs of expression change with his development and growth it becomes evident that he will identify himself with different art media during different developmental stages. Which are the attributes of an art medium which promote self-identification? Three points seem to me outstanding characteristics:

(1) The art medium must conform with the child's own desire for expression.

(2) The art medium and art expression must become an inseparable whole.

(3) No technique or material should be replaceable by another one.

Let us look, for example, at water color as the medium. The following seem to be outstanding attributes of this medium: water color is transparent in its use; it has a flowing, merging quality; since water colors merge easily they can be mixed easily into the finest gradations; because of these mixing and merging attributes water color changes easily in its characteristics; because of this changing condition water color has a vibrating, atmospheric quality; because of this vibrating quality it does not lend itself well to local color tones and surface appearance. The running and merging quality makes it unsuitable for purely linear expression; its transparency eliminates all types of working processes which call for work in layers where one layer or brush stroke ought to cover the other. These are only a few attributes of the medium commonly called water color. Let us now look, in the light of these characteristics and the aforementioned three points necessary for the child's self-identification with his art medium, at the effect which water color would have on a scribbling child, on an average child of eight years, on a child of twelve years, and finally on a youth of sixteen years. While a more detailed account of the relations between art media and expression will be given in each chapter on the different stages of creative development, it seems to me important to show in one example the necessary care which must be taken in stimulating self-identification through art media. Since the child's main urges during scribbling are to identify himself with motor activity, the material used should encourage free expression of kinesthetic sensations without any intruding technical difficulties. Water color, which has the tendency to run, would produce an indistinguishable blurred mass that renders the child's motions as such indistinguishable. The child, unable to follow or gain control over his motions and unable to identify himself with them, would become discouraged and frustrated by such a technique. He needs an art medium especially suited to give easy expression to his urge for motor activity. If he scribbled with water color, the lines he produced with the wet brush would have to be interrupted frequently, as he would have to dip his brush into the water and paint. Such an interruption would, without any doubt, interfere with an uninterrupted search for motor control. As he continued to fill his paper with brush strokes, the brush lines would run into one another, merging into a blurred, indistinguishable mass of colors in which the kinesthetic sensation and the child's urge for controlling them would become entirely invisible. As the child could no longer see what he desired to do, he would become frustrated in his desire for self-identification and would stop it altogether. Even at a later stage of his scribbling, when he has the urge to name his scribbles, when he has the desire to give his scribblings distinct meaning, water color would interfere with his experience. Separating motions which have different meanings can be done much more easily in a linear technique than with blurring colors. Thus, it becomes clear that water color would greatly interfere with the needs of a scribbling child and is, therefore, an entirely unsuitable art material for this age level.

An eight-year-old child wants to express his experiences by means of drawings or paintings which resemble nature only insofar as significant characteristics may appear in both the child's drawing and in nature. The child's relationship to his environment thus is signified by the child's urge for the search for his *own* concepts. Through repetition these concepts often become schemata. Yet, self-introduced repetition is of great importance to the child as it gives him the feeling of self-assurance that he *can* draw what he wants to draw. The resulting self-confidence is an important assumption for the development of leadership. This stage in which the child repeats the same form concepts for "trees" or "man" has, therefore, a great psychological significance. If we do not give the child the proper motivation to identify himself with his individual concepts, we would not do justice to the child's creative needs during this stage of development. Such form concepts of a "tree" or a "man" represent the child's knowledge of them and what is of emotional significance to him. Such form concepts consist of parts, all of which are meaningful to the child. These parts are not subject to any changes because of optical influences. A "man" or a "tree" will not change in sunshine or moonlight for a child of eight years. Illumination, light, or shadows do not influence the child's form concept. Therefore, any technical accident, such as unintentional shading or running of color, which destroys or changes his concept will interfere with his desire for expression. Unintentional changes are meaningless for the child of eight. They only destroy his concept, his relationship to his environment, his confidence, and his self-assurance that he *can* succeed in establishing his individual relationships.

As has been said before, the transparency of water color serves best to paint atmosphere and not definite form concepts. Its running quality introduces many accidents which do not lend themselves to repetition. Such accidents could be of a happy nature if the child could make active use of them as visual stimuli. Since the child in his painting is more concerned with expressing his own ideas than with visual stimuli, however, such accidents would only frustrate him in his feelings of mastery. It is in the nature of an accident that it cannot be repeated. At an age when this desire for repetition is most definite, the inability to repeat would only be disappointing. An unintentional change through the running of paint would render the child's established concept meaningless to him. What often seems of aesthetic quality to adults may seem spoiled to the child because he cannot identify himself with it.

It appears that only an art material and technique which allow the child to develop his individual concepts without unnecessary restrictions are suitable for this stage of development. The techniques used must permit him repetitions if he so desires. Since water color changes too easily in tone and hue and cannot be directed as easily as poster paint, for example, it impedes the development of free art expression in an average eight-year-old child.

A child of twelve years has discovered himself to be mentally and socially a part of the environment. He may still be a member of a "gang." He loves to discover new things, to experiment, and to read fantastic stories. In art he will give expression to his new social and mental awareness. He will show his trend for search and experimentation. What formerly appeared an accident in painting will now be considered stimulating. The flowing, merging character of water color will be investigated. The child of twelve will soon find that he can get "effects" with water color which he could not get with any other material. The child has become *visually* aware of his environment and will take great satisfaction in having found a medium by which he can give expression to this visual awareness. A "dramatic" sky will be made still more dramatic by letting the colors run as they want to.

The dynamic quality of water color lends itself perfectly to support the twelve-year-old child in his search for new discoveries, for dramatic expression in nature, and above all, in his drive for visual stimuli. He may be surprised by what he can do through the many happy accidents which occur when the wet paint runs on the paper and merges in unexpected beauty. The visually aware child will benefit from such "accidents."

A sixteen-year-old youth has become critically aware, not only of his environment, but also of the work he produces. He, therefore, has definite intentions, not only of *what* he wants to express, but also of *how* his final product should look. He might want to paint his visual environment and thus take into consideration all the changing effects of shape and color in distance and atmosphere; or he might want to *express* his subjective emotional relation to experiences and thus use color and form as pure means of expression. While for the one type of student water color may be the medium through which he expressed his desires without technical interference, the other type may not find in water color the strong opaque quality which he needs for the interpretation of his subjective relationships. Water color may be an obstacle to his expression. Thus, when art expression reaches the realm of conscious art approaches, it becomes a specific art medium, suitable only for a very definite type of self-identification. This shows very clearly that not all art students have to be able to use water color. While it may be *the* medium for the one, it may be frustrating to the other, depending on the type of self-identification with art medium and experience.

Five points seem to me important in regard to selecting and developing techniques:

(1) It is the job of the teacher to know and introduce the appropriate materials at a time when the child is most ready to use them in relation to his growth and free art expression.

(2) Every material or technique must make its *own* contribution. If a task can be done more easily by a different technique with a better effect, the wrong technique has been applied.

(3) The teacher should know that the *child* must develop *his* own technique and that every "help" from the teacher in showing the child a "correct" technique would only mean restricting the child's individual approach.

(4) An art material and its handling are only a means to an end. A technique should not be taught as such, separated from its meaning. Used at the right time, it should help the child in his desire for self-identification. Perfection grows with the urge for expression.

(5) The simultaneous use of many different kinds of materials which fit the child's needs in one classroom is of great advantage because it exposes the child to the variety of procedures, and makes him sensitive to the various possibilities which he may find in developing his technique.

It seems, however, essential to stress that it is not the material approach which should be emphasized in a materialistic period such as ours, but the human spirit which transcends the material into expression.

For appreciation

Art on all levels is an expression of the human spirit. It expresses the relation of the artist to himself and his environment; thus it expresses the experience of the creator with the thing and never the thing itself. Therefore it can only be understood and appreciated if we identify ourselves with the creator. This self-identification with the artist in understanding and appreciating his work will have to deal with three main factors, all closely interrelated:

a) The level of the appreciator
b) The subject matter
c) The means of expression

The level of the appreciator

It is needless to say that a creative product remains meaningless unless the individual can relate himself to it. As self-evident as this sounds, in most of the art appreciation practiced in our classrooms the level of understanding and emotional relationship of the appreciator are almost completely neglected. Art is handed over one-sidedly and it is not infrequent that the teacher speaks of a work of art completely oblivious of the fact that his listeners have not the least understanding of the high-sounding adjectives which he relates to it. I have witnessed classroom situations in which the teacher, so fully and sincerely involved in his *own* appreciation of the work, completely loses contact with his pupils by neglecting their level of understanding and comprehension. It has been demonstrated that children react differently toward objects or pictures on different developmental levels.[3] Not taking into consideration the child's own needs by neglecting his responses would indeed be a frustrating experience. It is therefore important to base any aesthetic appreciation on the reaction of the pupil, and expand his aesthetic level from there on. It must, however never be forgotten that the aim of art appreciation is not to "analyze" pictures or to "learn to understand" a work of art. It is much more important to make the individual sensitive to its values in order that he can relate himself to it meaningfully. "Relational statements are not on the plane of 'true' or 'false' inter-subjectively. The same picture (or object) may inspire me and disgust you, but both our statements would have to be accepted as long as the relational 'to me' were understood to follow our judgments and as long as we both gave sincere reports. It is to be hoped that neither of us would end our appreciative experience there, but we would nonetheless begin there."[4] Simple questions, such as, "How do you feel about

[3] Holland, Jean, "Children's Responses to Objects in Daily Living, A Developmental Analysis." Unpublished doctoral dissertation, The Pennsylvania State University, 1955.

[4] Beittel, Kenneth, "Appreciation and Creativity." *Research Bulletin,* The Eastern Arts Assoc., Vol. 5, 1954.

this picture, or object?"—"Of what does it remind you?"—"Do you like it?"—"Why?"—"Why don't you like it?" may well be the starting point for an appreciation which leads to a greater sensitivity of perceptual, emotional, and intellectual relationships.[5] This comprehension, however, is geared to the individual and *his* growing sensitivity to meaningful aesthetic discoveries and not to an evaluation of the aesthetic product.

The subject matter

The subject matter necessarily deals with contents. On all levels of art expressions subject matter contents have always been of the greatest variety. They may have social significance, they may be of religious origin, they may be historic, scientific, entirely individualistic, or purely abstract in nature. In every instance it is imperative for the creation of a work of art that the artist identify himself with his subject matter. In order to relive or appreciate his intentions we have to put ourselves into the situation of the creator. For an example: We cannot identify ourselves with the intentions of a child who depicts his home environment without learning of his home atmosphere; that is, the subject matter he has chosen.

While the choice of the subject matter has no influence on the intensity of self-identification, it is of prime significance for the creator. If the child chooses a subject matter in which he is not interested or to which he has little or no relationship, he will not be able to identify himself with it. The same holds true for the artist. Very often we hear that it does not matter what you choose for your creative production; "What is of final importance is the type of execution." To separate the content from its presentation would mean to deprive a body of its spirit and vice versa. In a creative work, subject matter and the way in which it is presented form an inseparable whole. In creative activity, the urge for expression usually depends on the intensity of the experience. The more intensive the experience, the greater is the desire for expression. Since the child's spheres of interest change with his development and also with his environment, it is of prime importance that a subject matter with which the child can easily identify himself be chosen. And conversely, the teacher will be able to see from the subject matter the child chooses just what the intellectual and emotional interests of the child are.

As has been said before, the subject matter may be concrete or abstract in nature. Even in simple experiences like "rowing a boat" the child can identify himself purely with the motion he feels in the boat, the subjective

[5] See p. 57, "Aesthetic Growth."

kinesthetic sensation, or he may become visually bound up with the spectacle of the environment. The creative result may be an abstract expression of the kinesthetic feelings he had while rowing. He may completely identify the abstract motions he produces on the paper with his experience in the boat. However, he may also produce a pictorial representation of his relationship to the environment in which he was rowing. He may place the self in value relationship to it. Thus, he may depict himself large or small depending on how significant he felt when he was rowing; or, he may give us an account of his feeling for nature. In every instance, we learn to understand and appreciate the child's relationship to his experience by identifying ourselves with the type of his presentation.

What has been said for the appreciation of the child's creative work is basically true also for the appreciation of great works of art. In bringing them closer to the child we have to know that we must first of all make it possible for the child to identify himself with the relationship the artist has had to his subject matter. It is, therefore, of little value for the appreciation of a work of art simply to determine the content of it. In so doing we have separated the soul from its body. One cannot exist without the other. By trying to identify ourselves with the *intentions* of the artist we shall come closer to the understanding and appreciation of his work. In this way we induce in the child the problems of the artist and by so doing we make him feel like the "creator" as he appreciates.

The means of expression

Self-identification with the means of expression for the purpose of a better appreciation of creative works may appear to be difficult for one who is not producing creatively. It is, however, essential for the appreciation of creative works. It will immediately become easier if we try to assign "life" to the different means of expression which a creator has at his disposal. For example, if we think that a line is something living, it may move, it may live in friendship with another line, it may go visiting certain places, it may become excited, jump up and down, it may be quiet and calm, it may be aimlessly wandering about, or it may be "on business," as it were, going directly to a predestined place. It may even establish certain relationships with its environment, dominating it or being a part of it. The same and many more signs of such living quality can be seen in all other main elements of expression as in color and space, for example. There should be no misunderstanding, however, that we experience a particular color as happy, sad, or lonely in relationship to its environment; it means that we should identify ourselves with the color as something living in the same way as we would identify ourselves with our friends. To follow the fate of a tone or theme in music as it meets others, passes them, or unites with them to produce chords and harmonies is a wonderful way of learning to appreciate music in its own realm.

In the same way as we can identify ourselves with colors and tones we can also identify with materials which we are using. In fact every child is doing it when whittling a bow. First, he carefully tries to "select" the right branch—he predicts his behavior—he knows how much he can bend it. He would not do the same with wire. Wire behaves differently. He knows what to do with wood if wood wants to "feel beautiful," when it wants to show its grain at its best—how wood would "feel" when covered with paint or how "insincere" it would be for wood to look like marble.

To identify himself with art media becomes even more important for the older child who is more consciously aware of the significance of the final product and the means with which he reaches it. Art materials and techniques will then always remain subordinated to expression. How materials "behave" under different circumstances and conditions will then become a fascinating part of art expression or art appreciation. Instead of talking of skills or design characteristics we would then be more justified in talking about the behavior of materials and elements of design under various conditions. This would immediately bring to light that lines, colors, spaces, or art materials have their own intrinsic characteristics and also their peculiar reactions just as if they were alive.

For social adjustment

It is well to remember at the final paragraph of this chapter on the significance of self-identification that one of the major concerns of art education is its effect on both the individual and society in general. To live cooperatively as well-adjusted human beings in this society and to contribute to it creatively have become most important objectives for education. It is impossible to live cooperatively and understand the needs of our neighbors without self-identification. As the child identifies himself with his own work, as he learns to appreciate and understand his environment by subordinating the self to it, he grows up in a spirit which necessarily will contribute to the understanding of the needs of his neighbors. As he creates in the spirit of incorporating the self into the problems of others, he learns to use his imagination in such a way that it will not be difficult for him to visualize the needs of others as if they were his own. In identifying himself with art media, by experiencing them in their living quality, the child will gain appreciation and insight into the meaningfulness of art and culture. As the child develops creatively, the other subjects in his learning will necessarily gain in importance by this process. The child does not distinguish in his desire between identifying himself in creative activity and in history, for example. History, too, will become alive for the child as he becomes a part of it. Most of all, however, it is important for this world that educators realize that our ability to identify ourselves with our work and the needs of our neighbors may ultimately be responsible for our survival.

THE MEANING OF INTEGRATION
IN ART EDUCATION

The integrated experience

In the process of total integration the single elements to be integrated unite to form a new entity. In Art Education integration takes place when the single components which lead to a creative experience become an inseparable whole, one in which no single experience remains an isolated factor. What are the single elements to be integrated in a creative experience? Four types of experiences seem to be outstanding:

(1) Emotional experiences
(2) Intellectual experiences
(3) Perceptual experiences
(4) Aesthetic experiences

None of them from the first beginning appears to be in pure form. Yet, it lies in the nature of a creative experience that they all unite to form a new entity. This intrinsic value of any art experience seems to be of great educational significance, since it promotes the natural tendency of growth. The child neither grows in single subject matter areas nor does he grow in a separate way physically, emotionally, socially, or mentally. Yet, in education simultaneity of growth has largely been neglected. Too early specialization, especially on the upper levels of education, has prevented the child's integrated growth and has made man "one-track-minded." In some areas he developed this specialization to such a degree that he lost contact with the society which has to handle his "achievements." This is particularly true for the sciences, where the inability to integrate them with our social growth has created the great discrepancy between social and scientific achievement from which our time so badly suffers. Integration in learning therefore, becomes of major significance since it may be responsible for leading our youth to a more unified and better adjusted life.

The integration of art and society

If we want to understand a period and its characteristics, we should look at its cultural, social, and scientific achievements and its art expression. If we want to understand fully a work of art we should look at the time in which it was created, the circumstances which determine its style and art expression as well as the individual forces which led the artist to his form of expression. This interchanging effect between period and culture, social, political and religious environment and art expression has always been of greatest significance for the understanding of both the period in which a culture was created as well as the culture itself. The total integration of all these aspects determines a culture.

If later generations would look at the interchanging effect between our contemporary culture and its bearers, they would get a most diverse impression. Gothic cathedrals are built between skyscrapers and most advanced fields in science are taught in buildings of styles or pseudo-styles long outmoded. It is quite obvious that in this way a discrepancy is created between teaching and action. This is true especially if educators are not conscious of this fact. "Learning by doing" also applies to teaching, for we cannot expect confidence from our youth if we accept different measures for *our* actions. By so doing teachers deprive themselves of the proper functioning of a most effective educational means—environment. In a well-integrated culture such discrepancies do not exist.

It is clear that this is not a discussion on styles or even aesthetic attitudes, since both are only expressions of the time and its spirit. The influence which the environment has on growth is not a new discovery either of educators or of psychologists. An environment without relationship to the period in which it was created is like a building without a foundation, or like an individual who has lost connection with his own growth and now escapes into a world of meaningless stereotyped patterns. Only if we are unable to face a new situation do we try to find refuge in the repetition of conventional patterns. While teachers are generally aware of how education in pattern inhibits and restricts individuality—one of the most precious goods of a democratic society—they often fail to realize that a carrying over of styles meaningless to the spirit of the present day consists of nothing else but an adherence to meaningless patterns.

This disunity between art and society, between education and environment represents one of the factors from which our present time suffers. On the other side this disunity is clearly expressed by an art expression which, because of its extreme individualistic character, almost loses its communicative meaning. Thus, two extreme antipodes can be found within one culture: the tendency toward a confirmation of traditional patterns and the extreme individualistic trend in contemporary art.

Home environment has always had the greatest influence on the growth and attitudes of youth. Here, too, later generations could find a most excellent expression of the lack of integration between contemporary life and culture. They would think that going from the dining room into the kitchen must have meant serious adjustments over the centuries on the part of the inhabitants. While the kitchen is the room into which the "modern age" has penetrated, the living room is usually filled with assembly line patterns of outdated pseudo-styled furniture. Yet we are not at all aware of the adjustment that has to take place in moving from the functionally designed kitchen into the outdated living room. The lack of awareness, too, belongs to the serious educational implications of our time, for we can only remedy mistakes if we see them. It is quite obvious that we distinguish between consciously appreciating former styles and even sentimental adherences to meaningful objects and the unaware acceptance of traditional patterns. These existing contrasts between actual life and home environment must seriously affect our emotional being.

It is obvious that no single individual can be made responsible for this lack of integration between our culture and scientific achievements, but these important characteristics of our time have to be understood especially by those who guide our youth. It is only when we see these discrepancies that we find the urge to change them.

In order to understand and appreciate the implications of these contrasting tendencies of art and society, let us compare some phases of the life of an educator of the present with one who lived in one of the previous periods and cultures. While the Church and the cloisters were the main focal points of education during the Middle Ages, our schools have taken over this function in the education of today. During the medieval period, the Church, the carrier of education, fostered the most contemporary architecture. The cloisters most often significantly influenced the building of their time. The children of this period learned in an environment as modern to them as any Frank Lloyd Wright or Gropius architecture may be for our time. When the Cathedral of Florence was built, one of the most modern architects of that time was appointed, and Giotto began the famous campanile which later was continued by Pisano. When Brunelleschi added the dome in 1462 as an entirely different concept of style and building, the first dome of its kind, he did something perhaps more revolutionary and modern than most anything compared to architectural changes of our times, for, apart from the change in style, there was no concrete or steel structure to carry the dome. Yet, there was no one who complained about the differences in styles even within the one building. At that time it was quite common in building to show several styles, even three, like in the St. Stephen's Cathedral in Vienna, which was started in Romanesque style, continued during early and late Gothic, and finished during early Renaissance. While most of our public school buildings progressively move toward a new contemporary style, in most of the institutions of higher learning we do not dare to erect a contemporary building on a pseudo-styled average college campus, because we are afraid to disturb a traditionally established pattern.

If our medieval educator wanted to leave his town, he could do so only by using horse-drawn coaches, the style of which was in complete agreement with the rest of his aesthetic environment, as a means of transportation. This uniformity of different areas of living determined the culture of the past. Today, no one who has the choice of selecting an automobile would select an "outmoded" model. Obviously the latest streamlined model would be the first choice of the average American. Yet, it is understood that no reference is made to the greater efficiency and power of later models, but to the aesthetic exterior, the upholstery, the styling of the dashboard, etc. Here we express a "taste" quite in contradiction to the one which we expect in most of our homes. Are we then split personalities who accept different styles in different living areas—old-fashioned chairs at home, modern seating comfort in our cars, streamlined simplicity in the kitchen, and complex patterns of ornamentations in our bedrooms? Why is it that the utilitarian areas of living have accepted our modern style, while our homes and social institutions still adhere to the past? Our medieval man could pray in churches full of spiritual and religious power, built in the most contemporary styles. The best and most progressive architects were chosen to design them. If one period changed, the style changed with its spirit. Today we pray in churches which mostly are poor imitations of times long past.

What is the reason for all these discrepancies in our modern social and cultural institutions? Apparently we have no confidence in these vital institutions, for if we felt the need to glorify them, the places that housed them would express this spirit. It seems that we have more confidence in our industrial power and institutions than in our religious forms, for we have quickly accepted the "new styles" for our factories. This, however, is significant in itself, as it reveals a most serious threat toward our ethics and civilization, especially as this is underlined by the fact that the home and family life of today have seemingly to find refuge in past periods. The apparent lack of confidence in our modern homes, too, constitutes a serious threat to our social forms of living. While the new look of our scientific laboratories and institutions gives evidence of their living character, our educational buildings, especially those of higher learning, are living in the past, in an irresponsible adherence to an environment to which our youth of today has no relationship.

It is quite obvious that denying the present would only mean to deny the self, to play ostrich. The consequences of such self-denial, of such an adherence to the past, are too serious to be overlooked. It would not only widen the gap between our industrial and scientific achievements on the one hand and our social and religious institutions on the other, but also seriously affect individual adjustments. Education must awaken before it is too late. If we cannot adjust our educational achievements to the environment in which they grew, our education will be doomed to die and with it our social and religious institutions, while science and industry will triumphantly bury them.

Integration and learning

From the foregoing the significance of integration for educational procedures can easily be seen, for without using integrative processes in educational procedures we will never arrive at an integrated culture. Only when we begin with a well-integrated curriculum in early childhood will we be able to succeed.

Integration means neither correlation with, nor interpretation of, other subject matters outside of art. This, to my knowledge, represents the greatest misunderstanding of the meaning of integration. Teachers often think if history is illustrated, or interpreted in the art lesson, integration of the two subject matters takes place. This is by no means true. In such a superficial situation neither history is explained, nor does a creative experience become meaningful. In fact, both may have suffered. Yet, integration might occur even in *such* a situation. Let us analyze the circumstances when integration occurs and investigate the elements which promote or impede integration.

As has been said before, the single elements lose their identity in total integration. What are the single elements of an historic incident which becomes a creative experience? These elements may be of great variety and complexity; they consist of perceptual experiences such as visual, tactile, kinesthetic, smell or taste sensations as well as aesthetic and other experiences. Let us for instance discuss the topic of the first settlers landing on our shores. An illustration of the incident in the literal meaning will neither integrate design elements (that is, how an experience is expressed in a definite medium) with the individual experience of landing at an unknown place, nor will it promote the integration of movement, like jumping from the boat, nor the integration of the smell and coldness of the atmosphere with all the other experiences. All these experiences will either remain undeveloped, disregarded, or as separate parts in a purely literal interpretation of a subject matter. Design, or the creative power of interpretation, remains isolated from the subject matter. Both are misunderstood concepts which are badly correlated. Design, the power to express an experience in a medium, has not become meaningful, nor has the subject matter succeeded in becoming a part of the individual's experience. Integration does not occur from the outside; integration is not "made" by "assembling" two subjects; *integration happens from within.* This shows clearly that integration can only take place by self-identification. The integrated art experiences of the settlers who landed on our shores will, therefore, be different with each individual, according to the type of self-identification which takes place in each individual. As a child expresses his fight with the waves as a kinesthetic design motive, the design becomes the carrier of his experience—so much so, that one can no longer be separated from the other. As one child identifies himself with the fight with the waves when landing, another's experience may be focused around the sensation of stepping on land after endless sailing. The way in which all these experiences are expressed and organized in art media, however, is intensely personal. Such integration cannot take place when the teacher says: "Children, let's draw the landing of the first settlers." It can only take place if the child identifies himself with the experience. "How would *you* feel if *you* were in the group that landed; if *you* were the child of a settler who would lower *you* from the big sailboat down into the rowboat, in a wet cold atmosphere of a dawning day?" "How would you feel being rocked in your boat up and down by the waves?" The wave may become the line, and the line, the wave; so intensely integrated that one can no longer be separated from the other. Such motivation of self-identification is necessary to create the urge for expression which ultimately may result in an integrated art experience.

It has been demonstrated how integration occurs within the individual. Yet, it has also been shown how such an integrative process may have its starting point in correlating different subjects. Published research studies have proven that a close relationship exists between reading achievement and creative expression.[6] It has been demonstrated that the children who show good spatial coordination are also the best readers. Such studies not only show the close relationship which exists between art expression and reading but should also encourage teachers to use both for the purpose of integrative experiences. This, of course, is not only true for reading; it should be done everywhere, with all subjects, in order to give the child a better opportunity for integrative experiences than he has in a presentation of clearly defined, separate subjects. Only through a well-integrated and digested knowledge will a well-balanced growth be possible. As long as emotional growth is separated from intellectual growth, the child will develop inconsistently.

An attempt has been made to make self-identification and integration two of the most important vehicles in the education of the child, with art expression serving as a catalyzer to bring together the forces which determine growth.

EVALUATION OF CREATIVE PRODUCTS

The purpose of evaluation

In evaluating the creative products of children we must first of all consider the purpose for which we intend to evaluate the child's work. Do we evaluate it for our own purpose of gaining insight into the child's growth, his experiences, his emotions, his interests? Or do we want to evaluate the child's work for the purpose of showing him his strengths, his weaknesses, his creative abilities, his skillfulness or his lack of skill; in other words, to classify him?

Two important factors in the meaning of art education should be kept in mind at the beginning of a discussion on the evaluation of creative products. The one is that what is of final significance is the influence of art education on child growth and concluding from this, the other, that in art education the working process is of greater importance than the final product. In other words it may happen that a most "primitive"—and from an adult viewpoint, "ugly"—work may be more significant to the child than a well-executed, to the adults' eye, pleasing work. It may have occurred in many classrooms that a child "finds himself" in a painting, and from this time on, an emotional block which inhibited him in his growth is removed.

[6] Russell, Irene, "A Study of Relationship Between Reading Achievement and Creative Expression." *Research Bulletin,* The Eastern Arts Assoc., Vol. 1, No. 1, 1950.

The child could identify himself—maybe for the first time—in his creative work and thus could face his own self which he previously could not do. Yet, the work he produced may be aesthetically insignificant. It is obvious that such a change in his life is of far greater importance than any final product. To call the child's attention to the "poorness" of his product would only have a discouraging effect. It may even put the child back to his former status. It would also direct the child's attention to the final product and thus make him aware of "qualities" which are either meaningless or inconceivable to him. By encouraging the child in his work only because he has acquired greater skills in technical performances than others we would signify that we are mainly interested in technical performances. We would thus neglect the most important meaning of art education in the elementary classroom—the promotion of the child's growth. On the other hand, if we recognize the significance which any creative product with which the child identifies himself has, however "poor" the product may be, we give the child confidence and encouragement and make him feel that he is on the right track. In this way he will gain the creative freedom which is necessary for his emotional growth and which encourages the type of independent thinking that is a part of his intellectual advancement. *Creative works must be evaluated on their individual merits.* This is highly significant and is true for all levels of teaching. *The meaningfulness of the work to its creator must never be disturbed by "objective evaluations."*

From that it also becomes clear that the kind of evaluation of children's creative works will not only differ from individual to individual but also from one stage of development to the other. An experience which may be significant but meaningless to a child of seven years may be meaningful to a child of twelve. It also becomes self-evident that evaluations of a child's creative works are only made by the teacher to gain insight into the child's growth and not in order to confront him with his weaknesses or strengths. The first will help the teacher in understanding his pupils in their creative intentions and also in many phases of life outside of art; the latter will only increase the child's difficulties in "finding himself" and gaining confidence in his creative expression. By discriminating "good" from "bad" without regard for the child's individual desires we would only set rigid standards. These "standards," well known to classroom teachers, encourage the child who lacks confidence in his own work to copy the preferred one. Unable to compete with it he will give up his work. The result of such practices is discouragement, lack of confidence and inhibition of the one group and a go-ahead signal to a selected few. This is in contradiction to any basic philosophy which intends to help the child in his creative and mental growth.

An evaluation of the child's work is only of significance if it helps the teacher to gain insight into the child's growth so that he may effectively motivate the child in his creative needs.

This states clearly that any criticism, encouragement, or discouragement should only be applied after knowing the child in his development as well as in his individual needs and intentions. Objective criteria can only be applied *after* these subjective evaluations have been carefully weighed. It therefore becomes important that we analyze subjective as well as objective criteria which help the teacher in his understanding of the child and his desire to create. Most important of all is the *increased sensitivity* toward the child's needs which grows from an intense study of the characteristics which comprise evaluative factors.

Psychological evaluation

One of the very first criteria in looking at a child's work of art should be whether or not the child identifies himself with what he does. Is there an *active desire* in the child to express himself, or does he just "draw something," or is he inhibited and says "I can't draw"? If an active desire for self-expression is present, it will not be difficult for the teacher to find the child's intentions. The easiest way of doing it is to ask the child: "Johnny, what are you doing? Tell me something about your painting." If Johnny is not verbally inclined, or does not want to talk, he should be encouraged to express himself verbally. This is a part of an integrated creative activity. "What does this mean in your drawing?" may start him off. Great care must be applied *not* to use suggestive questions: "Does this mean this or that?" is a question which will easily reveal to the child your lack of understanding or often has an imposing character. Let the child freely express and explain his work.

If the child, however, just "draws something" and does not show any visible desire for active participation, it must first be determined whether there is no desire or whether an active desire for expression is "hidden." This, too, is not difficult to find out. It can best be seen in the type of discrepancy between his verbal expression and his projection. If he says: "There is just a tree and a house" and does not give another comment, even when encouraged, then in most of the cases he did not intend to draw anything specific but "something." However, if he tells of things not represented or visible, then we have to search for individual symbols which may express what he said and often reveal even more. I saw a child, drawing a man horizontally, and to his left there were two circles, the one with some scribbles in it. When I asked the child, "What is this to your left?" pointing at the circles, he told me, "The one is a glass of water and the other a plate with cookies which I get to eat when I am hungry in bed." Immediately, this revealed not only the child's close identification with his drawing, which superficially looked meaningless, but also his perceptual experiences, his home atmosphere, and many other things. It revealed that "touching" the upper circle of the glass was more important to the child than seeing it. It also revealed that the child apparently was often left alone, perhaps in darkness, and given a plate of cookies as a "reward" which, together with the glass of water, was placed to his left on the night table. In the darkness the child apparently wanted to assure himself of their presence and repeatedly reached out to touch the objects. By touching them he became more conscious of the top of the glass and the plate than the "side view"; accordingly, he merely drew the two circles which he "felt" to the left of himself. Neither the bed nor the night table was included in the drawing. This is clearly an indication of the self-centeredness of the child. Thus, the drawing revealed his complete experience, his relationship to his environment, his feeling in darkness, and his perceptual experience of a predominance of the sense of touch. It also revealed a home atmosphere, which, as it was found later, was a great disadvantage for the development of the child. Thus, apparently insignificant creative works which do not immediately show a close relationship between the child and his work are often very revealing. Before we consider a child to be "detached" from his work and just "drawing something" we must make sure that the child had no other intentions but the visible ones.

The child who just "draws something" has apparently no particular relationship to his experience. The establishment of a relationship becomes therefore of utmost importance. This is done differently for the various developmental stages (and a general method of motivation appears in each of the chapters dealing with the stages of development under the heading "Art Stimulation").

To motivate children who at least "draw something" to establish a closer relationship between themselves and their work will not be found as difficult as to encourage children who have *lost* connections with their expression altogether and simply react with the usual comment, "I can't draw." Some interference has occurred with their desire for self-identification as well as with their ability to project it. As has been said before, most of these interferences occur in early childhood, when the initiative for self-expression is broken by "showing the child how to do things." "What shall I do when my youngster of four years continually asks me to draw something for him?" is a common remark. "If I draw something for him he appears satisfied." Yet, few of our parents realize that with such actions they may destroy the initiative of the child to express himself creatively. The reason for the "I-can't-draw-child" can also be found in the type of criticism which uses as its basis adult standards rather than the child's own. At any rate it will be of great help to the teacher to find the cause of the child's inhibitions if he is interested in using the evaluation of the child's creative work to help him in his growth. For the establishment of self-identification of the child with his work it is necessary to give him confidence in his experience. Since the self is the most immediate intermediary of the child's experiences, it is best to start with experiences which refer to the immediate self. In using the self and its relationship to environment the teacher has also the best opportunity to control and boost the experience until the child has won confidence in the newly established relationship. Even in stages beyond early childhood the motivation of experiences concerning the self is most effective in giving the individual enough confidence to project his experiences.

Evaluation of meaningfulness
of creative product

Another important criterion in the evaluation of the child's creative work is its meaningfulness, or *the degree* to which the child identifies himself with his experience and its expression. Degrees of emotional intensity are always matters of subjective value judgments. In regard to the child's creative work the degree of intensity usually can be found by comparing several works of the child with each other. The sensitive teacher will have no difficulties in recognizing the creative works with which the child felt most intimately bound up. To watch the child during the working process is, however, the most exact measurement. The more children ask questions, the more they look around, the more they look at others' work, the less they are bound up with their own works. The child who is completely involved in his own work has no interest in asking questions, no time to look around; he has so much confidence in his experience that he does not need to look for "inspiration" from others' work. He will work without interruption to a definite end.

Usually, technical performance goes hand in hand with the meaningfulness of the child's work. This should not surprise us, for it is the urge to express something meaningful which creates the desire for greater perfection. Technique grows out of the urge for expression. We know this very well also from other areas of activities. I have seen youngsters whittling bows and arrows, beginning in a very crude fashion but through an urge for greater perfection ending up with "professional" jobs. How can the meaningfulness be increased through motivation?

The meaningfulness of a motivation largely depends on two questions: (1) Is the motivation adequate to the *developmental stage*? (2) Is the motivation keyed to the *specific interest* of the child?

It is quite clear that a motivation which is not keyed to the child's level does not become meaningful to him. For example, a scribbling child being motivated by visual imagery would be unable to conceive of it in the same way as an eight-year-old child could neither understand nor conceive of perspective space. The only motivation which would be meaningful to the child is a motivation which is adjusted to his stage of development. This, however, is not enough for a meaningful motivation because it would also be useless or even detrimental to his creative work if we were to divert a child from his own interests. There are two types of interests which we always have to keep in mind. The one depends on the general developmental stage, the "group interest"; the other is determined by the single child, the "individual interest." For example, a child of six or seven years, according to his developmental stage, is necessarily self-centered. What is of immediate value to *him* is significant. Everything is focused around the "I" and "my." The meaningfulness of a motivation for a child of this stage of development will therefore depend on whether an experience is focused around the "I" and "my." It may, however, occur that a child has gotten a new doll to play with. Her individual interest and emotions are keyed to the doll. To divert her from it by imposing something on her to which she has no relationship would only be detrimental to her creative expression. This does not mean that a child who is interested in her doll cannot be effectively motivated in other spheres of her own interest. Such motivations, however, are only effective if the *whole* child is reached.

EVALUATION IN TERMS OF GROWTH

Although growth occurs simultaneously in its different components and affects the child in his totality, the different patterns of growth are discussed separately for reasons of greater clarification.

Very often the mistake is made of evaluating the child's creative work by only one component of growth, most often by external aesthetic criteria —the way a creative product "looks," its design quality, its colors, shapes, and their relationships. This is unjust not only to the creative product but even more to the child, since growth does not consist of external criteria and not at all of aesthetics only. Aesthetic growth, although very important, constitutes only one fraction of the total growth of the child. However, since art has traditionally been interpreted as being related mainly to aesthetics, this concept is greatly responsible for the neglect of the other factors of growth. In art education the final product is subordinated to the creative process. Its effect on the child is of significance in his total growth, and total growth consists not only of aesthetic growth.

It also needs to be pointed out that the different components of growth are almost never equally distributed. A child may be very free emotionally, yet he may not be very original in his approaches, his thoughts and feelings, and therefore not be very creative. Another child may be very creative and inventive but may have little feeling for organization, for design. His aesthetic component of growth has not been adequately developed. Again another child may be highly endowed creatively and also aesthetically, yet his lack of motor control, shown in his lack of physical skills, may hold him back in his creative expression. There are highly intelligent children whose intellectual growth has far out-ranked the remaining qualities of growth. Such children may be hindered in using their intelligence creatively.

In order to understand and evaluate total growth better, an analysis of the significance of the different components of growth is given in the following paragraphs.

Emotional growth

The emotional release given by a creative work to its creator usually is in direct relation to the degree and intensity with which he identifies himself with *his* work. Neither the degree nor the intensity is measurable, yet their effect can easily be recognized. Usually four steps in the degree of intensity of self-identification, and thus in the degree of emotional release, can be recognized:[7]

(1) Stereotyped repetitions
(2) Pure objective reports or generalizations
(3) Occasional inclusion of the self or substitutes for it
(4) The inclusion of experiences of the self

Frequent stereotyped repetitions are usually seen in the drawings of

[7] See also Naumburg, Margaret, *Studies of Free Art Expression of Behavior Problem Children and Adolescents As a Means of Diagnosis and Therapy.* Nervous and Mental Disease Monographs. New York, 1947.

children who have adjustment difficulties. Every adjustment to a new situation implies flexibility, flexibility in thinking and also in imagination. In severe cases of emotional maladjustments, the ability to adjust to new situations may be extremely low. There was a girl for whom the slightest change in her situation called for a serious adjustment. For example, when she was unexpectedly asked to get a glass of water, she withdrew into a cramped-like position, unable to respond to the request. For her "getting a glass of water" meant changing her position, getting up, stretching, going, finding a direction, finding the sink, the faucet, turning on the water, and many more changes of her present situation. Unable to face these changes and to adjust to them she withdrew into a stereotyped, cramped-like position. In her drawings, too, she felt most secure by repeating the same meaningless, stereotyped patterns of one and the same scheme of a figure.[8] This, too, expressed an escape into a world in which she felt secure. Only when her drawing became meaningful to her did her inflexibility gradually disappear; only when she was able to adjust to a new situation did her drawings show more self-identification. Emotionally maladjusted children frequently escape into a pattern-like representation. Such stereotyped patterns are neither adjusted to a particular experience of the child nor do they show a conscious desire for expression. The child simply repeats a schema in a rigid way because of his inability to adjust to a new situation. Such stereotyped, rigid repetitions thus express the lowest type of emotional release. Into this category of representation also belong all types of "copy-work." This, too, represents a stereotyped form of representation, a type of representation in which self-identification does not take place. Here, too, the child often is inhibited by adults, and, unwilling or unable to express his own world of experiences, he escapes into a world of patterns. Yet, copy work or tracing most often does not grow out of the child's inability to face new situations. Most often it is imposed and not a part of the child's behavior characteristics. Often, however, the continued use of copying methods deprives the child of his flexibility. The child, accustomed to depending on given patterns, no longer has the desire to adjust to new situations; he merely chooses the point of least resistance. Yet, if the child continues the use of given patterns, the end effect will be similar to the one of emotional maladjustment. Accustomed to dependency and rigidity in his creative work, the child's behavior reactions in general will reflect this tendency, because the child in his reactions does not distin-

[8] See Fig. 96a; see also Mattil, Edward, "A Study to Determine the Relationship between the Creative Products of Children and their Adjustment." Unpublished doctoral dissertation, The Pennsylvania State University, 1953.

guish between his different activities. They all reflect the total growth of the child. Thus, when copy work prevents the child from facing and expressing his own world of experiences, the child may ultimately lose confidence in his own work and resort to stereotyped repetitions as a visible escape mechanism.

It should, however, be kept in mind that there is a natural tendency for repetition in children's drawings during the schematic stage.[9] In the same way in which the child wants to assure himself, through repeated questioning, that he has found the right answer, the child also wants to assure himself that he has found his own form concept. *Stereotyped* repetitions, however, can easily be distinguished from the child's natural desire for repetition. *Stereotyped repetitions do not show any deviations,* whereas the repeated form concept during the schematic stage is used flexibly.[10] From what has been said, it becomes evident that the degree of emotional release in creative activity depends largely on the creative freedom of the child: the more frequently stereotyped repetitions occur in the child's creative work, the greater is the inflexibility of the child.

Individual satisfaction which the child obtains from his work is not always indicative of its meaningfulness for the child's growth. From what has been said in the foregoing paragraph, it can easily be understood that a child who escapes into stereotyped patterns may gain much individual satisfaction from the drawing of meaningless repetitions. The very escape from facing a world of experiences is a form of individual satisfaction, no matter how detrimental it may be for the child's growth. As we know from experience, emotionally maladjusted children most often feel greatly disturbed when something interferes with their escape mechanisms. When left alone, an emotionally maladjusted girl found apparent individual satisfaction in countless repetitions of stereotyped schemata.[11] Whenever she was diverted from them by being confronted with her own experiences, she became greatly disturbed. Yet, ultimately, this very disturbing factor brought her out of her own limitations and gradually adjusted her to life situations. Such cases are by no means rare. We find them daily in our schools—in children's, and also in teachers' reactions. "But my children love to draw from coloring books" is a well-known remark. An escape into a pattern is a "protection" from an "exposure" to the world of experiences. It is a false protection, the same "overprotection" which some parents impose upon their children. A continued overprotection conditions the

---

[9] See "Schematic Stage," p. 133.
[10] Compare Fig. 96a with Fig. 12.
[11] See Fig. 96a.

child to it and deprives him not only of his freedom but also of his ability to adjust to new situations. An overprotected child sent to camp may sit in a corner and cry for his protection, unable to use and enjoy the freedom to which he is exposed. While he apparently was individually satisfied in his overprotection, such individual satisfaction is no indication of the value of such methods. A child who loves to trace or do copy work may gain individual satisfaction from such an occupation. However, such satisfaction is based upon a false feeling of security and the fear of being exposed to new experiences. Instead of being actively engaged in his own world of experiences, the child escapes into a passive state of mind which is undesirable and unhealthy for life adjustment, citizenship, and a healthy personality.

If individual satisfaction does not go hand in hand with growth, it is of no value. If, however, individual satisfaction grows out of a feeling of achievement, if it is the result of one's ability to cope with a situation actively, it is a vital human experience which greatly contributes to the acquisition of self-confidence and happiness in life.

An emotionally dull or detached child will express his detached feelings by not including anything personal in his creative work. He will be satisfied by a mere *"objective" report*: "There is a tree, there is a house, there is a mountain"—nothing is included which may indicate his relationship to these objects. There are no other intentions but to represent the objects. Such "detached" art expression can be seen in first stages of child art as well as in developed forms of art expression. In the beginning stages such detachments can easily be detected. Usually the child adheres to mere schemata: trees are *all alike* with little or no deviations; so are houses and other objects. Figures are usually not included at all; if so, they neither show action nor variety in characteristics. In more developed art expression, the emotionally detached individual who objectively reports in his work without any participation on his part often "covers" this lack by skillful performances, or mannerisms.

An *occasional inclusion* of the self can be seen as soon as the child has achieved some emotional tie to his work and feels free enough to give it visible expression. Under "inclusion of the self" we understand any form of inclusion, direct or indirect.

In a direct inclusion of the self the child actually participates in his drawings, he may appear directly in his creative work, or he may transfer his feelings to someone else. A child may indirectly include the self by any form of personal participation. This may be seen in the characterization of objects: a house or tree which is meaningful to the child may have certain characteristics which other houses or trees do not have. A child who is emotionally free and uninhibited in creative expression feels secure and confident in attacking any problems which are derived from his experiences. He will closely identify himself with them and will with ease adjust to accidental situations which may arise from his work in dealing with different materials and media. Thus the emotionally stable individual is characterized by the great ease and flexibility with which he can identify himself with his own world of experiences.

Intellectual growth as seen in the child's creative work

Intellectual growth is usually seen in the child's growing awareness of himself and his environment. In children's drawings, the details of which the child can think are indicative of the child's intellectual alertness. The knowledge which is actively at the child's disposal when he draws may then account for his intellectual level. This knowledge changes with the chronological age of the child. Yet, even in children of the same age, a great variety of active knowledge can be seen. This difference usually indicates the difference in intellectual comprehension.[12] A child of five years who, when drawing a man, can think only of head and legs is intellectually inferior to a child who also includes the body and features. A careful account of the details as they refer to normal development is given in each chapter of the different developmental stages in the latter part of this book. There, it will be found that "details" refer to different attributes at different age levels. In the lower stages, "details" refer strictly to subject matter. A drawing full of subject matter details comes from a child with high intellectual awareness. This may not necessarily be a "beautiful" drawing. The details may often be scarcely recognizable. The child's feeling for aesthetics or his ability for skillful execution may often lag behind the intellectual comprehension. As the child grows, "details" will have a different meaning to him. "Details" may now refer to a greater differentiation in color and a more detailed account of size and space relationship, or a recognition of social issues. Yet, we must not make the mistake of thinking that lack of details of any sort in the creative expression of children *always* means low mentality. Very often emotional restrictions block the development of the child's intellectual abilities; or also, the child's tendency for too much reasoning and "intellectualizing" of his experiences may restrict his emotional freedom. In both cases the child's creative expression may suffer. It is for this reason that we often hear of children who

[12] Goodenough, Florence, *Draw A Man Test.* Worcester: Clark University Press, 1931.

are "very good in drawing" and seemingly poor intellectually, and others who are apparently "poor in drawing" and intellectually superior. For the development of a healthy personality it is of utmost significance that a *proper balance be kept between emotional and intellectual growth.* If a child is found to be restricted in his creative expression and yet high on his intellectual level, he must be given more art motivation in order to achieve the mentioned balance.[13] If a child is found to be rich in art expression but otherwise seemingly below his intellectual standard, he must be given help and confidence in his desire for intellectual achievements. Our present educational system suffers greatly from an overemphasis of intellectual growth. "Learning," that is, the acquisition of knowledge, almost exclusively stands in the focus of education. It is just as important for the child to gain freedom in expression as it is for him to get more knowledge. In fact, knowledge will remain unused, frozen, unless the child develops the urge and the freedom to use it.

Physical growth in creative activity

Physical growth in the child's creative work is seen in his capacity for visual and motor coordination; in the way in which he guides the line, controls his body, and performs his skills.

In the beginning, the mere coordination of body motion with the marks on the paper will be indicative of the child's physical growth from a state of passive enjoyment of uncontrolled motion to a level of coordinated body activity. In the later stages of development this coordination of body activities becomes more intricate. The sensitivity which often is necessary to make most minute changes needs the finest control of muscle coordination.

It is, however, not only this direct participation in body activities which includes physical growth in creative activities; the conscious and unconscious projection of the body self into the creative work and the complete self-identification of the creator with his creation accounts for much of the body control growing out of this type of creative activity. It can easily be understood that a child who puts motion into an arm of a modeled figure feels this movement in his own body. Thus, the child with a high and sensitive consciousness of body experiences will not only show good coordination and control of lines and brush strokes in his work, but will also project his ability for body control into his work. This conscious projection of body movements into creative art expression is accompanied by a kind of pro-

---

[13] A thorough discussion on methods of art motivations according to each stage of development is given in each of the respective chapters. See Table of Contents.

jection which apparently results from an unconscious presence of muscular tensions and general body feelings. Very often we can see that children with defects project these defects into their creative works. I have seen drawings of crippled children which clearly reveal the body defect by either an overemphasis or omission of the affected part. This projection, called *body imagery,* also shows the close relation between physical growth and creative activity.

Needless to say there are other forms of creative activity which entail physical growth to a much higher degree; for instance, creative dancing. The author, however, has limited himself to the discussion of drawings and paintings as one of the forms of creative expression and would not like to go beyond his limitations.

Perceptual growth as seen in creative activity

The cultivation and growth of our senses has been largely neglected in our educational system. Were it not for art education, the child would scarcely be reminded of the meaning and quality of his sense organs. Yet their proper use is of such vital importance not only for the enjoyment of life but also for vocational purposes, that we cannot afford such neglect.

In creative activity, perceptual growth can be seen in the child's increasing awareness and use of kinesthetic experiences, from the simple uncontrolled body movements during scribbling to the most complex coordination of arm and linear movements in artistic production. It can be seen in the growing response to *visual* stimuli, from a mere conceptual response as seen in early child art to the most intricate analysis of visual observation as seen in impressionistic art in which form, color, and space are subordinated to the impression of the total picture. Into this area of visual perception belongs the growing sensitivity toward color from the stage of mere enjoyment and recognition of color in early childhood to the ever-changing relationships of colors in different light and atmosphere.

Even auditory experiences are often included in art expression. This inclusion ranges from the mere awareness of sounds and their inclusion in children's drawings to sensitive reactions to musical experiences transferred into art expression.

Perceptual growth further reveals itself in the growing sensitivity to tactile and pressure sensations, from the mere kneading of clay and touching of textures to the most sensitive reaction in clay modeling and other forms of sculpturing and the enjoyment of the different qualities of surfaces and textures in interior decoration and other art forms. In addition to these factors of perceptual growth, the extremely complex area of space perception must be added. Space, for the child, means the immediate area around him, the area which has significance to him. As the child grows, the space around him grows, and the way in which he perceives it changes. An extensive discussion of the differences in space perception and how it can be seen in creative activity is given in each chapter of the various developmental stages.[14] Here it may only be pointed out that space can be perceived visually by seeing objects in various distances, or also nonvisually, by moving in space. We then distinguish between visual orientation in space and kinesthetic orientation, the type of orientation which is used by people who have no sight, or do not use it. Both of these orientations decisively affect art expression.[15]

Children who make extensive use of perceptual experiences include in their creative expression kinesthetic sensations, tactile, and visual experiences, and also a sensitive awareness of shapes, their colors, and the environment which surrounds them. In contrast to them are children who are little or not at all affected by perceptual experiences. Their creative products show timidity in lines and brush strokes as an expression of lack of kinesthetic enjoyment; they show poor visual imagery, little or no ability to observe, and no inclusion of experiences relating to tactile or other sense experiences.[16]

Social growth in creative activity

One of the factors of foremost significance in human growth is the individual's growing ability to live cooperatively in his society. This cannot be reached unless the child learns to assume responsibility for the things he is doing. Without his identifying himself with his own experiences, this is not possible. Therefore, the first step in social growth is made by facing one's own experiences. There is scarcely a better means for taking this highly important step than creative activity. It lies in the very nature of a creative process that the individual identifies himself with it. In this way he not only discovers his own self and *his* needs but also learns to identify himself with the needs of others. While the child's immediate self and his home environment will be the starting point for his creative experiences, he will soon discover that he is not alone and independent.[17] The inclusion

[14] See Table of Contents under "Space."

[15] See p. 271, "Visual and Haptic Space."

[16] Countryman, Calvin, "A Test on the Visualization of Tactile Sensations." Unpublished doctoral dissertation, The Pennsylvania State University, 1955.

[17] See p. 134, "Schematic Stage—Mass Consciousness."

of others in his creative work, the close self-identification with the needs of others, will lead the child to the discovery of the group. In it, he will find much satisfaction through group work, a very important part of creative activities. During the important period which we shall call the gang-age,[18] the child discovers his social independence with a group. The arts can greatly contribute, through cooperative work, in giving this newly discovered feeling a constructive meaning.[19] This feeling of social consciousness and responsibility is of great significance for the child's understanding of a larger world of which he will become a part.

In appreciating the arts of other cultures, the child will discover that "the arts are avenues by which the highest meaning of a whole society or culture can be felt, understood, and transmitted from one generation to the children and youth of the next." [20] He will also discover that "the arts supply the chief means by which the individual can identify and publish himself in the world." [21]

The creative works of children who are cooperative and conscious of their social responsibilities show a close feeling for self-identification with their own experiences and also with those of others. The products of children who are socially handicapped, or were suppressed in their desires for social participation, show their isolation by a lack of ability to correlate their experiences to those of others. Their work shows inconsistent, spatially uncorrelated items, and the inability to identify one's self with others in subject matter as well as action.[22]

Aesthetic growth

Aesthetic growth is one of the inherent attributes of any form of creative activity. Herbert Read calls aesthetic education "the education of those senses upon which consciousness, and ultimately the intelligence and judgment of the human individual, are based. It is only in so far as these senses are brought into harmonious and habitual relationship with the external world that an integrated personality is built up. Without such integration we get not only the psychologically unbalanced types familiar to the psychiatrist, but what is even more disastrous from the point of view of the general good, those arbitrary systems of thought, dogmatic or rationalistic in origin, which seek in spite of the natural facts to impose a logical or

---

[18] See pp. 183 and 184.
[19] See Read, Herbert, *Education Through Art*. London: Faber and Faber, 1943, pp. 274, 275.
[20] and [21] Midcentury White House Conference on Children and Youth. Conference Findings, Washington, 1950.
[22] Mattil, Edward, *op. cit.*

intellectual pattern on the world of organic life. This adjustment of the senses to their objective environment is perhaps the most important function of aesthetic education." [23]

Aesthetic growth thus is essential for any well-organized thinking, feeling, and perceiving, and the expression of these in communicable form. In fact, it is a part of any proper organization of whatever media we have at our disposal. Depending on the media, we then deal with the different art forms as expressions of this organization. The proper organization of words we call poetry; the harmonious organization of spaces we call architecture; of tones, music; of lines, shapes, and colors, painting; of body movements, dance. This organization does not start on any arbitrary line. It may start anywhere: in life, in play, in art. That is why our whole personality is affected by aesthetic principles. Wherever organization is lacking, the mind disintegrates. Aesthetics, therefore, not only affects the single individual but also our whole society. Aesthetic growth is organic with no set standards; it may differ from individual to individual and from culture to culture. It is this that distinguishes it from any arbitrarily set organization. Also in art, aesthetic criteria are based on the individual work. A creative work grows by its own aesthetic principles. If we attempt to regiment aesthetics, we arrive at dogmatic laws which have their expression in totalitarian rules. This has important implications for aesthetic growth. It implies that all set rules, rigidly applied to any creative expression, are detrimental to aesthetic growth.

In the creative products of children, aesthetic growth reveals itself by an increasing sensitivity to the total integration of all experiences concerning thinking, feeling, and perceiving. This total integration can be seen in the unity of a harmonious organization and expression of thoughts and feelings by means of spaces, lines, textures, and colors. Children who lack aesthetic growth show no feelings for organization either in their thoughts or feelings or in the expression of them.

From what has been said, it can easily be understood that aesthetic education should be one of the main forces in a democratic society.

Creative growth

One of the major distinctions between man and animal is that man creates and the animal does not. Creative growth mainly consists of the power to use freely and independently and to apply the six aforementioned components of growth for an integrated effort. Creativity is an instinct

---

[23] Read, Herbert, *op. cit.*, p. 7.

which all people possess, an instinct with which we were born. It is the instinct which we primarily use to solve and express life's problems. The child would use it to express himself even if he were not taught to do so. Recent psychological studies reveal that creativity, the ability to explore and investigate, belongs to one of the Basic Drives, a drive without which man cannot exist.

Creative growth starts as soon as the child begins to document himself. He may do it by inventing babbling noises, sounds which he produces, or he may do it by inventing his own forms which he may call "man," "house," or "mountain." It is *his* form, *his* invention which makes it a creation. From this simple documentation of one's self to the most complex forms of creations there are many intermediary steps. It is with these steps that creative growth deals.

In child art, creative growth manifests itself in the independent and original approach the child shows in his work. A child does not need to be skillful in order to be creative. Yet, for any form of creation, a certain degree of emotional freedom is necessary because creativity without freedom and fearlessness in subject approach and in the use of various media is unthinkable. Experimental attitudes are evidences of creative-mindedness. Children who have been inhibited in their creativity by dogma, rules, or forces resort to copying or tracing methods. They easily adapt styles of others as a sign of lost confidence in their own original power to create.

Since it is in the very nature of creativity that it is intuitive in character and freest when uncontrolled, creative growth does not parallel the chronological growth of the individual. Indeed, creativity is present much more in the child who has not yet been subjected to the rules of the society than in the adult who has to adhere to them. Most adults lose their creativeness and only few can save it. To preserve it and unite it with the mature mind of men is, indeed, one of the highest privileges of art education.

EVALUATION OF OBJECTIVE CRITERIA

In discussing objective criteria for purposes of evaluation we shall refer to the final product only, as the tangible objective proof of a creative development. However, it cannot be emphasized strongly enough that "objective criteria" can only supplement the "subjective criteria" discussed in the preceding chapter. Only by carefully considering both of these criteria can we do justice not only to the creative product but also to the child.

There are three important points which must be considered in the process of evaluation by means of objective criteria: (1) the stage of development; (2) technique and skill; (3) the organization of the work.

Stage of development

It is quite obvious that what may be adequate creative expression for an average child of five years can no longer be the art expression of the average eight- or ten-year-old child. As growth progresses the creative expression, a visible manifestation of growth, changes. In order to know the average criteria for purposes of evaluation, the creative development of the child must be studied in its single developmental stages. The discrepancy found between the average criteria of the respective stage of development and the chronological age of the child is indicative of the child's growth. For example, if we were to find scribbling with good and free motions done by a child of three years, we would consider this the normal form of expression. If, however, we should discover that the scribbling was done by a child of eight years we would consider the child backward in his growth in spite of the coordinated and free motions of the scribbling. This statement has only relative validity as applied to the average child. Yet it must be clearly understood that for the individual child and his development this scribbling may have provided just the right outlet. Therefore, it would have been wrong to discourage it. The mere recognition that the child of eight years should have long abolished the stage in which he merely enjoys motor activity and should already relate his creative work to his environment should be enough for the teacher to guide and motivate the child properly in his growth. It must always be up to the child to discover his own experiences and to grow by them.

Evaluation of the final product should then always be only a guide for the teacher and not a means for classifying or "grading" the child's work.

For the purpose of a more objective evaluation of the child's average creative development as compared to his chronological age a detailed discussion of developmental characteristics is included in the chapters on the different developmental stages. This discussion will refer to the representation of the human figure, the meaning of space in terms of all environmental experiences, and color. It is suggested that these paragraphs should be consulted regarding the average expectancy of levels in child art. It is self-evident that human development differs and that teachers must deal flexibly with such average expectancies, using them only as a guide.

Technique and skill

Three major considerations should guide us in the important question of evaluating techniques and skills:

(1) Did the child select a technique adequate for his expression?

(2) Is the technique used as an intimate part of the child's creative work?

(3) What degree of effort does the final product represent?

Even the most skillful child will become discouraged if he tries to express himself with wrong or inadequate means. It is up to the child to develop this sensitivity for what is possible in which type of material. Yet the lower the developmental stage, the more does the child need guidance in the selection of the right material. A more experimental attitude in letting the child "find" his media is important on the upper levels, where the satisfaction from the final product becomes more significant. How the teacher must develop a sensitivity for the child's needs has been discussed in the previous section on "Self-Identification with the Art Medium." The way in which he can guide the child in his desires for using an adequate technique for his expression must be approached from two points of view: (1) the *general* suitability of a technique for the kind of expression specific to the developmental stage, and (2) the *specific* way in which the individual uses a technique. This relationship among the child's growth, his art expressions and his specific needs for art materials and techniques is included in special paragraphs on "techniques" in the main part of the book as a part of the discussion of the different developmental stages. In these paragraphs the relationship between the child's creative needs and art expression specific to the child's level of development is analyzed.

The *specific* way in which the individual uses a technique to express *his* experiences must be considered separately. It is quite obvious that no general rules can be given for such a specific task. It is important, however, for the teacher to know the *intentions* of the child first before he gives him any suggestions. If the intentions of the child are contrary to his use of the technique, it is obvious that the child needs guidance. If, for instance, a child who paints "A Fair" in monochrome colors is unhappy because he cannot get the "noise" expressed, a discussion of what is "noise in color" could follow. Or, if a child who wants to express "racing" and surrounds everything by a static outline complains about the lack of movement, he might be given the feeling that the outline might restrict movement just as a fenced-in space would restrict movement. Such individual guidance, however, must always be of a general character. It is up to the child to apply it specifically to *his* work.

In the evaluation of the adequacy of a technique, both the *general* suitability of a technique for the stage of development as well as the *specific* way in which the individual uses a technique must be considered. *A technique must be an integral part of the creative work.* This means that a technique is never studied by itself, separated from the creative work. It is never merely a by-product. It *must* be a part of it. Its perfection grows through the urge for expression. We all know of youngsters who can make innumerable bows or slingshots and who will not stop until a perfect one has been accomplished. If this drive for perfection of a self-chosen object could be used also in the creative skills and techniques we would accomplish the desired aim. Our youngsters did not first learn how to whittle a stick without having a purpose in mind; there would have been no driving power behind a purposeless bending of rods. If, however, he had in mind to bend the rod for a slingshot, the use of the slingshot and the fun he gained from it would determine the power for the drive for perfection. It is not grammar which we learn first. There would be no use for it, were it not for the sake of expression. Once the desire for expression is awakened, the urge for greater meaningfulness will develop the desire for grammar. To find out that a sentence might change its meaning through the use of a comma may become an exciting experience for a child in whom the urge for expression is awakened.

From the foregoing it becomes evident that learning an art technique for the technique's sake would not only be senseless but might even develop in the child an aversion toward it. The best food will not taste good if there is no appetite for it. It may even cause indigestion. The same is true of an imposed technique. This is true for all levels of art education. The drive for expression must precede the learning of techniques. The more powerful is the drive for expression, the greater is the urge for technical perfection. Especially on the upper levels, this desire for greater technical perfection must be supported by the teacher. This support, however, must always be based on the individual desire of the student and determined by his work. There is no formula for drawing or modeling a figure. Also the study of it is intensely personal. There are scarcely two individuals who would look for exactly the same things. One might want to study shapes and forms, another the anatomical structure, a third the expression of it, a fourth might concentrate on movement, while a fifth may be interested in the figure as such only secondarily but will draw from it the inspiration for an abstract interpretation. The student has to be guided *in the direction* of *his* thinking. While it is true that we find many students for whom "almost any definite formula for drawing a figure or fastening two pieces of material together is more pleasing than a spontaneous experiment," [24] this represents only an uncreative escape. This type of regimented learning is contrary to any democratic spirit and may lead ultimately to a regimented society. Where else should we learn creative approaches if not in art education? Yet, skills and techniques are important, especially in the higher stages of development where self-criticism and critical awareness lead the individual to a greater emphasis on the final product. Important as skills and techniques may be, however, they must always remain a *means to an end* and never become the end themselves. In a creative technique "the hand cannot be separated from the eye and brain. It includes skilled vision, skilled imagination, skilled planning, criticism, and concentration of energies. The fault of most academic training in art has been that it neglects most of the elements necessary for a full technique. It fails even to realize that there is such a thing as the technique of artistic perceiving and imagining. It leads students too directly and constantly to the final stages of execution and expression, with too little attention to the preliminary phases of creative thinking. . . . The mental and manual are intimately bound together. Perhaps this is the main distinction between the artist and the uncreative worker, however skilled the latter may be in a mechanical way. In the former, direction of the hands and outer medium is controlled by an inner, self-developed aim and vision, whereas the factory machine operator can at times almost let his hands work by themselves, without conscious control." [25]

Especially in our secondary schools, where compartmentalized teaching of subjects still prevails to a great extent, we can find the same tendency for specialization in art education. It must be possible for *all* children and youth to participate in art education. That is only possible if we recognize the creative potentialities in each individual. Technique, after all, is only the acquisition of the necessary skills to execute one's own creative desires. This shows again that the individual determines his own standard.

In evaluating a product of art it is the teacher's task to find out whether the child or youth has reached his own standard. This is not always easy. We know from our own experiences that standards greatly differ and that not all children's drives are strong enough to reach the height of their own standards. Thus, we most often encounter a discrepancy between the child's

[24] Munro, Thomas, "Creative Ability in Art." *Fortieth Yearbook of the National Society for the Study of Education*, Bloomington, Ill.: Public School Publishing Co., 1941.
[25] Munro, *Op. cit.*, pp. 315–316.

potential creative ability and his actual work. This is a very important factor in the evaluation of a creative product. In an ideal situation the child always reaches his creative height; yet we know that there are many children who are skillful and uncreative, and others who are creative and not skillful. The one may, with little effort, achieve a pleasing result, while the other may put too much effort into his work and will achieve little. The relation between effort and ability must be taken into account. It would be unjust and undemocratic to neglect the efforts of the less gifted ones. As a guide for a just evaluation we should always ask ourselves, "Did the child reach his potential possibilities; is this the best *he* can do?" If not, in most instances it can be shown easily and explained to the child that into this part of his work he has put more effort and expression, while this part has been left "empty." In a former work the child may have reached his "high" point, while the present work does not show the same effort and concentration. This, however, brings us to the discussion of the last of the objective criteria.

The organization of the work

In evaluating the organization of a child's creative work we shall consider three major points:

(1) How meaningful to the child are the areas in the picture?

(2) Did the child follow a mode of expression consistently?

(3) Is the work a coherent whole?

How meaningful the different parts in a creative work are to the child can be found easily by asking the child the simple question: "What does this mean to you?" Yet, if the child is not present, we have to rely on characteristics which may help us to distinguish meaningful from meaningless parts. The meaningfulness of parts in general depends on two factors: (1) the literal content or, as we also might call it, the intellectual and emotional description of the subject matter; and (2) the way the part is placed in its environment.

Meaningless parts, which have no intentional meaning to the child, have little or no detailed description and in no way stand out in size and color. Parts which are meaningful as an experience and important in their contents are usually quickly recognizable by the emphasis on meaningful details and also by the size and color of each part in relation to the rest of the work. A child who attaches no special meaning to a house will simply draw its schema, which consists of his *general* interpretation of house. A child who has had a meaningful experience with a house will indicate this experience by an added relationship to a *specific detail*. In Fig. 18 the child slept on the upper floor and indicated this by the inclusion of a stairway. In Fig 7b the mother of the child usually kept track of the child by looking through the little window in the door. Aware of the significance of the window, the child included it as a special detail. In Fig. 13 size and color relationships indicate the significance the subway had to the child in relation to the "mass" of houses, which are all equal in regard to details but stand out in the difference of color and size.

We can receive an important insight into the meaningfulness of an object to a child from the way he places the object in value relation to its environment. Gustaf Britsch [26] gives a splendid description of the relationship between the "meaningful" and the "meaningless." He says: "Let us consider that someone places a bouquet of flowers on an empty table. He is not doing it just casually in passing by, only in order to pick it up again; rather he is doing it with the purpose of arranging it on the table. The majority of people will place the bouquet in the center of the table. In doing so they document this action by the fact that they had something meaningful in mind: the bouquet of flowers. The meaningfulness of it could have only been emphasized by separating it from a meaningless environment. In placing the bouquet in the center of the table, they changed the table into an unnoticed and unimportant environment." In Fig. 6 none of the parts is especially meaningful or meaningless. They seem to be placed casually on the paper. They are like a bouquet of flowers which was placed on the table with no specific purpose in mind. Table and bouquet had therefore equal meaning in their *presence* as *objects*. In Fig. 7c and Figs. 8 and 9, we can see that a definite value relationship has been established which distinctly places the meaningful object in a value relation to its environment. The objects are no longer present merely as isolated parts but have assumed *meaningfulness* relative to each other. This meaningfulness is somewhat different in Fig. 7c from in Fig. 8. In Fig. 7c the meaningfulness of the central figure clearly stands out. Yet, it is directed toward the other objects on the bottom of the drawing. The "empty" space around the figure is like the table around the bouquet. It is meaningless, unimportant, but serves the purpose of bringing out the central figure. In Fig. 8 the meaningfulness of the central figures stands out, too. In this case, however, no direction is given. The "empty" space around the figures also emphasizes them. However, the space is no longer as meaningless as the one in Fig 7c. Through the dots (snow) it has received a secondary meaning—like a table cloth would have if it matched the bouquet.

[26] Britsch, Gustaf. *Theorie der Bildenden Kunst.* München: F. Bruckmann, A-G., 1926, p. 29.

The second point raised regarding the evaluation of the organization of the child's creative work was related to the consistency of the child's work. The question of whether a child follows a mode of expression consistently needs some clarification before it can be answered. What do we understand by "mode of expression" and what do we call "consistent"?

A mode of expression can be derived from conscious or unconscious sources. It may "just happen" or it may intentionally be followed up. This is especially true of child art. Most often both intentional and unconscious modes of expression are combined. In Fig. 14 the conscious mode of expression was determined by the child's intention to *represent* apple pickers. He has done it consistently, since all parts in the picture relate to his chosen theme. Our questions will then be: (1) "Is there a central theme?" and (2) "Do all parts in the creative work relate to the central theme?"

In children's drawings unconscious mode of expression refers to *how* the child expresses himself. Later in the development, when the child becomes more concerned with techniques, this unconscious form of expression becomes influenced by a more conscious use of techniques. In Fig. 14 the decorative schema of the trees, the peculiar organization and distribution of the "spaces," was purely unintentional. But here also its consistency can be followed up by its uniformity. A mode of expression would not be consistent if one element fought another element; for instance, if a painting which mainly consists of bold brush strokes also had meaningful pencil lines. The intended meaningfulness of the pencil lines would be overpowered by the bold brush strokes. They would make the pencil lines scarcely visible. (Compare the consistency of Fig. 19 and Fig. 21.)

The third question refers to the wholeness of a creative work and its organization, its design. Does design refer to expression? Is the expression put forth in the creative work held together and carried by design? These questions are the most difficult to answer, and all theories concerning the meaning of composition, balance and rhythm will give only a superficial answer. In fact, what we usually find in such discussions only approaches the external quality of the wholeness of a creative work. We must always keep in mind that design is only the structure which holds all inherent qualities together. Only the interrelation between the meaning of a creative work and its design values makes the work a coherent whole. The only practical approach to this question seems to me to be the negative approach: would a change within the organization of the creative work affect its meaning? If it would, the work is apparently so coherent that any change would disturb its wholeness. As long as changes would not interfere with the expression and meaning of the work, it appears that the work is not a coherent whole. For instance, what would happen if we tried to change the position or the place of the apple picker in Fig 14? Let us try to put his hands into the basket; the space between him and the apple tree would then become too big. It would isolate him and thus would not carry the message of apple picking. We surely could change his position by moving the tree and placing him between the trees. This change, however, seems to necessitate another change. The figure in the center would create an almost symmetrical balance on the lower part, while the upper one would be completely asymmetrical. It would also change the meaning of the picture. This way, the boy appears to be somewhat of an outsider, a casual picker. Were he in the center, he would appear to be in the midst of the work, a permanent laborer.

The complete integration of content and organization, of design and its meaning, is one of the intrinsic qualities of a creative work. Any artificial influence on the part of the teacher would only cause confusion in the child. Such unity has to come from the child as a sign of his state of mind and should help the teacher only to gain more insight into the child's growth.

GRADING THE CHILD'S CREATIVE PRODUCT

Whenever the main attention is diverted from the child to the product which he produces, injustice must result both to the child and to his work. A child who may have been inhibited and frustrated in his expression, and for the first time crudely reveals his experience, might produce a creative product which scarcely shows the importance of this action. For the child this may have been the first tender beginning of a new life, a life in which he no longer has to escape into meaningless stereotypes, a life in which he can face his own self and freely express it. Yet, the beginning is difficult. It may just consist of some slight deviation from his former mode of expression, scarcely recognizable to the "naked eye." Yet for the child this first little step was decisive. We would not notice it in his final product unless we know the child and his former mode of expression. By looking at the product only, we would not only do injustice to the child but also to the significance which the process of self-discovery has for him. By comparing his work with the work of others in the same grade, we would completely neglect the individual child.

It is then needless to say that grading of creative products, however it is done, is harmful to the child because it diverts his attention from the creative process to the final product. It may add another blow to an inhibited child who for the first time has found himself in his creative activity, for his work does not compare with that of others. A poor grade, in addition to his inhibitions, indeed would not promote his freedom of expression.

Unfortunately, in most of our public schools, grading is required. If rigid numerical grades can be avoided and replaced by descriptive grades, it would be of great advantage. In descriptive grades the child's problems can at least be revealed. If numerical grades are required, the least harm may be done by grading the individual's progress, rather than by establishing "classroom standards." Such external standards only deal with the product and completely neglect the individual child and the effect which the creative process had on him. By grading the child's progress we at least deal with the child. By comparing the successive products we can draw certain conclusions as to the child's efforts, the meaningfulness of his *experience*, the *organization* of it, and the *skill* with which he used his media. Even then we might punish him for his inhibitions if we do not take into account that we deal with human beings and not with products.

EVALUATION CHART

The evaluation chart on pages 69–71 is of a general nature. It is more a summary of the chapter on evaluation. In it, only the general criteria are emphasized. Therefore, it can be used for all stages of development. The chart can be used for obtaining a child's profile of his growth by checking the answers and connecting the check marks. The right side of the curve represents the superior quality, the left side the inferior ones, and the center expresses average qualities. Evaluation charts designed to meet the specific needs of the different developmental stages are included in the discussion of the respective stages.

EXHIBITS AND COMPETITIONS

Natural competition

In every healthy classroom situation the child feels a part of the classroom spirit. It is obvious, therefore, that he will have a natural desire to improve this spirit by his own contribution. This contribution starts as soon as the drive to express himself in one or another medium is awakened in the child. First, he competes with himself, finding out whether he cannot do better than he has done before. Growth is a continuous competition with

GENERAL EVALUATION CHART

Objective Criteria	Little	Some	Much
Is the child's creative work adequate for his stage of development in representing the:			
1. figure			
2. space			
3. color			
Technique adequate for expression.			
Technique is part and parcel of child's work.			
What degree of effort does final product represent?			
Meaningfulness of single parts of work as detail.			
Meaningfulness of single parts of work as part of environment.			
To what extent did child follow a mode of expression?			
To what extent does any change upset the meaning of the work?			

GENERAL EVALUATION CHART (Continued)

Degree of Self-identification	Yes	No
1. Constant stereotyped repetitions		
2. Now and then stereotyped repetitions		
3. Mere objective reports		
4. Some inclusion of self by adding special characteristics to objective report		
5. Indirect or direct inclusion of the self		

	Attributes of Growth	Little	Some	Much
Emotional Growth	Free from stereotyping. Lack of generalization of objects (no trees are alike, etc.). Constant deviations from generalizations. Inclusion of experiences of the self. Use of free lines and brush strokes.			
Intellectual Growth	Inclusion of many subject matter details. Differentiation in color. Other indications of active knowledge.			
Physical Growth	Visual and motor coordination (how well he guides lines). Conscious projection of body movements (representation of them). Unconscious projection of body (body image). Skillful use of techniques.			

Perceptual Growth	Visual experiences: light
	                 shadows
	                 perspective space
	                 color differentiation
	Non-visual experiences: tactile
	                     texture
	                     auditive
	Kinesthetic experiences (body movements).

Social Growth	Faces his own experiences in his work. Identification with the needs of others. Inclusion and characterization of social environments (home, school, factory, office). Participation in group work. Appreciation of other cultures. Enjoyment of cooperation, directly (through work) or indirectly (through the topic).

Aesthetic Growth	Integration of thinking, feeling, and perceiving.
	Sensitiveness toward harmonious color.
	    " " " texture.
	    " " " lines.
	    " " " shapes.
	Preference for decorative design patterns.

Creative Growth	Independence without copying. Originality without imitating style of others. Creativeness and inventiveness in regard to content. Can immediately be distinguished from others in mode of expression. Is entirely different from others.

one's own standards and achievements. This is the most natural and healthy form of competition, especially at a time when the child does not approach his environment critically and with awareness. The family and the natural classroom situation already will confront the child with competitive experiences which often create difficult problems. The difficulties most often arise from the child's inability to conceive of achievements of others beyond his own level and to cope with them. If parents and teachers do not appreciate the child's own individual contributions on the child's own merits, complications such as jealousy or withdrawal of the child from active participation may result.[27] In creative expression not only the various stages of development differ but also individual modes of expression. Since the child's art activities merely serve for him as means of expression, and his individual mode of expression may greatly differ from that of his classmate, he often may be unable to conceive of and understand these differences.

The situation changes somewhat when the child grows older and the final product becomes more and more significant. While for the younger child the natural competition in the home and in the classroom often confronts him with difficulties which are beyond his comprehension, for the older child natural competition is one of the best characteristics of a good and creative home or classroom atmosphere. In the upper grades of the elementary school and further on, the stimulation which children receive from each other's creative approaches is an invaluable contribution to creative teaching. The child is simultaneously exposed to the many different "styles" and modes of expression which he now can evaluate in terms of his own experiences. Such natural competition which is not based on standards creates a most wholesome atmosphere.

Forced competition

Under forced competition we mean the type of competition which does not grow from a natural situation but which is introduced. Usually in forced competitions a certain standard must be met and prizes are given as stimulus and reward.

Since teachers often are confronted with this type of competition, an analysis of its educational meaning seems to be important. It is without any doubt that most of the competitions are sponsored with the best intentions—usually to give the child an additional stimulus to use the utmost of his abilities and to prepare him for life situations, according to the sponsors, for competition also plays an important part in life. Competitions further

[27] See p. 14.

reward him for his efforts, apparently comparing favorably with life situations. Some even say that such preparation is essential, because life is not easy and is full of competition. They say that it would be artificial to protect the child from the struggle to which sooner or later he will be exposed. Finally it is said that the child should see how his work compares with that of others. All this and more is said in favor of competitions.

Let us try to apply these arguments to the child's situation and the meaning of art education. Child art is highly differentiated. It is extremely individual. There are scarcely two children who express themselves entirely alike. One of the important aims of art education is to bring out these individual differences which make up the child's personality. Their suppression would inhibit the child's personality. In order to have *all* children participate in expressing their individual differences creatively, art education emphasizes the freeing process of self-expression and not the final product. Any competition which is based on the final product *must* immediately have the effect of diverting the attention of the child from the working process to the final product. Such a diversion is most harmful to the child since it confronts him directly with problems of evaluations of the final product which are inconceivable to him. A child who won a high award in one of the recent competitions could not recognize his own drawing. This is by no means rare. Children quickly change and therefore lose contact with their former mode of expression. Another child did not know at all *why* he won the prize; neither did the other children in the classroom. However, since the child who won the prize drew his animal—which won the award—with the flat part of the crayon, *all* children in the classroom drew with the flat part of the crayon from then on. Thus the competition not only directed the children's attention to the final product but stimulated them to imitate. This way, they lost confidence in their own ability to express themselves. A child has no understanding why somebody else's drawing won a prize. For him there are no "rights" and "wrongs" in creative expression. If some "standards" are imposed upon him, they will only harm his personality since they will suppress his individuality. Since the child does not use "techniques" consciously, an emphasis on the final product may make him conscious of "techniques" and take away his spontaneity. Very often the child expresses experiences in his creative products which are not visible even to experienced teachers, yet they may be highly significant for the child. In competitions, usually the aesthetically beautiful drawings and those which are "original" receive awards. "Original," however, has the connotation of standing out from others by means of external qualities. Those children who express themselves sincerely, but neither originally nor aesthetically, never have a chance to receive rewards in competitions. Yet, they might be the children for whom creative activities are most important. For they need the freeing of their personalities most urgently. Competition does not provide such a release since it is based on the final product whereas the child grows through the creative process.

The best preparation for the child's future life is to give him a "fair chance for a healthy personality."[28] No artificial stimulations—no matter how high the rewards are—can replace the sound *experience* which is necessary for any creative work.

For the upper levels, that is, when the child becomes more critically aware of himself and his environment, the meaning of competition may change somewhat. During puberty when the child's attentions grow more toward the final product, it can easily be understood that the final creative work assumes greater significance. Yet, we must contend with another factor which completely counteracts this growing significance. With this increasing awareness, during puberty, the youth not only becomes more conscious of the final product, but also of his inability to solve it adequately. We all know that this is the period where most of our youth lose confidence in their ability to draw or paint. Yet, one of the main aims of art education on this level is to preserve creative freedom beyond childhood and make art an activity for *all*. Shall we then continue to *emphasize* the dividing line between those who are "gifted" and those who are shaken in their confidence to create? Do we need the added stimulus of "rewards" for the gifted which harm the ones who have not found themselves creatively?

Competition may be a great incentive—and often also a discouragement—on the professional level. However, it seems a necessity which has not always brought out great genius, as the history of art will demonstrate. Nevertheless, exhibitions are one of the few means in which artists can reveal themselves to others. If we have especially gifted art students in secondary schools why shouldn't they participate in competitive exhibits. Should we concentrate, however, on the few by neglecting the others? No jury can take into consideration the meaningfulness of a work to its creator. It is this meaningfulness which is most important to the development of a healthy personality, especially at a time when the individual's confidence is shaken.

There is another aspect of competitions which needs to be discussed—the time-consuming effort required to prepare for them, and the pressure exerted to meet a deadline. I have seen schools which are constantly geared

[28] Main theme of the Midcentury White House Conference on Children and Youth, Washington, 1950.

to work for competitions. The results are: superficiality, stress on techniques, and overemphasis of the final outcome. All this overpowers any serious attempt for self-identification of the youth with his own creative experiences. The natural competition which takes place in every good classroom atmosphere remains the most healthy type of competition.

Classroom and school exhibits

If we speak of exhibits we mean the showing of works with no competitive aims. Such exhibits may serve two purposes: (1) to reveal what has been done, and (2) to follow a certain educational purpose. It is without any doubt that both objectives may be of great value.

Exhibits in classrooms are usually held for the children's sake. The child loves to see his own work displayed more than he enjoys that of others. Which works should be displayed? Should we display them indiscriminately —or should a selection be made? From what has been said before, it is quite obvious that no work should be displayed which does not express the child's own experiences. That is why all pattern or copy work should be excluded. If we have to make any further selection it by no means should be made from the viewpoint of "adult taste." Often the most expressive drawings may not appear beautiful to the adult. *All* child art should be displayed which expresses the child's own and sincere intentions. Classroom exhibits should frequently be changed for the child loses quickly the intimate relationship to his own work. Often children don't even recognize their own work after a short time span. It is not only senseless, but may even be detrimental to display children's "developments" for them, because their feeling for past experiences most often is gone and "old" drawings have become meaningless. For the teacher and the parent such displays of developmental series may be highly educational. It gives the teacher and the parent an excellent means to compare different stages in the development of children, to see the progress, or often to detect certain stereotyped repetitions or emotional blocks. Many important attributes which cannot be seen in the single work reveal themselves in the sequence of drawings.

If an exhibit is done for an educational purpose, the exhibit needs careful labeling and the purpose should clearly be visible. The following are some educational purposes for which exhibits can be designed:

Child Development
Individual Development
Aspects of Growth
Developmental Stages

Types of Expression
Use of Techniques
Styles of Expression
Normal Development versus Deviant Developments
Integrative Aspects
Trends in Art Education
Areas of Expression
Subject Matter Approaches
Schemes of Displays
Parent-Teacher Child Relationships
Socio-Economic Backgrounds as Seen in Art

Every exhibit is a visual organization of material. Not enough care can be given to its proper display. An exhibit in which too many things are shown is confusing. If the attention is supposed to be directed toward one piece, the piece should be clearly isolated. If a series of pieces belong together, the sequence should be brought out through the display. The educational influence of a well-organized display is very great. The very way in which the sign leading to the exhibit is lettered will reflect the type of the exhibit upon the visitor. A casual sign with poor lettering may immediately put him into a psychological state of non-attentiveness and casual reactions. A carefully labeled exhibit will psychologically create the feeling of orderly thoughts and organization. Casual labeling will give the feeling of casual thoughts, even in an educationally well-planned exhibit. Above all, the assembly line should not take over the exhibits. They should be small, frequent, and meaningful.

MUST A TEACHER PRODUCE CREATIVELY?

A work of art as a product of human spirit can be understood only when the driving forces which lead to its creation are understood. These driving forces vary with the individual and his developmental stage; they are determined also by the culture in which the work is produced and the medium in which it is created. To motivate the student wisely it is essential for the teacher not only to know these driving forces, but to identify himself with the creator and experience these forces as if they were a part of his own experiences. The more complex these forces are, the more difficult it is for the teacher to understand, analyze, and identify himself with them. Vice versa, it might appear that the more primitive the creative product, the easier it is for the teacher to identify himself with the creator. This is not quite so, however, for primitiveness may be more remote from our thinking than is a generally accepted art expression. The two main sources of difficulty for a teacher in this process of self-identification with the creator are a *discrepancy between his own way of thinking and experiencing and that of his pupils* on the one hand, and a lack of skill in thinking and *creating in the different mediums* on the other hand. While the first is a matter of psychological understanding and insight, the latter is of a purely artistic nature.

Psychological insight in art instruction

In teaching situations the *psychological insight* and the ability to *think in terms of different mediums* cannot be separated from each other. However, both of these attributes will vary in significance during different stages in human development. During childhood—that is, during the stage in which the child creates in an unaware, unconscious fashion—the handling of material, the thinking and creating in terms of different mediums is done without control. Thus any influence by the teacher on the use of materials and mediums would only interfere with the child's individual approach. For the teacher of the very young child thinking in terms of mediums is important for the understanding of creative processes, but it is the *psychological insight* of the teacher which in this developmental stage of the child and his creative activity is of utmost significance. A child who cannot express himself freely will not gain freedom in his creative expression merely through technical aids. Since the young child is totally unaware of technical procedures his inability to express himself is usually a sign of lack of self-confidence or inhibitions. Whatever the cause of these inhibitions or lack of self-confidence may be, it cannot be removed by technical aids. It is this interference with the child's creative activity through giving technical advice which so often characterizes the instruction of artists or teachers who think for themselves in terms of creative use of mediums and who do not have the psychological insight necessary for properly motivating the child. If a child lacks confidence in expressing himself creatively, the only way to remove his inhibitions is to get at the roots and find the cause. Usually this lies in the inability to establish a relationship between experiences and representation. If a child says "I can't draw myself throwing a ball," an encouragement of technique in terms of drawing mediums will not help him to establish more confidence. On the contrary, it may even widen the gap between his experience and the inability to express it. What the child needs is a boost in his experience. "Show me how *you* throw a ball—What did you do with your arms, your legs?—Let's try it again—

Now you threw it up high—What did you do with your hands?—Where did you look?"—and so on. Such questions will establish the child's confidence in relationship to his experience and will finally create the *urge* in him to express himself. *The "mastery" of a medium is only a result of the need for expression.* It is, therefore, of major importance to learn the child's needs. If these needs are understood, motivation becomes a simple procedure.

Can the elementary school teacher profit through his *own* artistic achievements? Yes, by all means, for producing creatively is to a very great extent a matter of identification with the expressed experience. In fact, as it was discussed in the chapter on self-identification, no creative expression is possible without identification of the creator with his work. It is this ability of identification which the teacher has to use when properly motivating the child; with the young child this can be best achieved through psychological insight without direct reference to skills.

As the child grows, the final creative product becomes increasingly significant to him. With the shift from the emphasis on the working process to the final product, thinking in terms of art mediums becomes a part of the creative process. It then becomes impossible for a teacher who has never gone through the experience of creating in a specific medium to understand the significance of thinking in terms of that medium—whether it is wood, clay, pencil, paint, plastics, or crayon. Nor will the study or the manipulation of elements in design such as line, space, color, lights, darks, and textures be enough—the *real* experience with them is what counts. A teacher who has never experienced the qualities of wood—its grain and texture, its elasticity, its characteristics of splinting—will never be able to motivate and inspire the youth who has failed to solve a poorly conceived problem in working with wood. To think *in terms of the material* is an important creative process, especially important during the adolescent years when the unity among concept, material, function, and purpose helps to encourage the youth in his desire to achieve a final product which he can appreciate. If this final product does not grow out of organized thinking, a thinking in which medium and expression are unified, the result will express a chaos in which the medium fights the concept, in which materials have ceased to be a part of creative expression. It is understood, of course, that the ability to think creatively in terms of mediums does not imply that every teacher must be practiced in all mediums. It is rather the intense experience accompanying any creative occupation which is important for keeping alive in the teacher his appreciation and understanding of creative experiences of his students.

I, myself, as a painter, have often experienced these creative compulsions—to form and express ideas with paint. Out of the desire to find myself in my paintings and the struggle with the medium, I have gained my most valuable insight into the nature of creativity on the level of awareness. Nothing can replace the value to me of these most precious hours of creative production for understanding the works of my pupils and students. Their struggle becomes my struggle.

Identification of teacher with child through his own work

Both the mental act of self-identification with the intentions of the creator and the ability to think in terms of the medium in which his intentions are to be expressed are important prerequisites for good motivation in art teaching. To speak of an extreme case: a person who has been blind from birth could never be motivated in his desire to creative expression by referring to color, perspective, and other visual concepts. Color and visual perspective are inconceivable to him. Being forced to express himself in these mediums would only have a frustrating effect on him. A teacher who identifies himself with the intentions of his blind students would never do this. While such extreme cases are rarely to be found in the average classroom, the principles involved in knowing the needs of the individual to be motivated are the same. Just as we would frustrate an individual who wants to express his inward feeling of a subjective relationship to his experiences by asking him to express merely visual relationships of objects in space, so a visually minded student would feel lost when confronted with the "must" of expressing himself subjectively or abstractedly. While the first fact is becoming generally understood by teachers, there is great danger in our progressive art schools that a modern "standard" is being created which excludes the visually minded individual from creative participation. Any rigid standard puts an end to creative production. The sincere desire of the teacher to identify himself with the creative intentions of his pupils will prevent him from adhering to such rigid principles, and his own experimentation in creative mediums may help him to refrain from setting up specific standards of validity.

The flexibility of the teacher

There is still another important factor which makes creative activity necessary to a good art teacher. A work of art is not the representation of the thing; it is rather the representation of the experiences which we have with the thing. These experiences change with our subjective relation to the environment as well as with the mediums through which these relationships are expressed. This holds true for the design and execution of a chair as well as for the design and execution of a picture. Any form of art expression is, therefore, a dynamic ever-changing process. It is this changing process which is of greatest educational significance, for through it the individual's mind remains flexible and adjustable. This is not only important for the student, but even more so for the teacher, who needs this flexibility both to understand and motivate the individual and to be able to shift and adapt his thinking from individual to individual.

From what has been said, it is clearly understood that the emphasis in this discussion is on the creative process and not on the final product. That the teacher of art sincerely experiments with the creative mediums in finding his own expression is, therefore, more significant for him than the final product he achieves. The most primitive and sincere outcome, therefore, will be of greater value for his teaching than a brilliant technical performance which lacks the self-identification which is so vital a part of sound creative teaching.

THE TEACHER'S NEED FOR KNOWING DEVELOPMENTAL STAGES

As has been pointed out, the need for properly stimulating the child derives from the basic psychological connection among the child's emotional experience, his mental level, and his creative expression. It is this psychological connection which we have to study. Since subject matter in creative activity has such a different meaning from that in other fields, a thorough clarification of the relation between developmental stages and subject matter is necessary. In arithmetic, for instance, only a gradual increase in the difficulty and amount of subject matter will allow the child to grasp it properly. According to the child's mental development, the amount and difficulty of subject matter is thoroughly balanced. The child starts by learning the single symbols for numbers. Then he learns to count, to add, to subtract, to multiply, and so forth.

How does subject matter relate to creative expression and how is subject matter in creative activity related to the mental stages of the child? Before answering these important questions, it is necessary to clarify the meaning of subject matter in creative activity.

Whereas subject matter in other fields is almost exclusively related to content, in creative expression it is quite different. The content, the "what" we represent, is trees, houses, plants, flowers, men, and so forth. In creative activity there is no changing subject matter which must be taught, because the same subject matter is used in all the various age levels. There is no orderly sequence of subject matter, as in arithmetic or other fields. A man can be drawn by a five-year-old child or by a sixteen-year-old youth. What then can be expected to be the difference in teaching a five-year-old child or a sixteen-year-old youth? The difference in teaching of arithmetic is evident. There, the child may first learn to distinguish between one and two, and later he will study the higher forms of mathematics. Subject matter in creative art, as stated above, does not change during the different age levels. It is determined by "man and environment" throughout elementary-school levels and beyond. "Man and environment" do not change. *What changes is our subjective relationship with man and environment.* It is this subjective relation between the world and ourselves that has to be studied in order to know how to stimulate a child properly according to his age level. A "man" to a five-year-old child means mainly the self, the ego, which needs a head for thinking and eating and two legs for running (head-feet representation). For a ten-year-old child, a "man" still means mainly a projection of the self. However, consciously aware of the variety of man's actions, movements, and body parts, the ten-year-old represents "man" accordingly. A sixteen-year-old youth, however, has already discovered that man is a part of environment and he represents "man" with conscious consideration of size and proportions in comparison to what surrounds him. So changes a tree—for a five-year-old child the tree is something undifferentiated, a trunk and something indefinite on top; for a ten-year-old, the tree is a trunk with branches to climb on; and for a sixteen-year-old youngster, a tree is a part of the environment, with which he is acquainted in detail. The subjective relation of these young people to the tree has changed entirely though it is still the same tree—the same subject matter. This makes it clear that it would be entirely wrong to teach how to draw a tree or a man. Moreover it would be beyond the comprehension of a five-year-old child to perceive or understand a tree in all its details as a part of environment. He would not even be able to take in an explanation of the realistic meaning of a tree. Accordingly a "perfect" drawing of a tree with all its details would be entirely out of place. "Perfect" is a relative value judgment, and in creative activity it means "perfect" in relation to the child's experience. "Perfect" for a five-year-old child is a representative symbol for tree. It would be unnatural if the child drew it realistically with all details. Hence, it is clear that "subject matter" must be more confined to the "how" than to the "what." In creative activity subject matter is based upon *the subjective experience of man and environment according to the various mental levels.* A proper application of subject matter in creative activity requires the study of the change of the subjective relation of the child to man and environment throughout the mental levels. There is no subject matter "tree," only the different ways a tree is experienced in the various years of life. However, since there are so many possible ways of drawing a tree in each school grade and since there are besides trees, an almost unlimited number of things in the environment, it will be necessary to investigate the common base of children's experiences. This investigation will lead to the understanding of all the various forms of expression used in their representations.

The answer to the question, "What makes the child express one and the same thing differently at different mental levels," will be of essential importance for the understanding of the child's creative work. It also will be significant for the nature of stimulation on the part of the teacher. What makes a child of four or five years express a man by drawing only a head and two legs? Does this really represent the child's knowledge of a human being? Certainly, every four- or five-year-old child knows that we have a body, two arms, hands, and even fingers. He even knows that we have fingernails if his attention is directed toward them. But no average child of this age would ever draw such details. *What the child draws is his subjective experience of what is important to him during the act of drawing.* Therefore, the child only draws what is *actively* in his mind. Thus in such a drawing of a "man" we get only a report of the *active knowledge* the child has of a man while he is drawing. *In other words, the drawing gives us an excellent record of the things which are of especial mental or emotional importance to the child.*

Still another factor has to be taken into consideration as an important means for the proper stimulation of a child's creative activity. The change of the child's *relationship* to environment involves *emotional* as well as *mental* growth. This is one of the most important facts in the child's emotional and social adjustment. The child, depending upon the help and care of others (at the beginning on the parents), does not feel the necessity of cooperating or collaborating with others. His most important experience is the experience of the self. That is why his spatial correlations are very indefinite in the beginning. The growing interdependence between the child and his environment is expressed in his drawings. If, in this emotional experience, the experience of perceiving environment sensually (bodily, kinesthetically, or visually) is included, the investigation of the child's relationship to what surrounds him is placed on a broader base. This investigation still lacks an important part if size, dimensions, distance, and relative proportions of the self to environment are not also included. The differences in the concept of size and distance of children and adults point clearly to the psychological importance of these questions. Distances and sizes which appeared large in childhood appear different to the adult. But since these psychological questions of the child's relationship to outside experiences can scarcely come under the heading "environment," all these experiences are put together under "space"—experiences in space or of space. To simplify matters, *all experiences that refer to things outside of our body will be regarded as experiences of space.*

As a result of this discussion, it can be understood why no proper stimulation of the child's creative activity can be given without a thorough knowledge of what changes may be expected, at the various developmental stages, in the child's subjective relation to man and environment.

GENERAL CLASSROOM PROCEDURES

Discipline

Much has been said on "self-discipline" as contrasted to rigid or "forced discipline." It is needless to say that it is part of our ethics to adhere as long as we can to the principle of "self-discipline," the discipline which grows out of the understanding of a situation and the desire to relate one's self to it, and not out of force. However, adhering to the principle of self-discipline under any circumstances would be as wrong as using "forced discipline," the discipline which is brought about by external rules, by force, or other means of punishment. It cannot be stressed enough that in any classroom situation, the "principle of extending the frame of reference," [29] that is, starting with the given situation and environment and gradually changing from there on, should be applied. This is especially important for the beginning teacher. One cannot suddenly "establish" self-discipline in a situation which lacks completely the understanding of and readiness for it. The education to self-discipline is a long and slow process, especially in an environment of rigid discipline. To try to establish "self-discipline" in an environment in which children have been conditioned to the use of rigid rules would be like swimming against the tide. "Self-discipline," not being understood and appreciated, would soon result in chaos. Indeed, chaos is worse than rigid discipline, for in chaos no learning is possible. It is therefore important that a new teacher, facing a school

[29] See p. 5.

situation of rigid discipline, initially continue this type of discipline. For, once he has established it, he can more easily, with educational means, move on from there. It cannot be stressed enough that the first contact with children is almost always decisive for the later conduct. Therefore, the first motivation must be given with the full attention of *all* children. It must not be started even if *one* child is not completely with the teacher. The greater this initial contact—even if brought about by a somewhat demanding, "Mary, I don't see your eyes," or, "Johnny, you are playing with your crayon," the easier it will be for the teacher to "ease-up" the atmosphere. It is needless to say that essential for any "creative unfolding" is a relaxed atmosphere in which children feel free to express themselves and communicate, when such communication is important for the exchange of ideas. It must be remembered that one of the important contributions of classroom learning consists of the free interchanging of thoughts, of the dynamics which develop in group activities. If this freedom is thwarted, creative activity will not thrive. However, we must clearly distinguish between chaos and the free exchange of ideas so essential for creative expression.

Preparation and distribution of materials

Matters of apparently pure technical importance, such as the preparation and distribution of art materials, may sometimes be decisive for the success or failure of an art teacher's ability to motivate his pupils effectively. In many instances, I have seen teachers very effectively motivating their children's sensitivity toward experiences and materials, completely wasting all their efforts by destroying their "creative atmosphere" by distributing the materials at the time when the children were just "bursting" to express themselves. The preparation and distribution of art materials belong as much to a good art teacher as the motivation. It is quite obvious that children on all levels should be used for the preparation, distribution, and in the end, collecting the art materials. A feeling of responsibility in each child to participate in such activities is essential in any democratic society. The extent to which children in the different grades can be used depends greatly on the preparation of the material and on the level of the children. The importance of materials as the means with which we express ourselves cannot be emphasized enough. Only through such emphasis can we expect to develop in our children the feeling for the wealth which is "buried" in every bit of material. The waste of materials is only a sign that the values have not been discovered for which they may serve. Teachers cannot start early enough with the creative use of scrap material if for no other purpose than to help their children discover the feeling of greater sensitivities in handling them, and in using their imaginations more flexibly. The greater our affinity to materials the more will we regard them as precious. This is not for mere economy but as an important educational means, for without this "emotional" relationship to art media, no art expression is possible. A violin virtuoso not only handles his violin like something sacred, because it is of material value, it is *his* means with which he can document himself. It is a personal relationship which the true artist develops to the materials with which he expresses himself. Some of this feeling cannot be developed early enough in our children, the feeling of love and affection for those means with which they express themselves.

No art motivation should be started unless all children have their material or media ready for immediate use. One of the most precious parts in any art motivation is the moment of tension before its transition into expression. If this gets lost, we lose an important part of the "creative atmosphere."

CHAPTER III

THE FIRST STAGES OF SELF-EXPRESSION

Scribbling Stages (2 to 4 years)

THE MEANING OF SCRIBBLING

IN ORDER TO UNDERSTAND THE MEANING OF SCRIBBLING, IT IS NECESSARY to know the importance of kinesthetic experiences in early infancy. It is known to everyone how definitely the baby is affected when the mother rocks it in the cradle or in her arms. Such *passive* kinesthetic experiences, in which the baby only experiences the effect of rocking, have a definite calming influence. *Actively* the baby, lying on his back, moves his arms and legs in an uncontrolled fashion. Also it has been observed by psychologists how great the satisfaction is which results from these activities. At some point, usually at about two years of age, the child, when given a crayon, will start to make marks on the paper.[1] These motions will be uncontrolled in the beginning, and their outcome is lines, which indicate these undirected movements. The first stage of scribbling thus is a *disorderly scribbling,* bold or dainty in its lines, depending on the personality of the child. The conclusion to be drawn from such scribbling is that

---

[1] Gesell, Arnold, *How a Baby Grows.* New York: Harper and Bros., 1945; Bayley, Nancy, "The Development of Motor Abilities During the First Three Years." *Child Development,* Monograph 1, 1935.

at this mental level the child has no control over motor activity. Parents and teachers should therefore regard disorderly scribbling as an indication that the child is not yet able to perform tasks that require proper motor coordination such as eating, dressing, sweeping the floor, and so forth. How often we hear complaints about children who cannot learn to eat properly! A glance at the child's scribbling would be very revealing. As long as the child has not reached a stage of scribbling in which he has established control over his motions, it is both senseless and harmful to teach activities requiring proper motor coordination. Such attempts would be similar to trying to teach a babbling baby to pronounce words correctly or even to use them in sentences. As clear and understandable as this fact appears in the realm of speech development, it is entirely neglected in the field of creative activity. Not only are there parents who have not yet discovered the causal interdependence of uncontrolled scribbling and the inability to perform controlled motor activities, but frequently even teachers encourage scribbling children to draw something "real" to satisfy their own adult imagination. Such imposition of ideas that are far beyond the abilities of the developmental stage of the child can be disastrous to his further development. *No child must ever be interrupted in his scribbling.*

GENERAL DEVELOPMENT OF SCRIBBLING

Without differentiation (Fig. 2a)

After the child has for a considerable time practiced scribbling (approximately six months after scribbling has started), he will at some point discover that there is a connection between his motions and the marks on the paper. Exceptions, however, with regard to the period over which scribbling is extended are quite frequent.

Longitudinal, or controlled, scribbling (Fig. 2b)

As soon as the child repeats his motions again and again, we may be sure that the child has discovered visual control over them. From this time on, the child draws his lines consciously up and down or left and right, frequently still mixing his now controlled lines with uncontrolled motions. Gaining control over his motions is a vital experience for the child. Not only does he gain confidence from this feeling of mastery, but also for the first time he experiences visually what he has done kinesthetically. This fact is highly significant for the guidance of the child on this age level, for it

Fig. 2a. Disordered scribbling of a two-and-a-half-year-old child showing no control of motions.

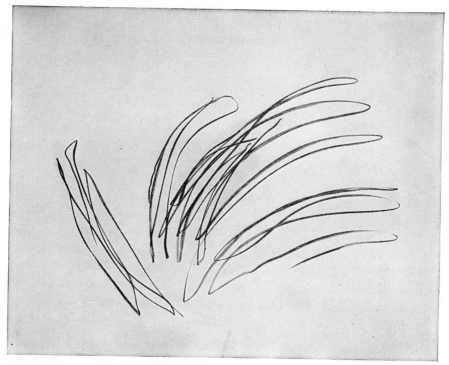

Fig. 2b. Longitudinal scribbling of a three-year-old child showing repeated motions and thus established control of motor activity.

is at this point that the adult will succeed in requesting of the child the proper execution of activities requiring motor coordination. The child will understand and enjoy the practice of the newly won experience.

Since motor coordination is one of the child's most important achievements during this period of age, we will readily understand that any discouragements in this activity would cause inhibitions. It also should be known that the child at this stage has usually no other creative intentions but to move his crayon on the paper. All his enjoyment is drawn from this kinesthetic sensation and its mastery.

Circular scribbling (Fig. 3)

Enjoyment of this new discovery stimulates the child to vary his motions. After having assured himself through constant repetitions, he now tries different, more complex types of motions. As an outcome of these motions.

Fig. 3a. Circular scribbling of a three-year-old child showing simply the urge for variation.

the child develops circular lines as an expression of the movement now usually executed with his whole arm.

Naming of scribbling (Fig. 4)

One day the child will start to *tell stories* while going through his motions of scribbling. He may say, "This is a train, This is the smoke," or "This is mother going shopping," although neither train nor mother can be recognized. This "naming of scribbling," however, is of highest significance for the further development of the child, being an indication that the child's thinking has completely changed. Until now the child was perfectly satisfied with the motions themselves, but henceforth the child connects with his motions imaginative experiences. *He has changed from a kinesthetic thinking* in terms of motions, *to an imaginative thinking* in terms of pictures. This decisive change can only be appreciated, if one considers that most thinking during a life span is concerned with thinking

Fig. 3b. Stereotyped motions, repeating the same rigid movement.

in terms of pictures. Mention of every noun, action, association of past experiences is usually connected with imaginative thinking. Surely, when such great steps occur in the mental growth of the child, we expect teachers to give confidence and encouragement in this new kind of thinking.

THE MEANING OF COLOR

From the previous discussion, it is quite obvious that the experience during scribbling is mainly connected with motor activity. In the *beginning,* the important experience was derived from the satisfaction of *motor activity, later* from the attained *mastery* and *visual control* of the lines. Color, therefore, plays a decidedly subordinate role in scribbling. It goes without saying that the child during this stage enjoys the use of color; however, it is likely, as we shall see in the next chapter, that the use of colors may also divert the child in the important experience of establishing motor coordination. The child too much attracted by color frequently interrupts his scribbling and begins splashing his paint on the paper. While this may release tensions and thus may be important for the child, it may become a habit if done too often.

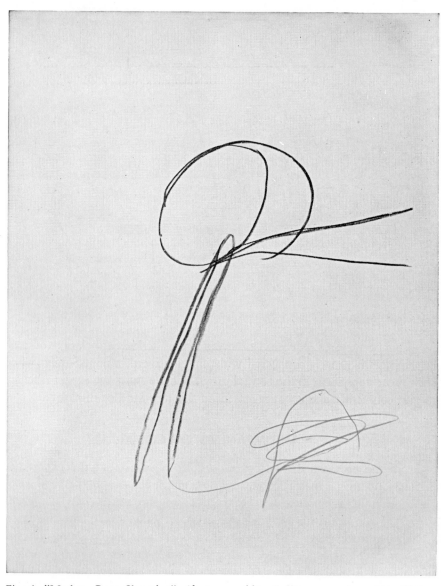

Fig. 4. "Mother Goes Shopping" (four-year-old). Indicates naming of scribbling. Notice the different kinds of motions.

ART STIMULATION

In the first stages of scribbling no other stimulation is necessary except the encouragement of the teacher to go ahead with the activity. As has been said before, scribbling should not be interfered with. This rule is important for the first as well as for the later stages, since such interferences would not only deprive the child of vital experiences, but would also inhibit him in his further work. Interferences, like the one mentioned, in which adults cannot soon enough see representations that are related to reality, may interrupt the growth of the child's motor activities in the same way as forcing the child to scribble with the right hand, when he prefers to use the left, may result in some neurotic behavior.

Larger motions are better for the development of freedom and should therefore be encouraged by furnishing proper materials, as discussed later. During "naming of scribbling," however, a definite stimulation is of great advantage. Since it is here that the great change in the child's thinking occurs, the *direction* of this new thinking should be stimulated. For example, when the child says, "This is mother going shopping," the correct stimulation would be, "Show me where mother goes shopping. What does she shop for? Are you going with her? Show me where *you* are. Are you helping her carry the basket? Where is the basket you carry?" The child will respond to each of these questions by making new motions. As it has been said, the purpose here is more the encouragement of the new imaginative thinking than the stimulation to draw recognizable objects. We are therefore perfectly satisfied with the motions the child is making while being stimulated in his thinking. However, it may also happen that this type of stimulation will also encourage readiness to relate scribbling to the world of representation.

Topics

From the preceding discussion it is evident that during the first stages of scribbling no topics are to be suggested, whereas almost any topic is suitable to encourage the imaginative activity during the last stage of scribbling.

Techniques

Any technique used with children must fit their needs. Since during scribbling the child needs to practice and experience kinesthetic sensations, the technique used should encourage free expression without intruding technical difficulties. Water color, for instance, is a very poor medium because these colors tend to run, giving an indistinguishable blurred mass that renders the child's motions as such indistinguishable. The child is unable to follow or gain control over his own motions and is discouraged by such a technique. Pencils are also unsuitable for this purpose because their sharp points prevent the proper gliding along the paper, apart from the fact that the points break easily. In many progressive kindergartens, finger painting is being used. The advantages of this medium are by no means great enough to justify its use in such *early* stages. During certain stages in early infancy the child likes to play with dirt or even with his own excrements. One of the great differences between men and animals is that men use tools and animals do not. The desire to use tools can be seen even in early infancy, and should be encouraged. In fact, children using finger paints during these early stages are frequently again encouraged to play with dirt, because the two materials are associated by similar physical consistency. Instead of progressing in control over their muscular activity, children become so involved in the enjoyment of the paste-like consistency that the activity for which finger painting was planned becomes subordinated. Finger painting might be a useful stimulant for maladjusted children, whose emotions need strong means of stimulation, but for the normal child, the best material in the early stages of scribbling will be big black wax crayons and smooth, large sheets of paper, or blackboard and chalk. The use of such materials permits the child best to follow his motions, because they give the clearest and most unblurred reproduction of the child's kinesthetic experiences. It might even be pointed out that, in the very beginning, the frequent use of a variety of colors may have a distracting effect. The child would frequently interrupt his motions to search for new colors, and such interruptions certainly would restrict flowing arm motion. It is needless to say that such advice should not be rigidly taken and frequent use of poster paint may serve an important purpose, as has been described before.

However, when the child begins to name his scribbling, the use of different colors may be stimulating, since the child frequently uses different colors to express different objects while scribbling.

During this age level three-dimensional techniques, such as clay or, better, plasticine (because of its less sticky consistency), are helpful. Experience in handling material for the production of three-dimensional objects is of significance because it gives the child an opportunity to use his fingers and muscles in a different way.

Beating and pounding the clay without any visible purpose is the

SUMMARY   SCRIBBLING STAGE—TWO TO FOUR YEARS

Stage	Characteristics	Human Figure	Space	Color	Design	Stimulation Topics	Technique
Scribbling (1) Dis- ordered.	Kinesthetic experience. No control of motions.	None.	None.	No conscious approach. Use of color for mere enjoyment without any intentions.	None.	Through encouragement. Do not interrupt or discourage or divert child from scribbling.	Large black crayon. Smooth paper. Poster paint. Finger paint only for maladjusted children.
(2) Longitudinal.	Repeated motions, establishment of coordination between visual and motor activity. Control of motions.	None.	None, or only kinesthetically.	Same as above.	None.	Same as above.	Same as above.
(3) Circular.	Self-assurance of control through deviations of type of motions.	None.	Kinesthetically.	Same as above.	None.	Same as above.	Same as above.
(4) Naming of scribbling	Change from kinesthetic to imaginative thinking. Mixing of motions with frequent interruption.	Only imaginatively by the act of naming.	Purely imaginatively.	Color used to distinguish different meanings of scribbling.	None.	In the direction of the child's thinking by continuing the child's story.	Colored crayons (four colors). Poster paint. Plasticine throughout scribbling stage.

95

parallel stage to the scribbling, called "disordered." As the child gets acquainted with the material and feels the need to control his activity, he starts to *break the clay,* sometimes without order, at other times watching the similarity of the pieces he breaks; or he may start to form shapes (coils or balls). This first conscious approach of shaping the clay without purpose or meaning can easily be compared with the second stage of scribbling, which is consciously controlled. At some point the child picks up one lump of clay and perhaps with accompanying noises, *calls it* an airplane or says, "This is a train." Psychologically, this is exactly the same change in the process of thinking as discussed in the "Naming of Scribbling." Whereas the activity of shaping or breaking was in the foreground in the previous stages, now the imaginative activity which is connected with the symbol (lump of clay) is predominant. Also here, the child has changed his kinesthetic thinking to an imaginative thinking. With this change he shows a readiness to establish a relationship between his representations and the things he wants to represent.

EVALUATION CHART

The chart on pp. 98–99 provides a basis for the understanding of the child's growth as seen in creative activity. A check mark should be placed opposite the question in the column which best indicates the answer to the question. "Much" indicates that the child is above standard; "some" indicates average; and "none" indicates that the child is below average and needs additional motivation. By connecting the check marks with a line and by turning the chart 90 degrees a profile may be obtained. If the growth characteristics obtained from this chart are correlated with those obtained from the general evaluation chart on pages 69–71 a more complete understanding of the child may be secured.

INTERPRETATION OF INDIVIDUAL GROWTH CHARACTERISTICS PERTAINING TO THE SCRIBBLING STAGE

Intellectual growth

In order to obtain an understanding of the child's intellectual growth, the average characteristics of scribblings as discussed in Chapter II and summarized on page 95 should be compared with the chronological age of the child. If there is a marked discrepancy, the child is either above or below the average. Let us, for instance, look at the scribbling in Fig. 2a. It says that it was done by a two-and-one-half-year-old child. We, therefore, look first at the column which refers to the mental age of the child. It reads: "Are there uncontrolled lines only?" We investigate the drawing and see no repetitions of lines which would indicate some control. Therefore, we put our check mark in the column: "yes." Since there is no discrepancy between chronological age and its respective creative expression, it appears that the child's intellectual growth is of average quality. If the child had been four years of age and still concerned with uncontrolled motions, it would have been a clear indication that the child's mentality has not grown beyond thinking in terms of motions. It would also indicate that the child had not even progressed to the level of mastering his motions, an important intellectual achievement. Furthermore, it would indicate that the child who should already be thinking "in terms of pictures" was still in a stage in which he merely produced uncontrolled motions. It cannot be emphasized enough that this is not merely a characteristic which refers to the child's creative expression. That a child whose imagery should begin to become concrete is still concerned with uncontrolled motions clearly indicates the child's intellectual status. The established thinking that a child's "weakness in art" does not affect him otherwise must undergo a decisive correction.

A child of four who is still concerned with uncontrolled motions is, therefore, below the average development. This does not mean that the child may not catch up in his development in a short time. The author has seen six-year-old children still scribbling and not only advancing up to the average level of development in a short period, but even going beyond it. *It should, therefore, be clearly pointed out that the results obtained by the evaluation chart are only indicative of the child's present status and do in no way predict the child's future growth.*

Emotional growth

There are some questions which can only be answered by observing and knowing the child and others by merely seeing his work. Suppose we know the child who produced Fig. 2a, and know that "he very much enjoys his scribbling." We know it because he is doing it whenever he has an opportunity to do so. We would, therefore, put our check mark on line one in the column which says "much." The second question asks whether the scribbling is free from stereotyped repetitions. Stereotyped repetitions are always a sign of rigidity. We must clearly distinguish between free repeated motions and stereotyped repetitions. *Free* repeated motions are usually *uninterrupted* (see Figs. 2b and 3a) while *stereotyped* repetitions consist

EVALUATION CHART *

Scribbling Stage

	Mental Age		No	Yes
Intellectual Growth	2–3	Are there uncontrolled lines only? Does he only pound or knead clay?		
	2½–3½	Are all motions controlled, repeated motions: longitudinal or circular? Does he form coils with clay? Does he enjoy breaking the clay?		
	3–4	Does the child name his scribbling? Does he name his pieces of clay?		

		None	Some	Much
Emotional Growth	Does the child enjoy his scribbling? Is the scribbling free from stereotyped repetitions? such as: Is the scribbling free from interrupted lines? Are the child's motions determined and forceful? Does the intensity and direction of the motions change?			

Social Growth	Does the child concentrate on his motions?				
	Is it difficult to divert the child?				
Perceptual Growth	Does the child show the desire for large motions? (Kinesthetic freedom.)				
	Does the child enjoy tactual sensations when working with clay?				
	Does the child control his motions visually?				
	When he names his scribbling, does he use different colors to differentiate different meanings?				
Physical Growth	Are the motions vigorous?				
	Are the lines bold?				
	Does the child use his whole arm?				
Aesthetic Growth	Does the child distribute his motions over the whole paper?				
	Does the child show a feeling for balance in his distribution of dense and loose scribbling?				
Creative Growth	Is the child independent in his scribbling?				
	When scribbling with other children does the child remain uninfluenced?				
	Is he generally opposed to imitating?				
	When naming his scribbling does he develop stories independently?				

* This evaluation chart can only be used if samples of scribbling are done in crayon.

of a repetition of *broken-up lines* like little hooks $\mathcal{W}$, or "h's" like $\mathfrak{n}\mathfrak{h}$ or $\mathfrak{r}\mathfrak{d}$ (see Fig. 3b). Such stereotyped repetitions indicate that the child has lost confidence in moving freely on the paper. As he has lost confidence in his ability to master, guide, and enjoy his motions, he escapes into stereotyped repetitions. By repeating the same patterns over and over again he escapes into a kind of "security" in which he feels undisturbed by new experiences and master of a situation. This false security, however, is harmful to his growth as it blocks any further development. *Stereotyped repetitions in scribbling, therefore, are indicative of emotional blocks* (see Fig. 3b). Needless to say, the scribbling in Fig. 2a does not show any indications of stereotyped repetitions. The check mark for this question would, therefore, be placed under "much." The next question, as to whether the scribbling is free from interruptions, is directly related to the discussed one, yet it is of far less serious nature. Usually, if a child scribbles in terms of stereotyped repetitions, his scribbling is also frequently interrupted. However, scribbling need not consist of stereotyped patterns in order for it to be frequently interrupted. A child who enjoys the free flow of motions continues his motions uninterruptedly. A child whose enjoyment of his motor activity is disturbed frequently interrupts his motions. *Frequent interruptions in scribbling show, therefore, a lack of the child's self-confidence.* In Fig. 2a the scribbling is entirely uninterrupted. We can assume that the child enjoyed his motor activity.

Experiments have shown that there is a very close correlation between the type of lines which the child uses in his scribbling and his character trends.[2] Children who are delicate and *timid* usually use dainty, undetermined, and *weak lines*, whereas children with *much will power* and drive use *forceful* and *determined lines*. The lines in Fig. 2a are throughout determined and forceful and show, therefore, that the child is full of will power and drive.

The last question of the evaluation of "emotional growth" deals with the change of direction of the line and its change of intensity. A scribbling can be very forceful and determined, yet if its direction is unchanged its forcefulness does not find release in the enjoyment of motor activity. The mind is, as it were, set. It is like an endless line on a pavement, or on a wall, in which no change of direction inspires the individual to greater coordination and control. Only through continuous "experimentation" with ever changing lines does the child finally discover that he can establish in his drawings a relationship with objects. It is essential, therefore, for his proper growth that the ever changing direction of his lines provides this

[2] Experiment reported on p. ix.

stimulation. Equal intensity of lines, too, shows that the child is not alert. An attentive child who is bound up with his activity changes the intensity of his scribbling according to his emotional state. *The changing of intensity and direction of lines, therefore, is indicative of the child's alertness.* In Fig. 2a a frequent change of direction and intensity of lines indicates the child's freedom and alertness which he kept up throughout his activity.

Social growth

Social growth in these early stages of childhood is difficult to detect because it does not reveal itself in the usual manner of cooperation or active participation in the family or larger society. The child is much too occupied with himself and his own activities to recognize the needs of his environment. As we have seen in our previous discussion, one of the most important assumptions for social growth is the ability to identify oneself with his own activities. It is only at a more advanced stage that identification with the needs of others follows.

In order to be able to identify oneself with his own activity, it is necessary that one possess the power to concentrate on it. It is for this reason that the question "Does the child concentrate on his motions?" has been placed at the top. This question can only be answered with certainty by direct observation. If the child frequently stops, looks around, and asks questions, he does not concentrate on his motions. Whether he frequently stops, however, can be recognized in the drawing by a somewhat "trained" eye. Knots in the lines, or interruptions, are indicative of stops. *Knots, small and aimless loops, and interruptions in the motions may give some indication that the child did not concentrate on his motions.*

The second question, "Is it difficult to divert the child?", can only be answered by direct observation. It is understood, however, that a child who closely identifies himself with his own motions cannot easily be diverted.

In Fig. 2a we can see no indications of stops or interruptions. The motions are free from knots and aimless loops. From observation it has been found that the child can only be diverted from his activity with "much" effort. From both reactions we can draw the conclusion that the child possesses important requisites necessary for a healthy social growth.

Perceptual growth

The growth of our sense apparatus is a vital necessity. One of the first important perceptual experiences is that derived from body motions. Parallel with this the sensitivity of tactual sensations develops. Both of these vital experiences reveal themselves in the child's creative work. If the child's scribblings show *continuously* small motions, the child is obviously restricted in his kinesthetic freedom. However, it seems to me important to point out that small motions, that is, a limited use of kinesthesis, may be either a character trend, or a sign of faulty motivations. Not all children have to make large motions! To force them upon the child is just as senseless as to try to change a delicate child into a robust one. While it is a more healthy sign if the child uses large motions, they cannot be imposed upon him. Any imposition creates unhealthy reactions. The child who made the scribbling in Fig. 2a visibly enjoyed his free kinesthetic experiences in large motions.

Whether the child enjoys tactual sensations when working with clay can best be seen from the way he contacts the material. Fearless contact indicates the child's enjoyment; the child who does not want to experience tactual sensations approaches his modelings shyly and with precaution. If we investigate the modeling, only slight indentations can be seen. The child who does not enjoy tactual sensations will avoid a too definite contact with different textures. In observing children who are modeling we shall see that those who do not enjoy tactual experiences only use the tips of their fingers, often only two, while the others use the whole hand.

Visual perception only starts when the child discovers that he *can* control his motions. From then on the child follows his motions with his eyes. Repetitions of motions are not always indicative of visual control, for motions can be repeated merely kinesthetically. Most often, however, the child's discovery of his ability to control and repeat motions goes parallel with his visual perception. With certainty, however, we can only answer the question as to whether the child controls his motions visually by observing the child during the working process.

The child who produced the scribbling in Fig. 2a apparently did not visually control his motions, for there are no signs of repeated or controlled motions.

Only when the child begins to name his scribblings does he have the desire to use different colors to designate different meanings. Color perception does not necessarily have to be connected with verbal recognition of color. One of the first stages of color perception is merely to distinguish between colors. This usually occurs during the stage of "naming of scribbling." In the case of Fig. 2a the child has not reached this stage. The column in the chart, therefore, remains blank.

Physical growth

In childhood, when means of compensation and sublimation are not developed as they are in adulthood, emotional and physical growth are closely related. A child who has physical impairments, or often is sickly, visually lacks emotional security and vigor. The adult often can compensate for his physical inadequacy and even overcome handicaps.[3] The child unable to participate in all the activities of his healthy environment generally develops a feeling of insecurity, often withdrawing from activities where he even could participate.

It will then not be surprising that some of the characteristics found in the scribblings of children which pertain to emotional growth will also be indicative of the child's physical growth. Indeed, it has been found that healthy children use vigorous and bold motions whereas children who are sickly and often ill generally express themselves by means of dainty and delicate lines. Usually the healthy child uses his physical strength whenever he has an opportunity to apply it. The pressure he puts on the crayon which results in a bold line may well be indicative of the child's health and his physical growth. Needless to say, this must never be the sole judgment for it. This merely should indicate how all faculties of growth reveal themselves in creative activity.

The last question in the evaluation chart under "Physical Growth" refers to the way the child scribbles. Whether the child uses his hand, his lower arm, or his whole arm for his motion, too, is indicative of the child's physical status. Children lazy by nature usually scribble by moving their hands only. Usually if children are healthy and active they apply the whole arm for their motions.

In general, it can be said that usually children in good physical condition most often use *vigorous* and *bold lines* applying their *whole arms* to their motions.

From Fig. 2a we can see that the child uses bold and vigorous lines. Whether he uses his whole arm could only be determined by observing him. From the scribbling, however, it appears that the child is active and healthy. It should, nevertheless, be strongly emphasized that oversimplification of such matters as health and physical growth would be very harmful. As has been said before, it is the intention of the author to point out the close relationships of all areas of growth to the creative expression of the child.

[3] See Chap. xii.

Aesthetic growth

While there is obviously no conscious expression of aesthetic growth in the early stages of childhood, some criteria may already be indicative of unconscious trends of aesthetic feelings. For instance, the way the child utilizes the space which he has at his disposal may be a sign of an early feeling for proper distribution and organization of his motions. If a child uses only a small fraction of the space he has at his disposal, he obviously has not developed the feeling for utilizing the rest of the space. This may be due to emotional restrictions, but it may also be a sign that the child's aesthetic feelings have not yet developed. Often it can be noticed that children develop early a distinct feeling for distributing dark or dense scribblings over their drawing areas. Such feelings are definite indications of aesthetic trends since they indicate a desire for a better organization and greater entity.

In the scribbling in Fig. 2a no such strong desire appears to be expressed, although the placement of the scribbling in the center of the sheet may indicate some trend toward aesthetic growth.

Creative growth

There are children who always need outside stimulation and others who seem to be always occupied on their own. There are children who are surrounded by toys and seem to be bored and others who are satisfied with a stick. While overstimulation and surrounding the child with too many things may take the initiative from him, we cannot deny the fact that there are from the beginning differences which point toward a greater or lesser creativeness. As early as during the scribbling stage we can observe children who are bound up with their motions and never seem to have a desire to ask how things should be done or even request a confirmation that everything is all right. Creative children scribble independently of outside influences. Even when they scribble in a group they seldom inquire, ask questions, or look at their neighbor's work. For them their own work provides all the necessary stimulation. But there are also children who constantly ask questions referring to the use of material and the ways things should be done. They are also the ones who are easily influenced by the work of others. If one child starts with big round motions, they will start to imitate him. Lack of self-confidence and independence in thinking are responsible for such easy influences. These are the children who lack confidence in their

Plate 1. "Mommy and Daddy." (4 years) Color is enjoyed for its own sake. There is no desire to establish color-object relationships during this stage of development. This child has just left the scribbling stage. Notice the circular motions used as "heads." The green "moustache" apparently established a significant relationship to "Daddy."

Plate 2. "I Am in a Lightning Storm." (6 years) The child has n
desire for "correct" color relationships. The use of few colors may ofte
satisfy his urge for expression. To direct the child at "proper" cole
relationships would be an interference with his expression. Let the chi
discover his own relationships. This discovery is a vital experienc
for the child. (Teacher: Jean Holland, Duke of York School, Toronto

creativeness. They are ready to imitate the works of others. They are the ones who would most need a boost in their creativeness, yet they are also the easiest victims of coloring books and of people who promote the use of patterns for they are glad if they can get at least a crutch to hide their lame creativeness. A healthy creative child is opposed to imitations because his own language is much more meaningful to him.

Especially when the child names his scribblings will his originality and creativeness become evident. He will develop his own stories and will not need the questions of adults.

In Fig. 2a no indications point toward an imitative trend in the child. The child apparently scribbles independently. If we had an opportunity to observe him in his group we would find that here also the child remains uninfluenced. The child appears to be creative according to the discussed criteria.

SUMMARY OF GROWTH ANALYSIS

According to the foregoing evaluation a knowledge of the single individual phases of growth has been received. For a better understanding of the child it is of great importance that the analysis of these single phases of growth should be followed by a synthesis. While the understanding of total growth could not have been achieved without relating the single components of growth to the creative processes and works of the child, it is of great importance that these single phases should be related to each other and looked upon as an entity. Needless to say, the best integration of all growth factors is seen in the creative work itself. However, it seems to me significant to relate the results obtained through the comparative evaluation of single factors. We can, perhaps, best do it by actually using the scribbling of Fig. 2a, which has been used all along for purposes of greater clarification.

According to the scribblings in Fig. 2a, we have found that the child's present intellectual capacity is neither superior nor is it inferior. The child closely conforms with the average performance. His intellect is carried by an emotionally flexible, balanced, and stable individual. The child, according to his creative work, pursues his desires vigorously, yet he is flexible enough to change his intentions whenever new experiences demand such a change. Socially he feels a beginning responsibility; at least he identifies himself closely with what he is doing. Apparently this emotional freedom of the child and also his capacity for a close self-identification with his experiences strongly influence the freedom he has developed in his perceptual experiences. That he can enjoy large motions is kinesthetically, as well as emotionally significant. While his bold motions would indicate a physically healthy and vigorous child, we would like to make this statement with care and reservation and leave the final word to the physician. In his aesthetic development the child has not shown anything of significance. We shall, therefore, closely watch his future aesthetic growth and expose him whenever possible to situations which can promote his feeling for organization and beauty. Creatively he seems to be very independent and free from disturbing influences. Apparently his emotional freedom and his intellectual status closely influence the confidence he has developed in pursuing his work originally. The child has a good foundation for a well-balanced citizen. Whether he will develop his leadership will depend on his future development of a more outstanding intellectual growth paired with a greater aesthetic trend toward a more sensitive feeling for organization.

EXERCISES

(1) Make growth profiles, using the evaluation chart also for Fig. 2b, Fig. 3a, Fig. 3b, and Fig. 4.
(2) Follow up the case history of a child by means of his scribbling.
  (a) Collect all scribblings of a child.
  (b) Write name and age on the back of the scribbling.
  (c) Attach to the drawing any remarks the child makes during scribbling.
  (d) Keep a notebook in which observations are recorded. Observations pertain to:
    1. Type of motion and technique.
    2. Concentrated or easily diverted.
    3. Physical execution (with joint of hand only, with lower arm and elbow joint, with whole arm from the shoulder).
    4. Emotions.
  (e) Observe the child's motor coordination in life situations: when dressing, eating, walking, lacing the shoes, and so forth.
  (f) Notice changes in scribbling.
  (g) Draw conclusions from your notes and scribbling of the child with regard to the child's growth.
(3) Collect many scribblings and classify them according to motions: disordered, longitudinal, circular, and naming.
(4) When child names his scribbling, try to observe whether he introduces certain lines or motions for certain things.
(5) Observe first relationship between drawing and reality.
(6) Find out the effectiveness of your stimulation during the period of nam-

ing by comparing one scribbling where you left the child completely alone and another where you stimulated the child in the direction of his thinking.

(7) Follow up a case history of a child by means of his modeling. Follow the same procedure as indicated for the scribbling of a child.

(8) Secure several evaluation charts as shown on pages 98–99. Collect several scribblings and determine growth factors according to the characteristics described on the evaluation chart.

(9) Compare growth characteristics obtained through the evaluation chart with personality data obtained from other sources.

LABORATORY WORK

Prepare finger paint consisting of:

1 part paint pigment
5 parts starch

Do some finger paintings yourself.

CHAPTER IV   **FIRST REPRESENTATIONAL**

ATTEMPTS

Pre-schematic Stage (4 to 7 years)

THE MEANING OF THE PRE-SCHEMATIC STAGE

For the psychology of the child

FROM THE DISCUSSION OF THE LAST STAGE OF SCRIBBLING, IT BECAME evident a discrepancy existed between the child's intention and his execution. The child intended to depict something, yet his representation did not reveal anything of this intention. But as we have seen, it was important for the child to become accustomed to and to be encouraged in his new type of thinking. Thus it will be obvious that the establishment of a slightest relationship to the thing intended to be represented will create a great feeling of satisfaction. In the beginning, therefore, the mere fact that *a relationship with reality has been achieved* will be of greater significance than the quality of the representation. A circular motion for "head" and longitudinal motions for "arms" or "legs," brought into functional relationship, will give resemblance enough to a "man" of living quality.[1] The mere fact that the child was able to relate his representation is exciting enough to fill

---

[1] Mott, S. M., "The Development of Concepts. A Study of Children's Drawings." *Child Development,* Monograph 7, 1936.

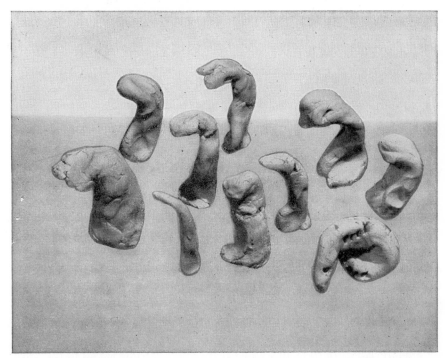

Fig. 5. First representational attempt in clay modeling: "Snakes." (Courtesy Educational Project, Museum of Modern Art, N.Y.)

his mind and emotion with a profound feeling of satisfaction. It may, however, be of interest that in many cases it is the round form of the head and the longitudinal form of arms and legs that are the first inspiration to realistic attempts. Henceforth, as the child establishes his relationship to the outside world in his representations, he feels the need to enrich this newly won discovery. It is extraordinarily interesting to observe how the child begins to abstract a line from the previous scribbling. Whereas circular scribbles becomes indicative of the head, longitudinal scribblings symbolize the extension of the body. This is how we must understand the meaning, both of the vanishing scribbling and of the beginning desire for representation. Scribbling loses more and more the causal relation between bodily movements and its result on the paper to make way for representation, which is related to the object. A different mode of drawing begins: the conscious creation of form. In this newly discovered relationship the child is constantly searching for new concepts, for which he will soon establish his own individual pattern, his *schema*. Before he reaches this stage—that is, during the pre-schematic stage, however, this search is clearly characterized in his drawings by a constant change of form symbols. The child will represent a man today differently from the way he will draw a man tomorrow. As yet, he has not established a fixed aspect, and we see at this stage in particular the greatest variety of form symbols representing one and the same object. Therefore, it will be easy for the educator to determine, for means of evaluation, whether the child is still in the pre-schematic stage or has moved beyond it (Fig. 7 a, b, c).

For the enrichment of the child's active knowledge

For the understanding of this chapter, it will be necessary to clarify what we mean by active knowledge. The child sees the world differently from the way he draws it. Even a very young child knows that a man is more than a head with legs and arms attached to it; he knows that a man has features, fingers, and even fingernails; but in his representations the child expresses only what is actively important to him during the process of creating. *In his drawings, thus, only the active knowledge, or what actively motivated the child, can be seen.* This is of decisive significance, because it permits the educator to record how far the child has proceeded in the grasp of himself and of the surrounding world. A knowledge of what actively motivates the child further reveals to the educator the emotional significance which the represented objects have for the child. *The passive knowledge,* however, is the knowledge which the child has, but does not use. Education, not only with regard to creative activity, consists to a great extent in activating the knowledge not used. Many people understand and enjoy reading the great works of Shakespeare, yet in their everyday language they use a limited number of words. Our passive vocabulary thus is large enough to understand the wealth of words which Shakespeare offers; actively, however, we are restricted to a rather limited vocabulary, depending a great deal upon the education received. Certainly a good teacher should be able to stimulate the individual to use words actively which hitherto were not used.[2]

During the pre-schematic stage the child is most ready to build up new concepts of form, to enrich his form symbols. As we shall see in the paragraph on "stimulation" in this chapter, it is most important during this age level, that is, as long as the child still is most flexible, to activate his passive knowledge through individual *experiences.*

[2] McCloy, W., *Passive Creative Imagination.* Psychological Monographs, LI, No. 5, 1939.

Fig. 6. "I am on the Street" (five and a half years). No spatial correlations are perceived. Proportions are drawn according to significance. Head-feet representation. Pre-schematic stage.

GENERAL DEVELOPMENT
OF REPRESENTATIVE SYMBOLS

Although the discovery of an established relationship between representation and the thing represented satisfies and fascinates the child in the beginning of the pre-schematic stage, we shall see that later this fascination loses importance and an eager search for the establishment of a definite concept of man and environment begins.

However, it is of great importance for the teacher to notice that all lines, although they are supposed to represent reality, are not in direct representational relationship to the object. The child establishes substitutes, lines which lose their meaning when separated from the whole. An oval might mean a body within the whole representation of a man, but when separated from the whole, the oval *loses* its meaning as "body." Such lines we call *geometric* since they refer to geometry, which is abstract. If such lines are used to represent something, they are "representative symbols." *Thus, a representative symbol consists of geometric lines which, when iso-*

Fig. 7a. "I am Running for My Ball" (five-year-old boy). (Courtesy Educational Project, Museum of Modern Art, N.Y.)

lated from the whole, lose their meaning. An important and extensive study has been made by Herbert Read[3] of the significance of these lines in relationship to the emotions and character of the creator. Since the development of the representative symbol frequently has its origin in scribbling, we can readily understand that in it are reflected some of the personal and even body characteristics of the child. Thus, the representative symbol of the human figure developed by a crippled child was distorted on the side which conformed with his own defect. The individuality of the schema has its roots not only in the body; in many cases it expresses the psychological constitution of the child. For instance, in the representative symbol of a man drawn by a timid child of delicate sensibilities, I could trace anxiety in the round, unclosed, uncertain lines just as much as I could find the characteristic resoluteness of another child in its rectangular representation of the body. Both representations are characteristic of the child's total personality structure. These facts show clearly *that even the earliest representational attempts are closely bound up with the individual self.*

[3] Read, Herbert, *Education Through Art.* London: Faber and Faber, 1943, p. 320.

Fig. 7b. "Mother is Looking for Me" (drawing of the same five-year-old boy). See frequent change of symbols. (Courtesy Educational Project, Museum of Modern Art, N.Y.)

Human figure

Out of the scribbling motions, circular for the head and longitudinal for the legs, the child develops his first representation of a man. These head-feet representations are common for a five-year-old child. With this representation, as has been said before, the child has merely satisfied a desire to *establish a relationship between his drawing and external reality*. To what extent the child will enrich this concept of a man depends on the child's mental growth, his sensitivity to stimuli and the proper stimulation by the teacher. The teacher has to use to the fullest extent this period in which the child is searching for his concept. Since the child is most flexible during this period, the teacher's task will be made easy by the use of the type of stimulation described later. (See Figs. 6 and 7a)

Space

For reasons of simplification *we call space everything outside of the body*. Therefore, all experiences that we have with or in environment are

Fig. 7c. "I and My Dog." Drawing of the same five-year-old child. Notice change of representative symbols, proportions of value, use of geometric lines. (Courtesy Educational Project, Museum of Modern Art, N.Y.)

spatial experiences. In the same way that the child is fascinated by the newly discovered relationship between a man and his drawing, he is satisfied with the establishment of mere relationships between objects and their representation. He is perfectly satisfied with the representation *itself* without relating the objects to each other. *In the earliest drawings of children the interrelations of things in space are not subject to any law.* The child thinks, "There am I. There is an ambulance. There are airplanes. There is the sky" (Fig. 6). No relationship between the objects has been established. The child did not think, "I am standing on the street. The ambulance comes along the street. Above there is the sky. The airplanes fly in the air." The child has not yet achieved an experience of space which is of general validity. He has not yet experienced himself as a part of environment.

Since the experience of the self as a part of environment is one of the most important assumptions for cooperation and visual coordination, the

Fig. 8. "I and My Sister in the Snow" (six years old). Space relations with sister have been perceived because of emotional significance. He is leading her through the storm; therefore "legs" are unimportant, and have been omitted. (Courtesy Educational Project, Museum of Modern Art, N.Y.)

child's inability to correlate things properly in space is a clear indication that he is neither ready to cooperate socially, nor has he the desire to co-ordinate letters or to learn to read. The teacher in the kindergarten will therefore use the child's drawing expression as an indication of the child's ability to participate in tasks which require cooperation. Forcing coopera-tion upon the child too early might create undesirable reactions rather than be of use for the group. First spatial relationships are usually experienced emotionally. Therefore experiences which refer to subjective relationships will be stimulating, as, "Do you like your doll?" "Draw yourself with your doll." In such drawings we might find no relationships among the objects outside of the child, whereas the emotional relationship of the child and the doll are clearly represented (compare with Fig. 8). Such reactions show that space relations in this early stage are to a high degree conditioned by value judgments.

Fig. 9. "Girl Picking Flowers" (five and a half years). Proportion of value. The girl is outlined in blue color.

THE SIGNIFICANCE OF COLOR

Also, in color no relationship between the object represented and its actual color has been perceived. A man might be red, blue, green, or yellow, depending on how the different colors appeal to the child (see Table 2). Surely there are deeper psychological meanings in the choice of color, but these meanings are so highly individualized and dependent upon subjective interpretations that such discussions fall outside of the framework of this book. Likewise, *first relationships of color are determined by emotional qualities*. Perhaps the only thing of objective color relationship in Fig. 6 is the red cross on the ambulance, which might be of emotional significance.

ART STIMULATION

Since all contact or communication with environment is established through the self, it is of greatest importance to stimulate the sensitivity toward the self. For the enrichment of the active knowledge of the self, it is necessary to stimulate the child's concept of *his body parts*. This is best done through the stimulation of the function of the parts by means of *individual experiences.* Once, during a visit in a first grade I saw children drawing just a line as a symbol for "mouth." Purposely I had a bag of candy in my pocket. After rattling the bag, I asked the children, "What do I have in my pocket?" "Candy," was the answer. "Do you think it is hard or chewy?" From the rattling the children deduced that it was hard candy. "Do you like candy?" was my question. "Yes," was the unanimous answer. Placing some candy on each child's desk, I asked them not to put it in their mouths until a given signal. "Now you may crush the candy, in order to find out how hard it is." And all the children bit the candy into pieces. After we had gone through this experience, I asked the children to draw "eating the candy." Every child in the classroom included the "teeth" in his representation. This *individual experience activated their passive knowledge.* This account should serve as only one example and should not be interpreted as meaning that such actual experiences are always necessary. It depends on whether the teacher is able to replace an actual experience by an intensive classroom motivation.

It is, however, of great value for the teacher to know *what outcome* she expects from her stimulation. It will prove to her whether or not she was successful in activating the passive knowledge of her children. This can easily be controlled by *comparing former drawings with those drawn after the stimulation.* If an enrichment of the form concept has taken place, the teacher was successful. Usually in classroom discussions it is preferable to create *first the general atmosphere* of the environment in which the action takes place and then gradually concentrate on the special topic. The following classroom stimulation will serve as an example. The topic: "Brushing My Teeth." As the outcome, an enrichment of the form concept of the "mouth" and a closer coordination between mouth and arm may be expected. Originality and individuality in expression are taken for granted. The general atmosphere is characterized by the *"where and when."* "Where do you sleep? What do you do when you get up in the morning? When do you get up in the morning? Where is your bathroom located? What do you see in your bathroom? What do you do to clean your teeth and protect them properly?"

The *"what"* (brushing the teeth) should always follow the general atmosphere. After the "what" has been discussed, *every stimulation should culminate* in a thorough discussion of the *"how."* "How do you brush your teeth? Do you brush them horizontally or up and down? How is your tooth brush? How do you hold your tooth brush? Show me how you brush your teeth." A short demonstration by one child would contribute to a more effective stimulation. "Now let us draw 'Brushing my teeth in the morning

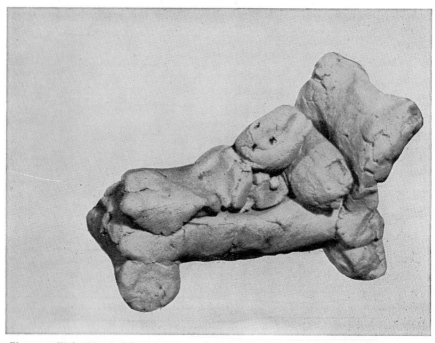

Fig. 10a. "I in My Bed." (Modeling of a six-year-old girl). Emotional relationship establishes proper spatial correlations. (Courtesy Educational Project, Museum of Modern Art, N.Y.)

in my bathroom.' " It is important at the end of the stimulation to include in the topic the formerly discussed environment, "where and when." In conclusion, every stimulation should contain first the *"where and when,"* second the *"what,"* and third the *"how."*

Topics

The following topics are suggested with the understanding that it is better to adjust a topic to a classroom situation than to choose it without regard to the class. The topics chosen during this age level are signified by the words *"I"* and *"my."*

I and My Mother (sizes).
I and *My* House (size).
I Am Brushing *My* Teeth (teeth).
I Am Drinking *My* Milk (mouth).

Fig. 10b. The use of materials is an important experience of children for they become sensitive to their specific characteristics. From the Children's Art Classes, the Pennsylvania State University. Dr. Edward Mattil in charge.

I Am Blowing My Nose (nose).
I Am Eating My Breakfast (mouth).
I Am Searching for a Coin *I* Lost (hand, eyes).
I Am Playing Ball (arms, hands).
I Am Hurting *My* Knee (knee).
I Am Playing Tag (arms, legs).
I Am Sitting on the Swing (body).
I Am at the Dentist (teeth).
I Am Listening to the Radio (ears).

SUMMARY   PRE-SCHEMATIC STAGE—FOUR TO SEVEN YEARS

Characteristics	Human Figure	Space	Color	Design	Stimulation	
					Topics	Technique
(1) Discovery of *relationship* between drawing, thinking, and reality. (2) Search for concept. (3) Change of form symbols because of constant search for them.	Circular motion for head. Longitudinal for legs and arms. Head-feet representations develop to more complex form concept. Symbols depending on active knowledge during the act of drawing.	No orderly space relations except emotionally. "There is a table; there is a door; there is a window; a chair." "This is *my* doll" (emotional relationship).	No relationship to reality. Color according to emotional appeal.	No conscious approach.	Activating of passive knowledge related mainly to self (body parts).	Crayons, clay, powder paints, (thick) large bristle brushes, large sheets of paper (absorbent). Also, unprinted newspaper.

I Am Reaching for an Apple (hand).
I Am Picking Flowers (hand, arms).
I Am Eating with Spoon and Fork (mouth).
I Am Swimming (legs, arms).
I Am Getting a Ring (fingers).
My Birthday Present (emotional relationship).
My Doll (emotional relationship).
My Party (emotional relationship).
I Am Tired (yawning, mouth).
I Am Led by a Policeman Across the Street (emotional relationship).

Techniques

For developing greater freedom, a *bristle brush, poster paint* (thickly prepared) on a somewhat *absorbent, large sheet* of paper are the best materials for this mental level. Absorbent paper is recommended because it prevents the paint from running. The desk, or if the desk is too small, the floor or easels, can successfully be used. If, however, large classes do not permit the use of these materials, colored crayons and smaller sheets are excellent. The quality of the crayon can be determined by the surplus wax that can easily be scratched off the paper. The more surplus there is, the poorer the quality of crayon.

In *clay work* (clay is now preferable to plasticine), the pre-schematic stage is also characterized by the search for a definite concept of form. Also here this search is seen in a *constant change of modes of representations* and representations themselves. *Pulling* out from the lump of clay all things that stand out, like noses, arms, and legs implies a *lesser consciousness* of the form than holding the form (nose, arm, leg) in the hand, forming it, and *adding it* to the body (Fig. 10a). Purposely, no decorative techniques are yet suggested, since on this level no child feels the conscious need for decoration. As long as the desire for the search of a concept of form and space is predominant, the desire *for decoration generally does not develop.*

EVALUATION CHART

The chart on pages 122 and 123 provides a basis for the understanding of the child's growth during the pre-schematic stage. The same factors should be observed as described previously on page 96.

EVALUATION CHART

Pre-schematic Stage

	Mental Age		No		Yes
			None	Some	Much
Intellectual Growth	4–5½	Does the child's representation of a "man" show more than head and feet?			
	5½–7	Does the child draw more than head, body, arms, legs, features? Are eyes, nose, mouth indicated? Are the features represented with different representative symbols?			
		As compared with previous drawings is there an increase of details? (Active knowledge.) Is the child's drawing representational? Does the drawing show details?			
Emotional Growth		Does the child frequently change his concepts for "man," "tree," or details like "eye," "nose," etc.? Is the child free from stereotyped repetitions? Are parts which are important to the child somewhat exaggerated? Is there a lack of continued and too much exaggeration? Is the drawing definite in lines and color, showing the child's confidence in his work? Does the child relate things which are important to him?			
Social Growth		Is the child's work related to a definite experience? Is there any order determined by emotional relationships? Does the child show spatial correlations: sky above, ground below? Does the child show awareness of a particular environment (home, school, etc.)?			

Perceptual Growth	Does the child use lines other than geometric? (Lines when separated from the whole do not lose meaning.) Does the child indicate movements or sounds? Does the child relate color to objects? Does the child start in his modeling from the whole lump of clay?			
Physical Growth	Is there a lack of continuous omission of the same body part? Is there a lack of continuous exaggeration of the same body part? Are the child's lines determined and vigorous? Does the child include body actions?			
Aesthetic Growth	Is the meaningful space well distributed against the meaningless space? Does the organization of the subject matter seem equally important to its content? Do colors appear to be distributed decoratively? Does the child show a desire for decoration?			
Creative Growth	Does the child use his independent concepts? If the child works in a group, does he remain uninfluenced? When the child is alone does he spontaneously create in any medium? When the child is alone does he refrain from imitating for imitation's sake?			

INTERPRETATION OF INDIVIDUAL GROWTH CHARACTERISTICS PERTAINING TO THE PRE-SCHEMATIC STAGE

Intellectual growth

A child who has reached the chronological age of four or five and still thinks in terms of motions has not advanced intellectually to his average stage of growth. That is why the question as to whether the child's drawings are representational is placed at the beginning. A child's drawing is considered representational as soon as a relationship with things is established. As has been said before, any lines or symbols may be used in establishing such a relationship. Let us, for example, look at Fig. 7b. This drawing was made by a five-year-old boy. He has definitely established a representational relationship. The check mark in the evaluation chart should be in the column "much."

The second question is concerned with the general tendency of drawing details. Children who are intellectually inclined express their highly active intellect by the desire to include many details. In Fig. 7b the child does not have a general tendency to fill his drawing with details. Excepting the eyes of mother ("Mother Is Looking for Me"), which consists of an outer circle with a dot in its center, nothing in this painting has an emphasis on details. Neither are the flowers differentiated, nor is the house divided into walls and roof, nor are the windows drawn with details. The check mark in the chart would then have to be placed under "some." The third question refers to either the age group of four to five and a half or to the five and a half to seven years. Since the child's age is five, we would look at the question which refers to children from four to five and a half years old. The child's representation of a man shows more than head and feet only. If we would like to be sure of answering this question correctly we would need more than one drawing from the same child. Figure 7a, as well as Fig. 7c, was made by the same child. From them we can see that the child's representation of a man usually shows much more than head and feet only. Our check mark in the chart would, therefore, be placed under "much"; although occasionally the child uses for expressive purposes the "head" only, for instance, in representing his "mother." In looking at the questions which refer to the child five and a half to seven years old, we would find that our child would more closely fit the level indicated there. The next questions refer to the modeling of the child. Also here it is of prime significance for the intellectual advancement of the child whether his creative concept is already concerned with imaginative projections. It has been found that children at this age who are more intellectually inclined model by starting with details, bringing the different parts into their consciousness, and relating them to each other. During this stage of development, children who model by starting with the whole lump of clay usually do not go into detailed expression, but rather remain with the "whole."

Emotional growth

One of the most important indications of emotional growth, particularly during this developmental stage, is the flexibility of the child. This can best be seen in the frequent changes in the child's concepts. The more frequently he changes them, the more flexible and adjustable is the child. For a more objective evaluation of this question, more than one drawing is necessary. If we look at Figs. 7a, 7b, and 7c we see very frequent changes of the child's concepts for "man" and his environment. For an example of this, the symbol for representing himself constantly changes. In direct connection with this question is the next question: "Is the child free from stereotyped repetitions?" The significance of stereotyped repetitions as an escape mechanism and an emotional block has been discussed previously.[4] Stereotyped repetitions during the pre-schematic stage are usually seen in repetitions of the same type of representative symbols without any deviations—for instance: if the child who drew Fig. 6 did nothing but repeat the same figure as expressed in his drawing. In extreme cases of stereotyped repetitions environmental representations are usually entirely omitted. The symbol appears repeated in an isolated fashion (see Fig. 96a). Needless to say, there are no stereotyped repetitions visible in any of the drawings reproduced in Figs. 7a, 7b, and 7c. That indicates that the child is entirely free from stereotyped repetitions. In our chart we would have to put our check mark under "much."

A child who reacts toward meaningful experiences in an emotionally sensitive way will show this emotional sensitivity in his art work. In his drawings he will exaggerate those things or parts with which he has become emotionally bound up. It can easily be understood that an oversensitive child who becomes too much bound up with one part may easily lose connection with the rest of the object. Too much exaggeration would be the result. Our child shows such a tendency for too much exaggeration. But since this type of exaggeration is not a continuous type of expression we

[4] See page 15.

would check the question which refers to the mere presence of exaggerated parts under "much," and the other which refers to a lack of continuous exaggerations with "some," since we found some tendency toward repeated exaggerations.

Children who lack confidence show their inhibitions by frequently interrupted timid lines. The lines in Figs. 7a, 7b, and 7c are bold and definite, showing the child's confidence in his creative work. Things which are emotionally significant are definitely brought into spatial relationship. The child is visibly hiding behind the house in Fig. 7b while mother is looking for him. The child brought himself into obvious relationship to his dog which he has apparently just found in his back yard, hidden by the high grass in Fig. 7c. It can easily be understood that this child never wants to copy, because copying would be meaningless for him.

Social growth

As has previously been pointed out, the first requisite for any degree of awareness of the responsibility for social functions is the ability to face one's own experiences and identify oneself with them. It is, therefore, of immediate significance for the proper social functioning of the individual whether or not he has the desire to relate his experiences to his creative work. In Fig. 7b the child relates every part of the drawing to a definite experience with which he closely identifies himself. We would, therefore, have to check this first question in the column "much."

The fact that the child relates himself to the outside world represents already a higher level of social consciousness. That he no longer conceives of his immediate ego only is indeed an indication that he has become interested in things outside himself. This interest may be very fragmentary, in no particular order, or, as has been said before, the order may be determined by the emotional significance. In all drawings (Figs. 7a, b, c) the child has introduced not only an emotional relationship between himself and things which were of significance to him but also a spatial relationship. The child clearly indicates the "above" and the "below," an awareness which is superior to his level of development.[5] Both of the questions in the evaluation chart which refer to correlation must be checked in the column "much." It is of further social significance whether or not the child pays attention to his *particular* environment. At least in Figs. 7b and 7c there are indications that the child treats different environments differently. Although no strong signs of a more detailed awareness are given, it is obvi-

[5] See page 140.

ous that the child is aware of the flower garden, the house, and even the pond (square above his head) in Fig. 7b, and the high grass of his back yard in Fig. 7c. We would place our check mark under "some." That means that he has developed some sensitivity toward his *particular* environment.

Perceptual growth

The mere presence of things in creative works is not indicative of perception. It may deal with conceptual knowledge or emotional relationships. However, the way in which things are represented is an indication of the type of experiences the child has had with them. A representation by means of mere representative symbols (parts which when separated lose their identity) usually is only of conceptual or emotional significance. As soon as the child establishes *more* than the mere *meaning* by *visually* relating his drawing to objects, visual perception begins. This can usually be recognized by the fact that the child uses lines other than mere geometric ones. In Figs. 7a, b, c only geometric lines are used. All details would lose their meanings when separated from the whole. The check mark in the chart would have to be placed under "none." Also, there is no direct indication of lines which represent movements or sounds, which would point toward special kinesthetic or auditive experiences. It should be pointed out, however, that in both instances in which hearing or listening is involved (listening for the bouncing ball in Fig. 7a, or apparent listening for the hiding dog in Fig. 7c) the ears are exaggerated. Nevertheless, this is not indicative enough of visual or auditive experiences to justify the writing of the check mark under another column but "none."

From the original painting we would see that the outlines of "mother" in Fig. 7b are painted in purple, while he himself is painted in blue only. In Fig. 7c his arms are yellow, the legs and the rest of him are outlined with blue. The body is colored purple, while the ears are painted black. His dog is colored red. From this it appears that no relationship between color and objects has been established. (See Plates 2 and 3.)

Children who perceive the whole rather than conceive of an object in parts usually start with the whole lump of clay. Starting from the whole lump can easily be detected even on the final product inasmuch as it does not show separate parts or seams, which would indicate that the modeling is "pieced" together. Children who model by starting from the "whole" usually are observers since the "whole" can mostly be perceived only visually. (See Figs. 24b and c.)

Physical growth

It has been demonstrated by several investigators[6] that continuous exaggerations or omissions of the *same* body parts usually point toward a defect or abnormality of this particular body part. Blind individuals quite commonly exaggerate the eyes in their creative works. A child with a deformed foot continually omitted the foot. Another child who was hard of hearing continually emphasized the ears in his creative work. There is a complete lack of continuous exaggerations or omissions of the same body parts in the drawings in Figs. 7a, b, c. Both of the questions in the chart which refer to these points must be marked under "much."

It is quite obvious that the lines used in Figs. 7a, b, c are generally very determined and vigorous, and point, therefore, toward an excellent and vigorous physical condition. Indirectly the child also includes such body actions as stretching the hands and reaching for the dog as illustrated in Fig. 7c. While the drawings of the child indicate his good physical status, it is again warned that the last word concerning physical growth should come from the physician.

Aesthetic growth

If we have before us a blank sheet of paper, the space on it is still undefined. As soon as we draw a square somewhere on the paper, the space within the square becomes a defined area, while the space around the square still remains undefined. Gustaf Britsch[7] in his excellent book calls these areas, respectively the "meaningful" and the "meaningless" area (*"der gemeinte und der ungemeinte Fleck"*). In any work of aesthetic significance these two areas should be in harmonious relationship with each other. If, for instance, the square were placed on the paper without any relationship to the surrounding area, no aesthetic or design value would be established. The child's relationships to the "meaningful" and the "meaningless" areas are established entirely unconsciously. Yet, we can see from the way in which he establishes these relationships how he develops aesthetically. In all three of our drawings the relationships between the meaningful and the meaningless areas are extremely harmonious. All areas are well defined and the meaningful parts extremely well distributed. There is no "empty" or "dead" area which we would rather like to cut off.

[6] Read, Herbert, *Education Through Art, op. cit.;* Kroetsch, Walter, *Rhythmus und Form in der Kinderzeichnung.* Leipzig, 1917; Munz, Ludwig and Lowenfeld, V., *Plastische Arbeiten Blinder.* Brünn, 1934; also Lowenfeld, V., *The Nature of Creative Activity.* London, 1952.

[7] Britsch, Gustaf, *Theorie der Bildenden Kunst.* Munich, F. Bruckmann, 1926.

While the distribution of the meaningful areas is very well done, there is no indication of the child's desire for decoration, as related to the next question in the chart. In Fig. 9 we would clearly see such a desire in the stripes put on the girl's dress. Nowhere in Figs. 7a, b, c do we notice such an attempt, except perhaps in Fig. 7a where the child decorated the ball. This may justify our putting the check mark under "some." Organization of subject matter and content seems to harmonize completely inasmuch as neither overpowers the other.

While the child does not relate colors to objects, he seems to change his colors frequently with a good feeling for a decorative distribution. He does not remain with one color on one side of the picture and with another on the other side. The blue outline of the body against the purple inside or the black of his ears in Fig. 7c is indeed very decorative. Without any hesitation we can place our check mark for the last question pertaining to aesthetic growth under "much."

Creative growth

Among other characteristics creative growth reveals itself in the independence of approach. During the pre-schematic stage the creative child will develop his independent relationships to things which are expressed in independent concepts. The creative child will never ask "how" to draw a mouth, a nose, etc. He will without hesitancy draw his own concepts. The child's own concepts can easily be distinguished from those taken over from other sources by the free and flexible use and frequent changes which he applies to his own concepts and by the stiff and repetitious way in which he uses foreign concepts. Needless to say the child independently applies his own concepts throughout in Figs. 7a, b, c. If we could watch the child working in a group we would see that he remains completely uninfluenced in his concepts.

In order to answer the third question in the chart, it is necessary to observe the child to determine whether he spontaneously paints or creates otherwise, or whether he only does it when motivated. However, it can be said with certainty that no signs in the child's work are indicative of any trend toward copying or imitating.

SUMMARY OF GROWTH ANALYSIS

In summarizing and integrating all growth factors it seems to me significant to look again at the drawings as a total experience of the child's. We have seen that the child's intellectual level seems to be far above the average inasmuch as his conceptual knowledge is far superior to the average expectation as outlined in the foregoing chapter. Emotionally he seems to be more than sensitive in his inner reactions as well as in those to his environment. In Fig. 7b he draws himself hiding behind the house while "mother is calling me from the flower garden." Mother is, therefore, closely attached with his mind. It is because of this emotional closeness that he draws her large. For "calling" him and "looking" for him, her body seems insignificant and, therefore, is omitted from his drawing. Looking for him first to the left and then to the right made him draw two pairs of eyes, a not-infrequent representation of motion. "She is in the flower garden" makes the flowers an important part of his experience. "I am hiding behind the house" determined the size relationship of himself to the house. The house consists for him in his drawings of a wall, pointed to an undifferentiated roof—his perceptual experiences never were of importance— with windows in it and a door with a peephole. This was apparently important to him. Seemingly, his mother used it for observing him while he was in the back yard. The only important thing in the back yard appears to be the pond. Apparently he was conscious of it for safety reasons. "Himself" he depicted without arms, with a somewhat exaggerated head. His increased attention when listening to the call of his mother seems to be responsible for the enlarged head, while it seems quite obvious that he does not need the arms for running around and hiding from mother. If we compare this depiction of the self with that in Fig. 7c where he, happy at just having found his dog, wants to pick it up with his enormously exaggerated arms, the flexibility of the child in using his concepts is striking.

From this analysis, the personality of the child as a well-adjusted, healthy, somewhat oversensitive human being, with high intellectual and superior social conditions, easily reveals itself. However, it is not surprising that his strong reactions toward emotional stimuli do not make him at all an observer. Visual stimuli do not mean much to him. His creative independence paired with his aesthetic trends makes him a child with highly desirable trends and over-all superior growth characteristics.

EXERCISES

(1) Collect several drawings by one child and describe the changing quality of his representative symbols.

(2) Show the different use of geometric lines in the drawings of this period.

(3) Analyze a child's drawing with regard to:

(a) Changing quality of representative symbols.

(b) Active knowledge of the child.

(c) Spatial relationship of objects: ability or inability to establish relationship; is relationship established on account of emotional connections?

(d) Color relationship.

(4) Find out how many different symbols for "mouth," "nose," and "eyes" you can find in one classroom. Can you relate them to personalities?

(5) Give similar topics, once without stimulation and then with the best stimulation you can provide. Did you accomplish a change in the child's active knowledge? Describe the amount and quality of the change.

(6) Analyze a child's clay work as indicated in step 3.

(7) Make growth profiles, using the evaluation chart, also for Figs. 6, 7a, 7c, and 9.

LABORATORY WORK

(1) Prepare "thick" paint by mixing pigments with water.

(2) Draw a "door," or the "entrance of the school" first without looking at it, and then after having looked at it. Has your active knowledge improved? To what extent?

(3) Paint other objects before and after individual observation. Control the growth of your active knowledge.

(4) Do the same in clay. Find also here the increase of your active knowledge.

CHAPTER V   **THE ACHIEVEMENT OF**
A FORM CONCEPT
Schematic Stages (7 to 9 years)

THE SCHEMA IN DRAWINGS BY CHILDREN

THE MEANING OF THE SCHEMA CAN ONLY BE FULLY REALIZED WHEN
we understand the child's longing, after a long search, for a definite concept of man and environment. This concept is, as has been said before,
highly individualized. There are scarcely two schemata alike. The wealth of
the concept of form, the schema, depends on personality and on the degree
to which the teacher was able to activate the child's passive knowledge.
Thus, a child can enter the schematic stage with a rich concept of man
and environment, but he can also arrive at the conclusion of a concept with
a rather meager schema. I use the term "pure schematic representation" in
cases where there appears to be no further representational intention
beyond that which is represented. Where such a further intention is present,
one can no longer speak of a pure schema. Thus, *a pure schematic repre-*
sentation is a representation with no intentional experiences represented.
We shall find a pure schema in a child's drawing, whenever the child's
representation confines itself to the object, "That is a tree; that is a man."
When he says, "This man is big and this one is small," the differences with

132

which the child expresses larger or smaller allow us to draw certain conclusions. Conversely, a study of the kind of modification undergone by the schema allows us to understand the intention underlying the representation. This method is of especial importance to the teacher, who ought, by this means of comparison between the schematic and subjective drawing, to study the effects of his teaching. *The schema refers in the same way to space and objects as it refers to figures.* The schema of an object is the concept at which the child has finally arrived, which represents the child's active knowledge of the object. Also here, the deviations from the schema he usually uses to represent the object express the experience which was of importance in this particular drawing. For example, a child might draw a house with roof and windows only. For a particular experience, however, the door might be of special significance. He will then change his schema and add the door. *Through this deviation from his schema the child has manifested his particular experience.* X

Human schema—the first definite concept of man

The term *human schema* is used to describe the form concept of the human figure at which the child has arrived after long struggles of searching during the pre-schematic stage. The child's schema of a man is the incorporation of all the knowledge that he, emotionally, connects with the thought "man." Every achievement becomes an achievement when it grows out of the unconscious realm into the realm of consciousness. We do not believe in our achievements unless, *through repetitions,* we convince ourselves of our mastery. The child, too, assures himself through repetition that he has arrived at a definite concept of the representation of a man. *Thus, the human schema is the form concept of a man at which the child has arrived and which he repeats again and again whenever no intentional experiences influence him to change his concept.* The schemata of the human figure consist of the most different and *highly individualized* form symbols.[1] As has been investigated in my work *The Nature of Creative Activity,* schemata are not arbitrary signs but are *intimately related to both the bodily and the mental constitution.* That is why we will find in a classroom as many different schemata of human figures as there are individuals.

---

[1] For a variety of schemata see Goodenough, Florence L., "Children's Drawings," *Handbook of Child Psychology.* Worcester: Clark University Press, 1931.

Space schema—the first concept of order
in space

What we have said about the human figure is very largely true of the schematic representation of objects as well as of space. The great discovery, however, of the child during this age level is that there is a *definite order in spatial relationships.* The child no more thinks "there is a tree," "there is a man," "there is a car," without relating them to one another as he has done during the pre-schematic stage. The child now thinks, "I am on the ground," "the car is on the ground," "the grass grows on the ground," "Bob is on the ground," *"we are all on the ground."* This first *mass consciousness of discovering that the child is a part of environment is expressed* by a symbol which we shall call *"base line."* From now on this consciousness, which includes all in a common space relationship, is expressed by putting everything, objects and figures, on this important space schema, the base line. This has, however, great psychological implications for the education of the child. *Consciously being a part of environment is the most important assumption for cooperation.* It is therefore highly significant to recognize that the introduction of this fundamental experience of the base line is a clear indication that the child is now ready to cooperate intentionally. It is also a sign of the child's ability to correlate objects properly with one another. This again has its psychological implications. For instance, in reading, this very same correlation is necessary in relating letters to one another in order to form a word symbol. Thus, whenever the base line is introduced by a child, it is an indication that the child has grown out of the ego into a world of which *he feels a part.* We can speak of schemata, however, only when the representation of an object or space *through repetition has become established.* The schema in space or objects can originate in visual or nonvisual experiences. In other words, the impression the child gets in *looking* at things might determine his schematic representation just as much as the *importance* or the *emotional significance* the child attaches to it. Very often, as we shall see, *kinesthetic experiences* or touch impressions also influence the concept of the schema. It is, however, important to keep in mind that we speak of *a space schema when space is represented by some signs or others which, through repetition, assume a constant meaning in the drawings of a child.* Because the child has not yet discovered in his drawings the three-dimensional quality of space, he is frequently forced to introduce lines, which are merely individual symbols.

These lines are supposed to substitute for the third dimension. Consequently, the space schema is almost entirely abstract and has only an indirect connection with reality.

DEVIATIONS FROM THE SCHEMA— EXPRESSION OF SUBJECTIVE EXPERIENCES

Highly interesting is that if we accept the schema as the concept of man and environment at which the child has arrived, every deviation from it will have to be investigated according to its origin and its meaning. From this understanding of origin and meaning of the deviations in their various forms, we can draw conclusions about the child's experience. Three principal forms of deviations can be noticed in children's drawings: (1) *exaggeration of important parts*, (2) *neglect or omission of unimportant or suppressed parts*, and (3) *change of symbols of emotionally significant parts*. It should be understood that exaggeration and neglect refer *to size only*, whereas the change of symbols refers to *their shapes*. (It is needless to say that all these characteristics refer to the way *we* see them. Indeed, Barkan is right when he says, "Children do not overstate; rather they create size relationships which are 'real' to them.") [2]
The origin of such deviations lies either in autoplastic experiences— that is, *feelings of the bodily self*, in the *importance of value judgments* with regard to certain parts, or in the *emotional significance* which this part has for the child (Fig. 15).
A particularly interesting piece of work which displays all types of deviations in a single drawing is shown in Fig. 12 titled "Searching for the Lost Pencil." [3] Fig. 11 shows the schematic representation of a man that the child has drawn when simply asked to "draw a man." Thus, in this drawing no intentional experiences are represented; rather is it the form concept of a man, at which the child has arrived and which he repeats again and again whenever asked to draw a man. In comparing this schema with the subjective drawing, "Searching for the Lost Pencil," we shall clearly see the deviations and the experiences that these deviations express. In this picture the arms and hands are the vehicles of expression, and by means of them four phases of the theme are symbolized. The intense experience of searching and of groping about after the pencil is expressed, on the one hand, by the different emphasis and exaggeration of the arm.

[2] Barkan, Manuel, *A Foundation for Art Education.* New York: The Ronald Press Company, 1955, p. 117.
[3] Discussed by the author in his *The Nature of Creative Activity.* See list of references at the end of this book.

Fig. 11. Schematic representation of "A Man." In schematic representations no conscious experiences are represented.

and on the other hand, by changes in the shape of the symbol for "hand." The enormously lengthened, groping arm shows how the representation of the hand has been modified by the experience of clutching. "With this hand he has just found the pencil," the child says, pointing to the other hand holding the pencil. The arm now shows a double line (compare with schema) indicating its special functional importance. The hand, however, is now less emphasized because the experience of clutching is no longer the dominant one. Notice particularly the enormously exaggerated pencil, showing the emotional importance it had for the child when he found it. "With *this* hand he puts it in his pocket," the child says, and points to one of the arms of the second figure which, in fact, represents the same figure as the first one.

In other words, the child has represented four temporal phases by means of two figures. He might just as well have given one figure four arms; but this would have contradicted his experience. The arm which is putting the pencil into the pocket is now far less emphasized and is represented by a single line only while the second arm of the figure, having no longer a function, has shriveled to a mere stump. Bending

te 3. "I Am Standing in My Backyard." (6½ years)
lor is used purely for enjoyment. (See page 116.)
tice first signs of color-object relationships of emo-
ially significant parts such as eyes, lips, grass, tree,
i sky. These are first signs for the establishment of
or schemata. Notice also the importance of the ego as
npared to the tree. (Courtesy Laboratory School, State
achers College, Indiana, Pa.)

Plate 4. "Lightning and Rain." (7 years) Color is related to objects (Schem
Stage). The color-object relationship often becomes rigid. Notice that
sky retains its color-object relationship of "blue" although it is raining. 1
is characteristic for a color schema. (See page 157.)

Fig. 12. "Searching for the Lost Pencil." The schema has been modified according to the experience. Emphasis on meaningful parts. Neglect of unimportant parts. Several sequences are expressed in one drawing. (Schematic stage). Use of geometric lines.

down and standing upright are represented by means of differences in the length of the legs. It would be difficult to find a drawing that more clearly shows in a single picture, the origin and meaning of the different deviations from the schema.

We can illustrate still another experience originating in bodily sensations. According to the child the left figure is supposed to be bent forward, and this is expressed by means of shorter legs and a lowered head. The other figure on the right is standing upright while putting the pencil in his pocket, and this is expressed by longer legs and an upright head. But when the head is bent forward, blood accumulates in it, and we become more intensely aware of it. This is expressed in the drawing by an exaggeration of the size of the bent head.

This example has shown clearly that the child does not fall prey to an inflexible schema, but by using his own individual experience, he creatively transforms the schema in the act of creation. Furthermore, it shows that "disproportions" nearly always result from some definite intention or, better, experience, though this does not mean that the experience is necessarily conscious. *We therefore no longer have the right to speak of "false proportions,"* since such a judgment is determined by our visual attitude, the attitude of "objectively representing the environment." On the contrary, as we have seen, it is only when we understand the reasons for these apparent disproportions that we are able to penetrate into the true roots of creativeness. *Naturalistic tendencies and conceptions therefore, are totally unsuitable means for the understanding of children's drawings.* The child is intimately bound up with the experience of the self, and experiences his world subjectively.

REPRESENTATION OF THE HUMAN FIGURE— GEOMETRIC LINES

We have seen that the schema is merely the form concept, the basis for the creative experience. The richer this concept, the more possibilities are at hand for its expression. If the representation of a "man," the schema at which the child has arrived, consists only of head, body, legs, and arms, the creative possibilities are very restricted. The child, then, has only the possibility of using these four form symbols for the expression of his experiences. Soon he will be condemned to a certain rigidity, which educators always see as an outcome of poor schemata. *Therefore the child should be kept flexible as long as possible until he has built up a rich source of active knowledge, which is the basis for a sound creative development.*

As has been said before, the type of representation to which a child comes depends largely upon personality development, body constitution, and, to a great extent, upon the stimulation the child has received. If for a child the symmetry of the body—the *two* arms, the *two* legs, the *two* eyes, the *two* ears—is of importance, the child's schema will be the front view. If, however, the experience that the nose is protruding was of greater significance, the child's schema will show the profile. The opinion that the profile represents a more advanced stage in the child's creative concept is, according to experiments, incorrect. I have seen numerous children starting out with a profile concept of a man. If the two eyes and arms and the protruding nose are all of significance for the child, he derives from this experience the concept of mixing front view and profile, and often includes both eyes and the nose (Fig. 12).

From this discussion it seems evident that such a concept has not only the right to exist, but represents a high form of active knowledge and should by no means be "corrected." It shows again that the child's concept of the world, during this mental level, is derived from visual experiences to a limited degree, if at all. This point is also revealed by the fact that the schema still consists of geometric lines, lines which, when separated from the whole, lose their meaning. Although I have seen some children include "dresses" or "clothes" in their schemata as part of their concepts, usually schemata of the human figure consist only of symbols for body parts. *There is, however, no limit in the variety of such form symbols.* I have seen ovals, triangles, squares, circles, rectangles, irregular shapes, thick or thin lines used as schemata for "body," and all kinds of shapes for legs, arms, clothes and so forth.

SPACE

Psychological aspects

The most important and basic experience of the child's spatial development is the discovery of an orderly and related space concept. The child now includes himself in his concept in the same way that he includes the tree, the house, the whole environment. This first common experience of space—"I am on the street, John is on the street"—*is sometimes a most deciding factor in the psychological development of the child.* His attitude now changes from a completely *egocentric* attitude to a *cooperative* attitude. The difference between these two stages can easily be seen in watching children of a kindergarten and comparing their behavior reactions with those of the elementary-school level. Kindergarten children play and work together or cooperate only when urged to do so. In freedom they will generally follow their own directions. Thus we see one child going in one direction, imitating a train, another child sitting on the slide, self-concerned, whereas a third child plays in the sand, scarcely noticing the others. The only collision occurs when one child wants the toy another happens to have. This is clearly indicated, as we have seen, in the spatial concept of children during this age period. *Whenever the first common experience of space has occurred, the child relates himself to others, sees himself as a part of the environment.* The child then starts to cooperate with understanding. He has discovered for the first time a definite order in space.

Fig. 13. "Street Scene." Base-line representation expressing first spatial order.

Introduction of the base line

As an indication of the child's conscious relationship between himself and environment, he places everything on one line, the base line. All things standing on the ground are now related on this important symbol.

The line upon which trees as well as human beings are standing represents, therefore, not only the base line on which the represented objects stand, but the street itself. We cannot, of course, assume that the child knew nothing about the width or other characteristics of the street, since every child of this age level has crossed streets on numerous occasions. This experience seemingly has not yet reached the active level of knowledge. I do not refer here to the three-dimensional concept and the "inability" to represent it. I refer rather to the lack of desire to represent both sides of the street with the space between. The child, however, expressed the street merely with one line, the base line. The line is merely a symbol for everything connected with "street."

In this picture (Fig. 13) we see both sides of the street. In order to understand that the space between the two base lines does not represent the surface of the street, refer to Fig. 14, which is also a picture with two

Fig. 14. "Fruit Harvest." "I am Picking Apples" (seven-year-old gifted child). Picture is divided in two sections.

base lines, representing an orchard. The two base lines are purely conceptual formulations, and the drawing is nothing more than the representation of *one* orchard, regardless of whether it has two rows of trees or not. The represented phases are the ones of main significance, "picking the apples" on the lower base line, and "carrying them home" on the upper base line. That the space between has no meaning (or the meaning "air") will immediately be realized when we notice that every base line has its own sky. In other words, this picture has "two skies." We can only understand this concept if we consider the two base lines not as boundaries, but only as *base lines*. "We stand on the ground and above is the sky." Since every ground has its sky wherever I may stand, every base line is related to a sky. That is why we never see children draw anything between base lines. Exceptions can only be seen *on an emotional base*—that is, when the child through a *special emotional experience* comes to the realization that the space between *is* meaningful. However, before we continue our discussion on the meaning of this important space symbol, it seems proper to discuss the origin of the base line.

Fig. 15. "I am Throwing Something into the Trash Basket" (seven-year-old girl). The hands are of significance, therefore exaggerated. (Courtesy Educational Project, Museum of Modern Art, N. Y.)

Origin of the base line

It is quite obvious that in reality neither objects nor persons standing on the ground are standing on a line. That is why we can clearly state that the base line can not have its origin in visual experiences. The investigation of primitive stages in the development of mankind has frequently been of great help for the understanding of the single individual. In creative products of primitive stages we often see the use of the base line as a means of indicating motion. I have seen in an early Indian drawing an Indian fleeing along a line, presumably indicating by means of this line the direction of flight. The use of the base line to indicate motion appears in the same way in Australian drawings made on the bark of trees, or in drawings of Arctic tribes. Many other such examples could be stated, and from them we conclude that *the first origin of the base line is the kinesthetic experience of moving along a line.* From the play of our early childhood we know, too, that we frequently connect with the experience of moving the thought of going along a line.

Fig. 16. "I am Climbing a Hill" (seven years). Base line "goes up and down," symbolizing terrain.

The base line and the characterization of terrain

When the child represents his space concept, the base line, he uses this line to symbolize at one time *the base* on which things stand, and at another time to characterize *the surface* of the landscape. In Fig. 16, one base line symbolizes *the plain,* another base line represents *the mountain.* In other words, the child wishes to indicate that this base line is elevated over the plain and represents the *surface character* of the landscape. How much this "mountain" is still a "bent" base line can be seen from the fact that the trees stand *perpendicularly* to the "mountain." The growing upward of the trees is bound to a base line. We can realize this experience most clearly if we would consider the base line to be a line of wire, a straight wire with flowers attached to it. If we bend the wire according to the kinesthetic experience of going up and down, the flowers attached to the wire stand out perpendicularly as we see them in the child's drawings. Clearly, it is not the "shape" of the mountain which is of significance, but the line itself.

Fig. 17. "Playing Checkers" (seven-year-old boy). The checkerboard is "folded over" because of its significance.

This is very characteristically expressed in Fig. 16, in which the flowers are drawn perpendicularly to the mountain. We can understand this only when we realize that the line representing the mountain becomes the base line for the house. Upon this base line the flowers are drawn vertically.

If, however, as in Fig. 18,[4] the line indicating a mountain is not intended to be a base line (the shading indicates that the mountain "as a whole" had meaning), a new base line is introduced for houses and trees. After making a trip to the hilltop, the child wished to indicate a shelter on the top of a hill. Seemingly, the top of the hill, with all the excitement of climbing to it, made such a vivid impression on the child, that he did not want to sacrifice the peak for the house, which would cover the peak. The conflict of having the house standing on the peak brought the child to this creative concept. He first drew the hill, using the lower edge as base line. Although the child usually does not shade, in this drawing he did shade the hill, thereby showing that in this case he did not intend to give a

---

[4] Because of its interest, this example is taken from the author's *The Nature of Creative Activity.*

Fig. 18. "A Shelter on Top of a Hill." Symbol for mountain. Symbolic association of the house with hilltop.

special meaning to the outline. Thus the child emphasized the space inside the lines that represented the hill. He had created a distinct representative symbol for "hill." After he had drawn the hill, he drew a base line for the house and trees which just touched the peak of the hill. In this way he wished to indicate that the house stood on the top.

The child's conception, determined by his emotional experience, may be analyzed as follows. In a plain (the lower edge of the paper also represents the plain in the form of a base line) there is a hill, the hill which he has climbed (representative symbol for "hill" is the shaded triangle). On the top of the hill stands a shelter and trees. But, since every house stands on a base, and there is as yet no such base present (the outline for the representative symbol for "hill" does not here function as a base line because the child did not want to sacrifice the peak), he had to create one. The house must stand on the hill, therefore, its base must be on the hill. Consequently, the base line of the house is drawn in such a way that it touches the top of the hill, and thereby indicates the relation between the two. *This drawing shows clearly that the base line is not a rigid symbol,* and that the child departs from the base line whenever an emotional experience interferes with it. How the child uses the "base-line experience" in still greater variety will be described in the following paragraphs.

Subjective space representations

We call subjective space representations all representations in which an emotional experience forces the child to deviate from his space schema. There are basically two different types of deviations. One type is that in which the base line still functions as the vehicle within the spatial concept of the child. Then base lines as such are still used in the child's representation, but in modified forms. In the other type of deviation the emotional experience overpowers so much the child's feeling of being a part of environment, that he drops his "base-line experiences" altogether and introduces a space relationship which is founded purely upon his emotional feelings. The frequently used process of "folding over" belongs to one of the typical deviations. *Under "folding over" we understand the often-used process of creating a space concept by drawing the objects perpendicularly to the base line,* even when the objects appear to be drawn "upside down."

Fig. 19 is a typical painting of a child which shows the process of folding over. In this drawing the child depicts himself as waving to the ferry. After the child had drawn himself waving his handkerchief, standing on one side of the creek, he felt the need to draw the boat. He fulfilled this need by turning the paper around (or better, going around the paper which was lying on the floor) and painting the boat seemingly upside down. *This concept can best be understood if we fold the paper along the base line.* We then get the perfect experience of the child standing upright

Fig. 19. "Norfolk Ferry" (eight years old). Space is expressed by "folding over" one shore line. Both sides of the creek are related to the middle.

and facing the boat. Since the other shore line is also standing upright, as the boat does, it is drawn accordingly. Also here the correct understanding can only be perceived in folding the paper along the base line, which represents the other shore line. We then receive a perfect model of the scene and we suddenly realize the interesting concept of the "two skies," one on the bottom and the other on the top of the paper. Under the condition of "folding over," both skies are on top above the houses Basically, the subjective experience of the child was of being in the center of the scene, seeing one shore to the left and the other to the right. This experience shows very clearly that it is of *great advantage to have children work on the floor or on desks, on which the drawing can be approached from all directions.*

The other type of deviation is characterized by the fact that a child who usually uses base lines in his space schema drops the lines altogether. As has been said before, the emotional experience can be so strong that it overpowers the feeling of being connected with the ground. Fig. 20, "On the Seesaw," is a typical example of such a drawing in which the child's feeling of being a part of environment was overpowered by the emotional feeling of swinging up and down. The sensation of this kinesthetic experience determined the spatial concept. The boy artist shows himself way up near the sky and sun. His emotions are visibly expressed by the exaggerated size of his body as well as by his facial expression: the mouth is wide open. "My older sister lifted me up so high," he said. With this he indicated that his "older" sister was at least heavy enough to lift him up high. Through the exaggeration of himself (a result of his own subjective experience) the size of his sister seems so small that she could not possibly lift him. Since the sister was sitting opposite, the boy painted her seemingly upside down. In reality, this is *his* subjective view and can be understood only if we fold the pictures of him and her along the little base line on which they are sitting (the ends of the seesaw). We then again realize what a marvelous space concept the child has created through the power of his subjective feelings.

If the principle of "folding over" is used frequently, we shall understand from what has been said before, that such children are depending upon their subjective, emotional tie-ups. It can be concluded *that children who often use this principle of space representation are usually egocentric.* They regard themselves as the center of the world and relate everything to themselves.

Another important means of subjective space experiences results in drawings with *the mixture of plane and elevation.* We can very well under-

Fig. 20. "On the Seesaw" (nine-year-old boy). Subjective expression of the experience of going up and down.

Fig. 21. "Amusement Island" (eight-year-old boy). Boats are grouped around the island because of the subjective experience of the boat ride.

stand this experience if we ourselves or our friends draw the following subjects:[5] "A Chessboard on a Table." Then turn your paper and draw on the other side "A Glass of Water on a Table." Since the chessboard demands the top view, usually the table is also drawn in top view. The glass of water, however, can better be seen in side view and thus will determine the changed view of the table. This experiment only works with persons who are subjectively minded. For visually minded persons, the table will not change whether there is a glass of water or a chessboard on it. The child, however, who develops an emotional relationship to his drawing, will become bound up with the chessboard (Fig. 17) and surely draws it from the top view. The table, however, would not be a table if it did not have legs too. The child then draws a table with legs and when necessary, folds over the top of the table to show its significance, thus mixing plane and elevation in one drawing.

[5] Of course it is important to stress at the beginning that it makes no difference *how* things are drawn.

Another drawing of great interest, which shows the same type of experience, is the drawing in Fig. 21, "Amusement Island." The child visited an island on which were all types of amusement, people playing cards, hot-dog stands, and so forth. There were also boats for rent, and in such a boat the child took a ride around the island. The drawing now shows a top view of the island (that the water surrounds the island is best expressed this way). Everything is standing out of the island; that is why all objects on the island are represented in side view. That the water surrounds the island was most important for the child because of his boat ride. This is clearly expressed in the drawing by grouping the boats around the island. Many other examples of such spatial concepts are discussed in *The Nature of Creative Activity*.

Space and time representations

Space and time representations are of different time sequences in a single space. The child quite naturally uses this type of expression whenever he feels the need. Just as the child has his own way of depicting two- and three-dimensional objects, sometimes by using plane and elevation at the same time, so he has his own way of depicting events which occur in different time sequences. The child who mingles plane and elevation fuses his space and time concepts. But the psychological origin of space and time is often somewhat different. We can mainly trace two different psychological roots, to each of which there corresponds an adequate formal representation. The knowledge of these two roots seems of importance to educators because it will offer to them a wealth of material for proper stimulation of the child, and especially for integrating art with other subjects.

The child likes both to listen to stories, and to tell them. One manner of space-time representation arises out of this urge for *communication*. That is why we find *different episodes represented by different pictures in one sequence of drawings.* The pictures are separate, like those in comic books, and it is of no significance whether the individual theme really has been divided by a line or whether the division is purely fictitious. It is characteristic of this *"story-telling" representation* that the action as a whole is drawn repeatedly, but usually with different surroundings. Journeys, trips, traveling episodes belong in this type of representation. In such topics, usually the most important events are characterized. *They describe* a complex event by means of separate pictures, whose relation to one another is one of content.

The second psychological root can be seen in the picture in which *temporally distinct actions are represented in one space*. This does not spring from the desire to communicate something; its origin must be sought rather in the emotional tie-up with the representation and in the act of drawing itself. The importance of the action diminishes the child's consciousness of time to such an extent that he is not aware of representing different time phases in one drawing. He is concerned only with expressing within one drawing what he regards as most characteristic about the action, in much the same way as alternations between plane and elevation are used to express what is most characteristic about an object. *In the one case temporally distinct phases, in the other spatially distinct impressions are fused and used for characterization.*

It is important to realize that in this type of expression the picture is confined to a single sequence of actions or movements. Placing the various aspects next to one another in one space is employed merely as a method of characterization. For a typical example of this type of expression, refer to Fig. 12, "Searching for the Lost Pencil," which we have already discussed. Here we are referring only to the content of this drawing, which deals with the expression of different time sequences within one space. "With one hand he is still searching, although with the other hand he already has found the pencil." This means, that in one person the child has represented two temporally different and distinct phases. He was emotionally so much tied up with the content, that the content overpowered his feeling for reality. The representation of one typical phase of the experience would not have served its purpose. The emotional urge—the strong experience he had with all phases of searching, finding, picking up, and pocketing—made him draw all phases. He used the next figure for the expression of putting the pencil into his pocket with one hand, and the other hand was used to signify that the experience was over. In other words, by means of two figures he represented four different temporal phases. He might just as well have given one figure four arms, as we can see it done in medieval manuscripts (Plate 65, *The Nature of Creative Activity*). But this would have contradicted his concept of a man.

In the paragraph on stimulation, we shall see that we can use the knowledge of the two psychological roots of space and time representations to great advantage in education.

X-ray pictures

In the very same way as plane and elevation are depicted at the same time to show the significant "views" while disregarding the impossibility of such a visual concept, the child still uses another most interesting nonvisual way of representation to show different views that could not possibly simultaneously be perceived visually. *He depicts the inside and outside simultaneously whenever the inside is emotionally, for the child, of more significance than the outside.* In other words, while he is drawing he becomes so much bound up with the inside that he completely "forgets" that there is an outside. In this case, he drops the outside altogether. If, however, the outside has also some meaning for the child, inside and outside are frequently mixed up. The picture then shows part of the inside, the part which has emotional importance, and part of the outside, as if it were transparent.[6]

That the child reacts in his drawings more toward the emotional significance than toward the visual is extremely important for education. It shows very definitely what stands out in the child's thinking. The adult's concept of surface phenomena and views is not the concept of the child. Educationally, in the teaching of art, it should give the teacher a tremendous opportunity to use this concept in integrating his subject matter of other fields into the realm of creative activity.

A group of children visited a factory in which was shown the manufacture of a product from the raw material kept in the basement to the finished product on the upper floor. When the children were asked to draw their experience, most of them developed a complete "plan" of the factory. The front wall was eliminated and the "views" into the different floors showed the different important working stages that had been discussed and experienced previously. These working stages, now actively in the minds of the children, had become a part of each child's knowledge and experience and could be readily used.

Another child had just come back from the hospital where she had to undergo an operation. She was first brought to the admission room and then to the X-ray room where an X-ray picture of her injured knee was taken. She was then brought by elevator into the children's ward, which was on the second floor, and from there into the operating room on the top floor. After the operation the child was returned to the ward, where she remained until she left. But before leaving, another X-ray picture was taken. When home, she drew the hospital and all the important events she had experienced. There was no front wall of significance. To her, the emotional experience overpowered all visual concepts, and her picture showed the basement, the floor with the ward in which she was lying, and the top floor with the operating room. All intervening floors had no significance to her, so they were omitted.

Fig. 22, "Coal Mine," shows a typical X-ray representation in which

[6] Eng, Helga K., *The Psychology of Drawing*. New York: Harcourt, Brace and Co., 1931.

Fig. 22. "Coal Mine" (nine years old). Subjective space representation shows also inside of the mountain. X-ray picture. Space-time concept.

inside and outside are completely mixed up according to emotional significance. The child from a mining area drew first the "outline" of the mountain as if it were a base line. Then she proceeded to draw the little trees and the house still dealing with the boundary of the mountain as with a base line. This can easily be recognized by the perpendicular way in which she placed trees and house on the base line. After that, she drew the "iron construction" above the "shaft" of the mine. When she drew the "iron construction" she suddenly realized that it is from here that the coal comes out of the ground. Thenceforth she became so absorbed in the interior of the mine that the base line completely lost its significance as an indicator of terrain, and became the "boundary" of the mountain. The emotional experience now shifted from the outside to the inside. She then drew the shaft with the horizontal pit in which the miners are working. (Notice the yellow artificial light.) She further wanted to indicate that coal is produced from this mine, so she divided the space around shaft and mine in sections, indicating her imaginative experience of the consistency of the walls of a coal mine.

Fig. 23. "Saying Good-bye." Different time sequences are expressed in one draw-ing. X-ray picture shows inside of compartment. Space "is filled" according to importance.

In the discussion that follows, we shall see how the phenomena which were the subject of foregoing pages can be fused into a single experience. Fig. 23 [7] was done by an almost-blind child. The topic was "Saying Good-bye." The child is saying good-bye to his father at the end of the holidays before returning to the Institute by train. He is concerned therefore with a profound experience. He begins by drawing the coach in outline, to indicate its limits. To characterize it, he adds the axles with their wheels—four wheels, of course, because that corresponds to his *knowledge*. Now he has before him the impression: railway coach.

Leonardo da Vinci said that every picture should somehow look com-plete in every one of its phases. He meant, I imagine, that every phase of the picture should leave behind it an impression of completeness so as to enable the spectator to relive the experiences underlying the creative process. In a sense other than that intended by Leonardo da Vinci this is particularly true of the education of children. By studying the genesis of a

[7] *The Nature of Creative Activity.*

picture we have the possibility of investigating the organic interrelationship of the things represented and in this way experiencing for ourselves the manner in which thought processes issue in pictorial form.

We see, then, that when the child had a complete impression of the coach before him, he considered it necessary first of all to put the railway coach on the rails in order to give it the basis which it had in his thoughts. A coach without rails is, after all, no coach. Next he divided the coach into three compartments in order to create the emotional center for his representation. Thus his attention was concentrated more and more on the true focus of his experience. The part that will ultimately take up his whole attention is treated in more and more detail.

While the other "compartments" do not interest him, he draws in the left of the picture one seat and luggage rack, then the steps. The inside, of course, is now emotionally of greatest significance. The outside, therefore, is neglected and an X-ray picture is drawn.

If the drawing had been broken off at this stage and we were to consider it as completed, our eyes would already be immediately guided to the focus of the event. Now the child draws himself. He has taken his place, in the preparation of which he has spent enough time. So now we see him sitting there, holding out his hand in greeting. He has put his luggage in order and has drawn it lying in the luggage rack. His father stands next to him in the compartment; therefore his base line has to be drawn. He and his father face each other. This we see from the profiles which are turned toward each other and note that the nose has been accentuated in its importance. "Father already wants to go," the child says, and in order to indicate this, he draws one foot (which he has made shorter than the other) higher. Next the father is outside and waves his hand. The child draws this quite clearly by overemphasizing the waving hand in comparison with the other hand, which has no function in the picture. Then his father remains on the platform. Consequently, the child has to have that important symbol—a base line.

Having now completed the expression of his main experience, the child notices the "empty compartments" and quite automatically lengthens the "luggage rack" and puts in two windows. From this final touch the experience dies down, and we can ourselves feel vividly the emotions he has gone through and which he has portrayed in this picture.

We must ask ourselves whether the feet of the figure representing the father have been neglected "on purpose" while he was supposed to be moving about inside the compartment, whereas while he is standing outside the feet have been carefully drawn in. The child gives us an explanation,

"My father puts everything in order in the compartment and then he waits down below until the train goes off." In saying this he indicates that he has represented *all* the most important *phases* of his experience within *one space*. We see again how, in one drawing, *space and time* fuse, the *inside* appears when it is of emotional *significance*, the base line serves as base *or* as rail, and *deviations* from the schema show the real experiences of the child. We further have seen how the tendencies expressed in the drawings of children follow laws of their own that have nothing to do with "naturalistic" tendencies.

THE MEANING OF COLOR

From a mere emotional relationship to color, as expressed during the pre-schematic stage, the child gradually discovers that there is *a relationship between color and object*. In all spheres of the child's development we see the awakening process of such a consciousness. In the drawing of the human figure the child has arrived at a *definite concept* that has crystallized in the schema. In experiencing space, the child has for the first time experienced that he himself is part of the environment. Also in color the child discovers such a definite relationship. It is no longer his subjective experience, or emotional binding, that determines color. It is a newly won objective relationship to man and environment that makes the child realize that there is a *relationship between color and object*. (See Plate 4.)

We could just as well call this stage in the child's development *the stage of objective color*. In the very same way as we have seen that the ability to repeat a newly won discovery creates confidence and self-assurance in scribbling, in the development of a schema or in life in general, we also see here that repetitions of same colors for same objects have their great significance. These repetitions do not have the meaning of stiffness or rigidity. On the contrary, they have the meaning of the discovery of a new experience and the enjoyment of *mastery*.

This enjoyment of mastery is one of the most important driving powers in education. It is not "happy accidents" that encourage the child in his work. They can have the very opposite effect when the child discovers the uniqueness of an accident, and his inability to repeat the "achievement," in the very same way as we do not consider accidental happenings in our life as real achievements. The child, having unconsciously the same feeling, gets very much enjoyment out of the mastery of a situation. If this feeling of mastery does not become satisfied, it has missed becoming an important psychological factor in development. The child unconsciously has the correct feeling for mastery, and through repetitions throughout his development satisfies this urge to achieve it.

Once we have understood this important and true meaning of repetition within the psychological development of the child, we will no longer briskly refuse the child's "eternal" questions with answers like "don't ask that again and again." *This self-assurance of an achievement* (here the achievement of an established relationship between color and object) *makes the child repeat the same color for the same object again and again.* This established relationship through repetitions we may call the *color schema* of the child. Thus, in the very same way as the child has come to a definite concept of form (the schema for form) through repetitions, the child also arrives at a definite concept of color (the color schema) through repetitions. Again we would like to emphasize that we are not dealing with single aspects in the development of the child, that we would rather like to see the child as a whole. Only with this in our mind are we continuing the analysis of the *meaning* of the color schema.

The origin of the color schema might be found in a *visual* or *emotional* concept of color. Important for us to know is that whatever experience was of significance at the time when the child *first* discovered the relationship between color and object will determine the color schema. If the child's relationship to "ground" was first established on a muddy ground of the backyard of a shack, the color schema for ground will then be indicative for the child's basic experience with "ground." *Through repetitions this basic experience becomes established* as an experience of general validity. Thus, all "ground" will be brown, regardless of whether there is grass on it or not.

This established color schema will not change unless a definite emotional experience induces a deviation in the color. Therefore, in the same way as we have discussed deviations in the analysis of space and form concepts, the deviations from the schematic representation give us insight into the emotional experiences of the child. It might, however, also be a visual concept which determines the color schema—that is, "the foliage is green." It was green at the time when the child first saw it, when it established the relationship between foliage and color. Now Fall has come and, assuming that the child is still in the schematic stage of development, he will continue to use his established color "green," disregarding the visual experience of the turning colors of the foliage or even the bare trees. Again, however, if the child has had an experience of emotional significance with the turned colors—maybe by making a wreath out of fall leaves and searching for particularly beautiful colors—he would then deviate from a schema of green to a visual concept of fall colors.

From this discussion, it is evident that the color schemata, in the same way as the space and form schemata, of children are *not rigid* expressions. Each child has his own *highly individualized* color relationships based upon very fundamental first experiences. Even within the established color schema we see that deviations are quite frequent whenever special experiences of *emotional significance* are dominant.

THE MEANING OF DESIGN—A NATURAL URGE FOR REPETITION

A *conscious* approach in using "fundamentals of design" during this age period, would not only be an artificial adult approach, but could, in the child, under certain circumstances, destroy the spontaneous act of creation. I have not yet seen a child of this age level spontaneously decorating an object with the purpose of beautifying it. All such attempts were forced upon the child, or "stimulated" by adults. It is true that the child is an "innate designer" [8] in the eyes of the adults, only the child does not know it. Or, as D'Amico says, one "factor responsible for weakening the child's native sense of design is the nature of teaching design, the imposing of fixed formulas on the child, now in general practice."

What is this innate sense of design? From our discussion we have realized that the child by no means deals with any formal aspects with regard to art. His main inclination is the use of art as a means of self-expression. That is why we expect that no teacher will ever use formal criticisms on products of children of these early ages. Such criticism would be the very death of any free creative teaching. In the very same way as formal aspects on proportions would be detrimental to the free development of the child, because they would interfere with the innate urge for expression, formal elements like "balance" and "rhythm," if used as a "stimulant," miss the purpose. This would serve as satisfaction only for the adult, who likes to see "beautiful drawings," but would be most harmful to the free development of a child.

How does the innate sense for design manifest itself? One of the most important attributes of design is rhythm; one of the simplest characteristics of rhythm is repetition. The innate sense for design thus seemingly has its roots in the very same psychological urge for mastery and self-assurance

[8] D'Amico, Victor, *Creative Teaching in Art*. Scranton, Pa.: International Textbook Co., Revised Edition, 1953.

that manifests itself in repetitions. We shall, therefore, notice that this innate sense for design receives additional meaning during this period, since the urge for repetition in drawing starts during the schematic stage.

During this age level, however, teachers will have merely to direct the natural urge for repetition into the proper channels in order to stimulate within the child the natural values of design. Fig. 14, "Fruit Harvest," is an excellent example of such a natural tendency for design, grown out of the urge for repetition. The "trees" are by no means intended to be designs: they are the child's form concept, the schema for trees which, through repetition, has become established. The new experience that has forced the child to deviate his schema was the apples. The apples, therefore, are irregular. This irregularity, however, prevents these trees from becoming monotonous. A real effect of a design has been achieved, without the desire or consciousness of a design approach.[9]

Another concept, contributing greatly to the unconscious achievement of design, is the way children during this mental level deal with space. The quite common division of the drawing space into sections, determined by base lines, also contributes greatly to an achievement of a design. All this is natural to the child as a part of his development. It is his innate *space concept* and his innate desire for repeating *form concept* (schema) that make the child an "innate designer." Surely one can be an innate, an intuitive artist, even without knowing it. The child is such an innate designer, but the difference lies in the fact that the artist may gain through a more conscious approach and the child can only be disturbed through it, because this consciousness is something strange to him, something which lies beyond his comprehension. One must not teach a child who is still in the babbling stage how to pronounce words correctly, the result would only be frustration. It is the same with design.

MODELING IN CLAY

Modeling is not merely another technique. Since it is three-dimensional in quality, it stimulates another kind of thinking. Modeling gains in significance especially during this period since it has a very definite function. A technique is used wisely only if it fulfills an original purpose. As long as the same thing can be done in a different technique, adequately, this special technique is not the best one. Thus, nothing should be done in clay that

[9] For excellent examples, see Cole, Natalie Robinson, *The Arts in the Classroom*. New York: John Day Co., 1940, or Tomlinson, R. R., *Picture-Making by Children*. London: The Studio, 1934.

Fig. 24a. Clay modeling. Schematic Stage. (Courtesy Educational Project, Museum of Modern Art, N.Y.)

can be painted, and nothing should be painted that can better be done in clay; or nothing should be done in clay that can be better done in wood. Thus, it would be disadvantageous and useless to model in clay a carriage with wheels that cannot be turned: it is a "dead carriage." If, however, the carriage would not be modeled as "carriage" but would merely serve to characterize a man pushing it, it is not the function of the carriage to roll, but to characterize the man.

The real nature of clay is its plasticity. Because of its plasticity it can be used most advantageously during this level, in which the child has found his concepts on all lines and in which the child should use clay most flexibly. Where lies the definite function of modeling? It lies in the fact that through the plasticity of clay the child has an easier means of deviating from his concept than in any other medium. In building up the figure, the child actually has the opportunity for accompanying it kinetically in some imaginary experiences. I have seen a child who was modeling a picnic scene actually imitating the effect of visitors "coming" and "sitting down" by moving the figures and bending them in the sitting position until the final modeling expression was achieved. Or, I have seen children actually moving up the arm to the position of "eating" when this was the desired representation.

Whereas, the drawing concept demands a simultaneous concept of "one event" (with the exceptions of space-time representations), the process of modeling permits a constant change. Figures can be added or taken away or changed in their position and shape. This is due only to the original meaning of the special material—clay. It is, therefore, important to use this great benefit in our stimulations, which should mainly be confined to "actions." Of course, these actions should be related to the child's experiences. Environment should be avoided because it has the same three-dimensional quality as the material. Distance in external reality would compete with "distance" in clay, the result of which would be small-scale models. Such works can be made, but only when they are meant to be *models* and not self-expression. In the realm of creative production, environment will be included only when it has emotional significance to the child. Thus only the immediate environment will be of significance.

Two different modes of expression can be observed, each of which exists in its own realm—the one of *"pulling out from the whole"* and the other of *"putting single representative symbols together into a whole"* (see Figs. 24b and 24c). Since both methods reveal different kinds of thinking, it would be disturbing and of greatest disadvantage to a child to be diverted from his own method of thinking. Pulling the clay out from the whole means to have from the beginning a vague form concept of the "whole" from which details will be developed through a continuous analytical process.

This method of pulling out the single details from the whole through analysis is called the *analytic method.* Since this type of thinking is psychologically the same as that applied when observing (seeing) things, we can assume that the thinking underlying this method is visual.[10] At this stage, however, thinking is not applied on a conscious level. That is why the creative product still deals with representative symbols, form symbols which lose their significance when detached from the whole.

The other method of expression described as "putting single representative symbols together into a whole" means that the child is *building up a synthesis* out of partial impressions. Because of the fact that the child arrives at a synthesis by putting single details together, we call this method the *synthetic method.* Since this type of thinking does not refer to observation (in observing we do not build up an image by adding single details),

[10] See p. 264.

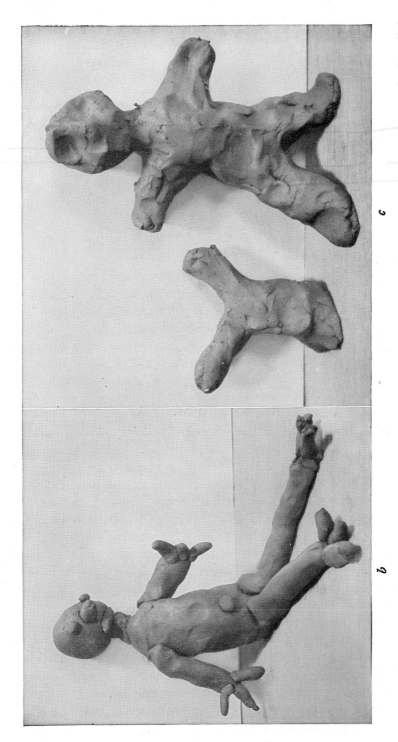

Fig. 24b. Synthetic method of modeling. The single pieces are put together (ten-year-old child).

Fig. 24c. Analytic process of modeling. All single parts are clearly pulled out from the whole form (seven-year-old child).

163

we leave it at this point with the statement that this type of thinking derives from nonvisual experiences. These nonvisual experiences can be of many different origins. They can refer to body experiences as well as to the mere activation of passive knowledge. From this discussion it becomes evident that "pulling out" or "putting together" is not a mere superficial technique but, as we shall later see more definitely, is deeply rooted in the child's thinking. Therefore any diversion from one method to another would only block the child's thinking.

ART STIMULATION

The kind of stimulation the teacher should apply during the different age levels grows out of the need of the child during each particular stage of development. We have seen that, during the schematic stage, the child has formed a definite concept of man, space, color, and objects on all lines of art expression and in his psychological development as a whole. This definite concept, through repetition, has become the schema.

The task of the teacher is to give the child an opportunity to *use* his concepts, not as rigid form symbols, but as living experiences. Thus, our stimulation must create an atmosphere in which the *child's consciousness of being a part of environment* is stimulated in the same way as *the function of the human figure*. The inclusion of actions in an orderly space concept will, therefore, be of the greatest significance. Our stimulation could be characterized by the words *"we"* (stimulating the consciousness of I and somebody else), *"action"* (meaning what we are doing), *and "where"* (referring to the actual description of the place, restricted to the characteristics only and not to depth or distance).

Knowing that it lies in the child's thinking to fuse time and space, it will be educationally and psychologically of advantage to use *time and space stimuli*. The stimulation for these time and space representations should be concerned with subjective experiences as hikes, trips, or personal experiences that include different time sequences. Later, there should be added stimulations that refer to objective reports, as the growth from the raw material to the finished product.

In the same chapter with a discussion of stimulation belong the many topics that refer to the representation *of X-ray pictures*. In such stimulations, inside and outside are of the same significance and should be stressed in the same way. Of greatest importance, however, is the need for creating an atmosphere that is strong and tense, and open and flexible to any suggestions from the child. Rigidity is the death of any creative method.

Topics

The following topics are presented only as a means of showing directions our thinking should take when stimulating children at this level. By no means are the topics to replace a close stimulation. The stimulation cannot be detailed enough. The more emotionally interested the child becomes in an experience, the better will the experience be for his work and his further development. The topics which follow are divided into groups under different headings which point out the type of stimulation to which the topic refers.

Action (to make form concept-functional)
Racing with My Friend on the Grounds ("we" (I and my friend) "action" (are racing) "where" (on the grounds)).
Jumping over a Rope Which is Held by Bob and John.
Pulling Myself High on the Rings in the yard.
Playing Ball with Bob.
Going to Church with Dad and Mother.
We Are Climbing a Mountain.
Carrying Something Home for Mother.
Planting a Tree, Anne Holding It.
We Are Sitting on a Sled Down the Hill.
Pulling the Sled Up a Hill.
We Are Skating on the Pond.
Recess on the School Grounds.
Climbing a Tree.
We Are Searching for Easter Eggs in the Back Yard.
Pulling Each Other.
Baseball.
Shaking Hands with Anne.
Saying Good-Bye to Mother.
Going to School.
Profile, Front view
Sitting on the Swing Holding the Rope (front view).
Going Between Mother and Dad (front view).
Holding the Umbrella in One Hand and the Bag in the Other (front view).
Playing Checkers (profile).
Eating Breakfast, Sitting Opposite Each Other (profile).

A Row of Soldiers Marching (profile).

Greeting by Shaking Hands (profile).

Space-Time representations

When I Leave My Home and Go to School.

From the Tree to the Board: Lumberyard.

From the Wheat to the Bread.

What the Early Settlers Did When They Landed.

When We Went to Visit the Market.

When We Went to Visit the Theater.

When We Went to Visit the Fruit Stands.

When We Went to Visit the Fair.

X-ray pictures

A Coal Mine (When We Were in One).

A Hospital (When We Were in One).

Going Upstairs.

In a Hotel.

In a Cave.

When We Visited the Different Floors of a Factory.

Stimulations characterized by "we," "action," and "where."

Techniques

Three things are very important with regard to developing techniques.

(1) The teacher should know *that the child must develop his own technique* and that every "help" from the teacher in showing the child a "correct" technique would only mean restricting the child's individual approach. The teacher's job is to introduce the appropriate material at a time when the child is most ready to use it.

(2) Every material or technique must make its *own* contribution. If a task can be done in a different technique with a better effect, the wrong technique has been applied.

(3) The teacher should develop economy in the use of techniques. In most books on art education we find that most materials are introduced and used from the very beginning of childhood. *At a time when the child is overwhelmed by his own creativity, when he is full of intuitive power, too many different media would not only be wasteful, but would often prove distracting as well.* As has been said during the discussion of the scribbling stages, the material must fit the needs of the child and must provide the best means for the child's expression. During scribbling we have seen that the crayon serves best to express the motor activity of the child.

The child at the age level from seven to nine years is neither concerned with plane nor with the representation of depth. What is most characteristic of this mental level is that the child has found a form, space, and color concept, which through repetitions develops into his schema. In the section on design, we have seen that these repetitions attain special significance in the development of design. It is therefore of the greatest importance that the child repeat the same colors for the same objects whenever he wishes to do so. A technique which does not afford the child the opportunity of experiencing mastery or self-assurance would not be a good technique for this developmental stage.

The consistency and texture of poster paint or tempera serve this purpose best, but crayon or colored chalk can also be used successfully. There is no reason whatsoever for introducing water color at this stage as many educators suggest. Water color is transparent, runs, and changes.

The transparency of water color serves best to paint atmosphere and landscape, but not design. Its running quality introduces many "happy accidents" which do not lend themselves to repetition—happy, however, only for those who can make active use of them as a visual stimulus. Since the child in his painting is more concerned with expressing his own ideas than with visual stimuli, these "happy accidents" would turn into "sad disappointments" because the child would not gain through this experience the feeling of mastery. Since we considered this feeling of mastery of prime importance for the psychological development of the child, we must not sacrifice these important gains to some happy incidents, regardless of their beauty. An accident cannot be repeated. At an age when this desire for repetition is most definite, the inability to repeat would be disappointing rather than inspiring. We shall see that at other age levels, when the urge for repetition is not important, water color will serve to inspire the child.

This discussion has shown again that technique is closely connected with the child's development and should not be introduced merely for the purpose of changing the material.

Also during this age period large sheets of paper give more freedom than smaller sheets. Since the child arrives at a more detailed concept, *hair brushes* with long handles are preferable to bristle brushes. As has been said before, *clay* is an excellent means for plastic expression. In this medium also educators, who know that the process of creating is of greater significance than the final product, influence the creative concept of the child adversely by discouraging modeling merely for the practical reason that a modeling produced by the "synthetic method" of putting details together cannot be fired in the kiln. Surely it cannot easily be fired because

EVALUATION CHART
Schematic Stage

	None	Some	Much
Intellectual Growth Has the child developed concepts for things familiar to him? Are his concepts clearly expressed? Has he a tendency to differentiate his schemata? (Hands with fingers, eyes with eyebrows, etc.) Does the child relate colors to objects?			
Emotional Growth Does the child use his schemata flexibly? Does the child vary the sizes according to the significance of the represented objects? Does the drawing show deviations from the schema by exaggerating, omitting, or even changing meaningful parts? Does the child use his lines or brush strokes in a determined fashion? Is there a lack of continuous "folding over"? Is there a lack of continued over-exaggeration?			
Social Growth Does he identify himself with his own experience? Has the child established spatial correlations? Does the child use base lines? Does the child characterize his environment? Does the child show awareness of his social environment in identifying himself with others?			

Perceptual Growth	Does the child mostly draw with continued uninterrupted lines, expressing kinesthetic sensations? Is the child aware of differences in texture? Does the child depart from the use of mere geometric lines? Does the child show visual awareness by drawing distant objects smaller? Does the child differentiate his color-object relationships? (Does he use different greens for different plants and trees?) Does the child model analytically?			
Physical Growth	Does the child show body actions in his drawings? Does the child show the absence of continuous exaggerations of the same body parts? Does the child show other signs which indicate his sensitivity toward the use of his body? (Joints, special details.) Does the child guide his brush strokes so that he remains within the predetermined area?			
Aesthetic Growth	Does the child unconsciously utilize his drive for repetition for design purposes? Does the child distribute his work over the whole sheet? Does the child think in terms of the whole drawing when he draws—not in terms of single details only? Does the child use decorative patterns?			
Creative Growth	Does the child create his own representative symbols (concepts)? Does the child vary his schemata? Does the child frequently change his symbols for eyes, nose, mouth, etc.? Does the child invent his own topics?			

169

SUMMARY   SCHEMATIC STAGE—SEVEN TO NINE YEARS

Characteristics	Human Figure	Space	Color	Design	Stimulation Topics	Technique
Discovery of a definite concept of man and environment.	Definite concept of figure depending on active knowledge and personality through repetition: "schema."	First definite space concept: "base line."				Colored crayons.
Self-assurance through repetition of form symbols: "schema."	Deviations expressing experiences can be seen in: (1) Exaggeration of important parts. (2) Neglect or omission of unimportant parts. (3) Change of symbols.	Discovery of being a part of environment: assumption for cooperation and correlation.			Best stimulation concentrates on action, characterized by "we" (I, John, tree), "action," "where" (characterization of terrain).	Colored chalks.
In pure schema no intentional experience is expressed, only the thing itself: "the man," "the tree," and so forth.		Base line expresses: (1) Base (2) Terrain	Discovery of relationship between color and object, through repetition: "color schema."	No conscious approach.		Powder paint (tempera, poster paint).
Experiences are expressed by deviations from schema.		Deviations from base line express experiences: subjective space: (1) Folding over (egocentric). (2) Mix forms of plan and elevation. (3) X-ray pictures. (4) Space-time representations.	Same color for same object.	Design forms received through repetitions, subconsciously.	Topics referring to: (1) Time sequences (journeys, traveling stories). (2) X-ray pictures (inside and outside is emphasized), factory, coal mine, and so forth.	Large paper. Hair brushes.
Use of geometric lines.			Deviation of color schema shows emotional experience.			Clay: (1) Synthetic. (2) Analytic.

of its slight cohesive qualities and the air bubbles in it, but it is absolutely an adult concept that products of modeling made by little children should be fired. If this concept would not have been developed by the adult teacher, the child would not care for it. During my 15 years of experience in teaching modeling to the blind, who, as a result of their handicap, model in a synthetic way, I have had no request for firing from blind individuals, who worked most enthusiastically and creatively.[11] From our discussion in the section on modeling, it became evident that the two modes of techniques express a different kind of thinking. *Changing the technique from synthetic to analytic would therefore mean restricting the child in freedom of expression.*

The preceding evaluation chart provides a basis for the understanding of the child's growth during the stage in which he usually formulates his concepts—the schematic stage. If this chart is correlated with the more general chart on pages 168–169 a deeper understanding can be obtained.

INTERPRETATION OF INDIVIDUAL GROWTH CHARACTERISTICS PERTAINING TO THE SCHEMATIC STAGE

Intellectual growth

One of the indications for the child's growing intellect is his understanding of the world which surrounds him. This world may be meaningful or meaningless to the child depending on his emotional relationship to it and his intellectual comprehension of it. Whether or not the world has become meaningful to the child then partly depends on whether he has at all tried to formulate his concepts. The first question, therefore, refers to this formulation of the child's concepts. If the child expresses in his drawings definite concepts (schemata) these can be seen in the repeated, yet flexible, use of them. The difference between the repeated use of a schema and the use of stereotyped repetitions is that a schema is flexible and undergoes any deviations and changes, while stereotyped repetitions always remain the same. Because of this apparently close relationship we have to be very careful in our judgment. We shall, therefore, always look first at the flexibility of the schema before we decide that it is the child's concept. For example, in Fig. 17 the child uses the same lines for representing himself and his brother while playing checkers. Yet, the sizes as well as the motion of the figures differ. We can, therefore, definitely say that the child

[11] See tables 35, 78a, b in *The Nature of Creative Activity.*

drew his concepts of "man" when he expressed "Playing Checkers." The second question deals with the *clarity* of his concepts. We consider concepts as clearly expressed if they as a whole *and* in their details clearly express their functional characteristics. If, for instance, "legs" and "arms" are drawn alike, with the same representative symbols, no clear concept has been expressed. The functional characteristics of the arms are different from those of the legs, yet they are drawn equally. In Fig. 17 the child did not have an altogether clear expression of concepts. We can find that the "nose" as well as the "eyes" are expressed with the same representative symbol—a dot. Yet they have different functional characteristics. Our check mark in the evaluation chart would have to be placed under "some."

Intelligent children never are satisfied with generalizations. The inquiring spirit often cannot go enough into details. The "active knowledge" as expressed in the child's concepts reveals the child's understanding of and interest in the world about him. The third question in the evaluation chart refers to this inquiring spirit. The degree to which a child has a tendency to differentiate his schemata, that is, the extent that he is not satisfied with generalizations and wants to find more detailed characteristics, is a clear expression of his inquiring spirit. In Fig. 17 very little indication—almost none—is given of greater differentiations in the child's concepts. Neither are the eyes characterized by differentiating the eyebrows, lids, or any other details, nor is the nose or the mouth indicated by more than a mere generalization. The only concept which shows some detailed characterization is the concept for hand. It consists of the "palm" and five "fingers." Our check mark in the evaluation chart would be in the column of "some" rather than that of "none," since some characterization has been achieved. However, we keep in mind that the some is not quite justifiable.

The "bodies" are painted yellow and are outlined with blue color. All the features are painted in the same blue color. The chairs and table are painted in brown color which may indicate some relationship to the color of wood. Apparently "some" relationship between color and object has been noticed, however slight it may be. Several drawings of the same child would allow us a much better judgment in this question.

Emotional growth

Rigid schemata do not lend themselves to the ever changing expression of the self. The flexible use of the schema is, therefore, the most important requisite for true self-expression. Because it lies in the nature of the schema, that it is the concept of the child which he uses over and over again whenever he needs it, the danger of becoming stereotyped is never as much a part of the natural form of expression as it is during the schematic stage. Flexibility is, therefore, the most important attribute of emotional growth to which special attention should be given during this period. The satisfaction, growing out of the discovery of a concept, expressed in its repetition, too easily leads the child into a stereotyped form of expression. The schema will always remain a flexible means of expression of the child's unless some interferences occur which prevent the child from using it flexibly. The difference between stereotyped repetition and schemata has been explained previously.[12] In Fig. 17 the child does not use stereotyped repetitions. In stereotyped repetitions no functional relationships are expressed, while in this drawing "playing checkers" is clearly indicated by the relationship of the children to the checkerboard. Several changes in this schema of "man" can also be noticed. The most important change is the free use of the arm while playing checkers. Otherwise not too many changes are apparent. When playing checkers, both of the represented children would without any doubt face each other, sitting in opposite directions. The child, however, had established a "front view schema" and could not adjust to the new situation by using his schema flexibly and adapting it to profile representations. The check mark for the first question under "emotional growth" in the evaluation chart should, therefore, go under the column "some" (flexibility).

Another form of flexibility and emotional response can be seen in the variation in the sizes of the represented objects. With such variations the child may indicate the significance which various objects have to him. There is not much indication of such value relationships of objects in Fig. 17. The checkboard may be slightly exaggerated. But there are checker boards which cover half of a table. The window may be neglected in size. Otherwise the size relationships of objects do not indicate any particular emotional response. In the evaluation chart we would place our check mark under "none." The next question deals with the emotional response toward the self (the human figure). Are there any value relationships, exaggerations, neglect, or omissions which would indicate the child's emotional response to a particular part? No doubt, the arms and hands are exaggerated. So are also the ears, which may indicate some attentive listening. We would place our check mark in the column under "much" (exaggeration of meaningful parts). The child definitely uses his brush strokes in a determined way, thus indicating that he had confidence in his expression.

[21] See p. 125.

The next question deals with the process of "folding over." As has been said before, a child who continuously uses this process regards himself habitually as the center. Therefore, a continuous use of "folding over" means too much self-centeredness. In Fig. 17 there is "some" folding over. The checkerboard is drawn in top view, while the rest of the drawing is represented in side view. To determine whether there is a continuous use of "folding over" would only be possible by more drawings by the same child.

The last question under emotional growth deals with "too much exaggeration," often also called pathological exaggeration because no longer do they represent normal responses. If a child becomes bound up with one part of the drawing by losing *all* ties with the rest of it, the response of the child is no longer emotionally normal. He then continues to draw the one part of the figure to such an extent that the main part only appears as an appendix. Children who frequently draw such pathological exaggerations are usually emotionally maladjusted.[13] There is no such sign of pathological exaggerations in Fig. 17. There is a complete lack of them. Our check mark would have to be placed under "much" ("lack of continuous and too much exaggeration").

Social growth

The self-identification of a child with his own experiences in his creative work is one of the prerequisites for the establishment of a desire for contacts outside of him. In Fig. 17 the child clearly identifies himself with his experience when playing checkers. He even "wants to show us" how he plays checkers, by folding over his checker board. The child went beyond the immediate ego by properly contacting his environment. The child established very good spatial correlations in his drawing. The table is on the floor; the chairs are by the table; the children "sit" on the chairs; the checkerboard is on the table; the window is on the wall and the "light" (circle above) is above the table. All these are sufficient spatial correlations for placing our check mark for this question under "much."

As has been previously discussed the symbol which first expresses a feeling of "mass consciousness" [14] is the base line. In Fig. 17 this feeling of mass consciousness, a very important requisite for active cooperation, is clearly expressed: "I am sitting on the chair which is on the floor; my friend is on the chair which is on the same floor; the table with the checker-

---

[13] See p. 489.
[14] See p. 139.

board is on the floor; *we all* are connected with the floor." Thus, he introduced a base line indicating this feeling of belongingness, an important characteristic of social growth.

A higher level of social growth expresses itself in the awareness of one's environment. This awareness usually is seen by the degree in which the child characterizes his environment. By this we mean the inclusion in the drawing of environmental factors which have *no immediate relationship* to the expressed experience. In Fig. 17 the child drew only the objects which are of immediate significance for his experience of "playing checkers." The only characterization of his environment, outside of his experience, is the "window." But even that might have been his source of light for playing. The child gave us *no* indication in what room he lives by adding some more characterizations. Since the child did not even characterize his own home environment, it is not expected that he would be aware of his social environment in which he would identify himself with the social group in which he lives. However, for a more accurate answer we would have to see several drawings by this child.[15] The check mark for this as well as the former question would have to be put in the column "none." That means that the child is not conscious of his social environment.

Perceptual growth

Kinesthetic sensations are expressed in the continuous flowing quality of lines. The most common perceptual experience during this period of childhood is the kinesthetic. The first question, therefore, deals with it. In Fig. 17 the child uses free flowing lines indicating his satisfaction from this type of perceptual experience. No indication, however, is given of the child's feeling for the differences in texture. The checker board apparently shows a conceptual experience (the dots indicate the different fields) and not a textural one.

The next question deals with the important issue of mere symbolic representation by means of geometric lines or of departing from them to more visual presentations. In Fig. 17 we see no departure from the use of geometric lines. All lines lose their identity when separated from the whole. From this we can draw the conclusion that no apparent visual perception influences the child's creative concepts. Whether the child intended to draw the window smaller as a result of greater distance could only be answered by looking at more drawings. From the way he uses his

---

[15] Compare with Fig. 22 in which the child of a coal miner clearly showed his higher level of social awareness by characterizing *his* social environment.

base line as well as from his adherence to geometric lines we would conclude that visual distance has not yet occurred to the child.

This child has not even established color-object relationships throughout his drawing. While the chairs, table, and floor are painted brown, the rest of the painting is not brought into any relationship to the objects. It is needless to say that no close differentiation of color-object relations has been established.

Children who model analytically are usually visually inclined. The child has in his mind the whole visual picture; he starts, therefore, with the whole and later differentiates the details. Even from Fig. 17 we could predict that the child's approach in his modeling would be synthetical, since also in his drawings he never uses common outlines but "pieces" his drawing together out of single details.

Physical growth

A child who is physically alert and not otherwise restricted will express this feeling in giving his figures movement and action. Especially during the schematic stage, where the child easily remains satisfied with having found his concept, such action may not always be immediately visible. Most of the schemata consist of geometric lines and, therefore, contain no joints. The drawing of actions or movements often consists of mere exaggeration of the representative symbols for legs or arms. In Fig. 17 action is depicted by such an emphasis on the arms and hands. However, "sitting" is only represented by bringing the "body" in contact with the "chair." Since only a rather limited amount of "action" or "movement" is expressed in Fig. 17 we would put our check mark in the column "some."

As has been said previously, continuous exaggeration of the same body parts may indicate some defect. The reader may be interested in the fact that the child who drew Fig. 17 was hard of hearing. He continuously exaggerated, or at least emphasized, the ears as seen in Fig. 17.

No other signs of body actions are indicated in this drawing except the mentioned contact of the "body" with the "chair" to indicate "sitting."

The last question deals with an important discipline: whether the child can guide his brush strokes so that he remains within the predetermined area. Very often we hear from teachers who defend the use of coloring books because such books teach the child to remain within certain predetermined outlines, a discipline which these teachers find highly significant. How often do we see children purposely scribbling outside the outlines because *they* do not see any need to remain with them? A child who creates his own outlines will feel the urge to stay within them. In Fig. 17 we see that the child has perfect control in remaining within his own outlines. His body control seems to be perfect. Yet, as has been previously stressed, great care is necessary in making statements about the child's physical growth.

Aesthetic growth

As has been said before, one way of emphasizing harmonious organization in pictorial representations consists of utilizing the elements of design. One of these elements is rhythm. Rhythm to a great extent consists of repetition, a natural type of expression during the schematic stage. Some children, especially those whose aesthetic growth is more developed, utilize this repetition for design, or better, decorative purposes. This can most clearly be seen in Fig. 14 where the repetition of tree schemata in the representation of an orchard becomes highly decorative. In Fig. 17 no such repetition is utilized for decorative purposes. However, since the subject matter, "checker players," would not promote any repetition, other drawings would be necessary to determine properly the significance of the omission. The next question under aesthetic growth deals with the distribution of the subject matter. In a well-distributed and organized pictorial presentation no changes in the distribution should be possible. In Fig. 17 the child showed extreme sensitivity in the organization of his presentation. None of the parts could actually be changed without doing harm to his presentation. The child unconsciously even balanced the taller figure to the right by placing a window on top of the smaller figure to the left. Organization seems to be one of the outstanding qualities of this child.

In answering the next question, it appears that the child who drew Fig. 17 thinks in terms of the whole drawing when he draws rather than in terms of details. If the child had not done so, he would not have placed the table and chairs as carefully related to the whole space as they appear in the final product. In general, this question can be answered from the way the child distributes main objects on his drawings. If he casually starts somewhere and either does not have enough space to place everything he wants to draw, or discovers that he has nothing to add and too much blank space, the child does not think primarily of the "whole," but of "parts." The child obviously does not use decorative patterns or designs. His use of pure geometric lines would not incite the use of decorative tendencies.

Creative growth

As has been stressed before, flexibility of thinking and originality of approach are some of the criteria of a healthy creative growth. Let us, therefore, examine the first question in the evaluation chart which deals with the originality of the child's concepts. There is no doubt that the child who drew Fig. 17 used his own representative symbols. He is entirely original in creating his own concepts. Our check mark pertaining to this question would, therefore, be placed in the column "much." The second question deals with the child's flexibility. Whether or not he varies his schemata cannot easily be determined from one drawing. Several drawings would allow a more valid answer. The indications, however, are that he varies his schemata "somewhat" but not much. The two checker players are almost alike in the use of representative symbols. We mentioned, however, some noticeable changes which justify our placing of the check mark in the column "some." He apparently does not frequently change his symbols for mouth, eyes, nose, or other details, which indicates that experiences are usually not strong enough to excite enough flexibility for such changes. Apparently, the child's mind is satisfied with his own "vocabulary" of forms. He has little desire to discover new characteristics. However, this criterion can only be stated with certainty if we have at least three drawings by the child, done within not too short intervals.

The choice of the topic, to which the next question refers, is apparently the child's own. Whether the child usually waits for suggestions or whether he determines his own topics can only be said by observing and knowing the child. From Fig. 17 it appears that the child closely identifies himself with his topic, which usually is only done when the child also chooses it.

SUMMARY OF GROWTH ANALYSIS

The best integration of the child's characteristics of growth is seen in his creative work. From it (Fig. 17) we can see that its most outstanding feature is its unity, its appearance as an entity, in which nothing can be omitted or even changed. We can say, therefore, that apparently the child's most outstanding quality is his feeling for organization and order. He also expresses a quite distinct feeling and understanding for spatial correlation. By placing the chairs in proper relationship to the table and by including himself and his friend in the base line concept he indicates his feeling of "mass consciousness." This awakening of a social awareness together with the child's distinct feeling for organization and order seem to point toward a cooperative individual. The "folding over" of the checkerboard, however, points toward the fact that in this cooperative spirit he will not forget the self, because usually only self-centered individuals use continuously the process of "folding over." Since we have only one work of the child at our disposal, the statement in regard to his own self must be made with reservation.

From the profile obtained from the chart it is clearly visible that all other growth factors are behind the aforementioned ones. The lack of differentiated details seems indicative of a low active knowledge, and this in turn points toward a not too active mind. This clearly is supported by a somewhat rigid approach expressed in an adherence to the schema, as indicated by the drawings of front views of the checker players, while profile views would be indicative of the experience and the topic. The child's lack of perceptual experiences even when only used to establish color-object relationships also fits into the picture of a not too active mind.

Indeed, all the aforementioned characteristics give us a very accurate picture of the boy, known to the author at the time when he drew the drawing reproduced in Fig. 17. He was an orderly boy, always much concerned with his homework and, while always willing to help, was always concerned with his own self. His desire to cooperate stopped when personal sacrifices began. He was not bright and by no means alert. Emotionally he was rather inflexible, not very excitable. Only when he personally became involved in an experience did it affect him. Indicative of this would be the exaggerated hands of the checker players. The child was physically healthy, more of the robust type.

All this precisely coincides with the profile obtained through the evaluation chart.

EXERCISES

(1) Collect the drawings of one second- or third-grade classroom and find out how many different schemata are used for "eye," "mouth," "nose," "body," "legs," "arms," and so forth.
(2) Collect the drawings of one child and show
   (a) Repetitions of schemata.
   (b) Deviations from schemata.
(3) Explain the meaning of deviations from schematic representations by means of several drawings.
(4) What percentage of children in a second grade are using geometric lines for their expression? Find out the percentage in a third grade. Do you find any change?

(5) Observe the relationship of reading ability and base-line expressions in one classroom.

(6) What percentage in your class has arrived at base-line representations?

(7) Do you find a difference in terms of cooperation between those who have discovered the base line as a common space experience and those who have not?

(8) Collect drawings that refer to time-space experiences.

(9) Make a profile, according to the evaluation chart, also for Figs. 14, 15, 16, 19, and 20.

(10) Show in drawings the meaning of "folding over."

(11) Trace the relationship between "folding over" and egocentric attitude.

(12) Collect the drawings of one child and find out whether the child uses always the same color for the same object. If he does not, analyze the reason for it.

(13) Find out in the drawings of different children how the repetition of schemata affects "design."

(14) Show the meaning of schemata in clay modeling.

(15) How many children in your classroom model analytically (by pulling out from the whole) and how many synthetically (putting parts together)?

(16) Can you establish a relationship (in terms of observation versus mechanical skills) between those who model analytically or synthetically?

(17) Analyze a child's drawing in using the following scheme (check the correct part).

Drawing Characteristics	Personality Characteristics
Geometric lines	Subjective
Realistic lines	Visual, objective
Base line	Cooperative
No base line	Noncooperative
Rich schemata	Intelligent
Normal schemata	Average
Poor schemata	Dull
Folding over	Egocentric
Frequent exaggeration	Emotional
Too much exaggeration	Emotionally unstable
No emphasis on particular parts	Dull
Frequent use of bright colors	Joyous
Frequent use of dull colors	Sad
Space-time representation	Subjective
Stereotyped repetitions	Emotional maladjustment
X-ray pictures	Subjective
Good organization	Well integrated and balanced

LABORATORY WORK

(1) Establish consciously through simplification a schema for "tree" and one for "house." Cut it in linoleum, placing it on a base line. By repeating both schemeta and distributing them properly, design a textile.

(2) Collect pictures of designs that are based on the same principle of repetition.

(3) Collect materials of different structure of the following main groups: (a) Metals. (b) Fibers—plant, animal. (c) Plastics. (d) Stones.

CHAPTER VI

THE DAWNING REALISM

The Gang Age (9 to 11 years)

THE CONCEPT OF REALISM

Before we discuss the special meaning of realism within the child's development, we shall clarify the use of the term *realism*. By realism we do not understand the imitation of nature in a mere photographic way. Within art, and especially within our discussion, we shall use this term *whenever an attempt is made to represent reality as a visual concept*. As visual concept we understand the concept which is influenced by the changing effects in nature. These changing effects are caused by *motion, distance, light,* and *atmosphere*. The question might arise whether such a concept is desirable from the viewpoint of modern art education, which stresses the imaginative unrealistic tendencies. This would be a complete misunderstanding of the tendencies of modern progressive art education. Progressive art education stresses all tendencies that lie truly and sincerely in the development of the child. It would be a misconception to say there are no realistic tendencies in the child. We shall see that a visual concept of reality is deeply rooted in a large number of growing adolescent children. During these decisive years, the art educator must prevent the child from engaging in mere photographic imitations, for photographic imitations do not express the child's individual relationships. A work of art is not the representation of an object itself; rather is it the representation of *the experience which we have with the particular object.* A mere photographic imitation would deprive the child of the opportunity of identifying himself with his own experience.

THE GREATER AWARENESS OF THE SELF

The significance of this stage of development lies in the child's discovery of "social independence." The awareness that he can do more in a group than alone, that he also is more powerful in a group than alone, is the basis for group friendships or "gangs." Because of different interests of boys and girls in our society, they are most commonly of the same sex. Boys often despise girls and vice versa. It is the time when children want to sleep out of doors, when they prefer to be among their own group and lead their own lives. They often build their own hide-outs, invent their secret codes or language, and not infrequently lead "wars" against each other. During this developmental stage arises the first real awareness of the sexes. Girls are more eager to dress, and like parties; boys prefer camping; they belong to their gangs that have rules of their own, and not infrequently lead wars against girls. Such wars, as we are well aware, are only compensations for awakening feelings of affection, forerunners of adolescent feelings though far from having the same meaning.

These important feelings of an awakening social independence are often in contrast to the desires of parents or adults who do not want to give up the close supervision and guidance of their children. It is mostly for this reason that adults consider this stage of development as undesirable and often as interfering with their own lives. Instead of giving support to this awakening feeling for group cooperation and the discovery of social independence, they often counteract it by prolonging close dependency. Instead of showing their sympathetic and warm feelings and interest for the desires of their children for group life, they often oppose it, not knowing that with such actions they only drive their children into secrecy. It is only by such methods that cooperation with adults reaches an apparent low peak, and because of it, "the peak of the delinquent period is usually said to coincide with the peak of the gang age at ten or eleven years."[1] Indeed, if adults could more identify with the needs of children, particularly during this period, and if they would understand the importance of them for future cooperation and citizenship, we would have less delinquency instead of a steadily increasing figure.

For the child, however, this may be a most dramatic and healthy period of discoveries, clearly seen in the child's creative work.

[1] Bowley, Agatha H., *Guiding the Normal Child.* New York: Philosophical Library, 1943.

Geometric lines, as used during the schematic stage, do not lend themselves very well to characterize boys or girls. Therefore, geometric lines do not suffice for self-expression. Indeed, the child removes quite abruptly from this mode of expression to a form of expression that *relates more to nature*. We see a definite lack of cooperation in the great number of children who *do not establish spatial correlations* in their drawings. In experiments which I conducted[2] 43.4 per cent of the subjects did not establish spatial relationships during this age level. The following topic was given to 400 children: "You are under an apple tree. On one of its lower branches you see an apple that you particularly admire and that you would like to have. You stretch out your hand to pick the apple, but your reach is a little short. Then you make a great effort and get the apple after all. Now you have it and enjoy eating it. Draw yourself as you are taking the apple off the tree."

The results showed, that without being influenced in any way, the children were freely able to display the pattern of their experiences. "Beautiful" trees and apples were drawn just as often as "misproportioned" people. The subject had allowed the children to be absorbed in the visual experiences of the beautiful apple hanging on one of the lower branches of the tree, as much as in the feeling of the importance attained by the apple when it is particularly desired. The body experience of grasping the apple could be expressed just as much as the experience of stretching the body while it was being picked.

I considered separately the representation of the individual human being, the representation of the tree and the relation of the two to one another. This experiment has shown that at the age of nine, 69 per cent of the children still draw according to principles of evaluation and not according to visual observation. That is, 69 per cent of the children at this age level disregarded entirely the size of the tree in relationship to the size of the child. However, the tendency was very strong to draw characteristics of the tree as well as of the self. Boys made distinct boys, girls wore dresses. From the reproduced drawing it is seen that this increasing conceptional knowledge of the external world and its significance lowers the child's capacity for coordinating visual experiences with the self in the drawing. This is borne out by the figures, for in the 10th year, 43 per cent of the children were unable to establish a relationship between child and tree (Fig. 25). *This period, then, represents the time during which the confidence of the child in his own creative power is for the first time shaken by the fact that he is becoming conscious of the significance of his*

[2] *The Nature of Creative Activity.*

environment. Teachers and parents alike believe this period to be critical. One of the most important tasks of the teacher is to inspire the child's feeling for cooperation by stimulating a more conscious feeling of spatial correlations in his drawings. How this is done will be discussed in the chapter on stimulation.

In the representation of the human figure

As has been noted, the mere concept of the human figure as expressed during the schematic stage, does not lend itself to characterizations. A schema is in its nature a collective expression, like the concept for "man." In it there is no place for individual details concerned with the characterization of the object. It is a *generalization* of the expression "man." At a stage where the child is eager to express characteristics of sex, as boys with trousers and girls with dresses, the schematic generalization is inadequate for this type of expression. The concept as such and the modes of expression are both inadequate. Geometric lines, as used before, are unsuitable means to characterize suits or dresses. As part of this crisis the child has discovered his inadequacy, and as a result moves toward a more realistic representation. It is dawning upon him that his representations can be adjusted to nature. But the child is still far from achieving a visual concept. The girls, in their representations, do not yet "see" that their dresses have folds or wrinkles or that the hem is uneven when walking. The "hem line" is always even in drawings of this period.

This shows clearly that the drawing is not an outcome of the child's visual observation, but that the child is rather eager, merely to *characterize* the girls as girls or the boys as boys. It must not, however, be overlooked, that such a drawing is the first step toward a realistic concept. Through this concentration on the "how," the child gains feeling for details, but loses feeling for action. Indeed, we see a *greater "stiffness"* in the representations of the human figure in drawings of children of this age. However it is significant that henceforth *every part* has its meaning, and *retains this meaning even when separated from the whole.* This is an important means of evaluation for the teacher, since he can easily recognize whether the pupil has attained the stage of "dawning realism." As has been noted, a symbol can be determined by separating it from the whole; it then loses its meaning. *Realistic or pseudorealistic lines do not lose their meaning when separated.* The child has reached the stage where the line has lost its mere symbolic significance (Fig. 26).

Fig. 25. "Picking Apples from a Tree" (ten years old). Inability to establish correlation between figure and tree caused by egocentric attitude. Emphasis on apples. (Dawning Realism.)

Fig. 26. "Man with Umbrella" (ten-year-old boy). Awareness of clothes. Stiffness due to emphasis on visual experience.

In expression of emotions

Through the growing awareness of a visual concept the child no longer uses exaggerations, neglect, or omissions as frequently as a means of expression of emotions. One cannot change a "hand" into another "hand," as the child has changed symbols to express emotional binding. Other means are now used more frequently to express the focal point of the child's interest. Although at nine years, the larger number of children still use changing sizes as a definite means to express quality, their number decreases rapidly after the tenth year, as the mentioned experiment with the apple tree clearly indicates.[3] The child begins now to substitute means of expression by an accumulation of details on those parts which are emotionally significant. We shall talk about this important means of expression in the next chapter.

[3] *The Nature of Creative Activity.*

Fig. 27. "Cutting a Tree" (eleven-year-old girl). Painted after hurricane had felled tree near her house. Notice exaggeration of tree. Awakening of visual awareness. (Courtesy Education Project, Museum of Modern Art, N. Y.)

In the representation of space

The plane and the base-line concept

In the same way as the greater awareness of the self led the child to realize that the geometric line is an inadequate expression for his needs, we also see in the representation of space a change from the mere symbolic expression, as seen in the base-line concept, to a more realistic representation. As a result of this dawning realism the child discovers that *the space between base lines becomes meaningful; the plane is discovered.* Thenceforth the base line loses its significance as the vehicle of space representations. "Folding over" is criticized as "unnatural." Trees and houses no longer stand only on the edge of the line. Though this form of representation still is in frequent use, the child also lets the trees grow from the "ground." The sky is no longer merely "above" but goes all the way down. This does not mean that the child has become aware of the meaning of the horizon.

The child of this age has not developed a conscious visual percept of depth, but he has taken certainly the first step toward such a concept. With the sky all the way down the child soon realizes that a tree, growing from the ground, will partly cover the sky. Hence he becomes aware of overlapping, and another step toward a visual concept has been perceived. Stimulated by the teacher, the child will soon apply this experience of overlapping in the sky to other experiences of overlapping. The best stimulation of this visual experience can be introduced through using the technique of paper cutting because as the different layers of papers are applied, they will cover one another. This experience of overlapping is important not only because it is a part of the growing spatial concept that leads to the representation of three-dimensional space, but also for psychological reasons. That one object can cover another is an important experience, because it implies an awareness of the existence of the other object. This is especially significant during a period in which cooperation outside the "gang" is at its low peak. Personal experiences are important to the child because he reacts emotionally to such experiences (Fig. 28a and Fig. 28b).

Spatial correlation and an egocentric attitude

One of the most important attributes of this age level is the tendency of many children toward losing contact with groups at large. Children who are misunderstood by their parents feel frustrated and as such have the tendency to withdraw within themselves. In drawings, this withdrawal expresses itself in the inability to establish spatial correlations. The more the adult prohibits the child from following his own inclinations, the longer will this period of resistance or non-cooperation last. It is important to know that every punitive measure causes reactions that are frequently more serious than the first cause.

As has been stressed in the Introduction, art education serves a double purpose: as a means of self-expression and as a therapeutical means. The inability of the child to establish spatial correlations should for the teacher be an indication of the child's emotional state. In most cases this is due to improper handling of situations with regard to the child's growing awareness of ego and his discovery of social independence. Stimulation of the child's will to establish spatial correlations in creative work will, in most cases, be accompanied by an improvement of the child's social behavior. Thus, the child may develop a greater consciousness and desire for cooperation also within his own group. Especially can this be encouraged through participation in group work. Group work, therefore, will be of special significance during this period. The teacher has to know that group work is only effective when the child gets the feeling that *he could not have achieved singly what the group has accomplished,* and that his contribution is an important part of the whole. If the child can have the feeling that he alone could have accomplished a similar work, the group work would not have fulfilled its purpose. On the contrary, group work might even have frustrated the child.

A group of boys worked on a harbor using the technique of paper cutting. Every boy of a class of 42 worked on a special boat selected as an outcome of a classroom discussion. Since this was done in a coastal area, the boys were very "boat-minded." One cut out a sailboat, others a PT boat, a cruiser, a battleship, fishing boats, rowboats, motorboats, steamships, and one boy made a ferry. At the end, 42 or more boats were finished. A few boys cut out the docks. The whole project was pasted on blue cardboard, and the whole class helped in the final arrangement. It was a grand harbor! Every boy had his own boat that looked much better in the group than by itself. All had the feeling that they could not have accomplished such a gigantic task alone. It helped greatly to increase the feeling for cooperation. If the child feels his importance, if opportunities are given to him to work and play with his companions, if he finds emotional outlets to express what he has on his mind, if his "gang" is regarded as a social unity and therefore respected, he will soon grow out of this age into a period of reasoning and greatest usefulness.

COLOR—SUBJECTIVE STAGE

The more the child moves toward the establishment of a *visual* relationship between color and object, the more are teachers tempted to misuse his dawning sense for "realistic" colors by teaching the child "how to use and to apply color." There is no place in the elementary-school classroom for the teaching of color theories by means of color wheels and other "scientific" helps. Such teaching would only destroy the child's spontaneous approach and would make him insecure in his own intuitive color experiences. The only way the child can be made more color conscious is through the emphasis of the child's own reactions to color. The more emotional the character of these reactions is, the deeper will be the experience.

How then should we introduce a knowledge of color, or is this not necessary? The answer depends on what we mean by knowledge. We should certainly make the child aware of his own achievements. To state

Fig. 28a. "Street Scene." Group work in paper cutting, emphasizing cooperation. Overlapping is an important experience.

an example: we visited a slum area, and upon our return, we talked about the people living there, the unpainted houses, the broken roofs, the shattered windows replaced by wooden boards, and the back yards filled with junk. After we had discussed these living conditions and their social implications, the children painted "One Day; Living in the Slums," the feelings they would have if they were supposed to regard such a place as their environment. Another time we went to a well-kept residential area and saw how the houses were well painted, with differently painted window frames, flowers in windows, curtains, nicely kept lawns, and back yards with garden furniture. The children painted this, too: "The House in Which I Wish to Live."

It is easily understood that the comparison of the *dull* atmosphere of the slums with the *bright* and joyous treatment of the house in which the child wished to live gave many opportunities to talk of *dull* and *bright* colors, not in an abstract way, but in connection with an experience. This certainly introduced a real, emotional relationship to the two color values —bright and dull, or if we would like to call it "happy" and "sad." Since

Fig. 28b. "Circus." Group work in paper cutting.

the child during this period is especially open for deviations from formerly held, rigid color schemata, he will use such emotional stimulations most willingly. He is visually not yet ready to react more sensitively toward colors which surround him.

The impressionistic, or visual, color scale is the last and most complex to experience. *The child's color relationship during this stage is related to his emotional reactions; it is highly subjective.* That is why we should use the most different moods with reference to color—calm and excited moods as well as monotonous and changing ones and discuss them in terms of color. For all these various moods, experiences can be found such as the one described above. Because of the highly subjective emotional reactions to color we shall call this stage the *subjective stage of color.*

DESIGN AND CRAFTS

Removal from mere symbolic expression to a more realistic treatment—that is, the conscious emphasis on dresses or suits as introduced by the growing awareness of the difference in sex—introduces a conscious desire for decoration. Girls more and more frequently begin putting patterns on their dresses. Only then, when the child herself indicated the desire for decoration, should we proceed with it in a more conscious way. Without disturbing the emotional approach to decoration, we would like to give it a sounder fundament. However, in the same way as we do not teach color theory in elementary grades by means of scientific helps, we will not introduce any formal teaching of balance, rhythm, or any other attributes of design. We might, however, encourage children to use reproducing techniques, such as potato prints or stencils to experience rhythm consciously. The simplest geometric pattern cut into the flat, cut end of a carrot will be more suitable than any complex "flower pattern." The only encouragement which the child should get by such prints, during this period, is the *conscious* understanding of repetitions. This feeling for repetition established in the former stage will readily be taken over into a conscious approach and used there freely and with understanding.

It is most important for the child to get from the very beginning the impression that this form of design serves the *function* of decoration. That is why it is necessary to relate this form of design to some kind of material. Printing curtains would be such a task even if the dots, or whatever is being used as simple prints, are somewhat "primitive." In this connection the child learns to understand the functional meaning and usefulness of a design. The repeating pattern used for it gives him the understanding of the nature of repetitions within design. The folds in the curtain will show how the pattern becomes dynamic through the nature of the material. This is one of the experiences the child has to get from the very beginning of the conscious design approach: *design grows out of the material!* Different materials demand different designs. If this is not recognized by the teacher he loses one of the most important aspects in design: *the specific function of each material.*[4] To identify with "the needs of materials," that is, to learn their *behavior,* is not only educationally important but also ethically, as it will promote a feeling for sincerity and truth. "What can paper do?"—"When does it feel fine—when neglected—and when does it feel thwarted?" A piece of paper "may be happy" when showing how it can fold, turn, bend; "it may feel" neglected as a sheet in the cupboard where nobody cares for it; "it may feel" insincere when it pretends to be wood as a wallpaper or thwarted when crumpled up in the wastebasket. "Let's make wood feel very fine!" "When does wood feel fine?" Excursions in the school's vicinity to discover "how materials feel" are important experiences particularly during this

[4] Emerson, Sybil, *Design, A Creative Approach*. Scranton: International Textbook Co., 1953.

stage of development in which the child becomes increasingly aware of his environment.

It is entirely unsuitable to plan the design first carefuly on paper and then "transfer" it to the chosen material. Planning a design implies a more "scientific approach" for which there is no provision within this period. Furthermore, a design that is determined for another material will look quite different on paper. By doing so, the teacher has missed utilizing one of the greatest stimuli—that is, the stimulation which the child derives from the nature of the material. If the child, from the very beginning, works on the material that he wants to decorate, he receives one of the most important inspirations from the *structure* and *nature* of the material itself. The result of such established relationships between design and material will enable the child to adapt intuitive qualities for design to any material with which he is confronted. *Crafts should never be separated from design.* In our greatest cultures, skill, design, and workmanship were inseparable. Today, we see again this tendency in modern streamlined articles, from simple household utensils to furniture, cars, and architecture in general. We have to stimulate the child in time to recognize these close relationships.

In these first experiments no realistic approaches to design are recommended. To be able to use products of nature, such as flowers, leaves, and so forth, for a design assumes that these forms of nature are well known to the child. There is the great danger, that instead of adapting these forms of nature to a design—that is, stylizing them, the child will make poor attempts to reproduce nature. There is no such danger in using materials for abstract forms. Collages, that is, the combination of different materials for creating harmonious relationships, will help the child in getting more sensitive toward the nature and behavior of materials. The technique of finger painting can now be introduced since the child will be mature enough to get pleasure out of the motions, texture, and color used, not out of the consistency as we discussed it during the early stages. However, finger painting should not be done for realistic purposes, for which it is unsuitable, but for its own sake or application to useful articles, as schedule cards, simple folders, or boxes.

The most important element of design at this developmental level is the emotional approach to it. Giving children paper plates and asking them to imagine themselves in the middle of the woods (using the inner circle of the plate as base line for the trees, with the self in the center, or sliding on a sled down the hill, again using the circle as a continuous base line for hill) would be a suggestion to which children react emotionally. At the same time they will carry over the experience of repetition, which they have gained with their reproducing techniques. With regard to the choice of color, children should not be disturbed by any formal suggestions or influences. We always should have in our mind that it is not the final product, but the working process which counts, and that an "odd" color scheme will not hurt the child whereas he might be disturbed by a criticism that he cannot comprehend.

With design new techniques and materials are introduced. The more inventive the teacher with the introduction of materials, the better. Open-mindedness in regard to material used for decorative purposes is one of the most important attributes of a good teacher. However, economy in its use will also be significant. But, since the mere opportunity of getting the "feel" of the material is of great importance, the mere handling of it with some simple decorative purpose in mind will establish the desired relationship. Merely twisting a strip of sheet metal for holding a candle will introduce the quality of metal. Bending two wires in wavy lines and attaching them to a wooden base will make a serviceable penholder. At the same time the child experiences the manner in which wood and metal can combine with each other. Children should then be given an opportunity to improvise on their own account combinations of materials which need not necessarily serve a useful purpose. *Getting acquainted with the different functions and qualities of materials is the main aim.* Work with different-colored wool of different textures will stimulate the children to different things in this medium. Even twisting several colors together into a knot can be a fine starting point for a discussion on the nature of weaving with regard to the different materials.

The use of clay for pottery will be stimulating to the child of this mental level. Simple plates or dishes can easily be shaped. Even casting with a one-piece mold can be applied. This, however, is suggested only when the children make their own molds.[5] The following procedure is recommended: In a class discussion about the different shapes of water glasses, the one with the best shape is selected. Keeping in mind the difficulties in casting irregular shapes, only straight water glasses should be selected for this purpose. A cardboard box of the size of the water glass is obtained. The outside of the water glass is sized with soap. The water glass then is placed into the box and plaster of Paris (mixed with water to the proper consistency) is poured around it. After the plaster has set,

---

[5] Inasmuch as this is not a book on Arts-Crafts, detailed instructions on modeling and firing pottery cannot be given. For such instructions, the teacher is referred to the many excellent books on the subject.

Fig. 29. Figures in Papier-mâché. (Courtesy Educational Project, Museum of Modern Art, N. Y.)

the glass should be removed and the box peeled off. The mold, after it has dried, is ready for use. Clay has to be mixed with water until it becomes slip—that is, clay of the consistency of thin cream of wheat. The slip is poured into the mold up to the top and after ten minutes, poured out again. Through adhesion, enough clay sticks to the wall so as to form the thickness of the wall of the pot. Since clay shrinks when it dries (the child should watch this shrinking), the cup can easily be removed from the mold. The *cup* must be "bone dry" before it is put into the kiln. If a school does not have a kiln, the firing method used by Indians is suggested. An old iron kettle is obtained. In the back yard of the school a hole is dug in which several layers of charcoal are placed. The kettle which contains the bone-dry dishes is put into the hole upon these charcoal layers and surrounded and covered by more charcoal. Kerosene will start the fire which is kept for approximately six hours. After it has cooled off, the pieces in the kettle are *fired*. If the children have no opportunity to glaze the ware it must not be glazed by adults as is customary in many schools, because the child would surely lose the feeling of its original production.[6]

This discussion has shown that there is no separating line between crafts and design. On the contrary, the very integration of both will give them proper meaning and significance. This is of special importance because it will also open the eyes of the child to modern means of design. Boys who are very streamline-minded when their thinking relates to cars, locomotives, or tanks, will soon apply their knowledge and understanding to other projects and materials. This is particularly significant for a time in which we encounter such varied attitudes toward design in our daily life. With regard to automobiles, the most streamlined model will not be "modern" enough. But the same person who could not live without this "modern" car chooses antique furniture or a terribly poor imitation of it. We have progressed beyond the horse and buggy, but not at home.

Great cultures have always been characterized by this unity of art and life. To create this feeling in our children from the very beginning is of greatest significance. The child cannot be exposed early enough to a harmonious environment. But we don't start with a conscious stimulation until the child is ready for it—that is, when his visual approach permits the conscious apprehension of the nature of good design. That is the time when the child by his own desire starts to decorate with the purpose of decoration. The meaning and influence of design on our daily life is tremendous, conscious or subconscious, and it is the duty of the teacher to awaken the innate feeling the child possesses and direct it into the proper channels.

MODELING

As we come into more advanced stages of modeling and see the child showing greater concern for formal expressions, the question of preserving the products will arise. Before answering this question, it seems important to analyze again the meaning of art, especially in modeling in the elementary-school classroom. It is important to make a distinction between modeling and sculpturing. *Modeling is the unconscious expression in clay or plasticine,* which serves as a means of self-expression in three-dimensional media. In the elementary-school classroom we use modeling, as in all other creative approaches, not as the final product, but as the educative process. This means for the teacher that he must not put the emphasis upon the preservation of the final product. If the teacher would not put

[6] For methods of glazing *How To Make Pottery and Ceramic Sculpture* by Julia Hamlin Duncan and Victor D'Amico, The Museum of Modern Art, New York, is recommended.

emphasis on the preservation of art products, the child would never care to have it done. *Modeled pieces basically are not for firing.* Most of the synthetically modeled pieces (those that are put together from single details) would not be able to stand firing. As has been said before it is not worth while to sacrifice the child's individual thinking to a mere procedure. The question may arise whether modeled pieces should be painted or not. This question may be especially important at this age level, when girls start to include dresses in their modelings and boys, perhaps, uniforms. The painting of modeled pieces should not be encouraged, since modeling is the expression of three-dimensional experiences, which mainly refer to the sense of touch. If a child, however, feels the need to paint his work, he should go ahead with it. Generally it is not necessary to inspire the use of paint and clay in one work during this period of age. But it might happen that, as an outcome of classroom discussions, the children would like to illustrate a scene. For example, they might want to imitate the life in an Indian village, in which they make the tents out of canvas and wooden poles, and model the Indians either of clay or papier-mâché. Under such circumstances it is better to encourage the use of as many materials as possible, to have real canvas tents and the costumes of the Indians made of material rather than painted on clay or papier-mâché (Fig. 29).

As long as we use clay modeling as a means of self-expression, we stress the self as the focal point of experience. By that we do not mean that the ego must be represented in the modeling, but that the experience of the self in any form should be included. Formal aspects, which refer to the nature of composition or sculpturing, should be excluded. It is therefore entirely out of place to introduce such formal aspects as "we begin with one figure and then make two until we arrive at group representations." The child must express himself freely, and stimulation should be in the direction of the child's thinking. Since during this age the child's needs are concerned with friendship and gangs, and with greater awareness of the differences of sex and the resulting lack of cooperation, the stimulation must be directed accordingly.

ART STIMULATION

The following aspects of the child's development will stand out at this age level: discovery of social independence, greater awareness of the self, a lack of outside cooperation. Stimulation during this period must stress the newly discovered social independence in order to give the child the feeling of self-esteem. The stimulation must give him an opportunity to express the new feeling for the difference of sex, and it also must inspire the child to use methods of cooperation as beneficial means for getting results otherwise unobtainable. In classroom discussions, therefore, we should relate spatial experiences of the newly discovered plane to the self. Playing football, for example, would refer not only to the football field (the plane on which the action takes place), but would also involve the self (boy) characterized by the special uniform of a football player. Or, sitting around a table at a birthday party would include both the emphasis on dresses and on the table with all its accessories.

To inspire cooperation, two means can successfully be used: first, the *subjective method* of cooperation which deals with the representations of individual experiences of cooperation; or *the representations of scenes in which cooperation is of importance* (Fig. 27). It is, however, vital for the teacher to know that much depends on the way in which such a stimulation is presented to a group. The atmosphere which the teacher develops during the stimulation contributes greatly to its success. Such topics as "The Help to a Wounded Soldier" or "Flood Victims" can be presented very dramatically.

The second method, the *objective method* of cooperation, *deals with group work*—a whole group works on one project.[7] Also here, the kind of stimulation is vital for its success. As has been pointed out, paper cutting is an excellent technique for group work. In order to be successful, the organization for group work must be well-planned. The following procedure is recommended. First, a classroom discussion is started about a planned topic, such as "Fair" (Fig. 28a and Fig. 28b). "What do we see at a fair?" The answers are written on the blackboard by the teacher. In the meantime a big chip board or pasteboard is prepared by some children who paint, or prepare with paper, the simple background of sky and lawn. Second, the teacher asks the children to choose from the blackboard notes: "Who would like to make the merry-go-round, the shooting gallery, the Ferris wheel?" When all topics are distributed, the children start to cut out their own projects.

Third, the children are asked to bring all pieces to the teacher's table. Children who have made simple tasks will have finished sooner and should be given an opportunity to cut out other topics. When most of the children are ready, the fourth step, assembling, starts. This can be done by a committee guided by the teacher. Since the children have cut out their different

---

[7] Cizek, Franz, *Children's Colored Paper Work*. New York: G. E. Stechert and Co., 1927

objects in sizes unrelated to one another, the teacher should unobtrusively select the smaller pieces for the background by asking, "Who has done this? Please paste it on the board. Where will it look best?" The group will be interested in how and where its things are placed. A few desks should be set aside for pasting, and several things may be distributed simultaneously in order that more than one thing will be ready for pasting. After all projects are assembled, some children may complain that part of their works are covered. At this point the teacher should discuss the nature of overlapping, both from the visual standpoint, as an experience of seeing, and from the social standpoint—that is, that not all can be in the foreground. Background and foreground are both important. The outcome of such stimulation must be a feeling of achievement in the children. Every child must notice his contribution to group work. But it is also important that everyone understand that he alone could not have accomplished so big a task in such harmonious organization.

Topics

As has been described in the section "Stimulation," the child's subjective relationship to man and environment has become characteristic also for this particular stage. Subject matter throughout the grades, however, is determined by man and environment. Our analysis has embraced the ever-changing subjective relationship of man to his environment. From this standpoint, the following suggested topics are indicative of the child's special subjective relationships during this period. Inasmuch as these topics are only meant to be suggestions, it is assumed that they always will be adjusted and subordinated to the particular classroom situation prevailing. It is important that the teacher surround the topics with an intense atmosphere leading them into an aesthetic experience.

CLOTHES, DRESSES Going to Church on Sunday.
Asking Policeman on Street.
Sailors on a Boat.
A Birthday Party.
Bathing.
Working in the Field.
The Conductor in the Train Asking for Tickets.
The Cook in the Hotel.
Elevator Boy Staying Overnight in the Hotel.
A Parade of Soldiers.

Plate 5. "We Are Playing on the Playground." (8 years) Rigid color schemata and form concepts most often go hand in hand. They are usually signs of emotional inflexibility. The child cannot adjust to a new situation and therefore repeats the same schema again and again. Notice the tendency in this drawing to express "running," "watching," or standing with the same stereotyped concept. (See page 173.)

Plate 6. "Our Family." (11 years) Color now characterizes and often gives meaning to objects. (Gang Age. See page 190.) Notice the blue puddles on the shaded ground. Parts when separated from the whole retain their meanings. (Teacher: Jean Holland, Duke of York School, Toronto.)

SPACE, MEANING OF PLANE	Crossing a Street.
	Going over a Bridge.
	Playing Football.
	Playing Basketball.
	Playing Baseball.
	Policeman Directing Traffic.
	Traffic Stopping by Red Light.
	All Celebrations in Open Air.
	Boating in a Lake Surrounded by a Lawn.
	Skating on a Pond Surrounded by Woods.
	Farmer Ploughing His Field.
	Planting a Garden.
	Sitting Around a Table for Supper.
OVERLAPPING	Looking Out the Window.
	In the Movie Theater.
	In the Trolley Car.
	In the Train.
	Also see paper cuts (below, Objective Cooperation).
SUBJECTIVE COOPERATION	Help to a Wounded Soldier.
	Nursing the sick.
	First Aid.
	Sawing Lumber.
	Building a House.
	Carrying a Log.
	Digging a Hole.
	Repairing a Street.
	Decorating a Christmas Tree.
	Praying in Church.
OBJECTIVE COOPERATION	We All Are Making a City.
	We All Are Making a Farm.
	We All Are Making a Circus.
	We All Are Making a Fair.
	We All Are Making the Ark of Noah.
	We All Are Making a Store.
DESIGN ON MATERIAL	*Reproducing:* Potato print (geometric) on textiles.
	Finger paint: folder, card, box.
	Emotional: Sliding Down a Hill, using inner circle of plate as base line.

Racing Down a Hill, using inner circle of plate as base line.
Maypole, using inner circle of plate as base line.
In the Woods, using inner circle of plate as base line.
Picking Flowers, on a pot.
A Carnival, on a pot.
Animals of the Ark, on a pot.

Experiences with different material:
    1. Decorating canes.
    2. Bending metal to spirals (candlestick).
    3. Work with papier-mâché.
    4. Collages.

CLAY   A Farmer.
A Football Player.
A Policeman.
A Soldier.
A Sailor.
A Dancer.
Two, Cutting a Log.
Digging a Hole.
Sitting at the Campfire.

LINOLEUM CUTS   All topics as suggested applied to this technique.

COLOR   Rich House—Poor House (bright—dull).
Rainy Day—Beautiful Day (bright—dull).
Storm, (excited).
Adam and Eve Driven from the Garden of Eden.
Desert—Oasis (monotonous—changing).

Techniques

The child has advanced beyond the use of geometric lines and base-line representations in their linear meaning. With the discovery of the plane, he now feels the need of filling in the spaces, as is seen in the representations of skies which now are painted down to the horizon. Dealing with planes renders crayon unsuitable, and this material is not recommended for use during this age level.

Poster paint is an excellent medium for filling in spaces. Thinner, prepared poster paint will give a better opportunity for mixing color, which now has become more important. Since the child concentrates now more on details, a hair brush is preferable to a bristle brush.

SUMMARY   STAGE OF DAWNING REALISM—NINE TO ELEVEN YEARS

Stage	Characteristics	Human Figure	Space	Color	Design	Stimulation Topics	Technique
Gang age.	(1) Removal from geometric lines (schema).	(1) Emphasis on clothes (dresses, uniforms), emphasizing difference between girls and boys.	(1) Removal from base-line expression.	Removal from objective stage of color.	First conscious approach toward decoration. Use in connection with material.	Self-awareness stimulated by characterization of different dresses and suits (professions).	Paper cutting. No crayons from now on because of removal from linear expression.
	(2) Lack of cooperation with adults.	(2) Greater stiffness as result of egocentric attitude, and the emphasis on details, as clothes, hair, and so forth.	(2) Overlapping. (3) Sky comes down to base line.	Emphasis on emotional approach to color.	(1) Reproducing techniques, emphasizing repetition.	Cooperation and overlapping through group work.	Poster paint.
Preadolescent crisis.	(3) Gang age.		(4) Discovery of plane.	Subjective stage of color. Color is used with regard to subjective experience.	(2) Emotional design using the meaning of repetition.	Subjective cooperation through type of topic: "We are building a house."	Flat colored chalk. Clay.
Dawning realism.	(4) Greater awareness of the self with regard to sex (boys and girls).	Tendency toward realistic lines. Removal from schema.	(5) Filling in space between base lines. (6) Difficulties in spatial correlations as result of egocentric attitude and lack of cooperation.		Acquaintance with materials and their function.	Objective cooperation through working method.	Papier-mâché. Linoleum cut. Wood. Metal.

EVALUATION CHART

Gang Age

	None	Some	Much
Intellectual Growth Is the child beginning to use details to characterize the self and environment? Does the child depart from the use of schemata? Does the child depart from the use of geometric lines? Do details retain their meanings when separated from the whole? Does the child characterize boys and girls as girls? Does the child depart from base lines? Does the child express the plane?			
Emotional Growth Does the child identify himself with the drawing? Does the drawing lack stiffness? Are brush strokes or lines used freely? Does the child still use exaggerations? Does the child's drawing show accumulations of details on those parts which are emotionally significant?			
Social Growth Does the child in his work identify himself with the group? Does he correlate figures to each other? Does he coordinate figures with space? (Environment.) Is the child socially conscious of his environment? Does he cooperate in group work by subordinating his work to the whole?			

Perceptual Growth	Does the child include the horizontal line? Has the child become aware of overlapping? Is distance expressed by the diminishing size of distant objects? Has the child become aware of the changing effects of light and motion? Does color indicate more than characterization? Has the space between base lines been filled in? Are textural qualities expressed?			
Physical Growth	Does the drawing indicate a distinction between sexes? Is there emphasis on secondary sex characteristics (moustache, hair, etc.) ? Does the child's drawing show body action? Does the child retain flexibility in body movements?			
Aesthetic Growth	Does the child use decorative patterns on clothes or elsewhere? Does the child relate material to design and purpose? (Or does he look only for function?) Does the child relate details to the whole? (Or does he become bound up with them?) Does the child relate colors to each other?			
Creative Growth	Does the child choose his own subject? Does the child experiment with different mediums? Does the child invent his own forms? Is the child inventive in using materials for new purposes?			

205

As has been indicated, a technique is only good if it offers a special original contribution that fits the child's needs and helps to express in the easiest way what is in his mind. Such a technique during this period is paper-cutting which offers two important stimulations not offered by any other medium. The natural way of stimulating the child to experience the meaning of overlapping (which is the first introduction into the three-dimensional space concept), has already been disclosed and cannot be replaced by any other technique. Stimulation of *cooperation* through group work is the second important technique. Also here it fulfills a specific purpose with original means. *Clay* will be used for modeling as well as for pottery. Forming with hands as well as using simple one-piece molds is suggested.

For crafts, finger paint in connection with *pasteboard* work is suggested.[8] Work with cotton and wool of a variety of textures and colors is recommended. Acquaintance with as many materials as possible, such as wire, sheet metal, wood, and papier-mâché, will stimulate the child to apply design to function and structure of the material [9] (Fig. 33a and b).

EVALUATION CHART

The chart on pages 204 and 205 should serve as a means to evaluate the child's growth during the gang age through his creative product. It should be kept in mind that certain criteria may be indicative of different characteristics of growth. For instance, a higher awareness of environmental details may account for the child's interest in his environment, which may be investigative—that is, intellectual—as well as social, if it is combined with an interest in his neighbors.

INTERPRETATION OF INDIVIDUAL GROWTH CHARACTERISTICS PERTAINING TO THE GANG AGE

Intellectual growth

As has been said before, one of the outstanding characteristics of the gang age is that the child discovers his social independence. He becomes aware of himself as a member of a group. This higher feeling of awareness

---

[8] Shaw, R. F., *Finger Painting*. Boston: Little, Brown and Co., 1934.

[9] Browne, Sibyl, Ethel Tyrrell, Gertrude Abbihl and Clarice Evans, *Art and Materials for the Schools*. New York: Progressive Education Assn., 1943.

brings about a departure from schemata. How much he has departed from mere schematic representation—how much he feels the need to characterize objects, figures, and environment—is indicative of his intellectual growth. It can easily be understood that a child of low mentality neither becomes aware of his changing environment, nor does he discover those character- istics which allow him to individualize objects or figures which otherwise would only be schemata.

The first question in the evaluation chart deals, therefore, with the child's ability to recognize details connected with the self and the environ- ment and to use them for characterization. In order to get a more concrete understanding of what is meant by details let us look at Fig. 27. First of all, the meaning of details changes during the different stages of develop- ment. As we have seen, details during the schematic stage are significant in that they show us the active knowledge of the child. Details have a different meaning during the gang age when the attention is focused on the group experience. The single individual in the group has subordinated meaning, especially when the feeling for the group is expressed as in Fig. 27. In this painting a hurricane had felled a tree and a group of children came to watch two workers cutting the trunk into pieces. In such a painting "details" mean characterization in terms of the facts which are most sig- nificant to the child. It has been emphasized previously that the discovery of the difference in sexes is an important characteristic of the gang age. Details which point toward this characterization will then be most mean- ingful. Indeed, we can see a great variety of details in Fig. 27 which point up the difference between boys and girls. Look at the emphasis on the dif- ferentiation of clothes. The girls are wearing nicely designed dresses; the boys wear pants and shirts. One boy wears short socks, the other half socks, while the workers wear long pants. What an interesting distinction in details is made in the differences of hairdo and "texture" of hair. We can, therefore, say that the child uses many details for characterizing the self and environment. Our check mark on the chart would then be placed in the column "much."

The next question deals with the criteria of departing from the use of schemata. In this painting the use of schemata has been completely aban- doned. There are no indications of repeating a form concept. Since the child no longer uses form concepts but develops the urge to characterize, geometric lines have become insufficient means. This child has completely abandoned the use of geometric lines. Most of the details retain their mean- ing when separated from the whole.

The next question deals with the child's ability to characterize boys as boys and girls as girls. The child who drew Fig. 27 not only characterizes them through their exterior (their hair and clothing), but also through their occupations. The girl has her doll carriage while the boys play with an old tire.

The child not only has departed from base-line expressions but distinctly indicates his feeling for the plane. The texture of the grass clearly expresses the child's consciousness of the meaning of the ground.

Emotional growth

Without the ability to identify oneself with his own experience no emotional tie with an experience can take place. The different steps and degrees of self-identification have been discussed previously.[10] According to these statements, the child of Fig. 27 closely identifies himself with his experience, the total experience as well as the experience with single details. In this case the child identifies herself as a part of the group watching the cutting of a tree. However, she also clearly signifies through differentiated actions and criteria which she gave the single features that she identified herself with them. The interesting motions of the boys in the foreground, in which one apparently wants to push back the other, clearly shows how much the girl put herself into the place of the boys.

It has been discussed in the former paragraphs that children who do not properly experience their newly discovered social independence easily become stiff and rigid in their drawings. This is often also a sign of a too great and sudden awareness of the need to characterize. In Fig. 27 we see some stiffness of this nature in the workers who are cutting the tree. Otherwise, we see a complete lack of stiffness in this painting. Nevertheless, we would put our check mark in our chart under the column "some." If we look at the total effect of the painting we can immediately see that action is not its outstanding characteristic.

The next question deals with the use of brush strokes and lines. Brush strokes and lines are used freely in this painting. This is especially true considering the relatively small size of the figures. Yet, seldom is a brush stroke or outline interrupted. This is a clear indication, at this stage of development, of the free use of brush strokes and lines.

Children now usually refrain from using as much exaggeration as they did before. In this painting we may say that the child used "some" exaggeration in the representation of the tree. Otherwise, naturalistic proportions are used. One of the characteristics of emotional interest in a particu-

[10] See p. 22–37.

lar part is the accumulation of details in this particular part. This can be easily understood, for the child uses more affection to characterize a part which is of emotional significance to him. In Fig. 27 we cannot see any greater accumulations of details in a particular part. In fact, the painting appears evenly distributed throughout.

Social growth

Social growth, during this period, is one of the outstanding factors of growth. This is the time when the child discovers his social independence, when he recognizes that he has more power in a group than as an individual. Yet, when something interferes with this new feeling of social belongingness, the child may withdraw and remain an outsider. Whether or not the child identifies himself with the group can be recognized by two factors from his creative work: (1) from the content of the work; (2) from the group participation in group work. Since we are dealing in Fig. 27 with an individual creative product we shall have to investigate its content in regard to group identification. The content of a creative work may directly or indirectly express group identification. Direct group identification is expressed when the topic actually represents group activities, such as: "We Are Making a Camp Fire," or "We Are Building a Bungalow," or "We Are Cutting Logs," or "We Are Playing Football." Indirect group identification can be seen in a common feeling of participation in an event, such as, "We Are Watching a Fire," or "We Are Watching a Game." In Fig. 27 we can see both types of group identification: direct and indirect. The direct group identification is seen in the representation of the two men cutting the tree. The child identified herself with both men's actions, that is, with the thought of getting a job done cooperatively. The indirect group identification is seen in the representation of the children who "all are watching the log cut." From this we can draw the conclusion that the child identifies herself with the group "much."

The next question deals with the correlation of figures to each other. In several instances such a correlation is present. The workers cutting the tree are well correlated. There is also a well-established correlation expressed in the two boys represented in the left foreground. The mark in the evaluation chart would go under "much." Not only are the figures well correlated to each other, but they are also well coordinated with the environment into which they are placed. The most complex environmental coordination is seen in the two figures cutting the log. However, the children also are well placed around the focal point of interest.

Whether or not the child is socially conscious of his environment is the content of the next question in the evaluation chart. This is often only expressed by implication. If the topic allows it, the child may express his social consciousness directly. He may want to paint the dreary look of a mining town, or the clean look of a residential area; he may express the smoky look of an industrial city, its slums, or its needed recreation facilities. However, sometimes the differences in clothes, social acceptance, or belongings indicate a feeling of social consciousness. In Fig. 27 "some" social consciousness is expressed in the differences in clothing. The contrast between the workers and the children is obvious and, therefore, indicative of social consciousness.

The last question under social growth in the evaluation chart refers to group work only. Only by observation could it be found out if the child cooperates in group work and subordinates his work to the whole. A clear indication of the child's subordination is shown in the kind of emphasis which he expresses during the working process. If he emphasizes only his part and his concern about its placement and meaning within the group work, it is a sign that he does not subordinate himself to the aim of the group. If, however, he emphasizes the work of the whole group by being concerned about the work of others and the total effect of the whole, then he obviously subordinates his work to that of the whole group.

Perceptual growth

The child's growing visual awareness and his beginning feelings for realism are part of his perceptual growth. One of the first indications of the child's visual awareness is expressed by the inclusion of the horizontal line. In Fig. 27 we would not be able to answer directly the question in the evaluation chart pertaining to the horizontal line. In this painting the child was so much interested in the work on the ground that she excluded the sky. By implication we could say, however, that if the child had included the sky it would only have been possible by drawing a horizontal line.

Another aspect of visual perception is expressed by the child's awareness of overlappings. In Fig. 27 the child expresses this awareness on several occasions. The worker in the foreground overlaps and therefore covers part of the tree. The saw clearly overlaps and covers part of the tree, while the tree partly overlaps and covers the worker in the background. Our check mark in the chart could, without hesitation, be placed in the column "much." The next question in the chart deals with the diminishing size of

distant objects, also an indication of visual perception. In Fig. 27 no diminishing sizes of distant objects can be found. The grass only appears as a
textural quality but has the same size in foreground and background. The
child apparently has not yet become aware of this visual factor. Also, no
difference in size can be recognized in the figures which would point toward
the awareness of an apparent visual diminution of distant objects. While
it is generally not expected that a child of the gang age should become
aware of the change effect which light and motion have on objects, a child
of outstanding perceptual growth may include some of the aforementioned
effects. In Fig. 27 no effects which refer to light and shadow are included.
Light and dark are merely used as contrasting elements. Also color, with
which the next question in the chart deals, is only used to characterize
objects or in its decorative meaning and not in its changing effects in light,
distance, and atmosphere.

In regard to space perception it can be said that the child clearly perceives the plane space; this being made clear by making the whole plane
meaningful with a textural quality. Both of the last questions, one referring
to space and the other to texture, could be answered with "much."

Physical growth

A part of the physical maturity of the child is seen in his awareness of
characteristics of his own body, especially in regard to distinguishing it
from the other sex. In Fig. 27 the child is well aware of these differences.
Short hair for the boy and long hair for the girls as well as distinct differences in clothing indicate her alertness. However, there is no particular
emphasis on outstanding sex characteristics as moustaches, manicured
fingernails, etc.

The child is clearly conscious of her body motions. In several instances
she emphasizes meaningful body actions. The girl holding the carriage,
the jumping rope, the boy holding the tire, and the workers cutting the tree
are ample evidence of the child's body sensitivity. Whether or not the child
retains her flexibility in her body movements could only be seen from several creative paintings by the same child.

Aesthetic growth

As has been stated previously, the gang age is the period of development in which the child becomes gradually conscious of the meaning of
design, especially in relation to environment. Usually, this reveals itself

first in the use of decorative patterns on clothes or elsewhere. The first question in the evaluation chart deals with this use of decorative patterns. If we look again at Fig. 27 we can see that the child made "much" use of such decorative elements of design. Almost every dress or shirt has a different pattern.

Regarding the next question, as to whether or not the child relates material to design and purpose, we would be in a better position to answer if we could see some of the child's products in material. However, we can state from this painting, which is executed in showcard color, that she uses paint to its advantage. She neither treated it like water color, attempting to use paint fluently and in its merging quality, nor did she emphasize a linear quality. She did by no means overemphasize technique, that is, the functional use of the material only. This would have led to the types of paintings in which the technical performance overshadows expression and content. This would be like a virtuoso who does not know what he plays. The next question in the evaluation chart deals with the child's ability to relate the parts to the whole, a very important aesthetic criterion. It is quite obvious that the girl who painted Fig. 27 was very sensitive in relating the parts to the whole; the way in which she painted the tree on the paper reveals that she had the total picture in her mind when she started to paint. The distribution of the branches left the space open for the spectators as well as for the workers. It further introduced a perfect balance of linear and spatial distribution: the big mass of the trunk moves upward, while the smaller branches together with the saw and the workers "move" downward, excluding the static group of the spectators.

From the original painting it could also be seen that the child is very sensitive in her color relationships. Not only are light and dark colors well distributed, but the choice of colors also shows that she has become aware of the decorative meaning of color.

Creative growth

It has been pointed out previously that the child's original approach is an important indication of his creative growth. Part of this original approach is the independent choice of subject matter. It is without any doubt that the child who painted Fig. 27 chose her own subject matter. The characterizations of details in the tree, in her workmen, and the spectators are clear indications of it. A child who did not choose her own subject matter could only have identified herself that closely with it had she made a "given topic" her own. Only then could the child include that many meaningful details which characterize the single items. The next question in the evaluation chart cannot be fully answered unless we know several creative works of the same child and find out if the child experiments with different mediums. However, it is not too difficult to detect rigid or experimental attitudes toward mediums even from one work. For instance, in Fig. 27 we can easily see how the child uses her material experimentally—that is, flexibly. She tried to use the paint solidly; now and then she outlined shapes to get better contrasts; she superimposed one color upon another, as seen in the figure in the center; she also tried to introduce different textures by stippling with the brush as seen in the representation of the grass. That altogether shows an experimental attitude. A child who has not developed the desire for experimentation usually deals with a medium consistently in the same way.

Whether or not the child invents his own forms of expression is not too easy to determine. One sure sign that he uses his own forms is the child's flexible use of them. The more stereotypes we can notice the more it is likely that the child has merely "taken over" some forms. While the child whose painting is reproduced in Fig. 27 changes details from figure to figure, a certain equal "pattern" can be seen in all of her figures. While it cannot conclusively be stated that the child has been influenced in her work by picture books or adult material, it seems that the child is not inventing *her* forms entirely without imposed influences. She appears to have a "pattern" for boys, one for girls, and one for "boys with long pants."

The last question deals with the child's inventiveness in regard to materials. Also, this question can better be answered after seeing many works by the child. She has not used showcard paint in any new or inventive way. However, this would not be altogether indicative for the child's general attitude toward inventiveness.

SUMMARY OF GROWTH ANALYSIS

In taking into consideration the detailed analysis of the child's work we would like to look again at the child's total work. In it all these details are integrated into a whole: the child's personality. According to all characteristics, there is a good indication that the child is advanced for her stage. It seems that she is moving out of the gang age into the "stage of reasoning." Intellectually the child seems to control and reason with her detailed observations. Her characterizations of the different sexes are also very mature and do not show any exaggerations which would indicate the newness of this discovery. This should not surprise us, for the child is already eleven years old and apparently a "gifted child," one who has no emotional blocks which prevent her free expression. While the child clearly identifies herself with her own experiences, we could notice some stiffness in the representations which are more remote from her own experiences as seen in the representation of the workers. Also, socially the child seems to be very mature. Not only does she coordinate her figures well, but she also relates them well to the environment in which they are placed. The child, however, seems to refer everything to her own particular social standard as seen in the one-sided depiction of types of children. Physically the child seems to be healthy in her growth. However, it should be pointed out again that the last word should be with the physician. The child appears particularly far advanced in her use of her senses—in her perceptual growth. She is well aware of her visual, textural, and tactile environment, as has been clearly found in the foregoing analysis.

While the child seems to be very sensitive aesthetically, as indicated in the organization of her painting and her sense for decorative patterns, her creative spirit is far behind. The child does not seem to be originally and inventively inclined. There are imitative trends in her picture. This, together with her intellectually advanced and socially dependent trend, may indicate a somewhat conventional child—one who may be more pleased to reach and adjust to certain standards than to create her own.

EXERCISES

(1) Collect the drawings of a fourth or fifth grade. Find out how many children have introduced clothes in their drawings.

(2) Collect the drawings of one child over a period of half a year. Record your observations on the progressive change from geometric lines to realistic lines.

(3) Check the percentage of children who still depend on base-line expressions only, and those who use the spaces between the base lines.

(4) Analyze the space representation on one drawing according to:
(a) Whether or not the child adheres to base lines.
(b) Whether or not the child uses overlappings.
(c) Whether or not the child establishes proper spatial correlations.
(d) Whether or not the sky comes down to the base line (or horizon). What conclusions can you draw from your analysis in reference to the child's ability to observe visually?

(5) Examine the children's relationship between behavior, character, and personality trends and drawings, with regard to (a) greater stiffness of figures and (b) lack of correlation in space.

(6) Do you find those children more egocentric who do not establish proper spatial correlations?

(7) Make growth profiles, using the evaluation chart also for Figs. 25, 26.

LABORATORY WORK

(1) Make an abstract design of different materials and structure.

(2) Make a simple object of wire, which shows the characteristics of the material.

(3) Do the same with (a) clay, (b) wood, (c) textiles, (d) cardboard, and (e) papier-mâché.

(4) Make several abstract finger paintings, using the motions of your hand and the different structures obtained by the impressions made by the surface of fingers and palm.

(5) Make a cardboard box, using finger paint for decoration.

(6) Tear a mountain chain from three matching colored papers and arrange them so that overlapping can best be seen.

(7) Make a paper cut, "City," by cutting different types of houses and arranging them properly.

(8) Make a cooperative paper cut, as suggested on p. 199.

(9) Model a mask, expressing yawning, laughing, and so forth, being guided by changes in configuration of your own facial features and muscles when yawning or laughing.

(10) Make a puppet from papier-mâché.

CHAPTER VII

THE PSEUDOREALISTIC STAGE

The Stage of Reasoning (11 to 13 years)

PSYCHOLOGICAL ASSUMPTIONS

T HE GREAT SIGNIFICANCE OF THIS STAGE CAN BE UNDERSTOOD ONLY when we regard it as a preparatory stage to the approaching crisis of adolescence. After the child has properly gone through the gang age he enters a stage in which he has developed enough intelligence to tackle almost any problem, yet, in his reactions, he still is a child. The difference between child and adult can best be seen in the diversity of their imaginative activity. This can best be observed in the different types of playing. The child plays hide-and-seek with the same unawareness as he uses a pencil, which he moves up and down while imitating the noises of an airplane. Such unawareness is characteristic of children. Quite obviously, their imagination transforms a pencil into an airplane. All children use their imagination in such an uninhibited way; if an adult would do the same he would be considered insane. For an adult, a pencil is a pencil and the pencil is for writing. The child's imaginative activity is unconscious. The adult's imaginative activity in its effect is controlled. This change in the imaginative activity from the unconscious to critical awareness, introduced by physical changes in the body, is one of the most important characteristics of the crisis of adolescence.

A healthy body can overcome the aftereffects of an operation much easier than a weakened body; therefore it is important to strengthen the body before undergoing a contemplated operation. We take this procedure for granted when dealing with a physical crisis, but it is all too often neglected in cases of emotional disturbances. Neither art educators nor psychologists give the necessary attention to preparing the child for the crises of adolescence. Yet this stage of reasoning is the appropriate period for such physical and psychological conditioning.

Since art education affects the whole individual, his thinking, feeling, and perceiving, the teacher has an excellent opportunity to influence its changes. Thus he may be able to help youth to overcome an important part of this crisis. Most commonly this change is seen in the fact that children are highly creative, whereas adults, because of their critical awareness toward their imaginative activity, generally lose their creative ability.

The important question will then be: How can we prepare the child most properly for this change that he can continue his creative production in spite of his critical awareness? Or, in other words, how can we prepare the child to create in such a way that he looks with pride on his work instead of being ashamed of it? During this stage for the first time the attention has to be shifted from the importance of the working process to an increased emphasis on the final product. Thus, the final art product becomes more and more significant with increasing age. This recognition of the growing significance of the final product is a clear demand on the part of youth, and it must be accepted by educators. The following graph might illustrate the interchanging effect of the importance of the working process upon the final product during the different age periods.

	AGE	2-5	5-7	7-9	9-11	11-13	13-15	15-17	17–
FINAL PRODUCT	Most Important								
	Increasingly Important								
	More Important								
WORKING PROCESS	Unimportant								
	Less Important								
	Important								

Another psychologically important factor comes into the picture. The closer we study adolescence, the more we see a distinction in the sensory reactions of the children toward their creative experiences. We see clearly a preference by some children for *visual stimuli* while others may be more concerned with the interpretation of *subjective experiences*. Visual experiences are defined as those which refer to our optical senses. They are concerned with the differences of color, light, and shadows, introduced through atmospheric conditions, as well as with the perspective interpretation of space. Subjective interpretations are those which emphasize the emotional relationship to the external world in reference to the body self. Visually minded individuals refer in their pictures to environment whereas nonvisually minded individuals are the expressionists. Children who have a preference for visual experiences feel as spectators, looking at their work from outside. Subjectively minded people feel involved in their work. As we approach the crisis of adolescence, during which preferences toward these different experiences crystallize, we have to pay increasing attention in our stimulation to both of these important experiences. In the same way that we would discourage a visually minded person by stimulating him in referring to subjective experiences, emotional qualities, or body experiences, in the corresponding way we would inhibit a subjectively minded person if we would stimulate him by mere visual experiences. Since traditional art education is mainly built upon visual stimuli, a great part of our youth must feel not only neglected, but frustrated. Many art educators use visual stimulations throughout the secondary level, not realizing that modern expressionist art is a clear indication of the importance of nonvisual stimuli in our present-day life. *Indeed, most of the children react in both ways with a preference for one or the other kind of experience.* The knowledge of this fact together with the increasing shift from the working process to the final product is of vital importance for art educators and educators in general who deal with this age level. A more detailed analysis with regard to proper stimulation will follow in the section on "Art Stimulation."

FIRST CONCEPT OF NATURALISTIC REPRESENTATIONS

In the human figure

From what has been said it becomes clear that only visually minded children who desire it will arrive at a realistic concept. Under realistic concept of the human figure we understand the concept that is determined by the *changing* optical effects experienced in different light, space, and atmospheric conditions. From this viewpoint, the drawing of clothes will become a realistic concept as soon as the changing effects which take place when we sit down are *observed*: the clothes fold or wrinkle at the bent parts, lights and shadows are determined by the changes of the sitting body, and so forth. Until he reaches this stage, the child usually employs clothes only for characterizations, to show that "this is a girl" and "this a man." Henceforth we shall see that the visual child gradually develops the urge to add to his characterization the optical changes already discussed.

The child starts to observe visually: thus visual observation starts where mere characterization ends. There is generally a confusion with regard to visual experiences on the one hand and mere recognition or characterization on the other. Stating that the dress is red does not imply a visual analysis any more than the bare statement "the boy wears pants." Both statements are mere characterizations. They will become visual experiences as soon as the changes of red are observed with regard to light, shadow, and distance; or if the changing effects which the "pants" go through while the boy is running or otherwise in motion are recognized.

Thus, observation is not the mere ability to see or recognize. It is the ability to analyze the visual image with regard to its changing effects in space. One of the first signs of the discovery of these changing effects is the drawing of joints. Usually during this age level children develop an increased desire to include joints in their drawings of the human figure. If this is noticed by the teacher, it is necessary that he include it in his stimulations by pointing to motions in which the use of the joints is of importance.

In later-developed stages of this age level more detailed observations are included. The child might even observe that clothes change with different motions. Thus the visually minded child will start to concentrate more on appearance. He will be eager to include "correct" proportions and motions. He will use exaggeration less frequently as a means of expression.

Whereas the visually minded child concentrates more on the whole and its changing effects, *the nonvisually minded child will concentrate more on the details* in which he is emotionally interested. In his interpretation of expressions he still uses the method of exaggerating important parts. The visually minded child sees the human figure as a whole, while the nonvisually minded child is particularly concerned with the details which are emotionally significant to him. Thus he refers more to the self and his body feeling than to the exterior qualities. His emotional binding dominates his art. His creative work belongs to the art of expressionism.

Since the best stimulation is the one which appeals most to the child, it is important to stimulate the child in the direction of *his* thinking and feeling. Thus, it would not only be fruitless to divert a child from his own feeling and perceiving but would be frustrating to him, for it would confront him with experiences which he cannot comprehend. It is, therefore, important to notice that mere visual stimuli would just as much frustrate the one group as stimuli which refer to the body self and its emotions would inhibit the other group since most children react in both ways. In a good stimulation, values of appearance which refer to the changing visual effects are just as important as the emphasis on body experiences, expressions, and emotions. That is why it is suggested that posing models be used during this age. But a pose should never be used merely for purposes of imitation! Every pose given to a group must have a definite meaning in order that those who are more dependent on their subjective or emotional interpretation might also have an opportunity of expressing themselves. The pose of a beggar who stands on a street corner should first be discussed with regard to body motions and exterior values. After that it is necessary to develop an atmosphere around the posing figure by discussing the life of a beggar and all its human or social implications. In such a way the teacher will be able to stimulate both reactions in his group—the visual as well as the nonvisual. The pose may be drawn with all visual criteria or it may be expressed as an interpretation of one's feeling, or both. If we would present the model merely in the common way as a visual stimulation (from the viewpoint of what we *see*), we would frustrate a considerable number of children whose approach is equally important. Although both tendencies are still not conscious to the child, it should be pointed out that this is a very important preparation for the stage of critical awareness, the stage of the crisis of adolescence (Fig. 30).

THE DEVELOPMENT OF TWO DIFFERENT SPACE-CONCEPTS

From what has been said before it must be borne in mind that children may have a preference for visual experiences or for the subjective interpretation of what they feel. A great number of children certainly will show both characteristics in their creative expressions, but most commonly we shall find a preference for one or the other. Only for the purpose of clarifying the differences in experience are the two concepts discussed separately.

The discovery of depth by the visually minded

With regard to the human figure, we defined visual experiences as the experiences that refer to the optical changes. In the same way, *we call the*

Fig. 30. "Beggar" (twelve years). Pose studied from life model. Othewise drawn imaginatively. Stage of Reasoning.

visual space the experiences that refer to the optical changes in space. One of the important optical changes is the apparent diminution of distant objects. Closely related to this discovery, however, is the meaning of the horizon. With the recognition of distance, space in its three-dimensional qualities moves more and more into the focal point of interest of the visually minded child. During this period, this move occurs almost entirely intuitively. The child merely follows his growing innate demand and power of observation. With it, light and shadows in their changing effects begin to come into the mental picture of the child. All this is done without awareness. Therefore the teacher should know that the stimulation with regard to the optical changes in space is not to be given on the conscious level of pointing toward perspective and its meaning for "constructing" three-dimensional effects, unless the child asks for it.

The seeing of depth must be discovered by the *child*. To take this discovery from him by "explaining" perspective to him would only mean depriving him of an important experience. The teacher must capitalize on the children's own findings and start on the child's own level. "What makes the tree more distant in your drawing?" Let the child become aware of his own discoveries; that he has drawn the tree smaller, because distant objects appear to be smaller to us; that he has included less detail, because we do not see as many details in distant objects; that he has given it a less intense color, because the air in between makes the color appear less bright. All this the child should find out for himself and should be used as a frame of reference for later experiences which may be less simple: "I want the road going to the house in the background, but it looks funny" may be remarks teachers often hear during this stage of development. "Let's see whether the road is doing the same as the tree" would be a good starting point, using a previous experience for new discoveries. The child will soon find for himself that the road as it goes into the distance does not grow smaller (that is, narrower) in his drawing as the tree does. It may also not be less intensive in color. Such discoveries should always be supported by real experiences in nature. It is, however, most important to keep in mind that the teacher has no right to deprive the child of his own discoveries. On the contrary, he must pave the way in providing the child with the right stimulus whenever the need for it arises.

Much of the precious creative unawareness of the child has all too soon been spoiled by teachers who cannot early enough see the child's taste adjusted to the adult's taste. Since it is necessary to prepare the child for the stages of critical awareness at a time when this awareness has not yet set in, such early intrusions into the child's development can be disastrous.

The change from the unconscious creative approach to the stage of critical awareness has to occur gradually. The more gradually the child can move from one stage into the other, the less is the shock the child suffers from the results of the changes in his imaginative thinking. Thus, if we can *stimulate the child in such a way that he comes in his unaware stages close to the concept which he will finally attain,* we have succeeded in bridging the gap between the unconscious approaches of preadolescence and the approaches of critical awareness which start during adolescence. It is, therefore, a question of preserving the child's creative power beyond the critical stages of adolescence. *If we can do this, we have not only saved one of the greatest gifts of mankind, the ability to create, but we have also kept one of the most important attributes necessary for proper adjustments: flexibility.* It is needless to say that the child's own desire is the best measure for his stimulation.

Apparent retrogression to base-line expressions of the nonvisually minded group

It has been observed in many cases that children who have advanced beyond the base-line concept at some point return to the very same kind of space concept. This retrogression to a former concept can only be understood if we study higher art forms of nonvisual art. There we would see that the base-line concept is no longer an unconscious "childish concept." In Egyptian, Assyrian, or medieval art expression, the base line becomes the vehicle of space representations. In this light, base-line expressions represent a higher form of nonvisual consciousness, not a retrogression. Indeed, the new base-line representations are the forerunners of a more conscious nonvisual art expression. The retrogression, therefore, is only apparent. It is in reality the very same step into the nonvisual sphere as the three-dimensional tendency of space representation is in the realm of visual perception.

In general, however, we shall see that nonvisually minded children concentrate in their representations more on the expression of the self and the emotions resulting from it. For them, space has significance only if it is necessary for their expression. From the very beginning, we will, therefore, be able to distinguish visually minded children from the nonvisually minded merely by the choice of representations. The visually minded child prefers environment, feels like a spectator. The nonvisually minded child concentrates more on the self and draws environment only when it has emotional significance for him.

Fig. 31a. "Moses Strikes the Rock." Nonvisually minded representation of a thirteen-year-old boy. Experience is focused at the self. The creator feels involved in the experience of striking the rock as the actor.

Both groups again develop a strong feeling for spatial correlations of figures in environment which was somewhat weakened through the lack of cooperation in many children during the gang age. Since the child is now in the stage of reasoning, he has overcome an egocentric attitude that prevented him from achieving spatial relationships. If we continue to meet with such drawings, we can be sure that we are dealing with children who have not overcome the frustrations they experienced during the gang age. The visually minded child now establishes his spatial correlations on the basis of visual experiences, whereas the nonvisually minded child establishes his correlations mainly through the body-self. The stimulation of spatial correlation is now entirely achieved through the choice of the topic. Dramatic stories set in environment are excellent means for stimulating the child's connection of the self to environment. This is the age level of "Western Stories." That is why stories dramatically introduced will be very appealing to the child.

Figs. 31a and 31b show dramatic illustrations from the Bible. Moses strikes the rock that water might gush forth. Such stories should be told in such a way that environment and dramatic action are emphasized equally.

Fig. 31b. "Moses Strikes the Rock." Visually minded representation of a thirteen-year-old boy. Experience is focused at the scene. The creator feels as a spectator.

Strong sentiments and feelings in the characters must be developed in the same way as mood, terrain, and atmosphere. Here also the two different reactions toward experiences can clearly be seen. In Fig. 31a, the painting by a nonvisually minded child, the experiences are centered in Moses alone and how in his anger he struck the rock so that water should emerge. Fig. 31b, on the other hand, the painting of a visually minded child, shows us a "spectacle." How grand it is to see that water flows out of the rock! In Fig. 31a, nothing but experiences of the self is embodied. The experience of form is intensely personal and finds its strongest expression in the lineaments of Moses. In Fig. 31b, we feel that we are taking part in this great moment as spectators. In the former, everything has been concentrated on expression and gesture; in the latter, it is the arrangement of the figures, the rich colors, the motions of the people, the water, the sky, and environment—all that is visually perceivable, that has become the main problem of representation.

We see the enormous effect the miracle had on the crowd. Some people have jars with which to fetch water, others are drinking it directly from the earth. *Many* dramatic episodes can be seen, but all are subordinated to the great miracle of the waterfall, the rock with the water gushing forth.

Fig. 32. "Carrying a Load." Neither visual nor nonvisual characteristics are dominant (thirteen-year-old boy).

Nowhere in this picture, however, do we perceive those intense personal sensations that hold our attention on Fig. 31a, in which even the water, the only object except the person of Moses, has been drawn in a compact mass as though it could be grasped rather than seen. The fact that in this picture the arm has been added later, also shows clearly the synthetic mode of procedure characteristic for nonvisual expression. This will be discussed in greater detail in the next stage.

The importance of stimulating both visual and nonvisual experiences becomes evident when we look at these two pictures. We will also realize how differently correlation has been experienced. In the drawing by the visually minded child, figures are correlated to landscape through the common spectacle, through the visual experience which is focused on the miracle. The nonvisually minded child, however, established correlation mainly through his intense body feelings and the emotions on which the whole picture is centered. Both pictures, however, have in common the strong dramatic effect which moved both children to realize their strong feelings for correlations. The unawareness of both creators gave them full freedom for expressing the dramatic effect so vividly.

It is needless to say that many children would be affected by visual and nonvisual experiences with a preference for the one or the other, such as in figure 32. In it we see a stronger tendency toward the expression of subjective emotional feelings. However, there is a clear indication of visual concepts as indicated by the changing quality of sizes and colors in the background.

COLOR—TWO DIFFERENT CONCEPTS

The child does not develop in particular directions only, but does so as a whole. If single trends are discussed separately it springs from the desire to present a more systematic approach and from the inability to discuss all trends simultaneously. However, space, color, and the self are fused in the creative development of the child, and form a unity, a part of the total growth of the child. After what has been said, the child's tendency will be understood if we see the same changing effects in color that were discussed in relation to space and the representation of the human figure.

Only the visually minded children show the tendency to see color in its changing effects. To have a visual concept of color does not mean merely to have the ability to recognize color. "This is green, red, or blue" means only that we can distinguish colors from one another, but not that we have a visual concept of color. To have a visual concept means that we notice the *changes* color undergoes under different external conditions. The same color appears different in light and shadow. The surrounding colors reflect upon the focal color and make it seem different. Red in blue light looks different from red in orange light. Red in the distance looks different from red in the foreground. Red on dull days appears quite changed on bright days. Countless other factors impinge upon color to make it relative to prevailing conditions. To notice these changing effects is one of the attributes of visually minded individuals. *During this important period which precedes the crisis of adolescence, the visually minded child will begin to adjust colors to his visual impressions, whereas the non-visually minded child depends greatly on his emotional reactions toward color.* Yet we must be aware of the fact that most of the children are between the extremes, and may show both characteristics.

Much has been written about the psychology of color, its emotional effects on individuals. Such emotional reactions to color are to a large extent determined associatively, through the effect of past experiences.

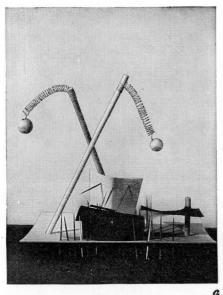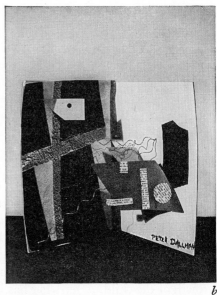

a   *b*

Fig. 33. Design in Material. (Courtesy Educational Project, Museum of Modern Art, N. Y.) *a.* fourteen-year-old boy; *b.* fourteen and a half years.

Thus, to one individual horror can mean red (he might relate it associatively to blood), whereas to another it might be green. Psychology has made it evident that all rigid theories which refer emotional reactions to color are to a great extent outmoded. At least generalizations should not be applied to teaching to deny the effectiveness of the use of color theories in leading to creative approaches. Emotional reactions to color are highly individualized. The nonvisually minded child uses color often in contradiction to nature according to his individual emotional reaction. Color, therefore, becomes highly subjective in its meaning.[1]

Also with regard to color, the main problem during this age period will be to find means of stimulation that gradually lead the child to the stages of critical awareness. If this is done gradually, the child will not feel the shocks resulting from the awareness of the discrepancy between his mental picture and his actual representation. If we now can stimulate the child effectively to see or feel color in the stage of unawareness, we will prevent him from being disappointed at his "inability" to express his mental picture. The better the color stimulation in the unaware and critical-awareness stages, the more have we succeeded in bridging the gap of the crisis

[1] Corcoran, Ambrose, "The Variability of Children's Responses to Color Stimuli." Unpublished doctoral dissertation, The Pennsylvania State Unversity, 1953.

of adolescence. How this can effectively be done will be discussed in the section, "Stimulation."

DESIGN

With the awakening concept for reality, the conscious approach toward design becomes increasingly significant. Whereas the visually minded child will more and more be concerned with the aesthetic function of design, expressed by the feeling for "color schemes, rhythm, and balance," the nonvisually minded child will more and more show the tendency to work either directly with materials and use them functionally or concentrate more on emotional abstractions. Both groups should be given the type of stimulation needed for developing properly (Fig. 33a). Since the child is still in his "unaware approaches," burdening him with theories would be out of place. The only effect would be an inhibited reaction at a time when the child still proceeds freely in his creative work. We shall see in the section, "Stimulation," how design and color are closely interwoven.

The visually minded child might start to relate forms of nature to design. The stylizing effect—that is, the process of simplification, might become a part of the child's experience. Since the laws of symmetry are more related to dogmatic periods, including periods of symbolism, it seems to be more and more out of place to include it at a time when individualism, emotions, and social changes dominate in our lives. Consequently, free forms invented by the child should be used for design purposes.

During this period it is important to confront the child with industrial products as examples of good functional use of different materials. From the kitchen utensil and furniture to the streamlined car or machine, the child should learn to adapt his design to the material. The child should be given an opportunity to use all types of scraps creatively, even if it is only for the pleasure of working out forms or shapes in different materials without relating them to a definite purpose (Fig. 33b).

If a potter's wheel is obtainable, the child will enjoy operating it. However, the child should be allowed to play with the wheel without being hampered by too many technical procedures. Skill and body coordinations definitely will greatly improve the child's confidence in his abilities, which is of so vital importance for the period of the crisis of adolescence. The creation of forms that can stand the critical awareness of the adolescent will further help to bridge the gap between childhood and adolescence.

In the section, "Stimulation," there is described an approach to the use of color for emotional abstractions which are a part of the design concept.

MODELING—TWO DIFFERENT APPROACHES

The meaning of modeling during this preparatory stage is of special significance. Here, better than in any other field, we can build a bridge between the unconscious approach to three-dimensional expression (which we called *modeling*) and the conscious approach (which we shall call *sculpturing*). This can be done easier in clay than in painting, since the difference between modeling and sculpturing is not as great as the difference in the approaches to painting, in which, especially for the visually minded, a whole transfiguration from the plane into three-dimensional space takes place. No change of such importance can be seen in clay work. Therefore, it is much easier to prepare the child in this field to face his work with critical awareness, with confidence, and without the shock which endangers his further creative production.

Since environment is excluded or, at least, minimized in sculpturing, visually minded as well as nonvisually minded children face the same subject matter. This also contributes greatly to make modeling a particularly effective means of stimulation. The meaning of clay work during this important period of transition is to lead the child from modeling to sculpturing in such a way that the child does not become aware of this transition. This can best be done by modeling either from real or imaginative poses. In real poses, the model is posing throughout the session. An imaginative pose is one that the model or the student subjectively suggests only in the beginning as a means of stimulation, but the actual modeling is done without the pose. The pose serves then only as stimulus and control. The latter procedure, if well handled, is by far the better one. In both cases, however, it is necessary to give the pose a definite meaning: "A man carrying a heavy load," "A scrubwoman," "Tired," and so forth. The procedure of stimulation will be discussed in the following section. Without giving the pose a meaning, we would frustrate those children who have a preference for emotional interpretation (Fig. 34a).

The difference between the visually minded and subjectively minded approaches can be seen both in working process as well as in the choice of subject matter. The visually minded group will concentrate on the changing effects caused by the differences of the motions of the posing figure in light and shadows. The nonvisually minded will use the posing figure merely as a stimulus and will model their subjective experiences of the "man carrying a heavy load," "the scrubwoman," and so forth. Whereas the visually minded child will most likely lean closer to the correct interpretation of the posing model, the nonvisually minded will give his own

Fig. 34a. "Jacob's Dream" (modeled in clay by thirteen-year-old boy). The motion was first experienced on the self.

subjective expression. With regard to the difference of the working method, we shall see that the visually minded uses more and more the analytic method of pulling out the details from the whole. Naturally, this corresponds to visual thinking. When we think of a tree, we first think of the tree in its entirety and then of the details—the structure of the bark, the branches, the kind of twigs, and the foliage. The synthetic method, however, will be used only by the nonvisually minded child. His thinking relates to the details that are of emotional significance.[2] He builds up his final impression out of a synthesis of partial impressions. It is therefore of vital significance not to divert to the analytic process a child who uses the synthetic method. We would only disturb or frustrate the child's thinking.

In the same way that we encourage the visually minded child in his modeling by directing his attention to the visual changes of form caused through light and shadow, do we encourage the nonvisually minded individual by stimulating subjective experiences. This way we gradually move from the unconscious form of modeling to the conscious approach of sculpturing. Henceforth no scenes which include environment and figures should be used. If such scenes are needed for illustrative purposes, they

[2] Zawacki, Alexander. "An Experimental Study of Analytic Versus Synthetic Modelings and Drawings of Children." Unpublished doctoral dissertation, The Pennsylvania State University, 1955.

Fig. 34b. "Cow and calf" (modeled by thirteen-year-old girl).

should no longer be done on a creative base, but more as scale models. Scenes like an "Indian Village" containing Indians no longer satisfy the approaching critical awareness. Modeling shifts gradually to sculpturing by eliminating all illustrative tendencies and by concentrating on motion and expression of the human figure.

ART STIMULATION

Since this stage seems to be of special significance for the further development of the child, especially with regard to the crisis of adolescence, the following generalizations will indicate clearly the issues involved. As is the case throughout this developmental level, the most important contribution art education can make toward the adjustment of personality is to help bridge the gap between childhood and adulthood. The more gradually this can be done, the less will this period be characterized by disappointments, frustrations, or even shocks. As we have previously said, one of the characteristics of adolescence is the change of the imaginative activity from uncontrolled to controlled, and can best be seen in the different ways children and adults play. If this change comes suddenly—that is, if the child

Plate 7. "Parade." (13 years) The visually minded child feels as a specta-
or, watching the parade. He uses color in its changing effects, mixing it
reely to express atmosphere and depth. Notice the glaring effect of
tmosphere achieved by "dissolving" the color surfaces. (See page 227.)
Courtesy Educational Project, Museum of Modern Art, N. Y.)

Plate 8. "My Barber." (14 years) The haptically minded
child uses color for expressing his subjective relationships to the environment. Color is often used purely
symbolically with no visual reference to the object. The
child does not feel as a spectator but is subjectively bound
up with his experience. He often uses plain color as in
this painting. He is not interested in depicting depth or
atmosphere. (See pages 265 and 266.)

becomes suddenly critically aware of his "childish behavior reactions" or his "uncontrolled imaginative activity," the usual result is a shock. As one of the consequences of this shock the child stops his creative work. He "can't draw anything" because his sudden critical awareness realizes the "inefficient" childish approach. The drawing expression seems "childish" and "ridiculous" because of the sudden awakening of an adult attitude.

The problem is how to make this change gradual. If we can stimulate the child's unaware production to such an extent that it reaches in his unaware stages a "creative maturity" which will be able to stand the critical awareness which once will set in, we have kept the child from making a sudden change, and have protected him from disappointments or shocks with regard to his changing imaginative activity. In general this can be done by making the child aware of his own achievements at a time when he is not yet aware of them. The graph below indicates more clearly the effect of proper art stimulation on personality development.

From this graph it becomes evident that if we did not prepare the child for the oncoming crisis of adolescence he would greatly fluctuate between unaware and controlled reactions as is indicated by the zigzag line in the graph. Such unstable behavior is typical for a crisis. The child feels torn between his childish reactions and his intellectual control. This behavior is typical of the adolescent youth. On the one hand he is ashamed to participate in childish play activities although emotionally he would love to participate in them, and on the other he cannot participate in adult activi-

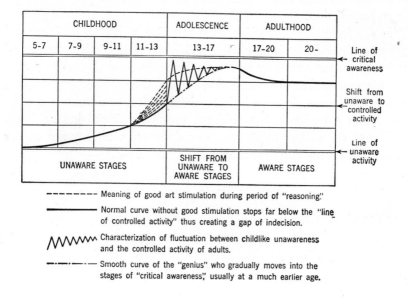

-------- Meaning of good art stimulation during period of "reasoning."

———— Normal curve without good stimulation stops far below the "line of controlled activity" thus creating a gap of indecision.

ΛΛΛWWW Characterization of fluctuation between childlike unawareness and the controlled activity of adults.

—·—·—·— Smooth curve of the "genius" who gradually moves into the stages of "critical awareness," usually at a much earlier age.

ties because he is not accepted as an adult. How often do we see those "lonely" boys who whittle their bows all by themselves or those girls who play with their dolls "secretly," because they would not officially participate in childish play activities and have not found social acceptance as adults.

The more we can raise the child's awareness during the stage of reasoning without doing undue harm to his creativity, the more do we condition the child to facing the crisis of adolescence properly. In the graph this raising of awareness is indicated by the many interrupted lines which show the different degrees of rise. In the motivation this is as simple as this: "Johnny, tell me *how* did you get this purple color?" or "Mary, tell me, what did you do to make your house look that distant?" or "Joe, how did you get this tense feeling in your figure?"—It simply means making the child aware of his *own* achievements.

It is self-understood that such motivations to raise the child's conscious approach must never occur *during* the creative process. There they would greatly interfere with the intuitive character of art. They must always occur afterwards.

It may be interesting to note that according to available research no such fluctuation occurs in the genius during adolescence. As indicated in the graph he moves smoothly from a stage of "lesser maturity and perfection" to one of greater without the "interferences" and "shocks" of adolescence. For example, the preadolescent Dürer or Mozart had already the characteristics of the more mature one. More research would be necessary to determine whether this characteristic can be used for purposes of guidance and prediction.

If in the following discussion on motivation a distinction is made between visually and nonvisually minded children it should be borne in mind that these two groups are by no means distinctly divided. On the contrary, as has been pointed out before, and documented by research,[3] these groups are on a continuum, frequently intermixed with a preference toward the one or other experience. It would not only be artificial but against the intention of the author to exaggerate a dichotomy. If they are discussed separately, it is only done for matters of clarification.[4]

Human figure

For the visually minded, the critical awareness during adolescence demands the drawing of correct proportions and motions with their chang-

[3] Lowenfeld, Viktor, "Tests for Visual and Haptical Aptitude." *American Journal of Psychology*. Vol. 58, 1945.
[4] See also page 263.

ing effects. The nonvisually minded require greater concentration on gesture and expression. How can we stimulate these factors without doing harm to the unaware, creative approach of the child? Three approaches are particularly valuable during this period. In "teaching" proportions at this age, *it goes without saying that proportions must never be measured.* Such a procedure would only inhibit his further creative work, since the child would start measuring proportions and apply rigid methods which are the death of any creative work. Therefore, means of stimulation should be found which make the child *experience* the correct kind of proportion. This can best be done by the choice of topics. *Topics that compare the sizes of the self to environment are best suited for such purposes.* Although it would not be useful to lead the child's attention consciously to the fact of comparing sizes, it will be important to include this factor in the discussion. As an example, we give the special meaning of the topic, "Fighting the Fire in a Burning House." After asking, "Who has seen a house burning?" we will receive many descriptions of burning houses.

These many descriptions should have a proper balance of visual and nonvisual experiences. Some children will be attracted by the beauty of the flames and their glowing colors, others will "feel" with the people who were living in the house and will become emotionally involved in the fate of those who lost their belongings. Still other children will be more concerned with the technical procedures of fighting the flames. Especially the boys might become interested in this angle. But at all times we will have opportunities to direct attention to comparative proportions with questions like: "How high did we have to climb to fight the fire?" "Did people jump out of the window?" "From what height did they jump?" "How long was the firemen's hose?" "How far up could they reach without climbing the ladder?" and so forth. Such questions will inspire both groups: the visually minded because they become visually aware of the comparative proportions, and the nonvisually minded because they refer in their drawings to the body actions and its emotional qualities. Many other topics like: "Sitting Under a Tree," "Reaching for an Apple on a Tree," "Sitting in a Rowboat," "Looking Out of the Window" and so forth, will stimulate the child to compare sizes. However, any "correction" of proportions by the teacher would only frustrate the child. If the child does not react to the mentioned stimuli, it is only a sign that the child is not affected by them. An imposition would not help him in his experience. Repeated trials, however, may make him aware.

The second approach suitable to prepare the child for the coming critical awareness of sizes and proportions is the use of posing models as a means of stimulation. Here, too, we must give both groups a possibility for self-expression. That is why the posing model should be given a meaning, as has been said before. As an example, we cite a particular pose: "Carrying a Heavy Load on the Shoulder." "Who carries heavy loads?" "Have you *seen* people carrying heavy loads?" "Have *you yourself* ever carried a heavy load? At what opportunity?" "Of course, workers on the docks carry sacks of flour, or a poor woman carries a bundle of wood on her shoulder, or refugees fleeing from their burning houses." "How do we carry a heavy load?" (Let the boy or girl pose while putting a load on his or her shoulder.) "You could not go upright, very well, could you? You would lose your balance. I also notice that you have your feet apart and not together. Why do you do that, for the same purpose of holding better balance?" "How do you hold the load? I notice your hands are close to the shoulder. I see, because in this way you have a better support on the shoulder than if you were to hold them out." "In what direction are you looking when you carry the load? Surely you have to look in the direction you are walking."

All these questions will bring the pose into a higher consciousness. The visually minded will draw what they, now consciously, see, whereas the nonvisually minded will refer to the experiences of the self. For both groups, however, it will be of benefit if the posing model does not keep the pose. The visually minded will have to concentrate much more on their visual experience by memorizing the image, and the nonvisually minded will use the posing model only as a stimulus, concentrating otherwise entirely on expression—that is, the mental picture he has formed, which is a resultant of his body feelings and emotional experiences (Fig. 35).

The third approach for getting the representation of the human figure more closely related to the adolescent stages, deals with a method in modeling. It is most stimulating to characterize first the personality of the modeled figure and let it then go through the motion as if it were a motion picture. For example: "A visitor (your grandpa) comes to see you. He sits down and tells you a story." The child would first model grandpa as he arrives and would actually put him then into the position which finally indicates telling a story. "How does your grandpa sit when he tells you a story? Does he hold a book in his hand? Does he support his head? Does he stretch out his legs or does he cross them?" and so forth. The plasticity of clay permits the expression of this kinetic experience. While going through the motions, the child will grow more consciously aware of them, and in turn will bring himself closer to a level of creative production capable of withstanding the critical awareness, which has to be expected soon.

Stimulation of space

The stimulation of spatial experiences again will have to be channeled in two directions. First, to prepare the visually minded child for a space concept that is more closely related to the adolescent concept of realizing the visual space. Second, to prepare the nonvisually minded child for the importance of the emotional tie-up of space and the self. We know much too well of the frightening effect which teaching of perspective has on some of our children. This effect is especially frightening for children who have no desire for the realization of such a space concept. This group, which is the nonvisually minded, has no comprehension of this way of perceiving space. However, *there is no need for including perspective in our art program as long as there is no demand for it* from the children.

For the visually minded, means of introducing a visual space concept should be found which excludes the dry teaching of technical data of perspective. To do that, it is most inspiring to refer even in the visual space concept to nonvisual means, to experience the different intensities of emotional experiences which are both far away and close to us. "What would happen, if one among us would suddenly die?" All children would immediately realize the tremendous intensity of this experience when it is so closely related to us. At the same time, the deaths of thousands of people on battlefields, in factories, and other places do not affect us much. The intensity of this experience grows and diminishes with the distance. Visual space, too, increases and diminishes in size and intensity, depending on the distance. However, in visual space this intensity depends only on the visual interest which we take in objects close to us, whereas in emotional experiences we can focus our greatest interest even on things that are not close to us. Thus, the intensity of nonvisual space is governed by the emotions we associate with the experience.

Most important, however, is that a good teacher must always start on the level of the individual and extend his frame of reference from there on. If for a child the expression of distant space, that is, perspective, has become important, the teacher must support the child's desire by using the child's present understanding and achievement of it, as has been pointed out on page 5. It would, however, be entirely wrong to impose such knowledge on a child who has no desire for it. We know too well how many children have been frustrated by their inability to comprehend perspective. To preclude the possibility of frustrating either experience in our stimulations, we have to refer to visual differences as well as to the different intensities of emotions.

Fig. 35. "Thinking" (thirteen years). The child still approaches his subject matter without critical awareness, yet his work shows a clear concept of the self. The motion is experienced on the self.

Color

Realistic color—that is, the color of the visually minded, can only be stimulated by actual experiences with nature. The different intensities—brightness and dullness and use of colors with regard to distance, shadows, and lights—can be brought into the consciousness only by observing them. Few children, and by no means all adults, can do that. We ourselves comprehend how little we see in comparison to some artist's concept of color. And some of us know that we are unable to see the "blue shadow" which we are supposed to see according to the old method of teaching. Not all of us can see the changing effects of colors, and there is no need for all of us to see them. What is a stimulation for one can mean frustration for another. There exist too many instances of frustrated children and unhappy adults, compelled to enroll in art classes in which they received visual stimuli only and in which they were forced "to see color."

Personification of color is a method that can be used for both groups, though it will appeal more to the nonvisually minded children. By personification of color is meant the seeing and dealing with color as if it were a living being. For example, the telling of some such story as the following would be effective. "Imagine you feel very happy and want to go on a hike. Everything around you is marvelous, just wonderful. Environment is beautiful, bright, and the atmosphere is happy. As you walk you see in the distance your friend, your most beloved friend. You thought how marvelous it would be to have him with you. And there he comes. Now you are talking about the most intimate things, and you become so friendly that you feel almost united with him. As you continue on your way, the atmosphere suddenly changes for the worse. It gets dark, dreary, and mysterious. And as you go on, someone stops you on the way and tells you that you are not permitted to continue; this road is not for you."

Now imagine that you are "red" in this story. How does red feel in a marvelous environment, happy and bright? What color would you choose as an environment for red to make it happy? How would you indicate to make red move on smoothly? What color is the best friend of red, whom red expected to meet? When red and his friend were talking so intimately, to which color would they unite? As they went on and the atmosphere darkened and the environment became mysterious, how would red change? How would its friend change? How would environment change with regard to red and its friend? What color would come in their way and prohibit them from continuing?

Of course there are hundreds of such stories. Almost any story can be translated into "color." This personification of color introduces it as a living symbol. No verbal theory can ever give as good an introduction into the living qualities of color as such personifications. Such an introduction into abstract design will also lead into the understanding of the nature of emotional abstract design. It is much better than music as a means of stimulation, since we have here means to refer to real living qualities. Such an interpretation of color will be highly individualized and the control by the teacher can only be in the direction of color relationships. "Is this really your friend? But he is quite different from you, isn't he?" Only such stimulations should be used to direct the child in his color intuitions.

Through such methods the child will not only gain more confidence in his use of color, but will also approach a more conscious relationship to it, which is vitally necessary for the proper adjustment to the coming stage, the crisis of adolescence.

The following list of topics should serve only as examples for the different kinds of stimulation, which all have the same aim—to bridge the gap between childhood and adolescence, unawareness and critical awareness, which so often has shown its disastrous effect on personality development.

Topics

ACTION FROM IMAGINATION
> Farmer Going Home Before Storm.
> Refugees Fleeing on Road.
> Trapeze Artist.
> Theatre Performances of Dramatic Content.
> Rowing a Boat.
> Fishing in Pond.
> Hunting Scenes.
> All Gymnastic Experiences.
> Men Working on the Street.
> Men Digging a Hole.

FROM POSING MODEL (NOT FRONTAL POSING)
> Woman Scrubbing a Floor.
> A Beggar on Street Corner.
> Woman Sweeping Floor.
> Tired from Work.
> Lifting a Heavy Load.

A Mother Feeding a Baby.
A Girl Reading.
Thinking at Desk.

STIMULATION OF PROPORTIONS

Sitting Under a Tree.
Burning House with Ladder Going up on It.
Climbing a Tree.
Reaching for an Apple on a Tree.
Looking Out of the Window.

DRAMATIC

Illustrations of books or stories.

COLOR

Before the Storm on the Field.
Impressions.
Cold in Winter.
Fall Storm.
Snow Storm.
Sunset.
Introduce moods.
Personification of color.

MURALS

Educational and historical related to subject
matter signified by words *from* and *to:*
From Raw Product to Final Product
(science).
From Birth to Death (history).
From Coast to Coast (geography, travel).

FRIEZES

All topics with continuity:
Pulling Sled up Hill and down.
Fruit Harvest.
Carnival Scene.
Races.

IN DESIGN

Characterize a profession by means of symbolic
designs (telegraph worker, tailor, shoemaker,
cook, physician, painter, architect, railway
conductor and so forth).

Use different materials in a functional way.

Abstract designs made from different materials
to learn their function: wire, sheet metal,
glass, wood, cardboard.

Knowledge of industrial designs: utensils, furniture.

IN CLAY

From posing model (topics as discussed).
Actions from imagination.

Kinetic motions:
Picking up Something (potatoes).
Mother Holding the Baby.
Getting Tired.
Sitting down, Reading a Book.

Techniques

As has been said before, technique is closely related to the need for
expression. The technique which does not help the child to express his
particular desires is not a good one. During this period, the visually minded
child relates his work more and more to reality. The most suitable technique will be one which easily permits the portrayal of effects in nature.
Since atmosphere and sky in nature are not opaque but have a transparent
character, a medium having such transparent qualities would be most suitable. This technique is *water color.* At this stage we can even encourage
the child to make visual use of the happy accidents which occur when the
colors in a sky run together and form "clouds" in the most different shapes.
At first the whole paper may be moistened with brush or hands before
the child starts to paint. Since the child now approaches his painting
visually, such accidents as the formation of clouds or the mixing of colors
will stimulate the child for his next work. Running of colors, which could
have been most discouraging at a time when linear representation dominated the pre-schematic or schematic stage, is now most stimulating.

Referring again to the quotation of Leonardo da Vinci to the effect
that an art work should look complete in every stage, will help in stimulating the visually minded child in building up a visual concept. The sequence
of how a picture is painted is here of deciding influence. For example, we
are thinking of a painting in which farmers rush home before the rising
storm. If we would ask the child to stop painting after he has finished the

stormy sky (which covers the *whole* sheet, of course), the sky as such could exist and could be called complete. If the child then added the field with its storm waves and we interrupted the child again, the picture again would look complete. The child might then add a farm or a tree and finally would paint the farmers in the foreground as they hurriedly leave the field. The picture has grown organically and looked complete at every stage. Besides that, we have the feeling that the sky is really behind the tree or the house without appearing to cut out the part of the sky covered by it. This *organic* growth of the picture is a vital part of a method of approach which will help to bridge the gap to which we have referred during this period so frequently. In order to paint on the sky, the child must wait until it is dry; otherwise the foreground would blur with the background. It is also of great advantage to use opaque colors, such as poster paint, for the foreground. This creates a still stronger feeling for the transparency of the atmosphere and the opaque quality of objects.

With regard to mural painting, it is suggested that either egg tempera or ordinary poster paint be used. If possible, murals should be painted directly, but if this is not possible, good craft paper tacked on the wall, or stretched on stretchers while it is moist (when it dries, it tightens) will serve very well. For painting directly on the wall, one or two coats of flat oil paint will serve as sizing. Bristle brushes for large spaces and hair brushes for details are advisable. Preferably, murals should not be carefully planned at this age level because careful planning destroys much of the intuitive quality and reduces interest. A small sketch, which tells approximately what will be on the mural, will be sufficient. Children should have all possible freedom in painting and organizing murals. Often it is good practice to permit two or more children to work on one mural. It must be remembered that *a mural is a decoration of a wall and that it should tell a story.* Sizes can differ with regard to importance. Since the child is still in the unaware creative stage, no further explanations should be given about the nature of a mural, but the teacher should have in mind that a naturalistic execution is contrary to the essence of decoration.

✓Techniques in clay refer to modeling, which gradually shifts to sculpturing and pottery. Also here, especially with regard to the latter, no planning should be done. Planning pottery belongs to the last stages and is most difficult. Both techniques have been discussed previously.

All other techniques such as linoleum cuts or designing in different materials should be continued in the direction indicated in the general discussion on design.

EVALUATION CHART

Stage of Reasoning

	None	Some	Much
Intellectual Growth			
Does the work indicate a complete absence of schemata?			
Is there a tendency toward a more conscious approach of subject matter?			
Does the child give attention to meaningful details?			
Does the child's work indicate an alertness either toward expressive details or differentiated appearance?			
Has the child become aware of the use of techniques?			
Emotional Growth			
Does the child identify himself not only with his experience but also with his environment?			
Is intensity of experience expressed either by exaggerations, or by differentiation of objects in distance?			
Does color serve as a means of expression either by using it symbolically or by referring it to mood?			
Is the child losing some of the stiffness of figures characteristic of the gang age?			
Does the child freely project either his emotions or his environment?			
Is the child experimental in his mode of expression? (Style.)			
Social Growth			
Has the child become aware of his social environment in his creative work?			
Does the child characterize environment or figures?			
Are spatial relationships obtained?			
Does the child identify himself with others in his work?			
Perceptual Growth			
Visual:			
Has the child become aware of his visual environment?			
Does the child express depth in his drawings?			

Perceptual Growth	Does the child include the horizontal line? Does the child include lights and shadows? Does the child observe wrinkles and folds in clothes when in motion? Does the child change intensity of line, color, and shades in distant objects? Has the child completely departed from base lines? *Non-Visual:* Has the child become aware of his own subjective relationships to his environment? Does the child express kinesthetic sensations? (Linear representations or movements?) Does the child express tactile or textural experiences? Does the child express body feelings? Does the child contrast darks and lights as means of expression? Does the child retrogress to base lines?
Physical Growth	Has the child become aware of the use of joints in his drawing of figures? Does the child clearly distinguish between the representation of boys and girls? Are characterizations according to differences in size and age visible?
Aesthetic Growth	Does the child distribute the parts of his creative work in a meaningful way? Does the child relate design characteristics to the meaning of the work? Is the technique used to its best advantage? Are colors related to each other? Is there a relationship among design, material, and purpose?
Creative Growth	Does the child's growing critical awareness keep him free from inhibitions? Does the child create without intellectual interferences? Is the child uninfluenced by his classmates? Can one easily distinguish this child's work from that of others?

SUMMARY   PSEUDOREALISTIC STAGE OF REASONING—ELEVEN TO THIRTEEN YEARS

Characteristics	Human Figure	Space	Color	Design	Stimulation Topics	Techniques
Developed intelligence, yet unawareness.	Introduction of joints.	Three-dimensional space expressed by diminishing sizes of distant objects.	Changes of color in nature with regard to distance and mood (visually minded).	Personification of color.	Figures in dramatic environment.	Water color.
Realistic approach (unconscious).	Visual attention to changes introduced through motion or atmosphere (visually minded).	Horizon line (visually minded).		Conscious approach to stylizing of industrial products (symbols for professions).	Actions from imagination and posing model (with meaning).	Mixed technique (water color and tempera).
Tendency toward visual- or non-visual-mindedness.	Proportion.	Retrogression of non-visually minded to base lines or expression of environment only when significant.	Emotional reaction to color of non-visually minded (not related to nature).		Relation of proportion of figures to environment.	Poster paint.
Love for action and dramatization.	Emphasis on expression of non-visually minded.			Function of different materials, and simple designs related to them.	Color moods.	Bristle brush.
					Color expression through personification. Illustrations of dramatic stories.	Hair brush.
					Murals ("from—to"). See design.	Linoleum.
						Clay.
						Materials for design (wood, metal, stone).

From what has been said it becomes quite clear that the more we prepare the child during his unaware stages to develop creative freedom and to use approaches in his art expression which can stand the stages of critical awareness, the smoother will be his growth into the stages of adulthood. The *undecided period*, however, in which the individual feels grown out of childhood and not yet fit for adulthood, one of the most decisive periods in life, will be discussed in the next chapter.

As the child becomes more critically aware of his creative product, there is an increase in the complexity of evaluating his creative work in terms of growth. Only the child produces in a straightforward fashion, projecting his total personality into his work without inhibitions. The adult usually wants to conform to certain standards. These standards do not exist for the child. It is for this reason that the child gives us a true picture of himself. The more the child becomes aware of external standards, the less will his work directly reveal his personality. The following growth analysis is made under the presumption that the child still creates without the intrusion of set standards and reveals himself in his creative work.

INTERPRETATION OF INDIVIDUAL GROWTH CHARACTERISTICS PERTAINING TO THE PSEUDOREALISTIC STAGE

Intellectual growth

For the purpose of better clarification, Fig. 30, the painting of a beggar painted by a twelve-year-old boy, is used for explaining the different growth criteria.

During the stage of reasoning the child has obtained enough critical attitude to make him aware of the world which surrounds him. This growing "realism" completely denies a generalization of objects or figures. That is why the first question in the evaluation chart is concerned with the mode of expression of the child. In particular, we are interested in the child's complete departure from using schemata. Indeed, in Fig. 30 no indications are seen of a conceptual use in representation of figures or objects. We can say, therefore, that the child's work indicates a complete absence of schemata. A child who still thinks in terms of generalizations (schemata) has intellectually been unable to penetrate into a visual world which recognizes individual differences. This recognition brings about a more conscious approach toward a subject matter of which the child has become more intellectually aware. In Fig. 30 the child visualizes a beggar who stands under a bridge. This is apparently an impression of which the child has become consciously aware while walking over the bridge himself. How much the child knows about a beggar is seen in the meaningful details which the child uses to characterize him. The beggar in Fig. 30 is characterized by many meaningful details. He stretches out his hand, he holds a cane in the other hand, he is apparently blind, he wears an old hat, long hair, and a beard. All these meaningful details show the child's knowledge of a beggar. The next question in the evaluation chart deals with the child's alertness toward expressive details or differentiated appearance. In Fig. 30 such differentiation is clearly expressed in the different treatment of the inside of the restaurant. A child who is not intellectually alert would have a tendency to treat such details alike. Whether or not the child has become aware of the use of techniques cannot be stated with certainty from one example and without observing the child. Indications are that the child who produced Fig. 30 is aware of the medium he uses. This can be seen from the different ways of using the merging quality of water color as well as the linear brush strokes which clearly stand out in the picture.

Emotional growth

Emotional growth during the stage of reasoning is characterized not only by the child's ability to identify himself with *his* experiences but also with those of his environment. This identification with the needs of others is usually seen in the intensity with which an experience is expressed. This can be done either by emphasizing important expressive parts or by differentiating the intensity with which objects are expressed. In Fig. 30 the child closely identifies himself with the blind beggar. He does it to such an extent that his feelings for the beggar's outstretched hand made him exaggerate this detail. As the emotional relationships to the different objects vary, so varies also the mode of expression. It is interesting to note that the people walking on the bridge are painted in silhouette only. This difference in dealing with details clearly shows the child's emotional interest in his main topic. The child may use color either to serve as a means of expression or as a means to characterize mood. In Fig. 30 the child has done both. By painting the beggar's face and hands in green color he has expressed a color symbolism rather than mere appearance. The mood of a rainy day is also expressed by gray and wet-looking colors.

The next question in the evaluation chart deals with the child's more flexible representation of figures as compared to the stiffer figures characteristic of the gang age. The child no longer is concerned with mere characterization of external features but has become interested in expression. In Fig. 30 "stiffness" has completely vanished. The child now freely projects his experience into his drawing. The realistic tendencies of this child, however, are clearly visible in spite of the desire to project his emotions.

The last question in the evaluation chart on Emotional Growth deals with the child's attitude toward his mode of expression. An emotionally free and flexible child should have an altogether experimental attitude. His style should not be a fixed one. While certain personality characteristics may always stand out in his work, the approach toward his mode of expression must never become rigid. We could better answer this question by looking at several of the child's paintings. With some reservation, however, we can say that this child's approach toward his mode of expression seems to be rather flexible. We can say that because he quickly changes modes of expression even in one drawing. The painting of the house is done almost completely in outlines. The silhouettes of the figures on the bridge and the bridge itself, which reveals the structure, are painted in solid colors only with some differentiated details. The beggar is painted solidly, partly in outlines, however, with clearly differentiated details. Such a difference in modes of expression in one painting may indicate that the child deals flexibly with his painting approaches in different drawings also. This is an indication of the child's ability to adjust quickly to new situations—an ability which is one of the most important criteria of emotional growth.

Social growth

Social growth during the stage of reasoning can most of all be seen in the child's ability to conceive of his social environment consciously. The first question in the evaluation chart deals with this ability. From Fig. 30 we can readily see that this child shows great awareness of social problems in his creative work. He has developed a great sensitivity toward his environment. This is expressed particularly in the different types of clothing which he gives his figures. But also, the whole arrangement of placing the beggar under a bridge over which several people are walking shows his social awareness. The child also characterizes his environment. He expresses this characterization by the careful choice of the environment as well as by the inclusion of meaningful details. The next question in the chart refers to the child's ability to obtain spatial relationship. A child who has difficulty relating objects or figures to the space in which they are represented usually thinks in terms of the figures or object in isolation. Since it is one of the most important criteria of social growth to posses the ability to cooperate, that is, relate each other's needs to one another, the ability to obtain spatial relationship is an important criterion of social growth. In Fig. 30 the child has demonstrated this ability by closely correlating the beggar and the space under the bridge. He also related the people on the bridge to the bridge and the beggar. In drawing the background and significantly contrasting the "restaurant" with the beggar he showed again not only his spatial but also his social awareness.

From the foregoing it becomes quite evident and obvious that the child who painted Fig. 30 could only have painted by closely identifying himself with the needs of the beggar. He thus signified his high degree of social consciousness. It seems apparent that all questions pertaining to social growth should be checked in the evaluation chart in the column "much."

Perceptual growth

As has been emphasized in the text, the stage of reasoning is characterized, among other things, by a tendency toward two different types of creation. These two tendencies show themselves best in the preferences for certain perceptual experiences. In the following growth analysis the different experiences are divided into "visual" and "nonvisual." We shall see, however, that extreme cases are relatively rare and most often both tendencies are present in one work. Yet there is rarely found an *equal* distribution of both aptitudes toward creative expression of experiences. In most of the cases there is a predominance of visual or nonvisual experiences, as we shall also see in Fig. 30.

In this painting the child does not approach his final product with critical awareness. The way in which he elongated the beggar's hands is a clear indication of it. The child himself is not yet clear about the type of experience which is most significant to him. To answer the first question in the evaluation chart, the child *has* become aware of his visual environment. An indication of this is the diminishing size of distant objects. The beggar being in the foreground is much larger than the restaurant in the background. The second question refers to the child's expression of depth. This question is difficult to answer. Certainly, the final impression of this painting is not one of depth. One has more the impression of flatness. The only part in the picture which continually extends from the foreground into the background is the sidewalk on which the beggar stands. However, this sidewalk is drawn completely flat. There is no indication of perspective space. It is, therefore, questionable whether or not the diminishing size of distant objects should be regarded as an expression of depth. Knowing that the child has not yet experienced perspective space it is also question-

able whether or not he includes the horizontal line. There is no indication
as to the meaning of the space to the left of the house. From the color it
appears to be sky. If this is the case, the child did not include the horizontal
line in his picture. On the contrary, there seems to be a visual contradiction
between the pavement on which the beggar stands and the background
of the picture.

The next question deals with the representation of light and shadow.
There are no clear indications of the child's desire to include and understand the meaning of lights and shadows. We have to make a distinction
between lights and shadows as an indication of visual awareness of the
three-dimensional quality of objects, and lights and darks as an indication
of the value of color. For this drawing, lights and darks clearly refer to the
value of color. This can clearly be seen in the light pale green coloring
of the face.

The observation of wrinkles and folds in clothes when in motion usually
is also an indication of visual awareness. A child who merely characterizes
a figure by means of its clothing usually does not include wrinkles and
folds. The child who produced Fig. 30 did not include wrinkles and folds.
The child, however, changed the intensity of lines, shades, and colors in
distant objects. This can best be seen if we compare the definite lines and
shades in the beggar with those of the people on the bridge and the people
in the restaurant. With regard to the next question in the evaluation chart,
the child does not seem to have completely departed from base-line expressions. As an indication of this we point to the base line of the house and
also to the bridge used as a base line for the people who walk on it.

The next four questions in the evaluation chart deal with the nonvisual
experiences of the child. Whether or not the child has become aware of his
own subjective relationships to his environment usually can be seen in the
emphasis which the child gives to meaningful objects or details. In Fig. 30
the emphasis on the beggar as the meaningful part in the picture is quite
obvious. Also, the amount of details which he uses in expressing the beggar
is indicative of his subjective relationship.

The next question deals with the child's kinesthetic experiences. While
they do not seem to be predominant, they can be found in the dominance
of linear expression. The line as such is of kinesthetic origin. Even by its
geometric definition a line is created by the movement of a dot. Usually a
predominance of the linear element in an art work is indicative of a strong
kinesthetic experience. Without any doubt, in Fig. 30, the line is an important means of expression. The other feeling for movement is expressed in
the representation of the rain.

While there is no explicit expression of tactile qualities, the body feelings which the child expressed by the elongated hands and the significance of the closed eyes are convincing. Also, the leaning toward the wall is clearly expressed by the omission of the other leg.

It has been said before that the child uses lights and darks as contrasting elements. This, too, is usually found in the representations of those individuals who have a preference for nonvisual experiences. The treatment of lights and darks as contrasting elements rather than three-dimensional ones indicates the emphasis on the plane. It most commonly accompanies the use of base lines, whenever space is indicated on the plane. Also, this tendency can be seen in Fig. 30. Nowhere, except on the pavement, is the space between base lines utilized.

Physical growth

As has been emphasized before, no component of growth develops in an isolated fashion. Growth affects the whole individual. Only for reasons of greater clarification are the components discussed separately. In particular, physical growth overlaps many other factors of growth. We have attempted to find questions more clearly pertaining to physical than to the other components.

The first question under "Physical Growth" deals with the child's awareness of his body. This is particularly seen during this stage in the use of joints. In Fig. 30 joints are neither neglected nor are they exaggerated. The child apparently has incorporated the use of joints into his natural form of expression. Part of the body consciousness shows itself in a clear distinction between the representation of boys and girls. A clear but not overemphasized distinction shows the child's natural relationship to the other sex. A child who has not yet become aware of these differences would still express himself by means of geometric lines. A child who is overconscious of differences in the sexes would exaggerate sex characteristics. The consciousness of the body self also brings about the reference to different sizes. The next question in the evaluation chart refers to the awareness of the child regarding the different sizes in the representation of children and adults. In Fig. 30 this awareness is clearly indicated in the representation of the adult and two children on the bridge.

Aesthetic growth

Aesthetic growth affects the total child. It shows his ability to make out of chaos a meaningful whole. In creative expression this meaningful whole is perhaps the most important criterion of a work of art. The first question in the evaluation chart under aesthetic growth deals with the child's ability and desire for meaningful distribution of the single parts comprising his creative work. The meaningful distribution in a work of art depends on two criteria: the design (meaningful space as compared with meaningless space) and the content. The pure design qualities of a picture can easily be evaluated if we turn the picture 180 degrees and forget its content by looking at it as a mere abstraction. If we do this with Fig. 30 we receive quite an interesting abstract design. The dark mass on the top (left) is excellently balanced with the dark mass (beggar). Hanging on it like a scale is the lower segment (bridge). The space in between is well taken care of by the decorative treatment of the squares (windows and restaurant). No part stands out or looks too heavy. The dark spots on the segment (people on the bridge) give the "scale" or "pendulum" a fine feeling of dynamic quality.

If we look at the distribution of the content we can see that the child unconsciously placed the beggar before the only "empty space" in the picture, thus isolating him from the rest of it. His feeling for the beggar becomes obvious by placing him under the protective arch of the bridge or underpass. This arch would be meaningless were it not characterized, by the people who walk on it, as a bridge or underpass. The restaurant in the background significantly relates to the blind beggar and the child's associative feeling of the significance of food for him. We now also understand the unperspective treatment of the pavement which in this context becomes a "pedestal" to glorify the beggar.

If we take both criteria together we arrive at a significant wholeness of this creative work. This also answers the next question: the child significantly relates design characteristics to the meanings of the work.

Technically, the painting is very simple. However, the linear quality of the brush stroke is well contrasted to the solid treatment of the beggar, the bridge, the windows, etc. The technique seems to be used to its best advantage. It would be difficult to paint or reproduce this picture in a different technique. That means that no other technique can replace it, which is a distinct sign of a good use of a technique.

Also, the colors are well related to each other to give the impression of a rainy day. Apparently the fluid brush strokes on the street and pavement unconsciously create a still greater effect of wetness.

The last question, which deals with the relationship among design, material, and purpose, strictly refers to products in materials.

Creative growth

Aesthetic growth more and more becomes a part of creative growth. It is also quite apparent that without emotional freedom the child will not grow creatively. Therefore, we shall frequently find questions which may have meaning for many areas of growth. Most characteristic of the child who approaches adolescence is his growing critical awareness. In children with a weak creative impulse this growing critical awareness may counteract the child's creativity. In Fig. 30 we cannot notice such an effect upon the child. On the contrary, we can see nowhere that inhibitions affected the child's creative freedom.

Often we find, not only in children, that too much reasoning takes away the spontaneity. This particularly refers to the stage of reasoning. There are children who would like to "explain" everything in their works by logical connections. Unable to do so, these children may lose the "feeling" for their creative works if proper motivation is not applied. In Fig. 30 we still see a childish spontaneity, even if the drawing or painting may already be somewhat controlled.

Whether or not the child is influenced by his classmates can only be established with certainty by looking at the rest of the drawings of the class. The drawing, however, looks very consistent and original in its concept and, therefore, seems to be uninfluenced. Creative works which are done under strong influence never show the consistent design criteria as demonstrated for Fig. 30 under "Aesthetic Growth." This problem is usually in close connection with the child's own original interpretation. In looking at the other reproductions in the book one can easily distinguish this child's work from that of the others.

SUMMARY OF GROWTH ANALYSIS

In looking at the total child and his work we can easily see that Fig. 30 has been produced by a boy well advanced in all areas of growth. While he seems to be more concerned with subjective interpretations, he is well balanced emotionally. His social awareness and capacity for self-identification together with his intellectual alertness and his emotional qualities may well qualify him for leadership. The only quality which may interfere with it is his trend toward subjective evaluations as indicated in the predominance of nonvisual perceptual experiences. He may develop great attachments in friendships but may lack objectivity important for leadership. This, however, may be counteracted by his outstanding feeling for organization as seen under "Aesthetic Growth." If we look again at the child's work as an entity, we may well say that the child's outstanding quality is his feeling for social issues.

EXERCISES

(1) Collect the drawings of a sixth or seventh grade. Find out how many children observe visually by drawing sizes for distant objects with "correct proportions" diminishing.
(2) Check the percentage that retrogress to base-line expressions.
(3) Check drawings in which houses, figures, and trees are represented according to proportion.
(4) Relate your findings to visual or nonvisual aptitudes among the children.
(5) Group the drawings of seventh grade according to a predominance of subjective trends, referring to non-visual experiences and visual predominance. How great is the percentage of either group? How many are in-between?
(6) Analyze one drawing, using the evaluation chart on pp. 244, 245.
(7) Make a profile according to the evaluation chart, also for Figs. 31a, 31b, 35.

LABORATORY WORK

(1) Model a woman scrubbing the floor, or performing some other action.
(2) Draw the same figure and think of an environment which fits best to the chosen topic.
(3) Make a cooperative design of a frieze, "Going Home from the Field," by asking each student to paint a worker with a shovel, a rake, or another tool on the shoulder. The drawing should fill the whole sheet of paper. Tack the series of drawings together around the room or along the wall.
(4) Design a symbol for a profession. Make a textile print from it by repeating the design.
(5) Make an emotional design using personification of color. (See p. 239).
(6) Make a functional form of a cup that lends itself for casting a one-piece mold.
(7) Make a one-piece mold and cast six cups.
(8) Design and execute a functional wooden knob for a drawer or door.
(9) Make a stage for your puppets.
(10) Make stage designs for a play, emphasizing different moods.

CHAPTER VIII   THE PERIOD OF DECISION

The Crisis of Adolescence
as Seen in Creative Activity

C RISIS MEANS PASSING FROM ONE STAGE TO ANOTHER UNDER GREAT difficulty. This is true physically, emotionally, or mentally. When undergoing an operation, the time the body needs to adapt itself to the new status created by the operation is called a *crisis*. Since adolescence is considered as a stage in the development of human beings, this crisis is connected with the difficulties of passing from one developmental stage to another, from the period of childhood to that of maturity.[1]

Because the crisis of adolescence is connected with bodily, as well as with emotional, changes, we deal here with a complex crisis in which body, emotions, and mind have to adjust to a new situation. Indeed, we can, therefore, say that this is an *important period of decision* in human development. That it is a period of decisive changes can be seen in the different behavior reactions and attitudes of people before and after adolescence. How often do we experience such sudden changes from happy, openminded children to shy and serious-looking youths. Much of this change is due to the degree of difficulty under which the individual has passed the

[1] Munro, T., "Adolescence and Art Education," in *Methods of Teaching the Fine Arts.* Chapel Hill: University of North Carolina Press, 1935.

crisis of adolescence. The less the child is affected by the changes of body and mind, the easier he can adjust to the new situation. The greater the difficulties were, the less was the child prepared to face the crisis properly. The question is, how can art education help to ease the crisis of adolescence? This can best be studied if we investigate the psychological changes which directly refer to the changes of the creative concept.

THE PSYCHOLOGICAL CHANGE IN THE IMAGINATIVE CONCEPT

If we attempt to investigate the psychological change of the imaginative concept, it is necessary to consider the facts which determine it before and after adolescence. It is especially important to stress those facts that cause this change. They can best be observed in the intermediary phases of representations expressing the pre- and postadolescent stages. For this purpose the topic "Playing Tag on the Schoolground" was given to a number of elementary-school children of the first three grades, high-school boys and girls of the junior high school, and college students, approximately 300 of each group.

Children and students were under no compulsion to draw the topic, but did so only if they wished. Individuals without prior special training in art were selected for this study. Of interest are the different ways of expressing the experience of catching and being caught, on the one hand, and the spatial representation of the school ground on the other. But it was also important to note that 95 per cent of all elementary-school children made some attempt to represent this experience, whereas only 35 per cent of the college students tried to depict this well-known game. Both facts—the different kinds of interpretation and the small percentage of the high-school, and the still smaller percentage of the college, students who attempted to draw the given topic (in contrast to an almost 100 per cent participation by the elementary-school children)—will give us a deep insight into the nature of this part of the crisis of adolescence.

In looking at the *children's* drawings, two striking features are apparent. (1) We see no attempt at realistic representations, neither in the representations of the human figures nor in the representations of the school ground. (2) The lower the age of the group, the less the attempt is made to indicate environment.

Let us select one drawing and describe it in greater detail, stressing some of the attributes more or less characteristic of all the representations of this age group. The child, a boy six years and six months of age, intro-

Fig. 36. "Playing Tag on the School Ground" (six and a half years old). Notice the exaggerated arm of the catching boy and the omitted arms of the captive. (Geometric lines. School ground is expressed by base line only.)

duced a representative symbol for "boy," an oval for "body" and a circle for "head." "Arms" and "legs" are expressed differently in the representation of the catching boy and the captive. Whereas the arms of the captive are omitted entirely, those of the captor are very much overemphasized, indicating the importance of the subjective experience of reaching out to catch. This finds its strongest expression in the exaggerated symbol of "the grasping hands" (Fig. 36). We also see a difference in the length of the legs in both figures. Looking at the other drawings of this age group, we frequently see the same difference in the representation of this part of the body—shorter legs for the captive and longer legs for the captor. We can conclude that "shorter legs" indicate "slower running" whereas "longer legs" mean "faster running." This confirms only what we have discussed in the chapter dealing with pre-schematic and schematic stages. The school ground is indicated by a base line only, which shows that the subjective feeling of being a part of environment is the only spatial experience the child has.

Fig. 37. "Playing Tag on the School Ground" (nine years old). Slight exaggeration of important parts. Characterization of environment (still base-line concept). "Clothes" replace geometric lines.

From this description as well as from our study in general, it is apparent that the child's creative expression is mainly connected with such subjective experiences as bodily feelings, muscle sensations, and touch impressions. It also is obvious that the child's way of perceiving space is determined by his subjective relationship to it, since the child's perception is derived from bodily, not from visual, experiences. The proportions in the child's representations are proportions of value, not the result of esthetic evaluations. That is why it can be assumed that *the child's world of imagination is mainly bound up with the self,* with subjective feelings, and subjective relationships toward surroundings.

Let us look at another drawing which will lead us a step further toward the period of adolescence. It is the drawing of a nine-year-old girl, and is another characteristic example chosen from the 300 of its kind. This drawing (Fig. 37) compared with the other, most obviously shows a greater relationship to "reality." The girls wear dresses. There even is an attempt to portray the flying hair of the running girls. Although unimportant details can be seen, there still is a clear overemphasis of the arm of the catching girl, thereby expressing the importance of this part. There distinctly is a greater emphasis on environmental objects. The school ground is indicated by trees and by a fence which surrounds the field. The space in the picture is divided into three sections. On the base line of the upper section there is the above-mentioned fence crossing the paper horizontally; then the middle section with the girls, as the focus of the experience; and the lower section with a fence standing on the bottom edge of the paper, which represents the base line. Although the fence is in the visual foreground, it is represented smaller than the girls, almost half the size. But if we consider the motion of the figures, we see a greater stiffness, even a lack of correlation between them. This is typical for the representations of this age group (see chapter on "Gang Age"). On the other hand, a greater emphasis on single details, such as the flying hair, shows the interest in things of significance. The nicely designed dresses of the girls, both in front view, hardly touch each other. If the somewhat exaggerated arm were not drawn, the topic would scarcely be recognizable.

From this representation we can assume that a definite *tendency exists to replace mere symbols* *("oval" for "body") by a representation which is more related to reality.* But as we have seen in our general discussion of this stage, this approach toward a realistic representation is due to a greater consciousness of the self deriving from the thought "I am wearing a dress," but is not a result of a visual concept. The proportion of value seen in the size of the girls who, compared with the trees, are drawn according to the degree of importance, still shows the lack of visual experiences, or at least a strong dominance of a subjective attitude toward the representation. Another fact seems important: the percentage of children who did not want to depict the topic has slightly increased, which shows decreasing confidence in self-expression. The temporary lack of spatial correlation is a result of a more egocentric attitude which, as we have seen, is typical for this age level, which we called the "gang age."

When we turn our attention to the drawings of the postadolescent college students, we see first of all that only a very limited number of students voluntarily depicted this topic (35 per cent). Those who did, tried to represent it as *realistically* as possible: some by the real movement of running with "well proportioned" figures including a part of the campus; others with the emphasis on the figures only, stressing the muscles and the function of the body (Fig. 38).

From this experiment it becomes clear that the closer the child approaches adolescence, the more he loses the strong subjective relationship

Fig. 38. "Playing Tag on the School Ground" (fifteen years old). Attempt at realistic representation.

to the world of symbols. The growing consciousness of his own body introduces a more critical awareness of the self. In some cases the higher consciousness of the self leads to a more detailed and determined expression of the body, whereas in other cases this growing critical attitude stimulates very strongly visual observation. *A conscious critical awareness now dominates the creative production of the postadolescent individual.*

There is, however, an intermediate stage, in which the individual has already lost the connection with his childish way of symbolic representation and has not yet found confidence in his own conscious approach. Through the strong desire of establishing a conscious approach, however, the child loses temporarily the subjective attitude toward his own creations. With this loss, the confidence in his world of imagination is shaken. Consequently, the drawings show this feeling of insecurity as a visible expression of the battle between the two impulses. This period in which the youth has neither an unconscious childish nor a conscious approach of self-expression is marked by a very profound crisis which sometimes shakes the whole self-confidence. This is the reason why so many individuals stop their creative work at this period. In the study of adolescence this particular phase of the crisis hardly has been recognized.

From the foregoing report it becomes clear that one of the most important tasks of art education during this vital period is to introduce means and methods of stimulations which would prevent the child from losing self-confidence. Proposals on how this can be done is the main thesis of this chapter.

THE DEVELOPMENT OF TWO
CREATIVE TYPES

We can now clearly distinguish two types of art expression both by the end product and by the attitude toward experience. When we investigate the artistic products of these two types in their pure forms we find that the visual type starts from his environment, that he feels as spectator, and that his intermediaries for experience are mainly the eyes. The other, which we shall call the haptic [2] type, is primarily concerned with his own body sensations and the subjective experiences in which he feels emotionally involved. In *The Nature of Creative Activity* I have demonstrated the existence of these two distinct creative types based upon two different reactions toward the world of experiences. In the course of this study it was found that imaginative activity, including the ability to give objective reference to creations of the imagination, by no means depends upon the capacity for perceptive observation. Furthermore, it was shown that the inability inspectively to notice "visual" objects is not always an inhibitory factor in creative activities. On the contrary, the very fact of not paying attention to visual impressions may become the basis of a specific creativeness of the haptic type. This is of greatest importance for art educators, especially for those who still are concerned with visual stimulations only.

A visually minded individual would be disturbed and inhibited were he to be stimulated only by means of haptic impressions—that is, were he asked not to use sight, but to orientate himself only by means of touch, bodily feelings, muscular sensations, and kinesthetic fusions. So much is clear, but what is not as obvious is that "seeing" may also become an inhibitory factor when forced upon an individual who does not use his visual experiences for creative work. Both facts are established by numerous experiments reported in the work referred to before.[3]

An extreme haptical type of individual—who is by no means rare—is normal-sighted and uses his eyes only when compelled to do so; otherwise he reacts as would a blind person who is entirely dependent upon touch and kinesthesis. W. Grey Walter in an encephalographical study reveals

[2] *Haptic* derives from the Greek word *haptikos* and means, "able to lay hold of."
[3] *The Nature of Creative Activity.*

that "individuals with persistent alpha rhythms which are hard to block with mental effort, tend to auditory, kinaesthetic or tactile perceptions rather than visual imagery. In this group of persons the alpha rhythms continue even when the eyes are open and the mind is active and alert." He administered a test to 600 individuals which made him distinguish between a "visualizer" (the M type) "with few if any alpha rhythms," a "non-visualist" (the P type) "with persistent alpha activity" and "a mixed type," (the R type) "with a responsive alpha rhythm." He raises the question "Why are the alpha rhythms so persistent when they appear in childhood?" He warns, however, that "we must be cautious about jumping to any such conclusion as that children only learn later to think in visual terms, although this is suggested by the extreme rarity of M type children." He continues that "evidence already available, both statistical and experimental, strongly suggests that the alpha rhythm characters are inborn and probably hereditary." [4] An *extreme* visually minded person, on the other hand, is entirely lost in the dark and depends completely on his visual experiences of the outside world. This distinction is true for creative types as well as for individuals in general, as has been reported elsewhere.[5]

Most people fall between these two extreme types. Investigations have proved, however, that only a few individuals have equal amounts of visual and haptic predisposition. Seventy-five per cent have an appreciable tendency toward one or the other. Since the tendency toward these two antipodes of experience is important not only for the proper stimulation in creative activity but also to life in general (especially, in the proper choice of occupation), we shall discuss this aspect of the problem in a separate chapter.

The result of an investigation in which I tested 1128 subjects by means of specifically designed tests for visual or haptic aptitude was as follows: 47 per cent were clearly visual, 23 per cent were haptic, and 30 per cent either received a score below the line where a clear identification was possible, or were otherwise not identifiable. In other words, approximately half of the individuals tested reacted visually, whereas not quite a fourth reacted haptically. These figures completely coincide with those of W. Grey Walter in his entirely independent study.

Thus, it would appear that one among four individuals depends more on his subjective reactions such as touch and kinesthesis than upon vision. Aside from its far-reaching significance in other fields, for art teaching

[4] Walter, W. Grey, *The Living Brain.* New York: W. W. Norton & Co., pp. 214–218.
[5] Lowenfeld, "Tests for Visual and Haptical Aptitude." *American Journal of Psychology,* Vol. 58, 1945.

this fact means that only half of the population can benefit from visual stimuli. The others either are not reached or may become frustrated by this type of stimulation. Each type should therefore be stimulated in the direction of his experiences and thinking. To do this, we should become acquainted with the nature of these two creative types, particularly because during the crisis of adolescence the individual is most unsure of himself. The kind of stimulation that is able to inspire him will not only contribute to his creative development, but will also instill the self-confidence necessary for a wholesome personality development. In spite of the fact that most people fall between the two types, with merely a preference for the one or the other, an analysis of each type in its pure form seems imperative for the proper understanding of their "mixed" forms.

Visual type

The main intermediaries for visual impressions are the eyes. The ability to observe visually does not depend entirely upon the physical condition of the eyes. Inferior visual awareness is not necessarily determined by a physical defect of the eyes. On the contrary, as experiments have proven, the psychological factor of having the *aptitude* to observe is of deciding significance. This is of special importance because it implies the fact that being forced to observe might possibly create inhibitions. Before one can remove inhibitions it is necessary to recognize them as such. Superfluous as this statement may appear, it should nevertheless be emphasized at the outset of the discussion on the two creative types. To be observed, for example, is that it would be completely wrong to attempt to set free the creative powers of a nonvisual type of individual by trying to remove his "visual inhibition" and anxiously attempting to familiarize him with visual impressions. One would in fact achieve the exact opposite, just as one would inhibit creative ability by forcing a visualizer to pay special attention to tactile impressions. *Not being able to see, or rather not noticing visual impressions, is not always an inhibitory factor.* On the contrary, we have seen that the very fact of not paying attention to visual impressions becomes the basis of the specific creativeness of the haptic type. Therefore, before the way is cleared for the development of creative ability, it is essential to ascertain which creative type is involved. From this it follows that naturalistic modes of expression should not be used as the only criterion. The use of such a criterion actually inhibits free creative expression. To ascertain the type being dealt with, the specific attributes of each have to be determined.

The *visual type,* the observer, usually approaches things from their appearance. He feels as a *spectator.* One important factor in visual observation is the ability to see first the whole without an awareness of details, then to analyze this total impression into detailed or partial impressions, and finally to synthesize these parts into a new whole. The visual type first sees the general shape of a tree, then the single leaves, the twigs, the branches, the trunk, and finally everything incorporated in the synthesis of the whole tree. Starting with the general outline, partial impressions thus are integrated into a whole, simultaneous image. This is true not only psychologically, but also for the act of creating. Thus, we will notice that visual types usually begin with the outlines of objects and enrich the form with details as the visual analysis is able to penetrate deeper into the nature of the object.

This visual penetration deals mainly with two factors: first, with the analysis of the characteristics of shape and structure of the object itself; and second, with the changing effects of these shapes and structures determined by light, shadow, color, atmosphere, and distance. Observing details, therefore, is not always a sign of visual-mindedness; it can be an indication of good memory as well as of subjective interest in these details. For visual-mindedness it is necessary to see the changes which these details undergo under the various external conditions as mentioned above.

Visually minded persons have a tendency to transform kinesthetic and tactile experiences into visual experiences. If, for instance, a visual-minded person acquaints himself with an object in complete darkness, he tries to visualize all tactile or kinesthetic experiences. "How it looks" is the first reaction to any object met in darkness. In other words, he tries to imagine in visual terms what he has perceived through other senses. A visually minded person who encounters an object in darkness thus tries immediately to visualize the object he has met. From this analysis it becomes evident that the visual approach toward the outside world is an analytic approach of a spectator who finds his problems in the complex observation of the ever-changing appearances of shapes and forms.

Haptic type

The main intermediary for the haptic type of individual is the *body-self* —muscular sensations, kinesthetic experiences, touch impressions, and all experiences which place the self in value relationship to the outside world. In this art, the self is projected as the true actor of the picture whose formal characteristics are the resultant of a synthesis of bodily, emotional, and intellectual apprehension of shape and form. Sizes and spaces are determined by their emotional value in size and importance. The haptic type, therefore, is primarily a *subjective type*. Haptically minded persons do not transform kinesthetic and tactile experiences into visual ones, but are completely content with the tactile or kinesthetic modality itself, as experiments have shown. If a haptically minded person acquaints himself with an object in complete darkness, he would remain satisfied with his tactile or kinesthetic experiences. Since tactile impressions are mostly partial only (this is true for all impressions of objects that cannot be embraced with the hands, where the hands have to move) the haptic individual will arrive at a synthesis of these partial impressions only when he becomes emotionally interested in the object itself. Normally, he will not build up such a synthesis and will remain satisfied with his haptic experience. If he encounters an object in darkness, he will merely withdraw, perhaps, with some feelings of the surface structure of the obstacle or with partial impressions of those parts that he has touched. Since the haptic type uses the self as the true projector of his experiences, his pictorial representations are highly subjective; his proportions are proportions of value.

In art education it is therefore of prime importance to consider these attitudes toward the world of experiences as significant as the visual approaches toward art. Thus a stimulation will be effective only if it includes haptic sensations as well as visual experiences.

THE DIFFERENT CREATIVE CONCEPTS OF THE TWO TYPES

To be able to separate pure optical perception from other sense impressions we need an object of contemplation that cannot be influenced or disturbed by other senses. But associatively almost everything in our surroundings somehow influences all of our sensations and experiences. We can therefore hardly ever speak of pure optical perception of things. Even color, regarded in isolation from any object, awakes in us dark, bright, cheerful, or warm feelings, and it seems self-evident that, for example, a tree waving in the wind awakes in us some knowledge of the elasticity of the wood, the nature of the leaves, and so forth. Thus Van Gogh writes in a letter to his brother, "Yesterday evening I concerned myself with the gently rising terrain of the wood, which is completely covered with dry, dead beech leaves. . . . The problem is—and I find this extremely difficult—to bring out the depth of the color and the enormous strength and firmness of the soil. . . . Out of this soil grow the trunks of the beeches which are a shining green on the side on which they are brightly illuminated, while on the shadow side the trunks show a warm, strong black-green. . . . I am affected and intrigued to see how strongly the trunks are rooted in the ground. I began to paint them with the brush, and was unable to bring out the characteristics of the soil, which had already been painted in thick colors. The new brush strokes simply disappeared. Therefore I pressed roots and trunks out of the tube and modelled them a little with my brush. There, now they stand in it, grow out of it, and have firmly taken root." [6]

We see here how the optical impression has been influenced and formed by other sense impressions, how intellectual apprehension of shape and form fused with optical and emotional experiences. Can optical perception, therefore, be adequately perceived by means of seeing with the eye alone? We shall have to conclude that optical perception in its purest form is only an extreme case of visual perception in general. We must therefore use the term "visual perception," when impressions coming from other senses are subordinate to those coming from the eye, and when visual impressions are the *dominant* feature in a percept.

The artistic representation of visual impressions always starts from optical perception. It is concerned with the subjective experience of the self only insofar as any creative activity is an individual mental act. "Being bound to the self" in this sense is not what we shall understand by the term later, because it does not seek its experience in bodily sensations, but *outside the body*. The self merely evaluates the experience.

"The further optical experience recedes into the background, the less important does the eye become as the intermediary of the concept. To the same extent the importance of the environment diminishes, and experience is more and more confined to the processes that go on in the body as a whole—bodily sensations, muscular innervations, deep sensibilities, and their various emotional effects. As the importance of the sense of sight diminishes, so that of the senses derived from the body as the intermediary between sensations and the concept increases. In what what follows, we shall mean by 'haptic perception' the synthesis between tactile perceptions of external reality and those subjective experiences that seem to be so closely bound up with the experience of the self." [7]

From the discussion it can clearly be seen that visual and haptic concepts are fundamentally different in their basic experiential content. Although we have pointed out that pure haptical or visual concepts are rarely

[6] Van Gogh, Vincent, *Letters*. Berlin: Bruno Cassirer, pp. 14, 16 and 17.
[7] *The Nature of Creative Activity*, p. 82.

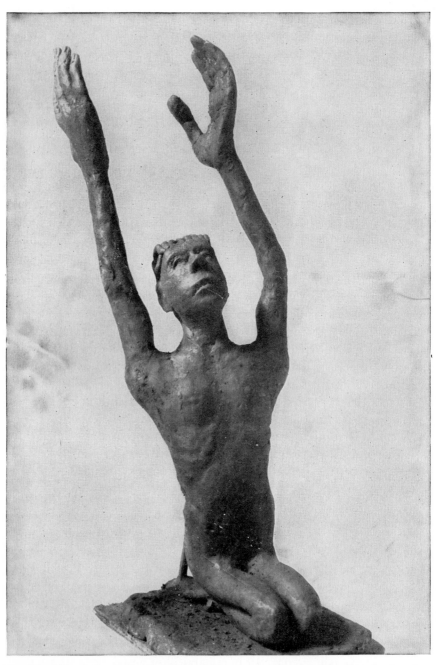

Fig. 39. "Youth Imploring." Sculpture by a seventeen-year-old girl, who has been blind since birth.

to be found, in our teaching experiences the tendency toward the one or the other can clearly be seen. As we are able to recognize them, we will be able to encourage the individual *in the direction* of his thinking, and thereby provide the guidance he sorely needs during the crisis of adolescence.

Human figure

For the visual type the human figure is a part of the environment (Fig. 40). As such, the human figure is exposed to the same phenomena as environment. The main experiences related to the representation of the human figure are the qualities that can be discovered with our eyes. "Correct proportions and measurements" are, therefore, of prime significance for the visual type. The changing effects of lights and shadows in the different motions are necessarily a part of the visual image. In art stimulation, therefore, the posing model is of different significance for the two creative types because the visually minded individual is mainly concerned with the visual analysis of his optical impressions.

The haptic type, however, uses the human figure as the interpreter of his emotions and feelings (Fig. 41). Since different parts of our body have various functions and importance, the proportions given these parts will assume the emotional significance assigned to them. The wounds on the hands of Christ are of such significance in a Byzantine mural that the hands dominate in size and in importance. Another experience related especially to haptic types is the intense body feeling expressed in the desire to get one's body transferred to another place (that is, when late; related to the wish of catching up with time and space) or the desire to catch something that is already out of reach by throwing one's arm after it. These typically haptic experiences are in strong contradiction to visual observations. They spring from body experiences and kinesthetic sensations. Since these experiences are highly subjective in their interpretations, the haptic representation of the human figure and its meaning is a highly subjective one.

In my *The Nature of Creative Activity* I have called attention to numerous examples of the works of the blind among whom haptic expression is much more common. In this book, I have demonstrated the meaning of autoplastic sensations, the sensations of drawing all experiences from the body, and the significance they assume. The figure of a "Youth Imploring" modeled by a girl who has been blind since birth will illustrate these viewpoints. Its most striking characteristic that we feel to be closely connected with the title is the over-emphasis on the

Fig. 40. "People Look at the Battleship Missouri" (twelve years old). Representation of a visual type. (Courtesy Educational Project, Museum of Modern Art, N. Y.)

imploring hands. We feel the strength of the elemental forces embodied in this figure when we regard the gradual increase in its proportions. It starts from the slender basis of the delicate legs and rising like a hymn to heaven finds in the great hands its mighty closing chord. The base has, as it were, been dematerialized: it is no longer earth-bound, and we have before us only the feeling "I implore!" (Fig. 39). In almost all sculptures by the blind we find that those parts of the body that have emotional significance are greatly exaggerated. We find, however, the same principles of representation in all epochs and cultures in which expressive qualities are of greater importance than visual ones.

In Egyptian murals the kings and other prominent persons are made larger in exactly the same way as in Byzantine paintings. In these cases large and small cannot be regarded as visual qualities: they are expressive evaluations; visual experiences have to make way for impulses lying outside of the visual sphere. This is especially true for modern art in which the emphasis again is on the side of expressive qualities. Then we will understand the true meaning of the complex creations of Picasso in which

Fig. 41. "People." Representation of a haptic type. No environment is represented. Experience is completely focused at expression. (Courtesy Educational Project, Museum of Modern Art, N. Y.)

space and time fuse, in which profile and front views are expressed simultaneously, in which the arm of a horrified mother becomes separated from the body as an expression of the intense feeling of reaching for her bombed child.[8] The nature of this art expression is at least as deeply rooted, historically and psychologically, as the visual interpretation of the world which surrounds us.

Since the stimulation of these subjective feelings is of prime importance for art educators who deal with the stage under discussion, there will be developed, in the chapter on stimulations, methods for bringing out and encouraging these important feelings.

Space

Space cannot be conceived in its totality. Its infinity is irrational and it becomes accessible to our senses only when we circumscribe it. At the center of space, with nothing whatever to surround us, space itself would

[8] Mural "Guernica," by Pablo Picasso.

be infinite and therefore nonexistent. The self would cease to be a measure of value in space. It would vanish to nothing in infinity. Our senses and our psychological attitude set limits to space, and each in its own way enables us to grasp space. *Visual space,* for which the eyes are the intermediaries, we perceive as the widest space. *Haptic space,* for which our organs of touch and our bodily sensations are the intermediaries, is the most restricted. Both spaces achieve a magical significance whenever the self is included in them through value judgments. In what follows we shall discuss the difference in the ways in which these two sensory spaces are pictorially represented. The direction of our investigation is determined on the one hand by the difference in the modes of sensory perception of these two spaces, and on the other hand, by the "restriction" of the extent of haptic as compared with visual space. Both points of view are necessary for understanding the kind of stimulation that the art educator has to use during this deciding stage in order that he will neither neglect nor frustrate either of these types.

In relation to its environment, the self grows or diminishes in size and in importance. Next to children we seem large, next to a skyscraper, small; unimportant in the world at large, important in our own circle; most important, perhaps, when we are quite alone. These attitudes vary according to our psychological state. The narrower, the more restricted, three-dimensional space or the space of our psychological experiences is, the more importance is assigned to the self. Haptic space is of necessity restricted. In it, therefore, the significance and the importance of the self are very much emphasized.

Among the differences produced by the eye in the visual image, is the apparent diminution of distant objects. In drawing, this apparent diminution of distant objects is achieved by using laws of perspective. The outer limits of visual space are represented by the boundary of the horizon line. How are distant objects represented in haptical space? Distant objects, in this kind of space, do not produce differences in size to the sense of touch or to emotional reactions. Thus, the visual image receives a decisive correction. When space is being explored tactually, distances can only have different values attached to them or seem of greater or less emotional significance. In haptic space, therefore, we find a predominance of subjective value judgments. In visual space (the space of appearances) distance is expressed by a progressive diminution of distant objects. The longing for freedom, however, grows with its remoteness. An individual without restrictions is unaware of boundaries. His eyes can easily rest on the horizon. The horizon of the sharecropper is his cotton field, the horizon of a laundry woman her tub. *The perspective of haptic space is a perspective of values.*

None of the creative interpretations of these spaces is true in a realistic sense. Both spaces are "distorted" by individual interpretations. Although philosophy has generally considered visual space as the more realistic, nevertheless it has less validity than the space of touch. Distant objects do not actually change in size, and the sense of touch truly records this truth. Visual experiences show an apparent diminution in the size of objects in space, but this is in strong contradiction to reality. Bushmen, who were confronted with photographs or reproductions of paintings of three-dimensional qualities, were unable to orientate themselves in the jungle of visual foreshortenings.[9] For them sizes do not differ with regard to distances. Their spatial interpretations, however, are not "true interpretations" either, since by them objects in space are evaluated according to significance. Interesting to note, however, is that we are completely one-sided in our judgments relating to the validity of our own visual space interpretations. Our civilization has become so accustomed to the photographic interpretation of space that we have to change completely our concept if we shift to the "unconventional" interpretations of haptic space, although these have been the conventional interpretations among historical cultures in which *expression* dominated in the realm of art.

THE TWO CREATIVE TYPES ARE PSYCHOLOGICAL—THEIR SIGNIFICANCE FOR PERSONALITY DEVELOPMENT

When we sit in a train, watching the swiftly passing landscape, we may or may not realize that the impression of the landscape as a whole exists only in our minds. In reality we do not see the whole thing, but only many little strips of landscape about the size of the window, each one quickly replaced by another. Some of us are quite satisfied with these many partial impressions and would even feel dizzy if compelled to integrate the fleeting glimpses into a whole. Others, however, do not need to be stimulated to put this "picture puzzle" together. While moving, they fuse all these strips together and see in their minds a whole landscape; more than that, they orientate themselves quite well in it.

Members of the first group not only lose contact with the parts of the landscape that are left behind, but often become irritated by the "ever-changing" picture. Many of us have experienced how this irritation contributes to the discomfort of train travel. It is not only the fresh air that

[9] Frobenius, Leo, *Kulturgeschichte Afrikas*. Zürich: Phaidon-Verlag, 1933.

Fig. 42. "Street Scene," painted by visually minded sixteen-year-old adolescent youth. Light and shadow, atmosphere, and visual proportions, determined by the law of perspective, govern this representation. (Courtesy Educational Project, Museum of Modern Art, N. Y.)

makes riding in an open car a pleasure, the smoothness of high-altitude flying that makes it more pleasant than the take-off; it is also the enlarged visual circle which permits better orientation and a fuller sense of physical security. The body likes to know what is being done to it. The driver of a car does not feel the sudden stop as much as the passengers do.

The traveler who sits either comfortably or painfully in his compartment seldom realizes that this ability or failure to produce a single, unified picture out of the many successive impressions of the landscape may classify him according to a definite psychological type, which differs from other types on this and many other points, as we shall see.

An air-pilot training candidate who failed in his examinations explained his failure as follows: "In high altitudes I feel secure. However, the closer I come to the ground, especially in landing maneuvers, the more I become confused. Since I cannot take in the whole airfield I lose orientation." This is exactly the problem of a blind sculptor, who, moving his hands over a face, receives only partial impressions. The inability of the pilot to

Fig. 43. "Lying on the Bed," painted by a haptically minded seventeen-year-old adolescent youth. Everything is focused around the self. Color has a subjective meaning; so have lights and darks. (Courtesy Educational Project, Museum of Modern Art, N. Y.)

integrate his partial impressions of the landing field into a whole, confused his sense of orientation. Having lost contact with the part of the airfield left behind, the pilot could no longer orientate himself.

In primitive, haptic, and expressive art the same attitude toward the experience of senses can be observed; however, with one striking additional factor. As a man sitting in a train loses contact with the area he leaves behind him, so does the haptic artist. But the train passenger, like the artist, may suddenly become bound up with something that quickly passes his eyes and strikes his personality, such as an old shack, or a hawk circling in the air. From this time on, the hawk will circle with him and grow in his mind as one outstanding, isolated impression of the many he has perceived in succession.

A blind person who made himself acquainted with a room became very much interested in a desk lamp. He could feel the bulb growing warmer when he turned on the light, and when he was asked afterwards to model the room in clay, the lamp was the most conspicuous part, even overshadowing the desk. This impression became outstanding and most of the others disappeared. The lamp may have been for him a symbol of the "unattainable," or better, the "unperceivable," which can easily change for the primitive man into any magic symbol. The creative result, however, shows the same expression for it: proportion of value.

Reference is again made to the sculpture "Youth Imploring" (Fig. 39) described previously (page 269). The world of expressionist art is one of expression, feelings, subjective processes: *of haptic experiences.* Bodily feelings, kinesthetic experiences, muscular sensations are clearest examples of subjective processes. The bodily feelings of these uplifted hands have become incorporated into the magic content of the expression of the whole sculpture. The same kind of expression can be seen in the works of modern masters such as William Lehmbruck, as well as in the exaggerated hands of primitive African sculptures. Or we might better say it can be seen in every art that originates in haptic rather than in visual experiences.

Thus, the two creative types are psychological which, independent of physiological factors, exist in their own realms. It has been demonstrated that there are completely and congenitally blind individuals who react visually or haptically in the same way as normal-sighted people react both ways. A blind person reacts "visually" if he is able to receive out of his touch impressions (which are partial impressions) a simultaneous image of the whole, like the visually minded, normal-sighted person who sits in the train and fuses all partial impressions into a simultaneous image. *Both final products are distinguished by the same visual attributes of emphasizing the external appearance.* Blind as well as normal-sighted haptic types, however, create entirely "from within." Their inward feelings are expressed in disregard of any realistic external qualities (see also p. 454).

It becomes evident that imaginative activity and even the ability to give objective form to the creations of the imagination by no means depend on the capacity to see and observe things. This is of vital importance for art educators because it will be an important factor in determining the methods of stimulation discussed in the following section (compare Figs. 42 and 43).

SIGNIFICANCE OF A PROPER ART STIMULATION

Proper art stimulation is always determined by the factors that influence the growth and development of the individual during a particular age period. During the crisis of adolescence the individual has to battle for many far-reaching decisions. He stands on the threshold of adulthood, reached under circumstances which often affect his life very definitely. Adjustment from childhood to adulthood usually occurs under difficulties, physiologically and psychologically. Neither one can be separated from the other because the body is closely related to our mind, and affects it greatly. We shall, however, be concerned only with the psychological effects and how we can influence them or, better, help the individual to overcome them by means of creative activity. Creative activity will thus become the natural outlet and means of expression for the individual. Art education during this important period should by no means be offered to only a selected group, but should be a natural means of expression for everyone. This conclusion is not in accord with common practice in the American high school, where art is taught to a small group of artistically "gifted" students. "Gifted" usually refers to skill, and conventional interpretations of objects of nature. If we can eliminate this attitude toward "art expression" and at the same time develop self-confidence in the individual to accept *art as self-expression according to individual needs,* we have succeeded in our chief aim of making art a common expression of mankind. In order to be able to do so, we shall have to study the psychological needs for the proper stimulation during this crucial period of decision.

CHAPTER IX   ADOLESCENT ART

W HILE OUR KNOWLEDGE AND CONCEPTS OF CHILD ART HAVE GREATLY
expanded during the past years, the understanding of the art of the
adolescent has been neglected greatly.

Child art has become a term meaningful to every teacher, parent and
psychologist. We know the attributes of child art, the forces which underlie
it, its developmental stages and above all, its meaning for growth. There
is no doubt that its educational value has penetrated deeply into our system
of kindergarten and elementary schools.

Many books have been written on child art. They all have contributed
in bringing it to our understanding. It has been demonstrated that child art
has its distinct attributes which—like childhood—represents a very important phase in our development. In general, it is the art which reveals
to us the unconscious, uncritical imagination of the child.

That we are far from having arrived at a similarly definite concept of
adolescent art can clearly be seen in the general confusion which is found in
both the junior and senior high schools of our nation and I may say, in the
whole world. It appears to be a universal problem. The underlying principles which determine the concept of *adolescent art* need to be clarified.
We know that adolescence probably is as distinct a period in human de-

velopment as childhood. There is, then, no reason why we should not be able to arrive at distinct attributes which determine adolescent art. It is quite obvious that the knowledge of such attributes can only result from careful investigation and research of the period of adolescence, its meaning for creative activity and an analysis of the work of adolescent individuals.

In general we can clearly see three approaches in our schools. One is mainly concerned with saving the precious attributes of child art. Teachers adhering to this method are anxious not to lose the freshness and unconscious approach of the child by creating an artificial "childhood atmosphere" at a level on which the adolescent is no longer proud to be a child.

While such motivations have produced interesting results, especially by highly intuitive teachers, there is no doubt that a retrogression to childhood in an isolated art situation is an undesirable artifice. It only is done to produce pleasing and "fresh" results and does not further individual growth. I have seen many such situations in which the classroom "atmosphere" is so strong that the single individual—completely a part of the general creative environment—creates like a child does. Outside of the classroom, however, when the intense atmosphere produced by the teacher is gone, the adolescent is ashamed of his "childish" production and realizes its "inadequacy"—until he again "succumbs" to the strong "motivation" of his teacher.

Such "push and pull" must certainly be detrimental to the growth of an individual. It contributes to the insecurity of the youth at a period in which by nature stability is at a low; when the adolescent neither feels as a child nor is accepted as an adult. Instead of giving him confidence in his art expression through encouraging his own trends, we often try to pull him back into a "prolonged childhood." As pleasing as the results may be, they do not serve the individual in this critical period of his growth.

The second approach, found in junior and senior high schools more commonly than the first, emphasizes perfection. The closer the art products approach "professional" standards, the better. In many instances, to the pride of the teacher, one could scarcely distingish between a high school art exhibit and the one of a professional art school. The teacher, realizing the drive of the adolescent youth to approach adult standards, is not satisfied with anything less than adult standards of high perfection. It is quite obvious that such practices not only deprive the adolescent youth of his own characteristics but completely counteract the democratic meaning of art education as an education for all and not for a selected few who happen to be able to conform to high standards of adult perfection.

The third approach also seen in our schools accepts the adolescent honestly on his own level. Neither is he artificially kept in a "childlike atmosphere," nor is he pushed into adult perfection. It is with this form of art expression that we shall deal more closely in this chapter.

In order to understand the nature of adolescent art and its place in our educational system, two problems need clarification. The one deals with the analysis and *meaning of adolescence as a stage of development* with special reference to creative growth; the other with the role of art education in our secondary schools. As has been said before, adolescence can be characterized as the stage in human development which is between childhood and adulthood. It begins with changes of the functions of the sex organs. These changes are usually accompanied by a greater consciousness of the significance of the maturing body and mind. This greater awareness of the self places the individual in a different, more conscious and critical relationship to his environment.

Imaginative activity also is greatly affected by these changes. How it is affected can best be seen in the different ways in which children and adolescents play. Children play without awareness of their action, using their imagination to make up for what reality does not provide. A stick may serve as an airplane, a machine gun, or almost anything. It is common and not at all disturbing to see children pushing a block or stick and imitating the sound of a locomotive, or using it, zooming through the air, as an airplane. As has been pointed out, if adults would do the same, they would be considered insane; such is the difference between controlled and uncontrolled imagery.

The adolescent, too, has outgrown the stage in which he uses symbols to substitute reality—like a stick for an airplane. However, *his* imagination is not yet as clearly defined as the imagination of the adult in regard to the goals and aims toward which he strives. In his play he refrains from using such over-simplified or abstract symbols. In life, however, he most often still adheres to unreal, dramatized romantic concepts. At a particular stage he wants to be a cowboy or forest ranger—with no other desires but to follow one of his romantic ideals. "The typical development of vocational interest is from active, exciting occupations of low prestige value—e.g. being a cowboy—to emotionalized ambitions having great prestige—i.e., being a famous trial lawyer." [1]

This attitude clearly coincides with the adolescent's choice of movies and books. U. H. Fleege made a study of adolescents' preferences in litera-

[1] Cole, Luella, *Psychology of Adolescence.* New York: Rinehart and Company, 1950.

ture and movies. He reports that adventure and romance far outrank all other types of presentations.[2] In *Adolescent Character and Personality* Robert J. Havighurst and Hilda Taba, in collaboration with the Committee of Human Development of the University of Chicago,[3] distinguished among five different personality types. In their study of ninety-four subjects, the "self-directive person" by far outnumbered all other personality types. Some of the tested attributes of this group of adolescents which appear to be of particular interest to our problem are: ambitious, persistent, introspective, self-doubting, self-critical. All these studies give evidence that the adolescent individual is by no means a realist who deals with facts and who lives in an objective world. Quite to the contrary, these studies point out that the adolescent has a tendency to withdraw from reality and to live in a world of his own. He is too "self-critical" to accept child standards in his creative work. Yet we must not make the mistake of moving too far in the direction of professionalism. A bottle, a book and a lantern or any other variations of still lifes will not satisfy his "introspective" tendencies nor will they help his desire for "romance and adventure." During a period most formative and important in human development we seem to miss meeting the needs of the individual completely.

It is quite clear that a junior and senior high school program, if it is to be effective, must be built upon the needs of the growing adolescent. Above all, it must provide the adolescent with opportunities for expression of *his* ideas and emotions. He must be motivated and encouraged to *experiment* in materials and art media in his own strive for "adventures" and discoveries without imposed perfection.

"Adolescents," says Dr. Cole,[4] "need outlets for their emotional interests and for self-expression. Their constantly shifting social adjustments inevitably put considerable strain upon them. They have a real need for such subjects as music, art, dramatics, writing. In these subjects, as in the sciences, a clear distinction must be made between the few for whom the subject is a specialty and the many for whom it is a means of self-expression. The object of the work in these fields should be to provide for such self-expression as can be indulged in by the 'untalented.' " Whether or not our classrooms will be filled or will only be attended by a few "talented" who chose art as an elective neither depends on the curriculum nor on any

[2] Fleege, U. H., *Self-Revelation of the Adolescent Boy.* New York: Bruce Publishing Co., 1945.
[3] Havighurst, Robert J., Hilda Taba, *Adolescent Character and Personality.* New York: John Wiley & Sons, Inc., 1949.
[4] Cole, Luella, *op. cit.*

external decision. Ultimately, it depends on the art teacher who can or cannot meet the needs of the adolescent. Adolescent art must become, like child art, the expression of its developmental stage. Only then will it have its adequate place in secondary school education.

From this and our previous discussion five important criteria stand out as vital considerations for the proper stimulation of creating self-confidence in the individual and thus making art a common expression of all: (1) The change from an unconscious approach to a critical awareness. (2) The change of the imaginative concept. (3) A reconsideration of subject matter. (4) The meaning of skills and techniques. (5) The crystallization of two different creative types or concepts.

THE CHANGE TO CRITICAL AWARENESS

During the discussion of the stage of reasoning, it was emphasized that the closer the unconscious approach in its intellectual and emotional apprehension can be brought to the stage of critical awareness, the easier can the child bridge the gap created by the crisis of adolescence. This gap, as we said, consists mainly of the undecided attitude of the individual, who feels torn in two directions: childhood and adulthood—childhood in his play and adulthood in his intellectual awareness. How often have we had the opportunity to see this contradiction in the attitude of youngsters who, while playing with airplanes and imitating sounds and motions, suddenly bring themselves up short and become ashamed because they are no longer supposed to engage in such childish antics. This distorted attitude can best be seen in creative activity when youngsters want to apologize for their "childish" drawings by an assumed mere "lack of skill." If discouragement did not as a rule accompany these "false" apologies, it would not be a harmful matter. But the apologies are usually symptoms of lack of self-confidence which is the end of creative expression. To avoid such discouragement we should introduce teaching methods that counteract this trend.

Before considering methods, the characteristics of a good method should be indicated. Methods that restrict the individual instead of making him free are poor. Methods having no relation to the individual needs of the student are rigid, and as such do not lead to the establishment of freedom. At the other extreme is the trend in progressive art education to throw overboard all teaching methods and to regard the unhampered creation by the individual as the only possible creative outcome of good education. Although such an approach may be applicable to some, it cannot become a basis for art education, especially during such a difficult period as the crisis of adolescence.

Other teachers try to avoid the basic difficulties by saying that the youth during this stage is particularly receptive to learning new skills and techniques. As a result of this attitude, they teach skills and techniques in order to cover the "poor creativity" of the pupils during this stage. As will be discussed later acquiring skills and techniques is an important aim of the teaching of art during this period because we should prevent the individual from becoming disappointed by the "inadequacy" of his final product. But if the techniques are not used as *means* to an end, but become ends themselves, they will only be façades without structure. Techniques should be developed, not taught; they must be born out of the need for expression.

With the complexity of expression the need for a more complex technique grows. This need can be satisfied by the individual only in his own individual desires. Techniques copied by students from teachers are taught, not grown, are rigid means of expression which obey inflexible rules. They are entirely unsuitable means of self-expression. What *can* be taught is the basic use of a painting or drawing material. Every student will find his own way of using materials according to his needs. As we shall see, oil painting will be used differently by visually minded and by haptically minded individuals. The one group prefers to use the complexity of an impressionistic color scale, but the other group is more concerned with the expression of "local colors." Within the visually minded group are numerous different approaches, as we know from the difference of pointillistic art of Signac and the paintings of Whistler or Manet. In the same way, we find extremely different approaches in the techniques of haptic art. Techniques of art will be discussed in greater detail in a subsequent chapter; what needs emphasis here is that teaching skills or techniques without the necessary emphasis on the creative foundation would be only an escape from the real problem.

A method of art is good if it brings out the innate qualities of an individual by developing self-confidence and the desire to go ahead. If the method is not applicable to a large group, it is of no use for our educational system. If the method does not grow out of the psychological development of the child, it is an artifice.

This statement characterizes the problems with regard to a good method. Generally, the first indication of critical awareness is in the inability to establish close correlations between imaginative thinking and the final product.

THE CHANGE OF THE IMAGINATIVE
CONCEPT

Much of the confusion of adolescent critical awareness in our society is due to the fact that, influenced by traditional concepts, art must by all means establish a "realistic" relationship to environment, a relationship which develops a "true" (photographic) picture of the external world. The concept of "truth" should be established from as many angles as possible, especially with the help of works of art of different epochs and cultures. It will then become evident that "truth" is relative, and that the word should be replaced by "sincerity." An African sculpture is as "true" to its creator as was the "David" to Michelangelo. The experience, however, which the African sculptor had with his work is vitally different from the experience Michelangelo had when he created the "David." Thus it is the difference in the experience that determines art expression, whether it be painting, music, architecture, or any other art form. To show and demonstrate this relationship between experience and art work in the greatest possible varieties is one of the most important educational means that may eventuate in an unhampered interpretation of experiences.[5]

A work of art is not a product of nature; it is a product of human spirit, thinking, and emotions, and can only be understood when the driving forces which lead to its creation are understood. These driving forces are of essential significance and everything else is only a by-product. If these driving forces are lacking, not even the most developed skills can ever replace them. That is why the works of the Primitives can be great works of art, while most skillfully executed works are not necessarily works of art if they lack the driving forces, the inner spirit that determines the greatness of an art work. They are like beautiful wrappers around nothing. It is therefore important to show the different qualities of these driving forces on the most diverse works of art of different epochs and cultures. It is important to show how in a Greek sculpture the highest adoration of the beauty of the body has been expressed. This can be understood only if we imagine that even a mother subordinated her feelings to the concept of beauty by disposing of a baby for the mere reason that its body was not perfect, as was the custom among the Spartans.

The driving forces which determined the expression of the "ideal" form and shape must be entirely different from those which determined

[5] Munro, Thomas, "Creative Ability in Art and Its Educational Fostering." *Art in American Life and Education.* Bloomington, Ill.: Public School Publishing Co., 1941.

religious expression (the medieval). "Ideal forms" disappear when expression dominates. When we cry, we do not care whether we cry beautifully. The driving force represents the need to incorporate all experiences deriving from expression into the single work of art to make it a symbol of expression. That is why, as we shall see, that in times when a general idea of expression was universal, like the general idea of religious expression during medieval times, the tendency toward symbolism or the general validity of expression is great. If the driving force, however, is individualistic—that is, when expression derives from personal experiences, art expression will be highly individualized.

From this angle we have only to compare Picasso with Rouault to see the strong differences in their individual expression based on the difference in kind of experience (compare Fig. 74a and Fig. 74b). Whereas many of the experiences of Picasso can easily be traced to body sensations and kinetic experiences (as the desire to paint dynamically, front view and profile in one interpretation of a head) Rouault concerns himself greatly with associations of past experiences in which medieval art is often brought into a new light. Its greatest and most powerful expression is found in the dark outlines as seen in the medieval stained windows. How different is the origin of the driving forces in an impressionistic picture in which the external appearance, the changes of light and shadows, the illuminating qualities of surfaces, the complex idea of the breaking of colors, reaches its climax. How contrasted to such external structures and appearances are the driving forces which make an African sculptor carve his idols, or an Indian his totems. An analysis of these forces leads the student directly away from the mere imitative urge of reproducing nature.

Youths during the period of adolescence are eager to give their thinking an intellectual backing. Although they will readily absorb those differences in the nature of the driving forces which determine the art experience, such a stimulation would not be enough for creating self-confidence in their shaken personalities. It would not be sufficient to awake in them the desire to express themselves in their own individual way. The personal experience in our everyday life must be included in the discussion of the difference of the driving forces which determine our imaginative experiences—that is, when we see a burning house, the driving forces which determine our experiences related to it will be quite different for different individuals. The one might be affected by the beauty of the blazing flames flaring skyward, their reflections, and the dancing shadows cast by them. The other individual is deeply touched by the fate of the people who are now without a roof over their heads, suddenly deprived of everything they could enjoy a few moments before. This individual sees the weeping mother holding the only thing she had been able to save: the baby in her arms. Still a third individual might leave the scene thinking only of what he would have done in the same circumstances.

From these different attitudes toward the same experience it becomes evident that the driving imaginative forces which determine pictorial representations are quite different. Whereas the one would merely approach the accident as a spectator (emphasizing visual experiences) the other might become involved in the struggle for existence, setting the ego as a value relationship into the focus of the experience. Haptic sensations determine his world of imagination. The third might be affected by both experiences.

For the proper approach toward art experiences it is of vital importance to distinguish between what is essential and what is unessential for the expression of an experience. *Everything is essential which directly relates to the expression of the experience.* Unessential are those factors which have no direct relationship to the creation of the work. To use these essentials as a guide for the complexity of a stimulation is the key for a proper art stimulation.

For example, our experience may be derived from a body motion: we were intrigued by a worker who carried a heavy load on his shoulder. Carrying a heavy load is now the most essential experience that we would like to express. Everything else becomes unessential. Thus, we do not care whether Mr. Smith or Mr. Jones carries the heavy load. Their faces might only detract from the essential expression in the same way as the face of the "Man with the Helmet" by Rembrandt would have contradicted his experience if it had overpowered the helmet. Rembrandt illuminated the helmet as the essential part, and put the face in deep shadows as if he wanted to say "under the helmet all faces look alike." It is not the portrait of Mr. Jones, it is the "Man with the Helmet." The helmet overshadows the face of the unknown soldier. If we compare this great painting with one of Rembrandt's portraits in which the face has to stand out and the headdress is almost a silhouette we will more definitely experience the meaning of these essentials.

Thus, while concentrating on the act of carrying a heavy load, we shall omit everything that does not contribute to "carrying a heavy load," and concentrate more and more on the experience itself. Although we are quite aware of the meaning of carrying, especially when going through the experience ourselves, we will soon discover that it is the lack of active knowledge which prevents the student from portraying his experience.

Fig. 44. Sketching from posing figure interpreting a topic. (See also *Fig. 32.*)

"What are we doing when we are carrying? Are we bent or upright? Do we have our legs together, or apart from each other, to gain better support? How do we hold our load? Do we need to bend our arms or do we have them straight? Do we look at the ground or forward?" Such questions will activate the passive knowledge of the individual and at the same time stress the essentials necessary for the expression of carrying a heavy load (Fig. 44). It will help those who have no definite concept and will not disturb or restrict those who have the natural gift of expressing themselves. It is much more stimulating and easier not to start to draw from nature but to use the experiences derived from the self.

The complexity of nature, its details and lights and shadows, deflect the attention from the essentials and may in the beginning be too complex and confusing. This way, we also will avoid imposing visual stimulations upon the whole group. Visual and haptic types will apply their individual application to this stimulation, which starts from the self. The visually minded individual will include environment in his visual concept and will project the experience of the self into his environment, whereas the haptically minded student will become absorbed solely in the qualities deriving from his own subjective experiences.

At some point, however, it might become essential to include more than one motion in a representation—for instance, if the repetition of a motion is essential for the atmosphere of the working situation. Digging potatoes and putting them into bags is a continuous activity requiring repetition. We would not do justice to the essentials to exclude this act of repetition. Sometimes monotony is one of the essentials; then we would not much vary the motions but would place them parallel. Another time it belongs to the essentials to show the type of motions workers go through while executing a job. Then we would find it necessary to show the characteristics of the motion by representing characteristic phases showing the rhythm, or working process, in one representation: "The Rhythm of Workers on the Road Swinging Their Picks."

The essentials might even become more complex if we include social atmospheres or emotional reactions. However, with gaining confidence the urge for expression grows, and the guidance of the teacher may diminish. Thus we shall see that the quality and sincerity of art expression are in close relationship to the urge for expression we were able to stimulate. Justice to details must grow out of the desire for expression, otherwise we are not dealing with creative activity. *The study of a detail must never be an aim in itself,* and in this respect art education often fails. The academic method, which used rules for creative production, starts with details. A mouth separated from its environment loses its meaning and becomes an anatomical part unrelated to art. A mouth is a dynamic part of the face and ceases to exist as such when separated from the whole.

Form and expression are a unit and can never be separated from each other without doing harm to either part. If a student who paints a picture of a man pulling a boat gets "stuck" because he cannot express the essential quality of a pulling hand, the study of a pulling hand grows out of the desire to incorporate this hand into the whole experience of a pulling man. He will then proceed with his study, not as a separated, isolated detail, but as a part of the whole which becomes fulfillment only when it unites with the rest. Studying details in the academic meaning becomes quite superfluous within a curriculum of modern art education. *The urge for studying details develops from the individual need for expression.* This need, however, is very diverse, individual, and highly subjective.

From the foregoing discussion, it becomes apparent that proper art stimulation relates as much to personality development as to creative expression itself. This double function of art teaching signifies the importance of aesthetic experiences within this decisive period of development, and shows clearly why art should not be confined to a selected group but should become a means of expression for everyone.

To understand proper art stimulation during this age with regard to the further development of an individual, we have only to consider individuals who did not receive the benefits of such a stimulation. They have lost not only the urge for creative expression, but in many instances also their creative and flexible responses to the outside world. Surely, many have regained these responses in a field other than art. However, it is still an open question whether even the latter would not benefit from art as a means of expression and activity that is completely different from their daily occupation.

A RECONSIDERATION OF SUBJECT MATTER

Considering the subject matter in an art curriculum which is centered on the adolescent individual and the promotion of his art expression, two factors appear outstanding:

(1) the needs of the adolescent in this society; (2) adolescent art as a special form of expression.

The needs of the adolescent in this society

There are two main needs of the adolescent with which art education should be concerned: the individual psychological needs of the adolescent and his needs in a highly specialized society. His psychological needs and how an art motivation should be geared toward them have been discussed in the previous chapter. In this chapter an attempt is made to develop an art curriculum of closely integrated experiences so vital in a society in which specialization, particularly in the sciences, is the dominating trend. To prepare students through integrative experiences to learn and understand the interaction and broader relationships in life's situations in general is then one of the important preparations for citizenship. That art experiences in general are integrative inasmuch as they combine thinking, feeling, and perceiving into an inseparable whole, has been extensively discussed in the section on "The Meaning of Integration in Art Education" (p. 37). We shall therefore keep in mind that it is the very nature of any truly *creative experience* that is integrative. In this connection we shall, however, attempt to present the *subject matter* as a unified, integrated program.

Integration in the following curriculum may be achieved in the indi-vidual by the numerous cross-references which appear as footnotes. With-out using these cross-references, the course of study loses its meaning.

The following areas of experiences appeared significant; however, an extension of areas or sub-areas is left to the creative reader who should consider this curriculum only as a starting point for a curriculum adjusted to his particular environment:

a) Experiences of the Self
b) Experiences in the Home
c) Experiences in the Community
d) Experiences in Nature
e) Experiences in Industry

Adolescent art a special form of expression

It has been pointed out that adolescent art has its own special character-istics, namely, that it is neither the unconscious childish mode of expression nor is it the art form of the professional artist and craftsman. It is much more the art expression of the adolescent youth regardless of whether or not he will later engage professionally in art activities. It is the art expression in which he engages whenever he has freed himself from the inhibitions resulting from his critical awareness toward his work. That such activity is highly personal and only in special cases of highly skilled and aesthetic qualities, should always be kept in mind in the use of the follow-ing curriculum. It is also understood that such a curriculum stands and falls with the *aesthetic sensibilities of the teacher,* his broad understanding for General Education and his qualifications to identify with the needs of his pupils.

EXPERIENCES OF THE SELF

    I.   Experiences of the Self in the Home

        A.   Understanding Myself

        Personal Moods

          1. Sculpturing: [6]
            a. Model a clay mask referring to the self:
               Yawning
               Laughing

[6] See "Sculpturing in the Secondary School," p. 354.

Thinking hard
Whistling
Crying
Singing
Smiling
Sleeping
Being frightened
Being angry

   b. Cast a mask in plaster, using a one-piece mold [7]
   c. Model a full head in which the position of the head also
      contributes to the expression
   d. Carve: [8]

Tiredness
Singing
Excitedness
Looking out

   e. Cut in soft stone:

Listening
Being sad
Turning around, searching for something
Praying

   f. Cast a head in plaster:

In a waste mold
In a piece mold

   g. Model a figure referring to yourself:

An action in your home: studying, carrying, getting up,
etc.

A movement of emotional significance

2. Draw with crayon, charcoal, conte crayon, pen or brush: [9]
   a. Reaching for something in your home
   b. Going upstairs
   c. Coming downstairs
   d. Yourself reading a book
   e. Being tired
   f. Lying on the couch

3. Paint in tempera, water color, oil, or combination of these: [10]
   a. How you feel in the morning
   b. How you feel on a rainy day
   c. How you feel in the evening

[7] See "Casting," p. 356.
[8] See "Carving," p. 360.
[9] See "Sketching," p. 340.
[10] See "Easel Painting," p. 342.

4. Design:
   a. Emotional abstractions of moods—gay, laughing, excited, calm, etc.
   b. Materials I love—a collage
5. Costume: [11]
   a. How I dress at a happy occasion
   b. When I feel let down
   c. To fit my personality
   d. Design a costume which may make me look taller or shorter
   e. A costume when I feel lazy

B. My Home Relations [12]

1. Model:
   a. A group of two friends
   b. Mother and child
   c. I and my brother (sister)
   d. I and my pet
2. Carve:
   My pet
3. Draw:
   a. An evening at home
   b. Playing with friends
   c. Listening to music
   d. A date
   e. Plan your home
4. Paint:
   a. Home life (farm home, city home, country home, mountain home, etc.)
   b. Saying "grace"
   c. Life in a cabin where I would like to be
   d. An abstraction of musical rhythms (jazz, dance, march, waltz) [13]
5. Design:
   a. Design type of home you would like to be in [14]
   b. Relate textures of different materials to each other such as satin, silk, linen, cotton, wool, burlap; different kinds of wood, metal, glass [15]
   c. Make a drawing to scale of the living room of your family.

[11] See "Experiences in the Community," p. 320.
[12] See "Experience in the Home," p. 300.
[13] See "Experiences in the Community," p. 319, also "Emotional Forms of Design," p. 374.
[14] See "Experiences in the Home," p. 303, also "Functional Design," p. 377.
[15] See "Experiences in Nature," p. 324.

Cut out the furniture to scale and move it on your drawing until it serves the function best and you also like it

d. Determine a color scheme for your room

6. Framing or matting:

One of your paintings or drawings

C. My Social Life

1. Paint:

a. In the play room

b. At the fireplace [16]

c. Dancing at a party

d. Going out with my friend

e. Watching television

f. At dinner

g. In our attic

h. Helping burn leaves

i. Shoveling snow

j. Mother cleaning the kitchen

k. Holiday preparations

l. A look out of the window

m. Different social atmospheres in different homes:

In different countries

In slums

In well-kept homes

n. Backyards belonging to a family who likes:

Gardening

To hang their laundry

To play

o. Characterize a family by its yard

2. Posing model with suggested topic: [17]

a. Raking the leaves

b. Pushing the lawnmower

c. Reading a book

d. Climbing a ladder

e. Carrying a log

3. Design:

a. How to decorate my house [18]

b. Curtains

c. A name card [19]

d. Make Christmas tree decorations out of scrap material

[16] See "Experiences in Nature," p. 324, also "Easel Painting," p. 342.
[17] See "Sketching," p. 340.
[18] See "Experiences in the Home," p. 305.
[19] See "Poster Work Lettering," p. 370.

    4. Grooming:
       a. For different occasions
       b. Try out color effects for different types and complexions
       c. What colors look best on me?
       d. How does clothing affect me?

II.   Experiences of the Self in Nature

   A. My Sensitivity to Form [20]

      1. Sculpturing: [21]
        a. Find forms of nature and bring out the innate qualities such
          as in rocks, shells, wood forms, etc.
        b. Make a collage of forms of nature
        c. Find forms in nature suggestive of phantasy
      2. Painting: [22]
        a. Cloud formations
        b. Different forces in nature
        c. Flat desert
        d. Mountains
        e. Sea
        f. Rock formations
        g. Plant forms
      3. Design—graphics:
        a. Snowflakes [23]
        b. Speed of wind
        c. Rhythm of movements in nature—waves in water, in fields
        d. The force of fire
        e. Different textures brought together
        f. Forms in plant life
      4. Photography [24]
        a. Close-ups of forms in plants
        b. Rocks and animals
        c. Leaf structures, moss, barks, etc.
        d. Crystals, surfaces of weathered rocks, crevices, etc.
        e. Shells
        f. Skins, webs, beehives
        g. Ripples on waves
        h. Shadows on different textures, etc.

[20] See "Experiences in Nature," p. 327.
[21] See "Sculpturing in the Secondary School," p. 354.
[22] See "Easel Painting," p. 343.
[23] See "Experiences in Nature," p. 327, also p. 324. "Emotional Forms of Design," p. 374.
[24] See "Experiences in Nature," p. 323.

B.   How Nature Affects Me

    1. Sculpturing: [25]
       a. Abstract forms in nature expressing personal meaning
       b. Forms which affect me positively
       c. Forms which affect me negatively
       d. Walking against wind
       e. Relaxing in nature
       f. In a storm

    2. Painting: [26]
       a. A hot day
       b. A dull day
       c. Wide open on a plain
       d. Between narrow gorges
       e. In a drizzle
       f. Walking in snow
       g. Different moods in nature
       h. Sandstorms
       i. Floods
       j. Twilight
       k. Moonlight
       l. Seasons, etc.
       m. Lightning

    3. Design: [27]
       a. Mobiles with gentle motions; with speedy motions
       b. Collages of smooth textures
       c. Collages of rough textures
       d. Abstractions of "feelings" in nature:
           Glowing
           Cool
           Lonely
           Gay
           Forlorn
           Spooky
           Wet, etc.

    4. Costume:
       a. Costumes for different seasons [28]
       b. Costumes for different climates [29]

---

[25] See "Sculpture in the Secondary School," p. 354.
[26] See "Easel Painting," p. 343.
[27] See "Design and Its Function," p. 377.
[28] See "Experiences in Nature," p. 327.
[29] See "Experiences in the Community," p. 317.

        5. Architecture:
            How nature affects housing [30]

    C.   My Social Life in Nature

        1. Drawing:
            Motions in outdoor sports: [31]
                Swimming
                Jumping
                Running
                Playing football
                Throwing
                Playing tennis, etc.
        2. Painting:
            a. Hiking in nature [32]
            b. Mountain climbing
            c. Skiing
            d. Skating
            e. Picnics
            f. Tenting
            g. Farming, plowing, haying, etc.
            h. Traveling in nature: by car, by train, horseback riding
        3. Design:
            a. Build a bench and tables for picnics [33]
            b. An outdoor bungalow
            c. Design garden furniture, etc.
        4. Costume:
            a. Different uniforms for sports [34]
            b. Costumes for hiking in mountains, in the tropics, etc.

III.   Experiences of the Self in the Community

    A.   Relationship of Self to the Community

        1. Painting:
            a. Visiting in stores
            b. My way to school
            c. Walking down the main street
            d. Helping in community drives [35]

[30] See "Experiences in the Home," p. 303.
[31] See "Experiences in the Community," p. 322.
[32] See "Experiences in Nature," p. 323.
[33] See "Experiences in the Community," p. 322.
[34] See "Experiences in Nature," p. 326.
[35] See "Experiences in the Community," p. 315.

      e. Going to church

      f. Dancing

      g. Using recreation facilities [36]

      h. Helping out with work in the neighborhood

      i. Looking for mail

      j. Going shopping, supermarket, etc.

      k. At the barber shop, etc.

      l. Going through slum sections

      m. Going through residential area

      n. At the fair

      o. Going to the movies

2. Sculpturing: [37]

      a. Praying in church

      b. Greeting my neighbors

      c. Planning a fountain for the school yard

      d. A football player

      e. What I want to be

      f. Listening to a concert, etc.

      g. A beggar

3. Drawing: [38]

      a. At the shooting stand

      b. Sitting on a roller coaster

      c. Swinging in a swing

      d. Stepping into a bus, etc.

4. Design: [39]

      a. Why I like certain buildings

      b. Why I dislike certain buildings

      c. Light patterns at night; traffic; neon

      d. A stained window for church

      e. Abstraction of how you feel:

            On a roller coaster

            When dancing

            When listening to music

      f. Studying historical places and buildings of the community, etc.

5. Excursions to: [40]

      a. Museums

      b. Factories

[36] See "Experiences in the Community," p. 322.
[37] See "Sculpturing in the Secondary School," p. 354.
[38] See "Sketching," p. 340, also "Experiences in the Community," p. 311.
[39] See "Emotional Forms of Design," p. 374.
[40] See "Experiences in the Community," p. 318.

     c. Recreation area

     d. Craftsmen

     e. Historical buildings

6. Costume design appropriate to the occasion and the individual:

     a. Sports clothes:

        Romantic type girl or boy

        Athletic type girl or boy

     b. Street wear:

        Stout person

        Slender person

        Tall person

        Slim or average

     c. Evening clothes to fit:

        Personality, build, complexion, and coloring

     d. Design costumes that will make tall person look shorter

     e. Design costumes that will be becoming to a short person

     f. Design a wardrobe for yourself (hat, bag, gloves, tie, socks, handkerchief, etc.)

     g. Design costumes for a special purpose:

        Sunday

        Easter

        Christmas

        Traveling

     h. Design a lounging costume for yourself

     i. Show how design affects appearance:

        Predominance of vertical lines

        Predominance of horizontal lines

        Predominance of vertical and horizontal lines

        Irregular curved lines

        Rhythmically curved lines

     j. Combine different textures of fabrics and furs

B. Relationships of Self to Other Communities [41]

    1. Painting: [42]

       a. Traveling by car

       b. Staying over night

       c. Waking up elsewhere

       d. Paint a mural of the important events of your visit

       e. How it feels being a stranger, etc.

       f. Visiting stores

[41] See "Experiences in the Community," p. 315.
[42] See "Easel Painting," p. 342.

IV.   Experiences of the Self in Industry [43]

    A.   My Adventures in Industry

        1. Painting:
           a. My impressions from a visit to the dairy, steel mills, coal
              mine, brick plant, coke oven, tannery, lumber mill, etc.
           b. How I feel while observing the operation of machines
           c. Identifying myself with workers in different industries:
              Being in a steel mill
              Serving the furnace
              Being on the assembly line
        2. Design: [44]
           a. Abstraction inspired by machine parts
           b. Abstraction inspired by motion, rhythm, and accuracy of
              industry, etc.
        3. Drawing: [45]
           a. Movements of workers
           b. Carrying a heavy load on the shoulders
           c. A group of workers on the highway
           d. Swinging a pick
           e. Pulling a rope
           f. Pushing a cart
           g. Lifting a bag
           h. Climbing a ladder
           i. Two persons carrying a log
           j. Digging a hole

    B.   My Appreciation for Tools and Processes in Industry [46]

        1. Pottery:
           a. Coil method
           b. Work on the potter's wheel
           c. Firing methods
           d. Glazing
           e. Decorating
        2. Textile: [47]
           a. Textile printing
           b. Block printing

[43] See "Experiences in Industry," p. 332.
[44] See "Emotional Design," p. 374.
[45] See "Sketching," p. 340.
[46] See "Experiences in Industry," p. 328.
[47] See "Experiences in Industry (Crafts); p. 328.

  c. Stencil printing
  d. Airbrush
  e. Silk screen
  f. Batik
  g. Tie and dye
 3. Weaving:
  a. Using different looms
  b. Hooking
 4. Woodwork:
  a. Design and execute a doorknob or handle
  b. A bowl on a lathe
  c. A simple, functional piece of furniture
 5. Metal:
  a. Use of wire and sheet metal
  b. Jewelry

C. Industrial Products Which I Buy and Use [48]

 1. Arrange a display of objects from your personal belongings which you consider good industrial design and contrast them with what you consider "poor" [49]
 2. Enumerate the differences
 3. Purchase from your local five-and-ten-cent store an article which you consider "good industrial design." [50]
  Defend it—"Why you think it is good"
 4. Select from advertisements good industrial products

EXPERIENCES IN THE HOME

I. Evolution of the Home

A. Evolution of Building Materials [51]
 Make a study of basic materials used in construction of homes during different periods and cultures

B. Evolution of Architectural Features (relating to different types of materials, such as mud, clay, branches, wood, bricks, stone, steel, glass). [52]

 1. Make a collection of pictures of homes built with different materials

[48] See "Functional Design in Decoration," p. 381.
[49] See "Experiences in Industry," p. 334.
[50] See "Functional Design in Decoration," p. 381, also "Experiences in the Home," p. 302.
[51] See "Experiences in Industry," p. 331.
[52] See "Experiences in the Community," p. 315.

2. Compare different kinds of covers (roofs) of houses which were used for protection in different periods and cultures

3. What kind of means did man invent to get from the ground level to other levels?

4. What kinds of doorways can you find in houses of different cultures?

5. How did hardware develop?

6. Compare a doorknob in:
   a. Egyptian architecture
   b. Greek architecture
   c. Roman architecture
   d. Medieval architecture
   e. Renaissance architecture
   f. Colonial architecture
   g. Modern architecture

7. What conclusions can you draw from this comparison?

C. Evolution of Furniture [53]

1. Show the evolution of a chair, a chest, etc.

2. Make a list of all movable furniture:
   a. In a colonial home
   b. In a contemporary home

3. What materials are used in the construction of furniture:
   a. In a colonial home
   b. In a contemporary home

4. What is the function of furniture toward better home life? [54]

5. Compare furniture styles with the change of home styles and home life

6. Find in several contemporary-designed chairs what was important to the designer and what determined his design:
   a. Material
   b. Function
   c. Design

D. Evolution of Utensils [55]

1. Make a list of utensils for various rooms:
   a. Which were adopted from an older civilization?
   b. Which are of contemporary origin?
   c. Which are functional?

[53] See "Experiences in Industry," p. 335, also "Functional Design in Industry," p. 385.
[54] See "Design and Its Function," p. 377.
[55] See "Experiences in Industry," p. 328.

2. Make a list of materials used in the making of utensils today and compare it with previous periods
3. Trace the development of a spoon through:
    a. Early primitive cultures
    b. Egyptian art
    c. African art
    d. Greek art
    e. Roman art
    f. Medieval art
    g. Renaissance art
    h. American Indian art
    i. Colonial art
    j. Contemporary art
4. Do the same with other utensils such as:
    a. A key
    b. A knife
    c. A vase
    d. A lamp

E. Art Activities

1. Design:
    a. Make a drawing to scale of the living room of your family and compare it with that of other periods
    b. Use a plan of a colonial living room and try to adapt it to present-day use
    c. What changes were necessary and why did you make them?
    d. Redecorate your own room or any other room with which you are well acquainted
    e. Make an abstraction of different steps or ramps
    f. Make a model mud hut
    g. Make an Indian village
    h. Make an abstraction of different building materials
    i. Make a textile print using the different textures of building materials
    j. Take a poorly designed piece of furniture and redesign it
    k. What changes were necessary and why?
2. Drawing: [56]
    a. Draw and study doorways in your locality
    b. Draw and study different kinds of stairways in your locality
    c. Draw and study different kinds of roofs
    d. Draw someone sitting in chairs of different periods and

[56] See "Sketching," p. 340.

observe how the posture is determined by the design of the chair:

"Sitting in a 'Sling Chair' "

"Sitting in a 'Contour Chair' "

3. Painting: [57]

   a. Identify closely with living in different home situations:

      How would you feel living as a hunter in a paleolithic cave

      Living on a Mississippi River houseboat

      Living in a colonial mansion

      Living in a contemporary home

   b. Paint abstractions using colors which refer to the different living conditions [58]

   c. Paint a mural: [59]

      Of the evolution of homes

      Of the evolution of stairways and ramps

      Of the evolution of the chair

4. Stage design: [60]

   a. Design interiors of various periods for specific plays

   b. Design costumes which are for plays of different periods

5. Photography:

   a. Gates of different periods in your locality

   b. Entrance doorways of different periods

   c. Houses of various ages

II. Planning the Site

   A. Home Surroundings [61]

      1. How does character of landscape influence and determine the essential features of house design?

      2. Collect samples of homes which are influenced by the character of landscape in which they are built:

         a. A house in a desert

         b. A house in the mountains

         c. A house on a shore

         d. A house on a hill

         e. Houses in warm climates

         f. Houses in regions with cold winters

      3. Collect samples of driveways and garages adapted to different surroundings.

[57] See "Easel Painting," p. 343.
[58] See "Emotional Design, Forms and Its Abstract Quality," p. 374.
[59] See "Mural Painting," p. 348.
[60] See "Experiences in the Community," p. 318.
[61] See "Experiences in the Community," p. 313, also "Experiences in Nature," p. 326.

B.   Location of Home on Lot [62]

    1. How can we best locate the house on the lot providing for:
       a. Privacy
       b. Sufficient garden area
       c. Outdoor living area
       d. Convenient garage
       e. Maximum benefits from air, light, and views
    2. Consider restrictions with regard to street or property lines
    3. What effective means for creating privacy do you know?
       Screens, levels, trellises, etc.

C.   Building Ordinances [63]

    1. Consider and study your community ordinances prescribing such factors as the location of house on lot, frontages, minimum costs, building materials, and window space
    2. Go through your community and compare the houses with regard to the restrictions of building ordinances

D.   Art Activities

    1. Design: [64]
       a. Design a home to conform to a particular area in your own community, keeping in a mind natural trees, lakes, ponds, streams, scenic beauty, and terrain
       b. Design a house:
           On a shore
           On a hill
           In a desert
           In warm climates
           In cold climates
           On rocky terrain
       c. Collect products of nature of your vicinity and combine them in an effective arrangement
       d. Design an outdoor living area for your own home
       e. Design an outdoor living area for a particular location:
           Mountain
           Shore, etc.
       f. Try to redesign your own house to make it fit your own lot better

[62] See "Experiences in Nature," p. 326.
[63] See "Experiences in the Community," p. 313.
[64] See "Functional Design," p. 377.

    2. Drawing: [65]
      a. Sketch various landscapes in your immediate vicinity and draw houses which fit the character of the landscapes
      b. Sketch various views from windows and try by changing the size of the windows to improve the view
      c. Sketch various outdoor living areas with various activities going on
      d. Sketch crowded areas and slums and show how you would improve them
    3. Photography:
      a. Houses on different terrains
      b. Houses with various landscaping
      c. Effective entrances using environment as part of design
      d. Views through windows, keeping the window still as part of the picture
      e. Views through doorways, of patios, of terraces
    4. Sculpturing: [66]
      a. Design outdoor sculpture for specific yards
      b. Design a fountain sculpture for the yard
    5. Poster: [67]
      a. Make posters emphasizing cleanliness, safety in buildings, health as it relates to building
      b. Make posters for community utility planning
      c. Make posters to promote better landscaping

III.   Interior Design [68]

   A.   Designing Rooms for Specific Families

      1. Zoning according to needs of the family:
        a. Diagram the inside area of your home according to activity zones and quiet zones
        b. What different zones would your family need:
           Entertaining
           Living
           Sleeping
           Studying
           Eating, etc.
        c. Design the needs of a family of five
        d. Exterior and interior of a house should harmonize:

[65] See "Sketching," p. 340.
[66] See "Sculpturing in the Secondary School," p. 354.
[67] See "Poster Work—Lettering," p. 370.
[68] See "Design and Its Function," p. 377.

Collect samples in which they do harmonize

Collect samples in which exterior design contradicts the interior

e. Does your room reflect your needs and personality?

f. How would you change it if you had no limits?

B. Structural Parts of Rooms (doors, windows, built-in units) [69]

1. What kinds of doors do you have in your home? Collect samples of doors.

If you could replace them for free-swinging, non-swinging, sliding, folding, all glass, flush-wood, paneled wood, etc., which would you prefer and why?

2. Collect samples of different kinds of windows:

a. Find out the different ways by which they can be opened

b. Picture windows should make the landscape a part of your daily enjoyment without interfering with your privacy. Go through your community or the outskirts of it and find out which of the houses which use picture windows adhere to these principles

3. What built-in units do you know of?

a. Collect pictures of various fireplaces; bookshelves which are part of the interior architecture; closets of various sizes serving different purposes; seating arrangements

b. Examine all these pictures with regard to the relationship of function, design, and material used

C. Choosing Colors [70]

1. Consider exposure, size, use and personal taste

2. Make a model room and experiment by changing the colors of the walls with different color schemes

3. What would you do to make the room appear wider, longer, narrower, higher, lower

4. Plan color schemes for different rooms serving various functions —a quiet room, a music room, a dining room, a bathroom, etc.

5. Plan color schemes for light rooms, for dark rooms, for different exposures

D. Considering Lighting [71]

1. Where is fixed lighting needed?

2. Compare different kinds of lighting fixtures with the design of of the home

[69] See "Experiences in Industry," p. 322.
[70] See "Experiences of the Self," p. 291.
[71] See "Functional Design in Industry," p. 385.

3. Compare fluorescent and incandescent lighting
      Where would you best use them?
4. Study different types of lamps, such as desk lamps, table lamps, floor lamps, wall lamps, ceiling lamps
5. What kinds of lamps would you like to have in your room and why?
6. Study the difference between the lighting in utility rooms (kitchen, bathroom) and living rooms

E. Furnishing Rooms [72]

  1. Study contemporary designs of furniture for different purposes
  2. Relate function, design, and material to various pieces of furniture*

F. Art Activities

  1. Design: [73]
      a. A table lamp. The base may be made of any material (plastic, wood, ceramics). The shade must belong to the base. In which surrounding will it be used?
      b. An outdoor light for a porch, entrance for a driveway, or a garage
      c. An outdoor light for illuminating house numbers
      d. A desk lamp with fluorescent light
      e. A magazine rack
      f. A footstool
      g. A coffee table
      h. A telephone stand and seat
      i. Book ends for a contemporary desk
      j. Drapery material for specific rooms
      k. Remake and refinish chairs, bookcases, etc.
  2. Draw: [74]
      a. A home plan dividing it into activity zones
      b. Activities in different rooms
  3. Paint: [75]
      When you look out of the window from different rooms:
         "My Room"
         "My Corner"
         A personal mood as related to your house or your room

[72] See "Experiences in the Community," p. 312.
[73] See "Functional Design," p. 377.
[74] See "Sketching," p. 340.
[75] See "Easel Painting," p. 342.

4. Print: [76]
   A linol block print, woodcut for drapery
5. Weave: [77]
   Place mats (combining different materials)
6. Turn on potter's wheel: [78]
   A vase, a bowl, dish, a pitcher
7. Make:
   A model of a one-story home with two bedrooms, kitchen, living room, bath, showing the division of the interior into rooms. Consider minimum hallways, traffic system, windows, storage, view, doors, built-in closets

IV. Home Life

A. Family Life

1. Sculpturing: [79]
   a. Model: "Mother and Child"
   b. Cut in soft stone: "Our Family"
   c. Carve: "Child and His Pet"
   d. Model: "I and My Hobby"
              "I and My Brother"
              "Praying"
2. Drawing: [80]
   a. With crayon, charcoal, conte crayon, pen or brush
   b. Going to church
   c. Going on a hike
   d. At the dinner table
   e. An argument
   f. Portraits of the family
3. Paint: [81]
   Identify with families of different incomes; how people live
4. Mural painting: [82]
   Family life from morning to evening
5. Costume design: [83]
   a. Working clothes
   b. Play clothes

[76] See "Linoleum Cut," p. 364.
[77] See "Experiences in Industry (Crafts)," p. 328.
[78] See "Experiences in Industry," p. 328.
[79] See "Sculpturing in the Secondary School," p. 354.
[80] See "Sketching," p. 340.
[81] See "Easel Painting," p. 342.
[82] See "Mural Painting," p. 348.
[83] See "Experiences of the Self," p. 298, also "Experiences in Nature," p. 326.

    c. A dress for marketing
    d. Slacks for shopping
    e. An evening dress

B. Things to do to Improve the Home

    1. Sketch: [80]
        a. Changes you would like to make in your home
        b. Changes in the landscaping of your home
    2. Design: [84]
        a. Bird bath
        b. Fireplace utensils
        c. A mailbox
        d. Towel rack
        e. A magazine rack
        f. Ashtrays
    3. Hanging of pictures:
        Hang pictures so that they can be seen, considering the best light; no interference by other items, the level of the viewer
    4. Flower arrangements:
        a. Consider relation of flowers to container:
            Color
            Size
        b. Consider combinations of flowers
        c. Display branches
        d. Plan arrangements of products of nature on trays:
            Moss, shells, rocks, foliage, flowers, etc.

C. Gardening and Landscaping [85]

    1. Divide your yard with regard to functions:
        a. Living area
        b. Recreation area
        c. Play area
        d. Gardening area:
            Flower
            Vegetable
            Rock garden
    2. Make a plan of your yard [86]
    3. Consider the lawn area in relationship to the planted area
    4. Consider the relationship among shrubs, trees, and flower area

[84] See "Design and Its Function," p. 377.
[85] See "Experiences in Nature," p. 326.
[86] See "Experiences in the Community," p. 322.

5. Design a rock garden
6. Sculpture: [87]
   a. An out-of-door figure
   b. A mobile
7. Painting: [88]
   a. Your impression of your garden
   b. Your feeling about flowers
   c. A close-up of the part of your garden which you like most
   d. What happens in your garden
8. Woodwork: [89]
   a. A bench for your garden
   b. Design and make a special fence—louvre fence, solid fence
   c. Design and make a bird house
9. Costume:
   a. Design an outfit for gardening
10. Design: [90]
    a. Use as an inspiration the textures, shapes, and colors you find in your garden and make:
       A collage
       An abstract painting

EXPERIENCES IN THE COMMUNITY

I.   Community Planning

   A.   Present Conditions

      1. Make a survey of present conditions in your town which need improvements
         a. Painting: [91]
            Traffic jam
            Slum areas
            Narrow streets
            Poor housing
            Poor working conditions
            Floods
            Lack of playgrounds
            Children playing on the street

[87] See "Sculpturing in the Secondary School," p. 354.
[88] See "Easel Painting," p. 342.
[89] See "Experiences in Industry," p. 329.
[90] See "Abstract Design," p. 374.
[91] See "Painting," p. 342.

How people live

Different social atmospheres

    b. Drawing: [92]

Sketch life on the street

A building in progress

Children playing on a vacant lot

  2. Make a survey of present conditions which you accept

    a. Painting: [91]

Your recreation area

Your playground

Newly designed streets

Our skating rink

A residential area

    b. Drawing: [92]

Our new school

Our airport

Our bus station

Our city hall

Scenes in open air

    c. Mural painting: [93]

For the school cafeteria

A cross section of our town:

Important activities

Important buildings

Important facilities

Important events

Important people

    d. Posters: [94]

For soap, a bottle of perfume, a dress or suit, cars, tires, foods, etc.

    e. Window display: [95]

Make a display that stresses uniqueness and quality

Make a display that stresses uniformity of quality

Make a good arrangement of a dress

Make a display for a "sale"

Make a good arrangement of a whole outfit

Arrange one window of a:

Grocery store

Women's store

Men's store

[92] See "Sketching," p. 340.
[93] See "Mural Painting," p. 348.
[94] See "Poster Work and Lettering," p. 370.
[95] See "Experiences in Industry," p. 333.

Drug store
Shoe store
Jewelry store
Department store
Arrange a window for:
Easter
St. Valentine's Day
Christmas

B   Future Improvements of Our Town

1. Painting: [96]
   Our future city
   Our future traffic
   Our future city at night
   Living in our future city
2. Design: [97]
   A future airport
   A future bus station
   A terminal
   Take a part of your town and redesign it as you feel it should be
   in the future
   A street sign
   A bridge
   A neon sign for a specific place in town
3. Poster design: [98]
   Study various types of print
   Distinguish between letters that are written and those that are
   drawn
   Use different lettering pens
   Try to letter with the lettering brush by using its specific char-
   acteristics (broad, flat, pointed)
   Make word illustrations, illustrating the meaning of the word
   by its design:
   Heavy
   Light
   Bold
   Strong
   Delicate
   Hurry
   Rough

[96] See "Easel Painting," p. 342.
[97] See "Functional Design in Industry," p. 385, also "Experiences in Industry," p. 336.
[98] See "Poster Work and Lettering," p. 370.

Smooth

Fun

Serious

Help

Dangerous

Apply the various characteristics found through these word illustrations to posters found in town, but for which you have a different idea

Apply your findings also to posters of various industrial products of your town

Make a "Welcome" sign for your town

Poster for "Backyard Campaign"

4. Sculpture: [99]

Model a monument for an important occasion:

World War

Certain achievements

Airport

5. Photography:

Compare new and old housing

Narrow and wide streets

Details of architectural designs

Search for interesting shadows

Search for textures, i.e., various pavements, various building surfaces

Search for contrasts: a lonely tree on a building lot, a church near a skyscraper, a bird in traffic, what else?

C. Architectural and Landscape Design [100]

1. Art history: [101]

Trace the influences on the buildings in your town

Find the oldest building in your town

Find the first building which broke through:

Traditional pattern:

What kind of building was it?

Is there some relationship of the building to the town?

Is it purely the initiative of a single person?

Did it affect other buildings?

What historic buildings are in your town?

Has your town a museum? If so find:

Paintings which refer to your town

[99] See "Sculpturing in the Secondary School," p. 354.
[100] See "Experiences in Nature," p. 326.
[101] See "Experiences in the Home," p. 300.

Objects which relate to your town
Crafts which are peculiar to your town
People who have contributed to your town

2. Design: [102]
A shopping district
Make a plan of an ideal farm
Make a model of a display window
Ask a neighboring merchant to allow you to decorate a window
Design an effective package for an industrial product
Design a seal or sticker to represent a store in your community
Design a public park with:
Landscape areas
Recreation areas
Play areas
A pond
Design a small city park in front of one of your public buildings
Design an entrance to a public park

D.   Transportation and Communication [103]

1. Design:
Invent your own road signs:
Stop
Curve
Steep Hill
Slippery
Crossroad

2. Posters: [104]
"Prevent Accidents"
"Watch the Red Light"
"Don't Play in the Streets"
"Drive Slowly"
"School Children"
"Hospital Area"
"Railroad Crossing"
"Bus Stop"

3. Mural painting: [105]
A mural for the airport
A mural for the bus station
A mural for the railway terminal

---

[102] See "Design and Its Function," p. 377.
[103] See "Experiences in Industry," p. 336.
[104] See "Poster Work—Lettering," p. 370.
[105] See "Mural Painting," p. 348.

The development of transportation to and from your town
A mural for the telephone building
A mural for the post office
Traveling through our county, or surrounding states
4. Make models of: [106]
An airport
A railway station
A bus station
A car design
A bus
An airplane

E.   Interaction with Other Communities and Countries

Where did the population of your community come from? Invite people from different countries to talk to your group. Find out about their customs and culture
1. Paint a mural: [105]
Where the people of your town came from
A community festival
The lives of people in various countries
2. Art history:
Show the relationship between art and life in the different periods of history in your town. Show the relationship between art and life in different epochs and cultures by looking at different houses and how life must have been in them
Show the connection between the form of a utensil and its functions and point out dominance of either one in the different epochs and cultures
Find out the relationship of characteristics of styles with their epochs and cultures. Start with the functional straight lines of modern architecture
Find traces in your community of other periods and cultures: in buildings, in furniture, in art objects, in merchandise, in utensils

II.   Education and Citizenship

A.   Health

1. Posters (two- and three-dimensional): [107]
a. "Don't Spread Colds"
b. "Keep Your Streets Clean"

[106] See "Experiences in Industry," p. 335.
[107] See "Poster Work," p. 370.

     c. "Don't Spit on the Floor"

     d. "Drink Milk"

     e. "Use your Swimming Pool"

     f. "Have Your Chest X-Rayed"

     g. "Cancer Drive"

     h. "Red Cross"

     i. "Prevent Accidents"

2. Sketch: Out-of-door activities: [108]

     a. Tennis

     b. Swimming

     c. Racing

     d. Other sports

3. Paint: [109]

     a. Contrast—"clean" and "dirty" (houses, restaurants, etc.)

     b. People at clinics

     c. Emotions or experiences during illness

     d. Unhealthy conditions in housing

B. Safety

1. Study: possible causes of accidents:

     a. On the street:

          Slippery pavement

          Falling objects

          Traffic accidents

          Neglecting traffic lights

          Speeding when driving, etc.

     b. At home:

          Fire

          Slipping

          Falling

          Poor use of tools resulting in injury

          Carelessness

     c. In industry:

          Crowded workshops

          Open fires

          Exposed wirings, etc.

2. Paint: [109]

     a. An accident:

          In industry

          On the street

          In traffic

[108] See "Sketching," p. 340.
[109] See "Easel Painting," p. 342, also "Abstract Design," p. 374.

At home
In recreation
3. Make posters: [107]
   a. "Prevent Accidents":
      At home
      On the street
      In traffic
4. Design: a safety measure

C. School Environment and Education

   1. Improve the appearance of your classroom by: [110]
      a. Reorganization of furniture according to better function
      b. Adding a well-designed display area
      c. Designing flower boxes
      d. Arranging an exhibit
   2. Plan exhibits of school art products in store windows with cooperation of merchants:
      A display of art books
   3. Arrangements:
      a. Make arrangements of products of nature for the classroom, using shells, rocks, moss, plants, flowers, etc.
      b. A display of book jackets
   4. Mural painting: [111]
      a. "The Development of our School"
      b. "The Life of an Educator"
      c. "The Development of Books"
   5. Costume design: [112]
      a. A dress for school
      b. A gymnastic outfit
      c. A band uniform
      d. A dress for a school party
   6. Illustrations:
      Illustrate your favorite story or book
   7. Visit to museums
      a. Views of local artists
      b. View the permanent collection
      c. Study the types of displays
      d. Learn how traveling exhibits are hung
   8. Exhibits:
      a. Make a class exhibit

[110] See "Design and Its Function," p. 377.
[111] See "Mural Painting," p. 348.
[112] See "Experiences in the Home," p. 308, also "Experiences in Nature," p. 326.

      b. Arrange an exhibit according to a specific topic:
         Skills
         Theme
         Material
         Subject matter, etc.
9. Excursion to: [113]
      a. Local artists, musicians, collectors
      b. Newspaper printing
      c. Local craftsman—carpenter, potter, jeweler
      d. Factories and industries
      e. Fire Department
10. Paintings: [114]
      a. Listening to a concert at the theatre
      b. Police helping children cross the street
      c. A visit to the museum
      d. Fire
      e. Extinguishing a fire
      f. Studying
      g. Reading in the library
      h. Helping in drives—Red Cross
      i. Helping flood victims
      j. In the school bus

III. Recreation

    A. Theater

      1. Formal aspects of stage design: [115]
        a. Study the effect of horizontal and vertical lines in relationship to mood
        b. Study the effect of different levels
        c. Study the effect of lighting in relationship to cast shadows
        d. Study the effect of lighting with regard to the illuminated part
        e. Study the meaning of big spaces versus small spaces
        f. The meaning of foreground and background
        g. The center of interest
        h. The emotional content
        i. The social atmosphere
        j. Period and style
      2. Design a stage set of a definite play according to the above principles

[113] See "Experiences in Industry," p. 328.
[114] See "Painting," p. 342.
[115] See "The Elements of Expression," p. 393.

3. Design a stage set and lighting for a dramatic scene:
   a. A graveyard
   b. A wilderness
   c. A prison
4. Design a stage set for a mass scene:
   a. A riot
   b. A festival
   c. A fair
5. Design a stage set and lighting for a small village square
6. Design a stage set and lighting for a scene in an industrial section or factory court
7. Design a stage set for a drawing-room comedy
8. Costume:
   Study the characters of one play and design the costumes and make-up
9. Masks:
   a. Make masks for a specific play:
      Fantastic
      Grotesque
   b. Study masks of different periods and cultures
10. Puppetry:
   Design stage set and characters for a puppet show
11. Architecture: [116]
   Design and make a model of an outdoor theater
12. History:
   a. Make a mural of the historical development of the theater
   b. Gather all available information about your oldest theater
   c. Make a study on the changes in film techniques from the beginning to the present

B. Music

1. Design: [117]
   a. Listen to various musical moods and paint your impressions by means of abstract designs
   b. Paint abstractions interpreting the sound of—a trumpet, a drum, a violin, a flute, etc.
   c. Try to catch the rhythm and mood of:
      A symphony orchestra
      A band
      A jazz orchestra
      A chamber ensemble

[116] See "Experiences in Nature," p. 326.
[117] See "Abstract Design," p. 374.

       d. Design a cover for a specific record

  2. Poster: [118]

      Design a poster for a music festival in your town; for a band concert; a choir; a chamber-music recital

  3. Sculpture: [119]

      a. Make a three-dimensional form suggesting music

      b. Model masks of:

         "Singing a sad song"

         "Singing a blue song"

         "Singing a happy melody"

  4. Paint:

      a. "Listening" to a concert

      b. "Jazz"

  5. Sketch:

      Motions of players during a rehearsal

  6. Layout:

      Make the layout for a specific program

C. Dance

  1. Costume Design:

      a. Design costumes for a creative dancer interpreting:

         "Mourning"

         "Industrial rhythm"

         "A clown"

         "Ecstasy"

         "Depression"

      b. Design a costume for a:

         Folk dance

         Social dance

         May festival

         Outdoor dance

         Formal dance

  2. Decorate for dance:

      a. Table arrangement

      b. Place cards

      c. Arrange a centerpiece

  3. Decorate for an outdoor dance

  4. Design abstract designs of various dance rhythms: [120]

      a. "Blue"

      b. "Tango"

[118] See "Poster Work and Lettering," p. 370.
[119] See "Sculpturing," p. 354.
[120] See "Abstract Design," p. 374.

        c. "Hot jazz"

        d. "Boogie woogie"

        e. "Ballet"

        f. "Creative dance"

    5. Sketch: [121]

        a. Dance motions from nature during a dance—one motion in time sequences

    6. Art history:

        a. Trace representations of dance through different periods and cultures

    7. Mural painting: [122]

        a. Paint a mural of the different meanings of dance:

            As a religious form

            As a national expression

            As a social form

            As recreation

        b. Paint a mural on the dance in different cultures

    8. Painting: [123]

        My personal feeling for dance

    9. Poster: [124]

        a. Design a poster for a:

            Dance festival

            Social dance

            Outdoor dance

            Spring festival

   10. Sculpture: [125]

        a. Model a dancer dancing a specific dance or rhythm

        b. Model an abstract form suggesting dance

D.   Motion Picture, Radio, Television

    1. Study a motion picture with regard to its intrinsic qualities, such as:

        a. Use of close-ups to direct attention to specific forms or actions

        b. Use of various spaces and times

        c. Use of movement

        d. Mass movements

        e. Insertion of seemingly unrelated parts underscoring emotions, such as clouds, storm

        f. Fading in

---

[121] See "Sketching," p. 340.

[122] See "Mural Painting," p. 348.

[123] See "Experiences of the Self," p. 293, also "Painting," p. 342.

[124] See "Poster Work and Lettering," p. 370.

[125] See "Sculpturing in the Secondary School," p. 354.

2. Study the various forms of films:
   a. Entertaining
   b. Instructional
   c. Documentary
   d. Historic, dramatic
3. Study the differences between stage production and movie making
4. Design:
   a. Enclosures for radio—table radio, portable radio, built-in radio
   b. Enclosures for television—table model, built-into a unit
5. Study television as an art medium:
   a. Compare with motion picture:
      The quality of intimacy
      The quality of spontaneity
      Audience participation
6. Design an art program for television which provides an optimum of audience participation and excludes imposed prescriptions

E. Outdoor Recreation

1. Study recreaton areas in your community:
   a. With regard to location:
      Away from industry, dust, traffic
   b. With regard to facilities:
      For children
      For youth
      For adults
2. Design a functionally spaced recreation area on a specific locality in your town:
   a. Areas for various sports
   b. Area for playing and games
   c. Area for sitting and eating
3. Design and build:
   a. A table-bench combination
   b. An outdoor fireplace
   c. Outdoor cooking utensils
4. Sketch: Actions from nature (sport and play)
   Paint:
   a. Life on a recreation area
   b. The feeling of noise and motion
   c. Cooking Outdoors
   Design: A fountain for a recreation area

EXPERIENCES IN NATURE

I. Interpretation of Nature's Principles

A. Changes and Growth

Paint: [126]
1. How plant-life growth or death affects the landscape
    a. Desert
    b. Barren land
    c. Farmland
2. Poster painting:
    a. Seasonal changes: summer, fall, winter, spring
    b. Sky and cloud changes as: effects of time of day on nature (morning, sunrise; evening, sunset) and cloud formations
    c. Forest fire prevention
Discuss and paint:
3. How increases in population affect our landscape: urban, rural
4. Effects of industry on nature: factories, strip mining, coal mining
Discuss:
5. Effects of rise and fall of population on nature
6. Mural painting: [127]
    The process of strip mining from the untouched landscape to the industrial change

B. Nature's Varying Moods

1. Painting or abstract design: [128]
    a. How we feel on rainy days
    b. How we feel on cold days
    c. How we feel on hot days
2. Mobiles:
    a. Varying winds, storms, tornadoes, and floods
    b. Sunshine after a heavy rain
    c. Shifting mists on the hills
    d. Changing courses of streams and rivers
3. Design:
    a. Reactions according to the varying moods of the day

[126] See "Easel Painting," p. 342.
[127] See "Mural Painting," p. 348.
[128] See "Experiences of the Self," p. 291.

4. Collage:
  a. Changing seasons
  b. Study through field trips how nature is affected by river changes. For example: a study through films, slides, illustrations of the Grand Canyon country, would possibly be good inspiration in forms, columns, colors, textures, space, etc., and lead into areas of painting or design

C. Nature's Motions

  1. Photography and mobiles:
    a. Effects of elements on nature as wind (how wind works on sand and snow; the moving clouds; the swaying trees and fields of grain) and water (raindrops on the walk and lake; waterfalls; swift rapids; whirlpools; dancing snowflakes)

D. Organic Actions

  Sketching: [129]
  Animal: graceful deer, jumping squirrel, hopping rabbit

E. Color and Light

  1. Abstractions of: [130]
    a. Seasons' colors
    b. Climatic effects on color and light: how weather affects our landscape (red hills, desert, mountains, snow coverage) and studying various lights of the rainbow, moon, sun, and stars
  2. Outdoor water color and oil paintings (art activity)

F. Texture

  1. Photography and design:
    a. Through weather and wear: sand and water ripples; rock and pebble forms; tidal effects (on coastlines, inland waters); snow formations (drifts, study an individual snow flake)
  2. Design: [131]
    a. Sea structures: sea gardens, sea shells
    b. Sea inhabitants and organisms compiled into an organized design
    c. Land structures: rock forms; landscapes; wood (dead or alive)
    d. Collecting dead tree parts, rocks or other products of nature

[129] See "Sketching," p. 340.
[130] See "The Meaning of Aesthetic Criteria," p. 392, also "Abstract Design," p. 374.
[131] See "Design and Its Function," p. 377.

to be worked into an interesting decoration, table piece, or lamp standards

3. Mural painting:
Texture qualities of soil through man's manipulation: cultivation, harvest time

G. Preservations

1. Posters:
   a. State and national parks
   b. Care and preservation of our woods and forests
2. Sketching:
   Possibilities and limitations for home and building sites
3. Design:
   Sketch and design houses on: a hill, a rock, in the desert, on the ocean, on a crest, etc.

II. Getting The Most From Nature

A. Conservation

1. Making the public conscious of the problems of conservation
2. Posters: [132]
   Save animals that are becoming rare
   Save flowers, do not pick them
3. Wise use of our natural resources, as wood:
   Discuss its many uses for building, paper, furniture, utensils, etc.
4. Mural: [133]
   Showing growth, wise methods of securing, and products from all parts of the tree
5. Utilization of land: [134]
   City planning to make the most use of a small amount of land to the best advantage
   Art activity:
   Plan, design, and build a model city of cardboard, wood, plaster

B. Natural Resources

1. Study the source of art materials and their use
2. Abstract design: [135]

[132] See "Poster Work and Lettering," p. 370.
[133] See "Mural Painting," p. 348.
[134] See "Experiences in the Community," p. 313.
[135] See "Abstract Forms of Design," p. 374.

       a. Materials of nature used as art forms; make an abstract design for an interior decorative piece from materials as bark, rock, leaves, wood, etc.

       b. Make a collage of natural materials stressing variety of line, shape, form, texture, and color

       c. Make pottery and ceramic pieces from native clay

       d. Using local wood, carve interesting shapes of realistic or abstract form

       e. Study the source of materials; provide experiences in making the materials—dyes, pigments, paper, tools (carving, modeling, construction, brushes, etc.)

  C. Landscape Design [136]

    1. Design:

       a. Plan an informal garden arrangement for your own home; paint it in oil, water color, gouache, pastel

       b. Make several color sketches that show plans for a year-round pleasing effect in a garden

       c. Plan, design, and build a model of a home that utilizes the landscape design as a purposeful part of the living arrangement to show an integration in architecture with nature

    2. Public landscape design:

       a. Design suitable landscape arrangements for a public building in your community; make a sketch in pencil, charcoal, water color, etc. to show the plans

       b. Plan a city park to include activities adaptable to many interests and age levels yet spacious-appearing; make color sketches of the various areas

       c. Plan a design to scale for a state forest conservation park; make an accurately-scaled drawing of your layout

    3. Outdoor social activities:

      Painting and stage design

       a. An outdoor athletic field day

       b. A festival setting such as May Day

       c. Adapt the surrounding landscape to an original play being produced on the grounds of the school

III. Clothing

  A. Outdoor Clothes

    Costume design

    1. A mining outfit, a farm outfit, a garden outfit

    2. Recreation as skating, skiing, hunting: [137]

---

[136] See "Experiences in the Community," p. 313.

[137] See "Experiences of the Self, p. 296, also "Experiences in the Community," p. 298.

a. Two- or three-dimension posters advertising correct clothes for outdoor occupations or recreation

b. Make a mural showing outdoor occupations for a guidance room

c. Build 9 x 12 dioramas showing the outdoor occupations or recreation, and the natural background

B. Climate

1. Seasons: consider your clothes with regard to weight of material, style, colors from nature

2. Weather: weather-proof materials, weight of materials, style, and amount of clothes

3. Latitude: weight of materials, style and colors as to highlands or lowlands, at different latitudes

4. Costume design:

Have the class design clothes for boys and girls for different seasons of the year, for the changes in weather and latitude. When designs are complete, have them make models of papier-mâché and exhibit in school showcases as visual education for students not participating in art activities

IV. Geographic and Climatic Influences on Culture

A. Nature's Way with Materials

1. Study the effects of weather and time on various materials such as: iron, wood, stone, paint, etc. Collect samples or take photographs of these. Which age or weather "gracefully"? Discuss the implications of weathering for architecture.

2. Collage:

Make a collage of weathered materials

3. Photography:

Photograph architecture with well weathered materials

4. Sketch: [138]

Show shapes in nature influenced by weather in their growth or through wear of the elements. A weathered rock, a weathered pine, a rock hollowed or shaped by a stream. Shapes of stalagmites and stalactites in caves. Look at weathered textures through a microscope.

5. Design: [139]

Use the textures of nature in an abstract painting

[138] See "Sketching," p. 340.
[139] See "Abstract Design," p. 374.

B.   Art History—Comparative Study of Cultures Influenced by Nature

   1. Art activities:

       Search for photographs of art work influenced by nature of different cultures as Egyptian, Greek, Chinese, Japanese, showing the use of materials peculiar to their specific location. Search also for photographs of the regions from which these works come. Wherever certain qualities in the one suggest the other, try to establish a relationship through an arrangement of these materials in chart or exhibition form. Try to list qualities common to the region, the culture, the art work

   2. Mural painting: [140]

       Do some thinking on the relationship of natural setting, culture and art work in America or in your own region of America. Make a mural on natural sources of art inspiration in your region—characterizing the variety of terrain, types of vegetation, climate, weather

EXPERIENCES IN INDUSTRY

I. Crafts

   A. Pottery

      1. Wedging the clay
      2. Coil method
      3. Work on the potter's wheel
      4. Firing methods
      5. Glazing
      6. Decorating
      7. Trace the history of pottery from the early beginning to contemporary designs of dinnerware and show its relationship to social changes
      8. Show the relationship among material, design, and function in:
         a. A Greek vase
         b. A Mexican pottery
         c. An Italian majolica
         d. An English Wedgwood
         e. A contemporary dinnerware
      9. Visit a pottery shop in your town and notice the different places where the pottery was produced

[140] See "Mural Painting," p. 348.

10. Find clay deposits in your environment
11. Try to make a simple outdoor kiln
12. Break up pieces of glazed pottery, and make a mosaic, sticking the parts to a paper, framing it and pouring plaster or concrete over it and then removing the paper

B. Textile Design

  1. Textile printing:
     a. Block printing
     b. Stencil printing
     c. Airbrush
     d. Silk screen
     e. Batik
     f. Tie and dye
  2. Weaving techniques:
     a. Hooking
     b. Needle point
     c. Gobelin
  3. Collect and discuss textile prints in different cultures and countries
  4. Discuss the changes a printed textile undergoes when flat and when hanging in folds
  5. Follow the history of the loom from the primitive self-made loom of tribal primitives to our modern cloth factories
  6. Try to relate the type of weaving, its pattern and design to the culture in which it was produced: compare a Mexican rug with a Persian rug
  7. Make a simple handloom and experiment in finding different patterns which grow out of the process of weaving
  8. Visit a rug store and find out where the rugs were made
  9. Trace the history of Gobelin and relate the technique used to its period

C. Work with Wood

  1. Carving
  2. Work on the lathe
  3. Carpentry
  4. Discuss the importance of the tool determining the shape of the object and, vice versa, the kind of object determining the tool with which it is made
  5. Show differences of carving marks in soft and hard wood

6. Carve:
   a. A "free form"
   b. A tray
   c. A wood sculpture
7. Turn on a lathe:
   a. A doorknob
   b. A lamp base
   c. A bowl
   d. A platter
8. Carpentry:
   Design and execute a simple piece of furniture such as:
     A table
     A chair
     A bench

D.   Paper

1. Folding the paper and cutting it
2. Shaping paper forms and combining them
3. Forming with papier-mâché
4. Trace the history of paper from the early Egyptian use of papyrus to the present day
5. List the different uses of paper and related material such as cardboard and fiberboards:
   a. Make foldcuts, folding the paper in different ways
   b. Try to predict the design produced by folding
   c. Make paper sculptures by combining the different processes of folding, shaping and cutting
   d. Experiment in using different lighting effects on the paper sculpture
   e. Use paper bags for masks and combine them with other processes, such as cutting, folding, or shaping
   f. Use papier-mâché for making a "free form," a mask, an animal, a figure

E.   Metal Work

1. Shaping:
   a. A copper bowl
   b. A wire sculpture consisting of round and flattened wire
   c. A brooch
   d. A ring with a setting for a stone
2. Forging:
   a. A metal frame for a chair

b. A fireplace set

c. A log carrier

d. A hot dog fork

3. Soldering:

a. Soft solder wire in wire sculpture

b. Hard solder in jewelry:

Pins on brooches

Settings on rings, etc.

4. Welding:

a. Metal sculptures

b. Metal furniture

5. Select historical work of arts and crafts and find the various processes which were used in:

a. A French gate

b. A forged English sword

c. An Italian Renaissance bowl

d. Mexican jewelry

e. Contemporary silverware

6. Visit metal shops in your town

7. Relate the process to design in various products of metal of different periods and cultures

F.   Synthetic Materials

1. Shaping

2. Pressing

3. Molding

4. Explore the use of different synthetic materials such as: plastics, vinyl, rubber

Plastics: make a simple platter

a tray

a bowl

a sculpture

5. Investigate the use of vinyl or rubber tiles in building. Experiment with new floor patterns for kitchen or bathroom floors

6. List as many objects now made of synthetic materials as you can think of. What were the materials from which they were made before the invention of synthetic materials?

7. Make a mold for making a form out of plastics

8. Design a car using plastic molds

G.   Relating Different Materials to Each Other

1. Make collages of different materials using processes as described above

2. Make a floor lamp using different materials
3. Explore various relationships of materials in furniture and architecture:
   a. Textile and wood
   b. Stone and metal
   c. Metal and wood
   d. Wood and stone
   e. Glass and metal
4. Trace the combination of different materials and processes through various periods and cultures

II. Assembly Line and Other Industrial Processes

A. Effect on the Self [141]

1. Discuss how the assembly line affects your standard of living
2. Discuss how problems of production were solved in the era preceding the industrial revolution caused by the assembly-line procedure
3. Name advantages and disadvantages caused by assembly-line production:
   a. Sameness of work
   b. Quality of work
   c. Effect on individual problem-solving
   d. Mass participation in inventions
   e. Serial housing
   f. Reduced prices
   g. Equalization of standards
   h. Individual differences

B. Effect on the Community [142]

1. Discuss how your community has been affected by industry:
   a. City planning:
      Mass settlements
      Apartment houses
      Cars
      Parking problems
      Smoke
      Population

[141] See "Experiences of the Self," p. 299.
[142] See "Experiences in the Community," p. 312.

Planning of homes:
Functional furniture
Kitchen and utensils
Bathrooms
Outdoor living
b. Environment:
Changes through:
Mining
Factory plants
Transportation facilities
Highways
Airports

III. Advertising [143]

1. Design container to hold a specific article such as perfume, auto parts, ink, milk, foodstuffs, mechanical instruments. Any product can be used; design the container considering the nature of the material or product
2. Make model package, consider proportions, color, public appeal, material, etc.
3. Advertise previously designed article: [144]
   a. Show-window display, show-card writing
   b. Illustrate and layout magazine page in any medium
   c. Illustrate and layout book page in any medium
   d. Illustrate and layout newspaper page in any medium
4. Study psychological appeal of advertisements by relating color to product. Example: perfume advertised in posters, magazines, billboards, etc.[145]
5. Advertise product of local factory: [146]
   a. Posters, abstract, or realistic, study lettering (for specific purposes), lettering character, consider character of product. Make silk-screen poster, airbrush, tempera, whatever available, including montage.
   b. Design trade-marks for local factory or specific industry; study good and bad characteristics of trade-mark, use iron and steel, textiles, foodstuffs and study differences
   c. Design letterheads for specific industry; study characteristics of letterhead, appeal, advertising value

[143] See "Poster Work and Lettering," p. 370.
[144] See "Design and Its Function," p. 377.
[145] See "Color, an Element in Composition," p. 414.
[146] See "Experiences in the Community," p. 314.

d. Design and set up window display, making and utilizing models, textiles, etc., for specific industry, correlate factory and product
e. Make posters for safety: for driving to work, in the factory. during work

IV. Consumer Education

A. Self [147]

1. Select in the dime store five household utensils of good design
2. Examine them with regard to the relationship among function, purpose, design, and material
3. Select from a furniture catalogue the table and chair which you like best and compare it with those which you consider worst
4. Name at least four attributes which are responsible for their differences
5. Select from a book on houses the house which you feel comes closest to your taste:
   a. State as many points as you can why you like it
   b. Did the house you selected utilize the space properly?
   c. Is the inside of the house in harmony with its outside?
   d. Are the materials used according to their functions?
   e. Are textures utilized?
6. Select and study a painting with which you would like to live:
   a. Why did it appeal to you?
   b. Is the selection you made in agreement with your environment?
7. Study appeal of various types of package design to people's tastes and personal reactions by showing them different designs and recording their reactions
8. Discuss the reactions and study ways of improving taste by showing:
   a. Relationship of design to content
   b. Avoiding cluttering effects
   c. Better layout
   d. Color relationships in accordance with content
9. Design a window display of a store of which you would like to be the owner:
   a. Show quality of article by displaying a few at the right place
   b. Show quantity for "sale" by repetitive pattern

[147] See "Experiences of the Self," p. 290.

B. Home [148]

   1. Study the proper choice of furnishings and household equipment, iron, washer, stove, table, chairs, lamps, etc. in relationship to income. (The best-designed washer or "easy chair" for the lowest, medium and high income group)

   2. Evaluate home furnishings with regard to price of product, design quality, material, and durability

   3. Select and discuss a home of good design quality for a low, middle, and high income group from the houses of your community

   4. Discuss poorly and well designed pre-fabricated houses

C. Community

   1. Redesign a poorly developed housing section of your community

   2. What effect has advertisement on the "look" of your community:
     a. Billboards
     b. Neon lights
     c. Advertisements on houses
     d. Window displays

   3. Select "good effects" on the "look" of your community and contrast them to poor ones:
     a. What are the characteristics of "good effects"?
     b. Why did you consider effects as "poor"?

   4. Study means by which you could make your community more "art conscious":
     a. Placing good paintings or reproductions in your town library
     b. Starting a display case in your library with good displays of various crafts, products or other well-designed articles.
     c. By starting an adult art program
     d. By asking stores to collaborate in the display of well-designed products

V. Transportation [149]

A. Mural Topics

   1. Depict the evolution of transportation

   2. Design mural for airline

---

[148] See "Experiences in the Home," p. 305.
[149] See "Experiences in the Community," p. 312.

3. Design mural for railroad terminal
4. A mural for a bus station
5. Discuss the evolution of car designs
6. Compare the evolution of car designs with other areas such as:
   a. Furniture
   b. Kitchen appliances
   c. Churches
   d. Schools
   e. Factories
   f. Laboratories
7. State similarities and dissimilarities in the evolution of contemporary design in various areas of living and working as compared to means of transportation

B. Design Topics [150]

1. Highway patterns resulting from intersections
2. Effective highway signs for intersections, or other warnings
3. Study the design of various kinds of transportation or means of hauling relative to their functions:
   a. Railroad, ship, truck, airplane
   b. Truck for lumbering
      for moving
      for hauling dirt
      for loading and unloading
   c. Airplanes for passengers
      for hauling loads
      for various war purposes
   d. Boats designed for passengers
      for carrying airplanes
      for carrying freight
      for various war purposes

C. Painting Topics [151] (the manner which best fits your expression)

1. Your personal feeling when traveling: [152]
   a. In a train—the landscape swiftly passing by
   b. In an airplane—cloud formations, patterns of various landscape textures

---

[150] See "Design and Its Function," p. 377, also "Functional Design in Industry," p. 385.
[151] See "Easel Painting," p. 342.
[152] See "Experiences of the Self," p. 291.

        c. In a car—highways—endless or rolling terrain—curves
        d. In a boat—water in its different moods—reflections
    2. At a:
        a. Railway terminal
        b. Bus stop
        c. Airport

D.   Graphic Topics [153]

    1. Identify with trucking at night
    2. Impressions on the highway
    3. A marshalling yard—at night in the rain, during busy hours, when idle

E.   Poster Topics [154]

    1. Safety posters:
        a. Do not drink when you drive
        b. Drive slowly
        c. Watch curves
        d. Dim your lights
        e. Intersection
        f. School children
        g. Highway construction

F.   Landscaping [155]

    1. Landscape a highway section
    2. Landscape a section dividing highways

G.   Model Making

Make a Model of:

    1. A bus station
    2. An airport
    3. A railroad terminal
    4. A harbor
    5. Underpass
    6. Various forms of intersections, clover-leaf forms
    7. Various means of transportation serving specific functions

[153] See "Graphics," p. 364.
[154] See "Poster Work and Lettering," p. 370.
[155] See "Experiences in Nature," p. 326.

THE MEANING OF SKILLS AND TECHNIQUES
IN THE SECONDARY SCHOOL

The development of skills appears of vital importance in the secondary classroom for it is through them that the adolescent individual gains confidence in his individual art expression. The characteristics of adolescent individuals developed by psychologists must be seriously considered in the motivations of adolescent art. Ambition, persistence, self-criticism, introspection, but also "a desire for romance and adventures" [156] are traits which will best be served by experimental attitudes toward skills and the use of techniques. It can then easily be seen that the crafts will assume a major role in any secondary school art program. It must, however, be kept in mind that a balanced program necessitates not neglecting the meaning of those forms of art where the adolescent individual can directly project his thinking, perceiving, and feeling. It is in this realm where we most often fail in recognizing the needs of the adolescent.

One of the most important factors in promoting freedom of expression during this vital period is the recognition that adolescents are afraid to use any method which *directly* projects their imagery. In countless cases, I have seen adolescent youngsters discouraged by the "primitivity" of their pencil drawings, but if the identical drawings were used for etchings or embossing, they were well satisfied (Fig. 45a and 45b). The *direct* form of expression apparently was emotionally too close to them and their self-critical attitude could not bear the "naïveté" which was in contradiction to their grown-up feelings. Etching or embossing introduced a procedure which brought about a somewhat more remote attitude toward the original and direct form of expression. This introduced distance, however, was vital to the acceptance of the work. Now it is no longer the naïveté which counts, but the technical involvement in the art expression of the adolescent. To provide adolescent youth with the opportunity of such technical involvement without losing the initial desire for expression is one of the foremost tasks of the teacher in promoting adolescent art.

Before discussing the use of techniques in secondary schools in greater detail, it seems essential to refer again to the distinction between mere procedures and techniques made previously. Procedures can be explained while techniques are highly individual and therefore develop according to personal desires.

The relationship of an individual to his technique is more an outcome of

[156] Havighurst, Robert J. and Hilda Taba, *Adolescent Character and Personality.* New York: John Wiley & Sons, Inc., 1949; Cole, Luella, *Psychology of Adolescence.* New York: Rinehart and Company, 1950.

b

a

Fig. 45a. "Primitive" drawing which does not stand his critical awareness leaves the adolescent youth unsatisfied.

Fig. 45b. Embossing it in copper, thus removing himself from the directness of expression by introducing a more complex technique, makes him accept his work. Children's Art Classes. The Pennsylvania State Univ. Dr. Edward Mattil in charge.

his experiences in the world which surrounds him than a result of learned skill. As long as technique is separated from individual expression, technique is only a handicraft which may even restrict the individual instead of encouraging him. If, for example, a haptically minded student is introduced to oil painting by being shown impressionistic methods of painting in nature, he will soon become discouraged because he will not see in nature the complex colors which are the results of visual analyses. His thinking and experiencing might be more related to the expressions in line than in color. *Technique and individuality are closely interwoven*: therefore, techniques should be *developed,* not taught. Technique is an expression of individuality, and as such, must contribute to, not hamper, the development of individuality. Consequently, the best technique will permit the individual to express himself most easily.

Since, as we have seen, art education in the secondary- and elementary-school classroom does not prepare for a profession but rather serves to develop the mental, emotional and aesthetic growth of the individual, the teaching of skills must be focused upon the problem of finding the kind of expression adequate for the student personalities. All skills, therefore, must be introduced with the purpose of fostering the individual's free expression.

Sketching

Linear

The line as such is an abstract expression. It can have *kinesthetic* origin but can also stand merely as a *symbol.* If it has kinesthetic origin, the line has more the character of *motion* (repeated lines with flowing character) ; if the line is an abstract of a form (an outline), it is determined mainly by expressive desires. The line which interprets visual experiences is usually a *sketchy line,* emphasizing the three-dimensional qualities of the form. For linear drawings, wax crayon (trade name, "Marking Crayon") is a good material. Since erasing is impossible, the student is compelled to concentrate more definitely on his concept. In expressive art, *every line* has significance. Even unintended lines have expressive qualities, perhaps the quality of "Fehlleistungen," [157] which play a major role in psychoanalysis. In expressive linear sketching, therefore, nothing should be covered or erased: everything should remain in its genuine original "hand-

---

[157] According to Sigmund Freud, "Fehlleistungen" are unintentional actions which are revealing with regard to the individual's subconscious reactions. Misspellings often belong to this category.

Fig. 46. Sketch of motions in black crayon. Free expression in lines.

writing." Wax crayon or lithographic pencil leads the student directly to this understanding, since he finds it impossible to "change" his concept within one drawing. If a concept does need a basic change, a new drawing must be started. This, however, is important, because it gives the student as well as the teacher an opportunity to see the growth of a concept, which is often revealing of the student's thinking and provides the teacher with a source of guidance (Figs. 46, 47, and 48). Since the character of the expressive line is in its truest one-dimensional meaning, smooth paper is preferable to paper with a rough texture because the latter would divert from the smooth, gliding, one-dimensional character of the line. This technique can be followed by brush and pen drawings; long-haired sable brushes and black drawing ink or drawing pens lend themselves very well to this purpose. Since the use of brush and ink demands more technical skill than that of wax crayon, the former can better be explored after the student has gained confidence in the use of wax crayons. This technique leads directly to etching or aquatint, which will be discussed under the heading of "Graphics" in a later section.

Three-dimensional

Sketching techniques that include shades of different intensities are usually techniques emphasizing visual reactions toward experiences. The essence of these techniques, therefore, is the emphasis on the quality of the visually perceivable appearance of the objects. Consequently, the technique must permit the easiest approach toward a visual image. Since the visual image changes with regard to mood, atmosphere, light, shadow, and distance, a material must be chosen which is more flexible and changeable. Such a material is *charcoal*. Charcoal, because of its adaptability to easy changes, is the material which can best be used where quick adjustment to an impression or an image is needed. The visually inclined student will, therefore, feel at ease with charcoal in his hand; whereas the expressively inclined, haptically minded student would feel unhappy with this "smeary" material. Charcoal can be followed up with graphite sticks or with soft pencil, in which the adaptability is no longer as great as in charcoal. For these techniques, coarse paper is preferable, because it diminishes the linear character and gives more easily through its texture the effect of depth and atmosphere. These techniques lead directly to the techniques of lithography, which will be discussed in a later section.

Easel painting

Imaginative

An easel painting is an intimate expression of emotions, ideas, or experiences in nature. It reveals the artist's direct relationship to his world of sensations. An easel painting, therefore, usually is not illustrative like a mural, which tells a story or an event, but is more the artist's direct approach to the world of his experiences. It is the most subjective approach in painting techniques.

Depending on personality, subject matter, and method of approach, different techniques will lead easiest to the desired expressive qualities. It devolves upon the teacher to recognize and guide his students into the kind of techniques that are most adequate to their desire for expression. Some students need models for visual inspiration. Other students are hampered by what they see, since they use means different from visual stimuli as starting points for their creative experiences. Their world is bound up with imaginative experiences which can basically be visual or haptical, the world of appearances or the world of subjective expressions. For both groups, however, different techniques will lead to their aim.

In general, for imaginative paintings—that is, paintings that are not done from nature, but purely from imagination, techniques must be chosen that lend themselves to a building-up process, to the possibility of going over the painting again and again without technically tearing the picture into uneven, heterogeneous parts. There are different techniques for utilizing such processes. They can be divided into techniques that can be carefully planned, layer by layer, and techniques that are not built up gradually, but are applied emotionally.

Techniques that are applied emotionally—that is, directly, without planning or contemplation, are technically the easiest to use. The aim of such a technique is to preserve the paint stroke in its original quality. Such pictures are usually painted *alla prima*—that is, in one sitting. "Painting alla prima aims from the very start at the final effect of the finished picture, and attempts to arrive at that effect in the shortest and most direct way." [158] If oil paint is used, the painter has to paint wet in wet to keep the homogeneous character. If the picture cannot be painted in one sitting, the binding media has to be of such quality that it permits only slow drying. In order to keep the painting from drying, a mixture of oil of clove (1 part) and poppy-seed oil (5 parts) is recommended. If, however, tempera is being used, it is suggested that the picture be sprayed slightly with thin emulsion or with water before continuing to paint on the dry picture, especially when casein tempera is used. Tempera gives sharper, clearer, and more illuminating qualities. Sharpness suggests the emphasis of the line— expressive rather than visual quality. Indeed, tempera does not lend itself well either to studies of nature or to "atmospheric" effects. An attempt to

[158] Doerner, Max, *The Materials of the Artist.* New York: Harcourt, Brace and Co., 1934; Hiler, Hilaire, *The Painter's Pocketbook of Methods and Materials.* London: Faber and Faber Ltd., 1937.

Fig. 47. Stiff, academic representation of head by Frank Stewart.

use tempera paint for realistic effects would, therefore, mean a waste of energy. Tempera will be an excellent medium in the hands of haptically inclined students, but will be a poor one in the hands of purely visually minded individuals. Of course, here also the teacher's understanding of the desires of his students should be the deciding guide.

Fig. 48. Free representation made by the same student, Frank Stewart, after apply-ing correct stimulation.

If the desire for careful planning is great, two techniques are suggested which truly satisfy this urge. The one technique is the use of oil paint in different layers in which the opaque and the transparent quality of the paint is effectively used. The other technique is a mixtechnique in succes-sive layers. This is the technique of the old masters, and is best seen in Il Tintoretto, El Greco, and Titian. It is the technique that uses the illu-minating and sharp quality of tempera paint as well as the quality of depth of oil paint. One layer is done in opaque tempera paint. When this is dry, a transparent wash or glaze is painted over it. This can be repeated again and again until the desired effect is reached. The wash—that is, the transparent layer, usually consists of resin, dissolved in turpentine. Mastic resin is excellent for this purpose. Since in this technique the final concept is built up layer by layer, this approach will be used by artists who prefer "scientific" planning and are otherwise more intellectually inclined. This technique is in contrasting effect to the emotionally used *alla-prima* technique in which the student has the immediate desire to give his emotions form and expression.

The *ground* used for oil and tempera paintings should be prepared. Whether paper, cardboard, pasteboard, canvas, or wooden panels (plywood) are used, the important job of the sizing material is to fill in the pores and prevent the sinking-in of the paint. Glue (1/10 in 9/10 water dissolved in a double boiler) will in most cases prevent too much absorption of paint. If the student wishes a gliding ground with a smooth and luminous surface, the ground must not be absorbent. For this purpose, the best material to use is heavy white paper on a stretcher, sized with a coat of glue. Works of great artists are painted in oil on paper and have kept perfectly. Before the paper is placed on a stretcher, it must be well moistened. In this condition it is glued to the stretcher. After it has dried, it stretches perfectly. Other smooth grounds can be achieved by painting a coat of white (titanium white or zinc white) over the coat of glue (oil ground). This especially is necessary when canvas is used. Gliding grounds are necessary for carefully planned work in which the brush stroke must have a clear and distinct character. If a rough impression is desired, the ground must be soaky (absorbent) in order to soak in the binding media as quickly as possible. Mixing some fine chalk or gypsum into the glue or oil paint will make the ground absorbent.

From nature

In painting from nature a quick approach is desirable. The technique, therefore, must be one in which final results can be obtained in the shortest possible time. That is why no technique that involves a building-up process in which one layer supplements the other lends itself for painting in nature.

Several techniques can be used for this purpose. Water color is good because its luminous effect lends itself very well for painting atmosphere. However, there is a difference between painting wet in wet, or wet on dry ground. If colors should merge into one another, wet in wet is the desirable technique. If sharp outlines are wanted, the ground has to be dry. Disregard of these quite obvious facts very often leads to failure and discouragement. Although much stimulation can result from accidental fusions of colors, the teacher should use such accidental happenings for explanations of what can be done consciously and how it is to be done. The ground (the type of paper) used for water colors depends on the desired outcome as well as on the approach. The more the student is inclined to give a rough and sketchy impression of a visual image, the coarser the paper can be. The more the student depends on the detailed effect of the scene—that is, the more he depends on the subject matter he wants to paint, the smoother the paper should be. Technically inclined students, who receive more enjoyment from the accuracy of depicting the subject matter than from painting impressions of nature which refer to mood and atmosphere, will therefore prefer the smoother ground. If these different attitudes toward depicting nature spring from the type and character of personality, students should not be diverted from their own approach. On the contrary, in both approaches there are strong values: each should be recognized and used to the fullest extent. Although the latter type, the one who is more dependent on subject matter, might be the less "artistic" type, it is of greater importance to foster personality trends than to "make" of everyone an "artist."

Pure tempera paint does not lend itself very well to painting in nature because its contours are too sharp and its colors not "atmospheric." Although there exist fine studies of nature in tempera techniques, its use for this purpose is not recommended. If more opaque colors are desired, a mixed technique of water color and tempera is suggested. If only tempera white is added to water colors, the technique is called "gouache." Although it is not customary to mix tempera and water color in one painting, there is no reason for not doing so if the student gets enjoyment out of the transparency of water colors and the contrasting effect of opaque tempera paint. In fact, many students through this contrast have come to a quicker and lasting understanding of the painting of "atmosphere." The experience of the changing colors with regard to distant objects has nothing to do with a surface experience of these objects. The main experience refers to atmosphere. Therefore, this can be best expressed by a technique that emphasizes the transparency of the air. A student might, however, become interested in the surface structure of a near-by object and there is no reason why he should not use a technique, like tempera, that permits an easier approach.

In oil, *alla-prima* techniques are the only ones which can be used in nature. There are two possibilities, depending again on the nature of the student. The one, mixing the desired colors on the palette and then applying them to the canvas; the other, using clear colors either with

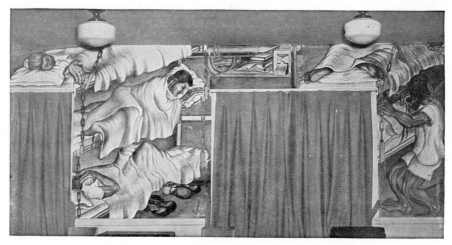

Fig. 49. Section of mural painted as part of architecture by John T. Biggers.

brush or with palette knife and putting them close to one another on the canvas. The final effect is reached through optical fusion in our visual apparatus. For visually inclined students who do not depend on detailed impressions, but rather depict mood and atmosphere, this technique is strongly recommended, since it permits the exercise of greater freedom in color and expression.

Also here, the student who finds most of his relief and enjoyment in detailed representations will prefer a smoother, nonabsorbent, meager ground. However, the student who prefers quick and rough sketches without details will find the rougher texture with some chalk or gypsum mixed into an oil ground more satisfactory. The teacher's understanding of the technical needs adjusted to the individual desires of his students will greatly contribute to their free and uninhibited development.

Mural painting and its techniques

The nature of a mural

Whereas an easel picture is an intimate expression of emotions, ideas, or impressions, separated from its surrounding by a frame which intimately closes it off from its environment, a mural is a part of "another whole"—architecture. The painter has to adjust to whatever problems arise from architectural conditions. This is the first decisive difference between an easel picture and a mural. No restrictions whatsoever are related to an easel painting with regard to size, technique, and subject matter. In a mural the size is determined by the architect (actually, the size of the wall). The technique has to be adjusted to the purpose of a mural—that is, its decorative effect, and the subject matter often depends upon the meaning of the building in which the mural is painted (Fig. 49).

Let us consider more closely these three characteristics that are decisive in distinguishing between an easel painting and a mural. The architect determines size and shape of the wall space for a mural. The first problem in designing a mural, therefore, is to adjust the composition to the architecture for which it is determined. This should not be felt as a restriction. On the contrary, it might become a basic stimulation, an inspiration, or at least a challenge to use a given shape for a composition. In a good mural, architecture and mural composition must be so closely interwoven that the one cannot be separated from the other. As soon as the architecture is felt as a restriction, the mural is as out of place as when the mural overpowers the architecture. Only when architecture and mural go together so well that one improves the other does the mural fulfill its purpose.

The second problem is technique in a broader sense, not merely as it is related to material. This problem can best be understood if we remember that the mural has to be a *part of the wall,* of the architecture as a whole. The painter must not work at cross-purposes with the architect by painting "a hole" in a wall, which would be the case if the painter emphasized distance or depth in his composition. The architect says, "There is wall." This wall is important in his architectural concept, and the painter must support this idea. Therefore, a mural cannot stress foreground and background effects, but should regard all parts as equally significant and distribute the composition over the whole wall space. In this sense, the mural is a decoration of the wall and should not conflict with its architectural meaning. That is why the mural technique must emphasize the line and its decorative meaning, and stress the luminous, expressive quality of the paint, not its atmospheric attributes. Finally, the mural must permit the emphasis of the surface of the wall as such, whenever it seems necessary.

The third problem relates to content. An easel painting can be removed from a wall whenever desired. It is something in itself, existing for no other purpose than for its creation. A mural is painted as a part of a whole and must be adapted to the purpose of the whole. The subject matter of a mural depends upon the space for which it is determined. This, too, can be felt as a restriction as well as an inspiration or challenge. Surely, confines of space on a wall were not regarded as a restriction during the early medieval age in which religious subject matter dominated in mural expres-

Fig. 50. Murals painted as a part of architecture. Group work. Hampton Institute.

sion. Since murals are painted as part of a whole architecture serving a definite purpose, a mural is destined for a larger audience whose members often (like in the churches) receive the impression simultaneously. A mural is, therefore, much more than a picture: it is a means of communication; it tells a story or transmits an idea. Also, from this point of view we will understand its technical approach toward a clear and definite depiction.

After this brief discussion of the nature of the mural, we shall proceed to a consideration of the different types of murals appropriate for the secondary-school level.

The planned mural

A mural that is planned for a definite architecture, painted either directly on the wall, and intentionally of lasting character, must first be planned in detail. A scale plan of the wall must first be made, and the mural composition adjusted to this plan. If the mural is painted directly on the wall, two techniques can be chosen: the "fresco" painting on the wet mortar, or the mural (or "secco") painting on a dried plaster ground.

Fresco painting is done on wet mortar, and on wet lime plaster in which lime is used as binding medium for the pigment. "The water evaporates, and at the same time the lime absorbs carbonic acid gas from the air. On the surface of the picture is formed a glassy skin of crystalline carbonate of lime, which incorporates the colors with the ground in such a manner as to make them absolutely insoluble in water, and at the same time gives to them the fine sheen peculiar to genuine fresco painting." [159] Although fresco technique is the most durable among all mural techniques, its application is too complicated for use in the secondary-school classroom.

A technique that is easily applied is commonly called "mural painting" (formerly, "secco painting"). A plaster ground is sized with a wash of lime. The binding medium is egg yolk or casein. Glue water can also be used in the proportion of 1 to 10. Two parts water for one egg yolk is the best mixture. The paint can be mixed before each painting session, or better, the paint pigment may be mixed with water to form a thick paste and then mixed with egg yolk whenever it is needed for painting. In this technique no white is necessary, since the white of the wall will be used not only to keep the feeling for the wall surface but also as "white," whenever it is needed.

[159] Doerner, Max, *The Materials of the Artist.* New York: Harcourt, Brace and Co., 1934, p. 265; Mayer, Ralph, *The Artist's Handbook.* New York: Viking Press, 1940.

Fig. 51. Mural by Charles Pickering. From the classes of the author.

The planned mural has tremendous educational values, which are partly due to the fact that the student has to adjust to given conditions, such as architecture and subject matter; and partly to the fact that almost any subject matter that lends itself for illustrative purposes is suitable for a mural. Thus, historic, social, religious, or scientific themes can be used very successfully for mural paintings, thereby providing an excellent opportunity to integrate learning in other fields with art (Fig. 51).

The direct mural

In contrast to the planned mural, in which every detail must be known before its final execution, the direct mural is applied directly to the wall without sketches or with only rough sketches. These murals are for special occasions, rather than for lasting memorials. Thus, theatre decorations, dance-hall decorations, or murals for special receptions come under this category. The best technique for this purpose is a casein ground and glue water or casein as binding medium. Transparent oil paint on white ground can also be used successfully. A rough sketch of the whole plan is designed first. This sketch, however, does not go into details, but leaves them open to special "inspirations" during the process of execution. Thus the direct mural gives the student considerable freedom for changes and permits him more flexibility than does the planned mural. Such a procedure corresponds to the environment and the purpose for which the direct mural is painted. Whereas the carefully planned mural is painted into a permanent architecture where it will remain as a part of the building, the direct mural will adjust to the occasions for which it is painted. It will be removed after the occasion is over and will be replaced by another. Its subject matter can relate to specific occasions whose rationale is unfamiliar to outsiders. The direct mural, conducted by enlightened leadership, can make an important contribution to the school life and its art consciousness. Because of its popularity and its direct approach it will be much easier understood and appreciated by the general audience. This, however, increases the responsibility of the art teacher for good guidance and leadership.

Both of the mural types described lend themselves also to group work.

The group mural

The fact that many students can participate in the creation of a group mural has distinct social values. Every participant subordinates his own contribution to the whole, yet all have the feeling of cooperative accomplishment. These values are modified by loss of artistic unity inherent in such a group project. The strongly creative individual can be hampered by "cooperation" with others. The planned mural, whose self-consistency and adaptation to the architecture to which it is related must be unimpaired, lends itself for group murals only when different students paint on different walls or panels. Students of mine executed several panels in the Department of Sociology, depicting the theme "Freedom" in various aspects: "Freedom Through Achievement," "Freedom Through Religion," "Freedom Through Evolution," "Freedom Through Revolution," "Freedom Through Expression," "Freedom Through Science," and so forth. Architecturally each window was a kind of niche, which we used for the different individual panels (Fig. 50). A few students painted the remainder of the wall, which surrounded the panels, with industrial designs, thereby integrating the individual panels into the whole architecture. In this way the planned mural lends itself to group work. If, however, such a subdivision into different separated wall spaces is impossible, the disadvantages of lack of unity and the overpowering of one student by another are much greater than the educational advantages derived from the co-operative project. Even when separate wall spaces can be obtained in one unit, there is still the problem of creating a unity among all panels.

The direct mural is the type to be preferred for group work. Since this mural is not planned for lasting value, lack of unity will not be disturbing. Usually determined for a specific occasion, it is subordinated to a definite "spirit." Whether the mural is for a reception, a dance, or a play the student has from the beginning the feeling that all students will subordinate themselves to a specific task. Proper organization is of prime importance. Group work does not mean that everyone can paint everywhere. The teacher or a committee should distribute the work properly. In this work the advantages of cooperation and social adjustments are very distinct. It is, however, important that all students participate in some functions, otherwise the effect might easily be negative.

Sculpturing in the secondary school

The three-dimensional expression of emotions, thoughts, or impressions of nature deals with methods of sculpturing. Naturally, this type of expression is more restricted in the choice of subject matter than painting, since it excludes the representation of environment. This restriction, however, is only superficial because many students who have little desire and understanding for expressing themselves in painting will find much relief and enjoyment in the realm of three-dimensional expression. Sculpturing lends itself to a choice of "living things," animals or men, as subject matter. The more visually inclined the student is, the more will he refer his work to nature and its appearance. The more haptically he is inclined, the more will he deviate from nature and concentrate on his subjective relationship to nature or the expression of his own feelings. The three-dimensional stimulation relating to subject matter and technique will, therefore, be different for those whose desire it is to approach surface appearances and for those who want to express their subjective relationships to their experiences. Whereas the former group receives its best stimulation from nature, the latter group will draw its stimulation from its own feelings.

The stimulation for the visual group, therefore, will refer mainly to appearance or aesthetic evaluation, dealing with structural differences as well as with the meaning of sizes and proportions. The stimulation for the haptic sculptor will consist of directing his attention to the feeling of muscle sensations, kinesthetic experiences, and emotional relationships. However, the chief aim of teaching sculpturing in the secondary-school classroom is to promote personality growth through self-expression, not to give special professional training. We will, therefore, discuss those technical questions only that lend themselves for this purpose.[160]

[160] Putnam, Brenda, *The Sculpture Way*. New York: Frederick A. Stokes Co., 1939.

Sculpturing versus modeling

A distinction has already been made between sculpturing and modeling, especially in the more advanced stages and grade levels. The expression of an unconscious approach—the stages without critical awareness—has been called "modeling," whereas the conscious expression in three-dimensional media has been called "sculpturing." In modeling, the working process is of greater importance. In sculpturing the emphasis is laid upon the final product. In modeling as well as in sculpturing two definite techniques, which are closely related to different kinds of thinking, can be observed: (1) The building up of partial impressions to a synthesis of a conceived form—that is, the synthetic technique and (2) The process of gradually cutting out from the whole form all unnecessary parts until, through this analytical process, the final form is reached—that is, the analytic technique. Synthetic thinking refers to a concept in which the partial impressions add up to a unity, whereas analytic thinking approaches the outer surface as a whole in its appearance. The difference between modeling and sculpturing, as has been pointed out, is that in sculpturing the thinking is consciously related to the technique ("building up from single part" or "cutting out from the whole" in clay, wood, or stone), whereas in modeling the working process is purely instinctive.

This means that in the secondary-school classroom we will deal with techniques of *sculpturing* only, since the student should approach his media with the proper understanding and knowledge of its meaning for expression.

Sculpturing in plastic media

The number of plastic media on the market has grown considerably during the past few years. Although clay is still the most popular material, it is by no means the most satisfactory, especially for use in the secondary-school classroom in which facilities for keeping clay in moist condition are not always available. If sculpturing is done only once or twice a week, as in most of the country's secondary schools, constant attention is necessary to keep the clay and the unfinished products workable. There is another disagreeable attribute of clay: it needs to be stiffened or supported by "armatures" (wire structures that hold the sculpture in the desired position). This technically necessary evil keeps the student from making spontaneous changes. It also makes casting necessary, because the clay sculpture cannot dry with the enclosed armature. Since clay shrinks during the process of drying and the wire maintains its volume, the clay would break. Furthermore, wire and clay are of such different nature, that often when the student prepares the armature he gets involved in the creative process of dealing with a "wire sculpture" and thus forgets that *his concept should grow out of the clay*. This is one of the basic criticisms of the use of an armature. It diverts the student from one of the most important creative principles. *The creative concept must grow out of the material from which it is created.* In this respect a clay sculpture and a stone plastic involve different creative principles. Thus the most organic clay sculpture would be one which is soldily built, with no parts standing out, so that an armature is superfluous. Certainly in ceramics sculptures, which are fired and glazed in the kiln, wire structures cannot be used.

If plasticine can be obtained in large enough quantities, it has some advantages over clay. It is stiffer and therefore does not need support by armatures. It does not dry out. This, of course, is an advantage for schools in which art is taught only once or twice a week. Furthermore, plasticine does not shrink, hence it can stay on an armature indefinitely without cracking. Plasticine has, however, a disadvantage in that it is not of a permanent character. Either it must be used for experimentation purposes only, or it must be cast into another material.

Victor D'Amico reports[161] a new cohesive clay invented by Arthur Baggs, ceramics artist at Ohio State University, that "holds together at the slightest contact and needs no firing." Only experiment and time will prove whether this is the great invention that makes casting unnecessary. Certainly with the growing need for plastic materials, sooner or later we will arrive at the final solution of how to preserve the sculpture in the form and material in which it was created. It is to be hoped that such a badly needed material soon will be discovered, but in the meanwhile, casting, or the transference of a clay sculpture into another medium, will remain necessary.

Casting

Casting is a very old means of reproducing three-dimensional objects in different media. The simplest example of casting is the seal. The seal is the equivalent of the negative or mold, whereas the impression of the seal on the sealing wax is the reproduction of the positive in the different medium. Casting always has been considered as a mere craft, a skill necessary to put a sculpture in a more permanent form. We speak of

[161] *Creative Teaching in Art.*

Fig. 52. Masks. Facial expression as organic start for sculpturing and casting.

a plaster cast if the material used for casting is plaster of Paris; we speak of a bronze cast if bronze is poured into the mold; and so forth. Casting, however, is in strong contradiction to a functional relationship between creative work and material. In modern art we emphasize again and again that the work of art should organically grow out of the material from which it is created. Especially in architecture, where we deal with so many different materials, do we want to give each material its specific function. We have definitely given up wearing wigs and making wooden columns appear like stone. If we build a frame bungalow we emphasize, instead of hide, the beauty of the wood. When we build a brick or stone building, we desire to show the function of the materials. From this point of view, the practice of pouring a clay sculpture in plaster or bronze (materials having different attributes from clay) on which we cannot see the imprint of our hands or tools, is to be condemned. With such a cast bronze sculpture we pretend it is possible to treat this material as we do clay. This is incompatible with a functional concept of creative activity in relationship to the material used.

As long as casting is treated as a mere technical transference into another material, casting itself is not an art form. If, however, casting is technically treated as an art form in its own right, it will become a new form of sculpturing. A stained window, for example, has an art form of

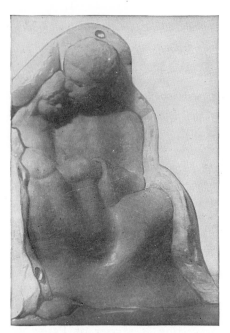

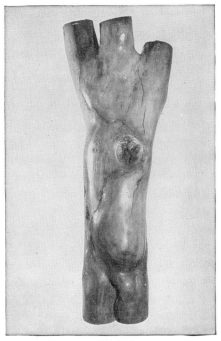

Fig. 53. Casting of a clay sculpture showing good characteristics of clay. (Sculpture by Samella Sanders.)

Fig. 54. "Victim." Wood sculpture by Henry W. Bannarn, showing excellent use of the structure of the material.

its own in which the lead, while holding the glass pieces together, determines the linear composition. In casting, the creative concept should also grow out of the technique, or vice versa, thus representing a new form of art. In this new form of sculpturing the seams which heretofore have been carefully removed on the final product, would become a part of the creative concept. Instead of removing them, one should allow them to fulfill their linear function in the same way as does the lead in the stained window.

The simplest approach is to cast a piece without undercuts.[162] A piece without undercuts needs only to be cast with a one-piece mold. A mask, in which facial expressions can best be studied and taught, would therefore be the most organic beginning for casting (Fig. 52). Over the clay mask plaster of Paris is poured to a thickness of approximately three inches. If many pieces are made from the same mold, it is advisable to build in a screen to hold the plaster together and prevent it from breaking. When the

[162] Daugherty, John Wolf, *Pottery Made Easy.* New York: Bruce Publishing Co., 1940.

plaster is dry, the clay can easily be removed. The mold is then carefully cleaned and sized with sizing soap, a substance which fills up the pores completely, thus preventing any material from sticking to it. After this is done, the casting material (in secondary schools only plaster of Paris is advisable) is poured into the mold. To facilitate the removal of the finished product from the mold when it is hardened, it is suggested that a handle of thick wire be built into the casting material. If only one piece is to be poured, the original mold can be chipped off. This is called a "waste mold."

If a piece has undercuts, which is to be expected in any round sculpture, the mold must consist of two or more pieces. Before casting is done, the sculpture has to be divided into sections with no undercuts (Fig. 53). These sections must be marked by clay walls approximately one inch high and then each section has to be filled with plaster. Before an adjacent section is done, the clay wall must be removed until the whole sculpture is enclosed with plaster. The more organic a clay sculpture is made, the more simply can it be cast. The more the clay sculpture grows out of the material "clay," the fewer parts will stand out, since clay in itself has too little firmness. Such sculptures, which have no separated or "attached" parts, are naturally "closed" as a functional outcome of the dealing with the material from which they are formed and lend themselves best for casting.

If casting is included in the secondary-school curriculum, it is most important to relate it from the very beginning to sculpturing itself. If this is not done, serious disappointments will result from the many obstacles that may arise from too many undercuts or pieces that stand out from the sculpture. I have seen students of college classes develop a horror, or almost a class psychosis, when too many pieces which were too difficult for casting were destroyed or damaged in the process. When a cast is well done, *nothing should be corrected on it.* If whole sections have to be made over again, the unity of the creative work suffers, while the creator feels frustrated owing to technical insufficiency which has spoiled his work. The work with armatures greatly contributes to such frustrations, since armatures represent factors working against the spirit of the material. If casting is introduced (and in my opinion it should be, because it offers not only creative but also industrial stimulations) armatures should not be used. They only offer obstacles, technically and creatively. What should be done if a student insists upon representing motions that cannot be formed without "stiffening" the clay? If, for example, a student would like to have the arm standing out, we can only tell him that his creative concept is not suited for execution in clay. He should either execute it in a different material, or create the same expression in a concept that grows out of the clay. Similarly, an architect of the medieval period could not have built Gothic towers out of wood. The modern architect will not build a stone building with the concept of a frame bungalow. He will not even plaster wood in order to give a wrong impression of the nature of his building material. To stress this point also in sculpturing is psychologically important because it is another way of emphasizing "truth" in the creative concept. A clay sculpture should be modeled so that it looks like a clay sculpture. This is not a new idea, but a neglected one in the creative concept of modern "functional" art, which emphasizes again and again the interdependency of material and creative concept without doing justice to this particular material. If the concept of a clay sculpture is really adjusted to the qualities of clay, casting is a simple matter.

Although I have seen classes which were disgusted from the frustrating effects of poor results of casting, I have also seen groups that became enthusiastic about the wonderful and inspiring process of transferring a clay sculpture into a work of durable material. It all depends on the way casting is presented. It is most important that the student receive his inspirations for good sculpturing in clay from the way the sculpture lends itself to casting. This experience, therefore, is a vital art experience, and by no means should be turned over to "professionals" but must remain a part of the student's experience.[163]

Carving in wood and cutting in stone

Carving in wood and cutting in stone have their places in the secondary-school classroom if they are used merely as an inspiration for working in a different medium and a means of feeling out different approaches. From this angle, however, it should be noted that there are decisive differences among the processes offered in clay work. In plastic material, the student may either choose to build up a sculpture out of partial impressions or to form it from the whole. In carving or cutting, the student has only one possibility, one psychological approach, and this is the analytical one, which starts from the whole and arrives at the final product by the process of elimination. Not all students are able to form such a concept; therefore not all students can be asked to do work in carving or cutting. The analytical mind works differently from the synthetical one. Whereas the analytical mind has from the beginning the impression of the whole

[163] Toft, Albert, *Modelling and Sculpturing*. Philadelphia: J. B. Lippincott Co., 1936; Glass, Frederick James, *Modelling and Sculpture*. New York: Charles Scribner's Sons, 1929.

simultaneously before him, the synthetical mind gradually builds up a sculpture into a whole. Thus, a student who very efficiently builds up a sculpture of numerous parts might feel frustrated during the process of carving or cutting, since it is contrary to his thinking and concept (Fig. 55a and 55b).

Carving in wood and cutting in stone must again "grow out" of the special material in which it is done (Fig. 54). Carving in soft wood is different from carving in hard wood. Not only do the different woods have different grains, but they also have different cutting qualities, which should be used to the fullest extent in a wood sculpture. There is no good reason for cutting small details with great difficulty in a kind of wood which lends itself best for subjects of rough texture. Using the grain as a part of the wood sculpture is an outcome of the relationship of the creative concept to material. To neglect this quality of wood means taking the beauty from the wood. Most commonly used woods for carving are apple, oak, and yellow pine. Walnut, mahogany, pear, and chestnut are also excellent for wood sculpturing. Very often the shape of the wood block or the branches or the log itself can be inspiring to the student. The material must be dry because carving in moist or damp material would be too difficult and discouraging.[164]

The process of cutting in stone is psychologically the same as carving in wood. It is the process of elimination, an analytical process. However, the material and the tools are different. Here, too, the creative concept should grow out of the material. A work in granite will naturally not lend itself to fine and detailed executions, since the texture of granite is rough and its spotty surface may divert attention from such delicate detail. This stone is most effective for colossal statues, or for sculptures that have the effect of a rock. The fine and smooth surface structure of marble, however, lends itself excellently for delicate work.

Although working in stone is considered as sculpturing in its best meaning, it is rarely used in high schools because of the many difficulties connected with the material and the use of tools. Cutting in plaster can, however, serve as an adequate substitute, although plaster itself is not very beautiful. Soap sculpture, although popular, is not recommended because the smallness of the size often results in the feeling of restriction.

The question often arises whether sculptures can be painted. From what has been said, it is quite clear that painting a sculpture would be the same

[164] For more technical information, see Leland, Charles G., *Woodcarving*. New York: Pitman Publishing Corp., 1931; Jackson, James, *The Handicraft of Woodcarving*. New York: Pitman Publishing Corp., 1921; Sowers, J. T., *Wood Carving Made Easy*. Milwaukee: Bruce Publishing Co., 1936.

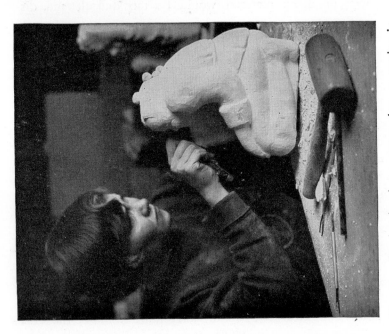

362

Fig. 56. Medieval sculpture. Painted wood. Group composition; part of an altar.

as making a wood building look like stone. Emphasizing the beauty of the material and its special characteristics is an important practice of modern art. A sculpture must be so convincingly done that nothing need be added, particularly painting, because sculpturing is entirely in the realm of three-dimensional expression.

However, when a figure is used for purposes other than that of mere self-expression color may be added to it. When three-dimensional works are used in relationship with another functional whole, as in theater decorations, or as a group in an altar (during the medieval age), the sculpture loses its intimate meaning as an expression itself and becomes a part of another symbolic or realistic form of expression. In this relationship surface structure or beauty of the material becomes entirely subordinated to the literary or interpretative meaning of the work of art (Fig. 56).

In this connection, mention should be made of the educational meaning of puppets, which can be carved in wood, made from clay, or formed out of papier-mâché and painted—a most inspiring and useful art form. The educational value of puppets is not only great because they lend themselves so very well for the integration into other school subjects (English, history) but also because of their wide range of expressive qualities. Successful, satirical self-portraits have been made in the form of puppets; psychologically they have been proven successful because they made the students more aware of themselves. If acting is included, such creative enterprise can contribute to a better feeling toward oneself. To make historic figures come to life again, puppets or marionettes can be used most effectively. However, naturalistic means of interpretations would be entirely against the spirit of puppets and marionettes because both are designed for stage effects. In this connection, painting marionettes or puppets has not the meaning of making them more "natural." Color is used in this relationship only as a means of expression.[165] Stage design, therefore, should always be included to show the final effect of the puppet in its proper environment.

Graphics—The reproducing techniques

Not all graphic techniques fit different student personalities. We know from the history of art that some artists were masters in linear techniques, but that others preferred black and white in its three-dimensional effect. This different attitude toward the use of techniques should be known by all teachers. The line itself can have many different qualities, as has been pointed out previously. But from all these qualities two are outstanding: the line as an abstract interpretation of expressions, and the line as the interpreter of visual experiences. In the first, the line itself has the function of expressing feelings or emotions, whereas in the latter the line, as the boundary of forms, characterizes their three-dimensional quality. Both types of artistic expression lead to different techniques.

Linoleum cut

The linoleum cut is the technique of cutting with differently shaped knives and gouges into linoleum. Depending upon the personality of the student, the cutting of lines or shapes might be more important than the effect of light and shadow, so often characterized as the aim in linoleum cut. From this it becomes evident that there are two techniques in a linoleum cut which are quite closely related to the creative types of students. For one the experience of cutting and its expressive quality, together with the relationship of shapes, is of main significance, whereas

[165] For more information on puppets or marionettes see Kennard, Joseph S., *Masks and Marionettes*. New York: The Macmillan Co., 1935; Flexner, Marion W., *Hand Puppets, A Practical Manual for Teachers*. New York: S. French, Inc., 1935; MacIsaac, Frederick J., *The Tony Sarg Marionette Book*. New York: The Viking Press, 1921.

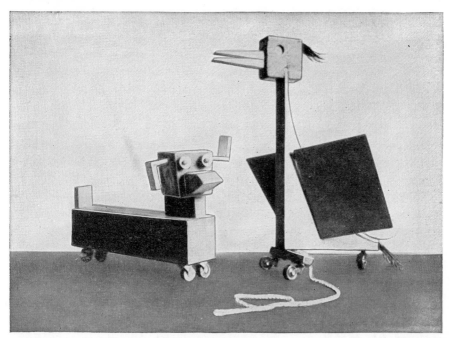

Fig. 57. Toys made in the Home Economics Related Arts Classes under Professor Amy Gardner, The Pennsylvania State University.

for the other, the visual interpretation of forms expressed in light and shadows (black and white) is the chief aim. Whereas the one student, who is inclined to express emotional qualities in his cuts, would feel frustrated when asked to translate his world into an experience of lights and shadows, the other student might find this technique precisely the one for which he was ready.

As is the case with other media, the technique of the linoleum cut must result from the experience of cutting into linoleum. Therefore, the students should not be required to first make a detailed drawing preliminary to cutting, but should try different things on scrap material with the knife without preliminary drawings. Later a brief drawing, which indicates the roughly outlined creative concept, should be sufficient for making a linoleum cut. Only when the student has experienced and digested the nature of the technique can he paint his creative concept with brush and black ink, because only then will he be able to use his brush and ink according to the functional lines made by the knife.[166]

[166] For more technical information on the linoleum cut see Frankenfield, Henry, *Block Printing with Linoleum, A Practical Manual.* Camden, N. J.: C. Howard Hunt and Co., 1940; Dobson, Margaret Stirling, *Lino Prints.* New York, London: Sir I. Pitman and Sons, Ltd., 1931.

Fig. 58a. Linol cut showing repetition as a natural outcome of printing (twelve years old).

If there are students who demand a more detailed structure than can be achieved with linoleum, woodcutting is the technique for them. In principle, however, woodcutting is the same in wood as linoleum cutting is in linoleum. For the secondary-school classroom, only in rare cases will the student want more detailed studies and structures than linoleum can offer (Fig. 58a and Fig. 58b).

Etching and lithography

The following discussion will not cover technical procedure of etching and lithography.[167] In this section, only the meaning of etching and

[167] For more information on etching and lithography read Pennell, Joseph, *The Graphic Arts.* Chicago: The University of Chicago Press, 1921; D'Amico, Victor, *Creative Teaching in Art.* Revised Edition. Scranton: International Textbook Company, 1953.

Fig. 58b. Linol cut with organic lines of cutting (thirteen years). Miss Kathryn M. Royer, Instructor.

lithography for personality development within the secondary-school classroom will be discussed.

Both techniques are far less popular than linoleum cutting because their use requires a greater variety of materials and tools and a greater technical knowledge by the teacher. These difficulties, frequently arising for no better reason than an unwillingness to try something new, should be overcome because etching and lithography are important means of creating self-confidence, specially during the period of adolescence. Drawings that often look "poor" or inexpertly done, can be greatly improved by converting them into an etching or lithograph. This is true not only because the etched line appears more permanent or "professional" but because the determination of the tone and shading of an etching is often influenced by accidental factors. Furthermore, those who have less creative talent should emphasize the skill factor of the technical procedure. Adolescent boys, especially, will find much pleasure in observing and going through the steps of etching and printing.

Roughly speaking, there are two techniques in etching: the dry-point process and the etching process. Technically, the dry-point process is much simpler than the other. In fact no etching is involved in the dry-point process. The drawing is simply engraved into a copper, zinc, or plastic plate and then printed. The softer the plate, the easier it is to engrave with the dry-point needle. Although the dry-point process is less durable than the etching process, we do not need to produce works for eternity. The less durable plastic material has many advantages, especially of transparency, which permits the student to use any sketch he has spontaneously made. He simply puts the sketch under the transparent plate, uses it merely as a guide, and removes the plate soon after to go over it freehand. It is important that etching, or better, engraving, should not merely be a technical transferring of a creative concept. Again, the technique must grow out of the material, and sketches should be used only for rough guidance.

The other technique, genuine etching, although more complicated, offers a far greater variety of experiences than the dry-point technique. The zinc or copper plate is covered with a wax or asphaltum preparation to protect the metal from the acid, into which the plate is immersed after the drawing has been transferred to it. Since the drawing is made in wax, only the merest pressure is needed to incise it into the wax. The acid eats the metal where the slight incisions in the wax have exposed the plate. The depth of the engraved line depends on the time the plate is left in the acid solution—the longer the time, the deeper the lines. The depth of the engraving determines the boldness of the line on the print. Some lines can be covered again with asphaltum while the others stay open. If the process of etching is repeated, only those lines which were left open will be engraved deeper. This partial etching increases the interest, creatively and technically. Important elements of the design can be made more bold and outstanding, and unimportant elements can be made recessive.

After the plate is etched or engraved, preparation for printing should be made. First the asphaltum should be removed with turpentine and then the plate while yet warm, should be inked with etching ink by means of a leather roller or "inker." After that the ink should be wiped off, leaving filled only the engraved lines. The plate, still warm, is then covered with damp paper (ordinary drawing paper will do) and placed under layers of thin felt. The whole "bed" is then slowly pulled through the printing press under great pressure. The pressure forces the damp paper into the etched or engraved lines and draws out the ink onto the paper.[168]

All this can be made very exciting, adding interest to the creative part,

---

[168] For more information read West, Leon, *Making an Etching*. New York: The Studio Publications, Inc., 1932.

particularly at an age level in which the desire for "professional" work and technical skill is great.

Whereas in etching the emphasis is on linear expression, in lithography, the form with light and dark shadings predominates. The simplest lithographic method that is suitable for the average secondary-school classroom consists of drawing with lithographic crayons directly on an aluminum plate having a prepared grained surface. This surface is treated with a special acid solution. When the ink is applied with a roller, it sticks to the crayoned part only, but is repelled elsewhere. The print is made as in etching but with somewhat less pressure.[169] All other lithographic processes are too complicated for secondary schools. The process described above, however, is simple enough to be used successfully without special training, and at the same time gives the understanding of the principles of lithographic processes.

Silk-screen as stencil technique

As we have seen in the discussion of graphic techniques, the creative and emotional qualities find visible expression through the technique itself, but this is not the case in silk-screen when used as stencil technique. Here, emotional qualities are mainly subordinated to the decorative. This, too, naturally grows out of the technical procedure of cutting an accurate stencil. Whereas the creative concept can be given full freedom in engraving an etching plate or in drawing with a lithographic crayon, the cutting of a stencil, a design, or lettering on the film for later transfer to the screen is predominantly a technical procedure. In this silk-screen technique flat spaces are used. Since this is essentially two-dimensional, silk-screen work should not be used "to compete" with painting. This type of silk-screen technique can be used effectively in its own realm for decorative designs. Unfortunately this technique has been overdone by those who do not understand its true characteristics. Naturalistic tendencies are entirely out of place in connection with the use of silk-screen printing.[170] Use of too many colors (and therefore also stencils) to produce realistic effects is inefficient and is indicative of a misapprehension of the nature of the medium. The simpler the technique used, the more effective it is in its own realm. The texture of the screen should be a contributing, not a distorting, factor. Again, the decorative qualities of the silk-screen technique cannot

[169] For more information write for *Multigraph Duplicators*. Cleveland, Ohio: Multigraph Corporation.

[170] For more information read Shokler, Harry, *Artist's Manual for Silk Screen Printing*. New York: American Artists Group, 1946.

compete with the emotional qualities of painting techniques. It is needless to say that there are other most fascinating silk-screen techniques but they appear too complex for the secondary classroom.

The same holds true for the stencil techniques, which are more popular than the silk-screen because stencils are merely cut out of stencil paper and are therefore easier to handle. A stencil can be moved around at will, and unless this is done freely, the possibilities of the technique will not be understood. The use of one stencil in repetitions is another characteristic of the technique. Inasmuch as repetition is an attribute of design, a naturalistic concept cannot be adequately executed with the stencil. However, brushing along the outline of the stencil toward the inside often produces quite attractive shading, but only if it does not attempt to imitate nature. Also, the shading must remain in the realm of design. Decorative qualities are only weakened, not improved, by naturalistic principles. To start out with two or three stencils of abstract shapes (namely, three circles of different sizes, one circle and a square, or a triangle) which are repeated in the same or different arrangements at equal intervals, is much better than using complicated flower patterns induced by naturalistic imitative urges. A textile is neither a place for a still life nor should it lose its characteristics by the emphasis of three-dimensional effects.

Poster work—lettering

Since one of the essential elements of a good poster is its lettering, we shall discuss first the principles of good lettering.[171]

Pure lettering, defined as being concerned only with the formal representation of a word, is writing rather than drawing. In contrast to this formal representation, we shall see that lettering can also *express* the word's meaning, at least to a certain extent. In this connection lettering moves from pure representation to a form of expression.

That lettering should be *written* in itself indicates the technical approach—that is, use of a pen, letter brush, or wooden spatula. The letter then should organically grow out of the pen's shape, without twisting or unnatural motions or turns. The simpler the type of letters, the better it is for the beginning as well as for later stages of lettering. To begin with capital letters only has many advantages: a simplified alphabet, to mention only one. Simple letters are derived from the simplest lines—the straight line and the circle. Since the circle often occupies too much space, it can be

[171] Chappell, Warren, *The Anatomy of Lettering*. New York: Loring and Mussey, 1935; Holme, Charles G., *Lettering of Today*. London: The Studio, Ltd., 1937.

Fig. 59. Lettering. Samples by Laura Zirner, Institute of Design, Chicago.

   a. The shape of the letter is determined by the tool—

   b. Free lettering with the pen.

   c. Designed lettering.

replaced by an oval. However, as soon as the oval is introduced, the problems posed by irregularities multiply. Outlining the letters and later "filling them in" is contrary to the spirit of pure lettering. It can be done only when lettering serves other than formal representations of words.[172]

Also important for good lettering is its "spacing"—that is, the distribution of the single letters within a whole word or sentence. We distinguish between closed, half-open, and open letters. Closed letters have a perpendicular line on both sides, such as *M, N, I,* and *H.* Half-open letters have a perpendicular line only on one side, such as *K, L, B, D,* and so forth. Open letters have no perpendicular lines on either side, like *C, A, G, O, S,* and so forth. When two closed letters adjoin, the space between them is

[172] Friend, Leon and Josephine Hefter, *Graphic Design.* New York: Whittlesey House, 1936.

much smaller than the space between two open letters. We conclude, therefore, that only the optical space counts—that is, the space that actually
is between the two letters, like *M N* or *K L* or *O C*. These optical spaces
should be equal in good lettering.

Good spacing in lettering consists, therefore, of a balance of the *optical*
spaces between letters in order to make the spaces appear equal. Most of
the irregularities of poor lettering derive from irregular letters and poor
spacing. Only after the student understands what good letters are and how
the letters should be spaced should variations of letters in different styles
and sizes be introduced. With regard to the lettering in different sizes,
writing "in block" introduces many possibilities in good spacing. Writing
in block consists of lettering several lines in such a way that they finally
form a rectangular or square block. One block can consist of lines of lettering of equal sizes as well as of lines which have different-sized letters.
A book title, for instance, in which the title can be largest, the subtitle
smaller, and the author and publishing firm again in different sizes, all
written in block, would be an example of such lettering. This is not only
of importance for the teaching of good lettering, but has also great educational value, since it compels the student to adjust one situation to another,
the smaller lettering to the larger, and so forth. Title pages, letterheads
for stationery, signs of different types would be practical examples in
which the principles of spacing can be applied.

If, however, lettering is not used merely as a means of formal representation but as an *expressive symbol* in itself, no limitations with regard
to technique should hamper the expressiveness of the letter. A very good
approach to this type of *letter drawing* is *word illustrations.* The students
are told to illustrate different meanings of words by adjusting the type of
the letters to the word's meaning (Fig. 60). Contrasting words like
"strong" and "weak," "bold" and "timid," "heavy" and "light," "night"
and "day," "rough" and "smooth," "deep" and "shallow," "narrow" and
"wide," "high" and "low," and "thin" and "thick," are very good suggestions for the beginning. Later on words can be introduced that stand for
themselves, like "fire," "speed," "excitement," "storm," "fear," "shock,"
"drowning," "trembling," "suffocating," "heat," and so forth. Through
illustrating such words the student will achieve an understanding of lettering as a living and expressive activity. With this in mind he will approach
poster work in a different way. For the beginning of poster work it will be
good to bring such word illustrations in contrast to the formal and written
lettering. A poster for a movie, "Storm over Asia," "Drowning in the
Swamps," and the "Whispering Shadow," which not only contains these

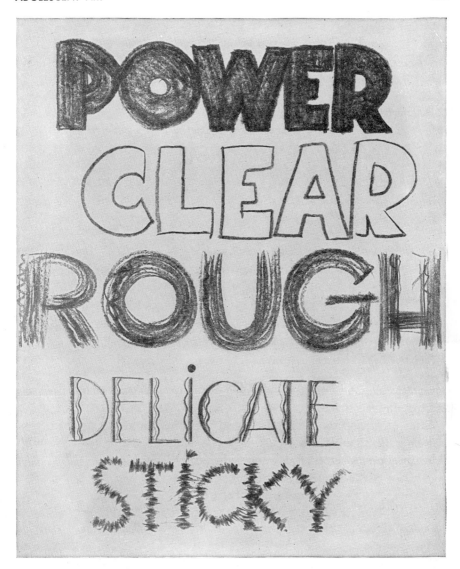

Fig. 60. Word illustrations.

suggestive titles but also the name of the theatre, actors, admission price, and so forth, will give opportunities for such contrasts.

Spacing in designing a poster is of great importance. A poster that is equally covered with lines of lettering will be monotonous and not effective. Emphasizing and isolating important from less important parts is a means of directing attention to specific contents while breaking the

Fig. 61a. Emotional Design. Made by entirely inexperienced students under supervision of Professor Sybil Emerson, The Pennsylvania State University.

monotony. A good poster should also contain contrasts between ordinary and meaningful spaces.

After practicing on posters of literary meaning, a poster of more general content should be chosen. Other techniques, such as work with airbrush and silk screen, can be introduced.[173]

Techniques for design

Emotional forms of design and its abstract quality

Any material will be suitable for emotional forms of design or abstractions which permits a free use of design forms, without restricting the individual to rigid patterns. Especially in the beginning, much emphasis should be placed on techniques that facilitate a direct connection between kinesthetic experiences (the way the arm is moved while producing lines or shapes) and other body sensations (Fig. 61a and 61b). Flat colored chalk that can be used for lines and shadings, therefore, is an excellent material

[173] For more information on poster techniques see Mangan, James T., *Design, The New Grammar of Advertising*. Chicago: Dartnell Corp., 1940, p. 73.

Fig. 61b. Emotional Design. More controlled and organized. Made in the classes of Professor Sybil Emerson, The Pennsylvania State University.

since it records without difficulties body motions and the different pressure put on the material to receive different qualities of shades. Techniques like tempera, which easily produce uneven surfaces and do not readily obey the flowing quality of an introduced rhythm, should be saved for later experiences.

Finger painting is also an excellent introductory means for the stimulation of emotional qualities in abstract design, if this technique is not misused. All too often one can see finger painting used in competition with other forms of painting—that is, with naturalistic tendencies. Finger paint consists of the direct transference of motions into lines, shapes, and colors. Although it is an excellent means of stimulation when used in its own right, it can entirely miss its purpose when used to imitate nature.

The work with the airbrush, too, offers excellent possibilities if its special qualities are recognized. If the limitations of this technique are realized, no landscapes or portraits will become victims of a misunderstood technique. Sharp lines can be produced even with the best airbrush. If sharp outlines are wanted, stencils have to be introduced. Stencils, as we

Fig. 62a. Functional design in wood.

have seen, are entirely unsuitable for expressing realistic tendencies. The airbrush, therefore, can function best in the realm of design, particularly industrial design, since the technical procedure destroys most of the direct emotional qualities.

Since structure, too, is one of the important qualities of design, work with material of different texture will be very stimulating. Scraps of wood, metal, textiles, plastics, and paper can be arranged in such a way that they produce an excellent "symphony" of textures and shapes. Because texture is closely related to the sense of touch, students should go through the experience of finding different textures purely by the sense of touch. What a fine sensation it is to touch the softness of velvet after feeling the smoothness of a fine curved glass. Such experiences will greatly stimulate the visual experience associated with different types of textures, as different grains of wood, weaves of textiles, and so forth. Such designs will necessarily use the three dimensions as well as the plane. In its abstract quality it is a form of design in its own right, but it can also be used to create a better feeling for the use of different materials in interior decoration. But this leads to the next section, functional design.[174]

[174] Perry, Evadna Kraus, *Art Adventures with Discarded Materials.* New York: Noble Publishers, Inc., 1933; Smith, Janet K., *Design, An Introduction.* Chicago, New York: Ziff-Davis Publishing Co., 1946.

Fig. 62b. Pottery. From the classes of **Dr.** Kenneth Beittel. Dept. of Art Education. The Pennsylvania State University.

Design and its function

Functional design must always be *in close interdependence with the material from which it is made and with the purpose for which it has to function.* Thus a design made for textiles should be made directly with the material, or designed in the spirit of the function of the textile for which it is intended. Since this relationship between design and material is of prime importance, it is best, particularly at the beginning, to design with the material in hand, without preliminary planning. Only when the nature of the material is thoroughly understood can plans on paper be introduced. A design for a vase, therefore, must be adjusted to the function of the potter's wheel and the nature of the material, "clay." In the same way a design for a piece of jewelry must grow out of the possibilities which different types of metal offer with regard to texture and flexibility.

The word "functional," therefore, refers to three different relationships that are equally important in any functional design: (1) the relationship between design and material, (2) the relationship of design to tools or machinery, and (3) the relationship between design and purpose.[175]

Let us discuss these qualities on one object of design. We may select for this purpose a piece of pottery made on the potter's wheel, glazed and fired in the kiln. The relationship between design and material seems to be clear as soon as we relate the plasticity of the clay to the working method on the potter's wheel. The process of turning is perfectly adjusted to the plasticity of clay. The relationship of design to the tool or machinery, in this case the potter's wheel, will be expressed only if we do not cover up what the potter's wheel has achieved. How often do we see the beautiful form created on the potter's wheel spoiled by denting some parts of the vase without any reason. Still more often do we find the surface quality, which the clay receives through the turning process, carefully removed and replaced by a smoothness which destroys the dynamic whirling effect which is a natural and functional outcome of the process of turning. The object will conform better with the true principles of functional design when this true relationship between design and potter's wheel is realized (Fig. 62b). The more we hide the effects of the tool and its function, the more we move away from the truth of functional design. Finally, the design must have a relationship to the purpose for which it is made. The purpose of a vase may be purely decorative. The only thing then which we have to consider is that the vase must not tip over easily: it must be able to stand safely. If it is to serve as a flower vase, however, its glaze must neither compete with the colors of flowers, nor can its shape be too wide on the top and narrow on the bottom. Such considerations must be applied to all pieces of design, each in its own realm with regard to material, too, or purpose (Figs. 63 and 64).

The greater the variety of materials with which the student works, the wider will be his range of experiences. In general, materials are distinguished by whether they are inorganic or organic. Inorganic materials consist of various rocks and metals dug out of the earth and generally refined or in other ways made suitable for working. Such materials and products give rise to three principal divisions of industrial art: pottery, glass, and metalwork.

The logical French mind sometimes classifies these arts as "les arts du feu," the arts of fire, because firing is an essential process in their manufacture.

[175] Emerson, Sybil, *Design, A Creative Approach*. Scranton: International Textbook Co., 1953; Kahn, Ely Jacques, *Design in Art and Industry*. New York: Charles Scribner's Sons, 1936; Holme, Geoffrey, *Industrial Design and the Future*. London: The Studio, Ltd., 1934.

Fig. 62c. Functional design in aluminum and glass.

The organic materials are by-products of vegetable and animal growth, such as wood and cotton from trees and plants, and wool and skin from animals.

Other divisions, such as *leatherwork* and *paperwork,* are of minor importance, and the aesthetic principles applicable to them are easily deduced from the general principles that arise in connection with the other industrial arts.

In addition to the materials mentioned above, one group, which cannot be placed in either of the foregoing groups because it is derived mainly from chemical processes, is becoming increasingly important. The principal

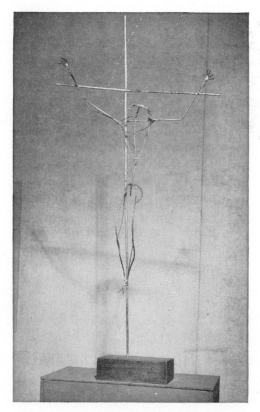

Fig. 63a. Wire sculpture by Karl Hoffa. From
the classes of Professor Yar Chomicky, Dept.
of Art Education, The Pennsylvania State University.

materials which belong to this group are referred to most commonly as
synthetic materials, mainly *plastics.*

"In addition to the arts which arise out of the working of these various
materials, there is an art which consists of assembling and combining ready-
made units from the primary industrial arts. This art we may call the art of
construction, and this art includes anything from combining metalwork
and woodwork on a piece of furniture to the building of a house, a factory
or a city." [176]

Functional design, therefore, refers to the relationship of this wide

[176] Read, Herbert, *Art and Industry.* New York: Harcourt, Brace and Co., 1938, p. 43;
Cheney, Sheldon and Martha Candler Cheney, *Art and the Machine.* New York: Whittlesey
House, 1936.

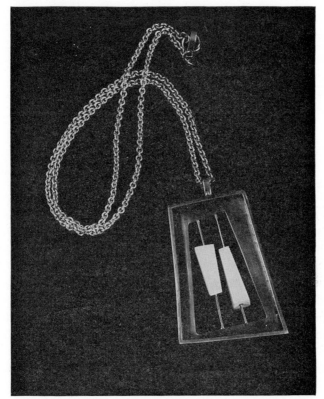

Fig. 63b. Contemporary jewelry in silver and ivory. From the classes of Professor Florence Penn, Dept. of Art Education, Miami University, Oxford, Ohio.

range of materials and their working methods to the purpose for which the design was created.

In the secondary-school classroom it is not only important to show this wide range of materials but also to introduce as many different working methods as possible and to relate them to the particular functional application of the specific material. It is important, moreover, to direct the attention of our youth to man-made objects which show the effect of functional design in its relation to material and purpose.

Functional design in decoration. A piece of jewelry is not a necessity of life although it may make life more beautiful and enjoyable. Such pieces of design in which the decorative quality dominates shall be discussed in the framework of "functional design in decoration." How can

Fig. 63c. Modern design of jewelry by Karla Longrée.

a piece of jewelry have a functional design if its function is merely decorative? "Functional" here refers more to the functional relationship of material and design than to the purpose for which it is made. Quite often in decorative design, the purpose for which an object is made plays a major role. Let us take for example a lamp base and the shade. A lamp base must not tip over easily. Therefore, a well-designed lamp base must be designed to stand firmly. Beyond this function there is not much more to consider with the exception of the adjustment of the type of design to the material

Fig. 63d. Modern table setting.

Fig. 64a. Daily objects, such as staples, rubber bands, toothpicks, paper clips, etc., are used as stimulations for textile prints. From the classes of Professor Sybil Emerson, Dept. of Art Education, The Pennsylvania State University.

Fig. 64b. Hooked rug, showing different textures achieved by using different yarns. From the classes of Professor Yar Chomicky, Dept. of Art Education, The Pennsylvania State University.

Fig. 64c. Cane-seat chair. Designed by Marcel Breuer. (Photo, courtesy Museum of Modern Art, N. Y.)

from which it is made and to the environment in which it will be placed. With regard to the shade, however, it is most important that it permit good lighting. Therefore, its design and material will not only have to serve aesthetic or decorative functions but also a definite purpose. That is why we can rarely speak of a merely decorative purpose in design because some functional purpose is always related to objects which deal with our daily living. The design of a piece of jewelry or a rug is not only dependent upon the material but also upon the purpose for which it is determined. A ring must be designed in some proportion to the finger or hand for

Fig. 64d. Interior. Designed by Dan Cooper, N. Y. (Knickerbocker Photo Service.)

which it is made; an earring is designed in relationship to the ear on which it hangs. Still, we can say that there is no necessity for wearing earrings, and therefore we can put earrings into the category of decorative design.

Functional design in industry. Every design in industry which has a definite relationship to the necessity of living is called "functional design." That is why the design of a toothbrush with a functional handle and bristles that reach into all crevices between our teeth is as much an industrial design as the functional organization or planning of a city. Both are of equal significance as educational means.

But here also it is of importance to show the before-mentioned relationships. These can best be demonstrated by the designing of functional gadgets which are in our daily use, like a doorknob, different handles for different purposes (drawers, teapots, towel racks), electric switches, hinges of functional quality in design, keys, silver (spoons, forks, knives), clothespins, hangers for suits or coats, and so forth.

Fig. 65a. Functionally designed one-family house. Architect Raymond Hall.

To direct attention to such details is most important because they often are overlooked in their significance for our daily living.[177]

Educators have an important mission to encourage the necessity of modern functional and well-designed furniture. Nowhere do we find such an adherence to the "old time" as in the average American home. Modern style in the American home has not penetrated beyond the kitchen and bathroom door. Kitchens, however, and bathrooms in general have functionally designed furniture and utensils. The average American is rather technically minded when it comes to the point of finding a better kind of transportation—the newest streamlined car cannot be new and modern enough—or a better kind of gas range, refrigerator, and so forth. In his living room, however, he wants to be surrounded by his ancestors. Although well-designed and functional modern furniture is far superior in comfort to any period-styled furniture, it has not yet found its way into the American home. It is no excuse to say that modern furniture is as yet too expensive for the average income. Period furniture is relatively less expen-

[177] Weinbrenner, Kenneth D., *Jewelry Making as an Art Expression.* Scranton: International Textbook Co., 1952. Faulkner, Ray, Edwin Ziegfield, and Gerald Hill, *Art Today.* New York: Henry Holt and Co., 1941.

Fig. 65b. Oslo. Business houses.

sive because the great demand for it has justified the application of mass-production methods for its manufacture. A refrigerator, for example, is more expensive than an old-fashioned icebox. If there would be a great enough demand for modern furniture, the production would necessarily have to be increased and the prices would fall. The question is more one of introducing the correct type of modern furniture to a public which will gradually open its mind to the advantages of the new era. This can only be done by acquainting our youth with the spirit of functionally designed modern furniture.[178]

What are the characteristics of well-designed furniture? The main characteristics are the same as in all other forms of industrial design: a relationship among *design, material, tool,* and *purpose.* This means that meaningless ornaments are omitted since they do not contribute to the purpose of living with and in them. On the contrary, as dust collectors they would only be detrimental to living comfort. The design itself grows out of the beauty of the different materials used. The beautiful and natural qualities of wood are never covered, but are preserved as much as possible. They are contrasted with other materials, such as glass, textiles, and metal, each being used in its own right. Simplicity in line, therefore, is an important principle of modern functional furniture. Variety in decoration is not introduced by ornamentation but by the use of different materials. The

[178] Mumford, Lewis, *Architecture.* Chicago: American Library Assn., 1926; *Sticks and Stones.* New York: W. W. Norton and Co., 1933; Frankl, Paul T., *New Dimensions.* New York: Brewer and Warren, Inc., 1928.

Fig. 65c. San Francisco. The Golden Gate. (Photo M. D. Ross, State College.)

purpose of the furniture determines its design qualities, and vice versa. Therefore, one of the main characteristics of modern furniture is that it serves a purpose in such a way that the material used is being shown in its best light. Functional lines are always beautiful. Workmanship naturally is necessary to bring out the above-mentioned qualities. Finally a fine piece of furniture depends on both the quality of the materials used and above all on the creative power of the designer.[179]

[179] Moholy-Nagy, L., *The New Vision*. New York: W. W. Norton and Co., 1938; Read, Herbert, *Art and Industry*. New York: Harcourt, Brace and Co., 1938; Agan, Tessie, *The House*. Philadelphia: J. B. Lippincott and Co., 1939

SUMMARY   CRISIS OF ADOLESCENCE—THIRTEEN TO SEVENTEEN YEARS

Stage	Characteristics	Human Figure	Space	Color	Design	Stimulation Topics	Techniques
The Stage of Decision Crisis of Adolescence	Critical awareness toward environment and representational outcome. Clearer identification of visual and haptic types or "in-betweens." *Visual Type* Intermediaries: eyes. Main creative concern: impressions of environment in which creator feels as spectator. *Haptic Type* Intermediary: body. Main creative concern: subjective experiences, emotional expressions in which creator feels involved.	*Visual Type* Emphasis on exterior proportion, surface appearance, visual interpretation of light and shadow. Depiction of a moment's impression. Sketchy techniques or realistic interpretations of objective validity. *Haptic Type* Emphasis on inside feelings as contrasted to outside appearance. Depiction of character and expression, often of symbolic qualities. Proportions of value. Individual interpretations.	*Visual Type* Perspective space representation. Apparent diminution of distant objects. Changing intensity with distance. Meaning of horizon. Emphasis on three-dimensional qualities. *Haptic Type* Retrogression to base-line expressions. Perspective of value in relationship to the self. Value relationship of objects to one another.	*Visual Type* Changing qualities of color with regard to environment. Color reflections. Analytic attitude toward color with regard to distance, mood, and so forth. *Haptic Type* Expressive meaning of color. Subjective color expressions. Emphasis on local color. Psychological and emotional significance of color.	*Visual Type* Aesthetic interpretations of form, balance, and rhythm. Decorative quality of design. *Haptic Type* Emotional interpretation of abstract quality of design. Functional design. Industrial design.	Visual and haptical stimulations. Environment and figure. Posing model with interpretations. Sculpture. Graphics. Design. Poster work.	Sketching in crayon. Oil paint. Tempera. Water color. Sculpture in: clay, wood, plaster castings. Graphics: linoleum cutting, etching, lithography, lettering, poster work. Silk screen. Airbrush. Stencil. Design: decorative functional in: stone, metal, glass, textiles, wood, paper, leather.

WHY NO EVALUATION CHART IS INCLUDED IN THE STAGE OF DECISION

The more the emphasis is shifted from the working process to the final product, the greater are the interferences which stand in the way of a free creative expression. Formal considerations like composition, style, and type of technique and presentation disturb the "unconscious" production. An evaluation of growth no longer can take place on the basis of the general criteria. They may be right for the one who still unconsciously and without external interferences produces creatively, but they may be completely wrong for the other whose creative medium no longer stands the critical awareness with which he approaches it. Acquired knowledge has now mixed with the many conscious experiences in life and art to the extent that the "mine and thine" no longer are clearly distinguishable. Creative expression has either been controlled and inhibited by intellectual forces, or it has grown from the realm of personal manifestation of the child to that of a consciously created aesthetic product. In neither sphere are "evaluations of growth" applicable. In art education the process of creating is a dynamic force in which all elements are included. An attempt has been made to evaluate it in order to help the child in his growth. The final product of the adult stands or falls on its own merits and no factor necessitates its evaluations.

EXERCISES

(1) Compare drawings of a fifth grade and eighth grade by pointing at characteristics which show the critical awareness toward the creative work of the eighth-grade student.

(2) Collect the drawings of a junior-grade high school and classify them according to their creative types.

(3) Study the characteristics of haptic drawings with regard to:
(a) Preference of topics.
(b) Proportion.
(c) Subject matter and its presentation.
(d) Meaning of color.

(4) Study the characteristics of visual drawings with regard to the same characteristics.

(5) Make a study of the meaning of the line throughout the history of art, by selecting one example of each category:
(a) The line in its kinesthetic function in primitive drawings.
(b) The line as base line in Egyptian or Assyrian drawings.

(c) The line in its expressive quality in early Byzantine murals.

(d) The line used as boundary to separate forms.

(e) The line expressing three-dimensional qualities as seen in perspective.

(6) Make a similar study of lights and darks by selecting one example:

(a) Lights and darks in their decorative qualities.

(b) Lights and darks expressing three-dimensional form.

(c) Lights and darks expressing dramatic effects of illumination.

(d) Lights and darks expressing mystic effects as illumination.

(e) Lights and darks in their expressive qualities.

(f) Lights and darks to express atmosphere.

(7) Make a similar study of the meaning of color by selecting one example of each type:

(a) Color in its decorative quality.

(b) Color in its dynamic, dramatic qualities.

(c) Color in its expressive quality.

(d) Color to express atmosphere.

(e) Color bound up with form.

(f) Color used abstractly.

(8) Show sample of time-space representation in art:

(a) Different time sequences used in one representation (mainly in murals).

(b) Space-time representations in motion pictures.

(c) Mixtures of plan and front views (especially in Egyptian art).

(d) Outside and inside representations.

(9) Relate one picture of each art period to the time it was created with regard to:

(a) Subject matter.

(b) Technique.

(c) Mode of representation

(10) Show the functional use of stone, metal, clay, and wood in sculpturing. Selecting one sculpture of each material and describe it.

(11) Collect pictures of industrial products with functional use of the material.

(12) Make a study of the use of different building materials in modern architecture.

CHAPTER X   **THE MEANING OF AESTHETIC CRITERIA**

Q UESTIONS OF AESTHETIC CRITERIA WITH REGARD TO PICTURE MAKING cannot be separated from the creative development as a whole. They, too, develop according to the specific need of the individual and *should not* be taught, but must grow out of the individual work of the student. They are closely bound up with personality. If these criteria are taught academically—that is, as a subject matter in itself detached from the work, they become dead knowledge which will inhibit rather than help an intuitive urge. Thus teaching of composition will be more harmful than useful at precisely the time when freedom is more important than rigid rules. If, however, composition grows out of individual needs, if it becomes a means of expression that helps the student to express what is in his mind, it will be an important tool, more for the *teacher* than for the *student*. It is not the student but the teacher who must learn the meaning of composition, and understand it, in order to guide the student. In this way, certain qualities or needs of expression or aesthetics can be achieved with the least effort and discouragement. Therefore, we shall proceed with a discussion of those problems of aesthetic criteria the teacher must know for guiding his pupils. Although composition unifies all elements of expression into a whole, we

shall not be able to understand and analyze this unification without knowing the meaning of the single elements. We therefore start with a discussion of the meaning of the single elements such as line, space, color, and
their different relationships to one another.

The elements of expression in picture making

Growth is on an everchanging continuum.[1] Aesthetic growth appears to
be the component of growth responsible for the changes from a chaos on
the lower end of the continuum to the most complete harmonious organization on the upper end. This striving for higher forms of organization does
not necessarily refer to the elements of art; it may also refer to a more
intense and greater integration of thinking, feeling, and perceiving and
thus be responsible for our greater sensibilities in life. Indeed, one of the
distinctions between the basic philosophies in art education and those in
the fine arts may be a difference in emphasis regarding harmonious organizations. Art education primarily deals with the effect which art processes
have on the individual, while the so-called fine arts are more concerned
with the resulting products. It is then quite logical to say that art education
is more interested in the *effect* of a greater and more integrated harmonious
organization of the elements of art on the individual and his development,
while aesthetic growth in the fine arts generally refers to the harmonious
organization of the elements of art themselves.

Herbert Read calls aesthetic education "the education of those senses
upon which consciousness and ultimately the intelligence and judgment of
the human individual are based. It is only in so far as these senses are
brought into harmonious and habitual relationship with the external world
that an integrated personality is built up." [2] Thus, Herbert Read refers in
his statement to the effect which aesthetic growth has on the individual
rather than to the aesthetic product which he produces. While we are lacking basic research in this area, there seems to be a strong indication of an
intimate relationship between the two. Thus aesthetic growth appears to be
essential for any well-organized thinking, feeling, and perceiving, and the
expression of these. Depending on the media used, we then deal with the
different art forms as expressions of this organization, such as, words,
spaces, tones, lines, shapes, colors, movements, or any mixture of these.
Aesthetic organization does not start at any arbitrary line. It may start at

[1] Beittel, Kenneth, "Appreciation and Creativity." *Eastern Arts Assoc. Research Bulletin,*
V:1 (1954).
[2] Read, Herbert, *Education Through Art.* London: Faber and Faber, Ltd., 1943, pp. 274, 275.

any level, conscious or subconscious, and anywhere, in life, in play, in art. That is why our whole personality is affected by aesthetic growth. Wherever organization is lacking, the mind disintegrates. Aesthetic growth, therefore, not only affects the single individual but also, under certain circumstances, a whole society. Aesthetic growth is organic with no external set of standards; it may differ in its expression as well as in its meaning from individual to individual and from culture to culture. "One must strictly refrain from forming a fixed code of laws to which one can submit artistic phenomena from the beginning on." [3] It is this that distinguishes it from any arbitrarily set organization. Also in art expression, aesthetic criteria are intrinsic to the individual work. It may, therefore, be said that a creative work is governed by its own intrinsic aesthetic principles. If we would attempt to regiment harmonious relationships and organizations, we would arrive at dogmatic laws. This has important implications for aesthetic growth in art education. It implies that all set rules rigidly applied to any creative expression are deterimental to aesthetic growth. Yet, in most of our schools—on all levels—such matters as proportions, balance, or rhythm, are still regarded as separate extrinsic entities with no relationships to the intrinsic qualities of the individual aesthetic product or the intentions of the creator and his developed sensibilities. Proportions, when "corrected" on the basis of external, most often visual attributes, may be in complete disharmony with the aesthetic entity of a creative product and the innermost expression of the creator. Rhythm, according to generally applied "principles," may be in utter discord with the harmonious integration of an individual's desire for expression.

How then can aesthetic growth be fostered in today's art education, if there is no apparent set of rules which can readily be applied to any individual? The most decisive aesthetic education does not take place merely by the criticism or guidance an individual receives for his aesthetic product. It is much more a total task of education, in which the individual's sensitivity toward perceptual, intellectual, and emotional experiences is deepened and integrated into a harmoniously organized whole, so that his "senses are brought into harmonious and habitual relationship with the external world." However, in this educational process art can play a major role, inasmuch as no art expression is possible without a heightened sensibility toward the external world and our ability to bring our inward senses in harmonious relationship to it.

[3] Fiedler, Conrad, *On Judging Works of Visual Art.* (Translated by Henry Schaefer-Simmern, University of California Press, 1949.)

The meaning of the line and its relations

If we draw a line, it would be a creation—very primitive, but a creation nevertheless because this line expresses something related to our feelings or ideas. The line might be bold, black, and direct, starting and stopping at definite points and thus showing *decision* of character. The line might be timid, dainty, wavering, *indefinite* like a child just starting to take his first steps, not knowing where he will end. Or the line might be *dreamy,* as it seems to us when we are suddenly at a place without knowing how we reached it; or the line might be *sketchy,* consisting of many parts, whose synthesis finally might approach the mental image which it followed step by step; or it might be an *intellectual* line, well thought over and carefully controlled; or it might be a *calm* line in which everything is quietly and carefully but determinedly drawn like the uniform waves of the calm sea; or it is an *excited* line in which no motions can be predicted, ever-changing as our emotions change when we live through great excitements; or a *felt* line drawn unconsciously, just *intuitively* following an emotional drive; or we might have drawn the line with a *utilitarian* purpose in mind, perhaps to separate two areas, as an architect who wants to indicate that this space has to be divided; or did we have in our mind a *symbolic sign* like the "minus," thinking only of its function or meaning, which through repetition has received general validity? Or were we aware of its *quality* as it flowed from our pencil as we can see it in the signatures of *vain* persons, who play with the line like a lady who never can handle her powder puff elegantly enough when she feels conscious of being observed? Or is it an *interrupted* line, drawn in two or many continuations, showing thoughts which are not spoken out as we do it in letters in which we like to express continuations of thoughts by merely adding a few interrupted lines? Or is the thought so important that we have to *underline* it; or did we draw entirely *mechanically* as we do it when doodling while waiting at the telephone for an important call; or did we want to emphasize *rhythm* by placing one line parallel to another, weighing carefully the different widths of the lines as we do when designing; or were we finally *unsatisfied* with the whole approach and did we cross it with two bold strokes indicating that it no longer exists?

These are only some of the distinctions of lines which will lead to a better understanding of the individual and his work; however, we would not do justice to the meaning of the line within a composition without discussing the different relationships of lines among one another. Such a discussion of merely the meaning of the line itself without its relationship to environment would be like a life story that is concerned only with the facts which deal directly with the person, and not with the interdependent causal connections that determine the life of an individual, like: "Up to this date Miss X was a student at this college. She could not continue her studies." That really is like an interrupted line. But why is it interrupted? Was she compelled to interrupt her studies or did she do it voluntarily? Will it be merely an interruption or won't she come back at all? What tragedy sometimes lies behind such simple words as "she could not continue her studies." Lack of money, illness, death, or whatever the reason, we never would be satisfied with a life story that only mentions the facts. The circumstances under which she interrupted her studies will make the facts interesting and dramatic to us. In the same way that we would like to see the accompanying lines in her life, we also would like to see the circumstances under which lines are interrupted, or in general, the relationships of lines to one another.

Two indefinite lines that finally meet at a definite point after long and many interruptions are like two friends who, after long interrupted contact, meet again. If, however, these two lines are definite, starting at a definite point, steering consciously toward the meeting point from the very beginning, their meaning is quite different. It is the same as if two persons would reach for something they already have in mind. The more this something is removed from their reach, the more inaccessible it becomes. It is the same with the two converging lines of a Gothic arch whose meaning has gone into the realm of inapproachable religious faith. People and ideas can meet under diverse circumstances; so can lines. The line becomes a living symbol, and as soon as we have reached this point, we need no longer ponder over this symbol's meaning, because we can draw our experiences and relationships directly from life.

We know from the very beginning of creative activity, from scribbling, what *repetition* can mean. In scribbling, repetition meant a greater consciousness. But we know from life how different the meaning of repetition can be, depending upon the circumstances under which something is repeated. If a bold line is repeated by a dainty sketchy line, it might mean mere imitation, like one who tries to imitate the original but is not quite sure of himself. However, repetition that is done over and over with the same degree of certainty might have the same effect as the uniform ticking of a clock which creates a monotonous rhythm that is noticed only when the clock stops, or when the rhythm changes. Thus it might mean equality or pure rhythm, depending upon the circumstances under which the lines repeat themselves.

If I have lost something valuable to me, and I ask someone to help me search for it, we both would do the same thing—we would search for the lost article. The emotions, however, with which both are participating are of different intensity, since the lost object belongs to me. Thus parallel lines would not do justice to such an expression. We would both search differently. How different it would be if the emotional factor would be cut out, as with the workers in a field who harvest potatoes or grain all day long! Here, the parallel lines would get their real meaning: of an *ever-lasting* repetition. If we would interrupt these parallel bent motions by upright figures, these interruptions would then introduce a pause, as Millet did in his famous picture, "The Gleaners." The more upright the line (or the figures), the more definite is the interruption as shown in the illustration.

If, however, we deal with parallel lines that are in perpendicular relationship to a base line, the meaning of the parallel lines changes again. (|) The perpendicular line, the most *absolute* line which is neither influenced from the left nor from the right, expresses the same *stability* that a flagpole expresses as the bearer of the symbol of the country. If those lines of stability are repeated at equal intervals, they will have the same meaning as soldiers, in whom *equality* and *stability* are unified. If, however, *one line stands out* from this uniformity, it immediately catches our attention like one civilian in the midst of a row of soldiers. The circumstances under which this line is standing out will determine its meaning. It might be an odd line with a little slant, as a felled tree falling in the midst of a forest of skyward-growing trees has *lost its stability;* or it might *stand out* in height overlooking all other lines like the officer on horseback. We might, however, just as well raise the base line in a convex curve like a hill overlooking the valley, or we might introduce a *protecting* line, a concave line like a protecting hole.

If the relationship of lines is well balanced, if one line takes care of the other, as in a building in which all stones hold together, we speak of *static lines;* if, however one stone is removed all other stones start moving. We then speak of *dynamic lines,* lines that are no longer balanced but moving. Lines might be *open, receiving* like our arms when we meet again after a long separation. But just as we might not be quite sure whether the person we are about to greet is indeed the long-unseen friend, since he has changed during his absence, so will the circumstances determine the meaning under which the open lines are drawn. Or lines might *be closed*. This could mean *protection* as well as *prison,* depending on the kinds of lines expressing the meaning of closing. If they are bold, rough and determined like bars of a cell, we surely associate them with "prison"; if they are round, carefully surrounding the hole, they will be protecting. If, however, one *line breaks through* such a protecting line, like the arm of Adam by Michelangelo which reaches out from the earth to communicate with God, the circumstances under which the line breaks through will determine its meaning; it might be a tree breaking through the horizon, reaching skyward, or it might be the hand of Adam.

In this connection the different height of the horizon in a picture might receive its real significance. A high horizon which because of its height will not be interrupted, serves as a protection, whereas a low horizon makes the landscape stand out, and with the frequently interrupted horizontal line, introduces a more unquiet and restless atmosphere. A high horizon may include all people living in this space as a protecting line. A low horizon, however, exposes man to the elements.

Although this discussion on the meaning of the line and its relationships is by no means exhaustive—since life can never be discussed exhaustively—it has shown the close interdependence of line and experience and has thus demonstrated that the line, as a vital element of expression, can be understood only as a part of it.[4]

The meaning of space and its relations

As long as space is not defined in its qualities, it can generally have four meanings: (1) in its unlimited quality, (2) within a restricted boundary, (3) the relationships of spaces of different significance, and (4) we in the space, or our subjective relationship to space.

The unlimited space cannot be conceived in its totality. Its infinity, the universe, is irrational. Space becomes accessible to our senses only when we circumscribe it, or when we assign to it a definite meaning. As long as we think of the inaccessible space of the universe, space remains irrational. As soon as we think in terms of "sky," we relate the sky to a definite atmosphere or mood, we have assigned to space a definite meaning, and as such, it becomes accessible to our senses, especially to our optical sense. If we think of restricted space, like the space in a room, it becomes accessible not only to our eyes but also to our kinesthesis or acoustic reactions.

[4] D'Amico, Victor, *Creative Teaching in Art,* Revised Edition. Scranton: International Textbook Co., 1953.

This space can be measured and, therefore, objectively determined in its sizes. The quality of this space, however, depends upon our subjective relationship to it. *Objective* space is space perceived *optically*. Its pictorial representation is governed by the law of perspective. Its clearest depiction is produced by the photographic camera. *Subjective space* is the space in which we include the self. In it, therefore, we find a predominance of subjective interpretations or judgments of value. They can refer to sizes and their subjective values, or they can refer to the qualities of spaces as expressed through different emphasis on light and shadow and color.[5]

A simple story will illustrate the meaning of these subjective relationships and their interpretation in art. You and your friend are standing in front of a door not knowing what or whom you will meet when the door is opened. Your present relationships to the space inside of the door, therefore is *undetermined*. The only thing you know is that you and your friend will soon enter a room. In art we would say that a *definite* space experience is contrasted to an *indefinite* one, thus creating the same tension and interest that we feel now as we are waiting in front of the door. The door opens! We enter a small, low room. The room is bare and empty. No one is living there; people have not yet moved in. This room has two doors. Your friend goes through one, you through the other. You enter a very small room, almost the size of a closet; your friend, however, enters a big hall. Both of you are compelled to stay in your rooms for some time without being able to leave them. After you have lived in these rooms you come back into the room from which you entered. Your impressions are different. You find this "small room" very large; your friend, accustomed to his big hall, finds it smaller than before. Your subjective relationship to the size of the room has changed. Through the inclusion of the self the spatial relations to the sizes of the different rooms have become subjective.

In art these subjective interpretations of value relationships in space are of prime significance. Not only does the significance, which is assigned to the self, change with regard to the importance it has in relation to environment, but the spaces also change with regard to the emotional significance they have to us.

Before discussing this experience of spatial relationships with regard to sizes in its pictorial representations, I would like to continue the story about the rooms, adding to the subjective relationships of sizes the relationships of qualities.

Again you and your friend are standing in front of the same door. The difference in your impressions then and now consists of the fact that you

[5] Wiggin, R. G., *Composing in Space.* Dubuque, Iowa: William C. Brown Company, 1949.

both have now *different* but *definite* feelings of what will meet you when the door opens. Having lived in the "closet" for such a long time, you will have in your mind a comfortably sized room, whereas your friend, having lived in the big hall, will remember this room as small. The door opens, and how surprised you both are when you discover a very nicely and comfortably furnished room with a fine rug and well-designed furniture. Again you don't stay in this room, but each of you enters one of the two doors that lead into the rooms well known to you both. Again how great is the surprise to find your very small room as beautiful as you ever could imagine a room to be. It has changed to a perfectly designed room, a room as comfortable as you never could have dreamed it, and at once you feel quite at home. Every glance reveals something new, gives more satisfaction of well-spaced and perfectly designed environment. Your friend, in the meanwhile, has entered his room. The big hall has not changed except that it now appears barer and grayer than before. The walls have become dirtier, the atmosphere more gloomy. He feels quite lost in this big hall and anxiously awaits the time when he will be allowed to leave. How different are your impressions when you both return to the middle room. To you, coming from your most perfectly designed room, the middle room, though larger than yours, will appear quite common, neither attractive nor distinctive in any respect. How different is the reaction of your friend. He will be delighted with everything in this room; everything will appear wonderful to him. Though he comes from his big hall, the middle room now seems to him better than anything he could imagine.

We conclude from these two stories that *big space* may mean *much space* and *freedom,* as well as *being lost* and *restricted* (in one's comfort). *Small space,* however, may mean *restriction in space* and in *freedom* as well as *greatest satisfaction* in being in a world of one's own. These problems could be further complicated by the addition of the problem of different personalities and their emotional reactions. The latter is the problem of Beethoven who wrote, "I hate the world at large, with its grimaces; how well I feel in my four walls"; as well as the problem of the little dancer who sits at home weeping because she cannot find the way to the world at large.

How are the subjective relationships expressed in art? To concretize the discussion, these compositional elements will be analyzed by means of three pictures representing the same subject in different space relationships. The topic is the same, "A Wood Chopper," and we shall see how his spatial relationships determine not only the meaning of the pictures but also change his character and emotional relationships.

a   b   c

Fig 66. "Wood Chopper."

The problem is the same as with the rooms. Like the entrance room in the former story, here the woodcutter remains in fact unchanged. What does change is his relationship to the surrounding spaces. Fig. 66a shows the relationship between sky and earth; in Fig. 66b, the immediate space in which he lives becomes characterized by a higher horizon; and in Fig. 66c, the space around him becomes restricted. If we investigate these changes we shall find phenomena closely parallel to the problems developed in the story of the rooms. Vast space, as expressed in Fig. 66a, means here *unrestricted freedom.* The space surrounding the woodcutter is almost unrestricted. In this space, in which he is uplifted by the convex line of the hill (see discussion on "line"), he stands out as a symbol of power, a master over nature, cutting wood, chopping trees at his own will. No one interferes with him. How different is the effect of Fig. 66b, where he is no longer surrounded by free air in free space. Through the raised horizon he has become a part of the earth, of his earth, characterized by stumps of trees and lumber. It is his earthly life that surrounds him. In Fig. 66a we were able to forget that woodcutting is a job with which to earn one's living, but in Fig. 66b we definitely are not only reminded of that but become aware of what it means to cut wood all day long. The self is struggling with its environment. No one is victorious, and the only thing standing out above the horizon is the axe, a reminder that in it lies power and that with it the man earns his living. The subjective relationship of the wood chopper to the space that surrounds him has changed. It has narrowed his field of vision and has brought him down to his daily occupation. How this relationship has changed in Fig. 66c! Now even the horizon has disappeared. The trees stand like the bars of a prison. The man has become the victim of his occupation, perhaps of society, a prisoner of the trees, which seem to take away from him air and freedom. How small he

a   *b*   *c*

Fig. 67. "Coming Home."

appears now; how beaten down by his environment, especially if compared with Fig. 66a.

However, as we have learned from our story about the different rooms and their relationships, much space not only means freedom but may also mean the feeling *of being lost,* whereas restricted space may mean greatest satisfaction derived from the feeling *of being in the world of one's own.* These relative value judgments in art are of great significance. They help in understanding the works of art and provide the teacher with the proper perspective for criticizing and evaluating art products of children. How often do we see a student struggle for a definite expression, without even being aware of the problems involved. Being aware of such psychological principles in the use of the elements of composition will help the teacher to protect his students from such unnecessary struggles. How this different expression of much space with the meaning of being lost, or of restricted space with the meaning of feeling happy in one's own world is shown in art, is demonstrated by means of the following three illustrations. Again the central figure remains unchanged. The topic is "Coming Home."

Fig. 67a, which corresponds to Fig. 66a, shows the person standing out from the horizon and exposed to storm in the vastness of space. But here, unlike Fig. 66a, where standing-out meant power, the same spatial relationship means loneliness, the feeling of being lost in the vastness of almost unrestricted space. In Fig. 67b the horizon is moved up as in Fig. 66b, and characterizes more the immediate space of action. But unlike Fig. 66b where it meant more restriction, it now has the significance of greater protection. The man can no longer feel as lonely and lost as in Fig. 67a, for he is surrounded by protecting elements. This feeling of security is increased in Fig. 67c, "Home-Coming," where the space is completely restricted. It is not the restriction of a prison as it was in Fig. 66c; it is now complete protection, which creates the feeling of happiness, in contrast to Fig. 66c.

How can the same space relations create such divers impressions? It is exactly as in the story of the rooms. Here also, all depends on the circumstances under which these space relationships occur. If we compare Fig. 67c with Fig. 66c, we will immediately recognize that in Fig. 66c restriction in space is expressed by lines that are determined—determined and bold because they start and stop at definite points, going over the whole length of the picture, as the trees do. They are dynamic and exciting lines because we cannot predict where they will start, where they have their base. This gives us the feeling that even trees might come closer and closer, thus expressing *unlimited* restriction. How different are the lines used in Fig. 67c, where restricted space expresses obviously the feeling of protection. Here we have the restricted space expressed by utilitarian static lines, lines symbolizing the boundaries of the room; by lines that are not in contrast to the central figure (as the trees are contrasted to the woodcutter), but which unite with him. They find in him their continuation, as it can be so well seen in the arms of the boy and the motion of the woman. All lines either *unite* or *protect*.

The very same difference in the use of lines holds true for Fig. 67b and 66b, and Fig. 66a and 67a. Whereas in Fig. 67b the lines are all curved around the central figure as if to frame him almost like a protective umbrella, in Fig. 66b the lines are all opposing the central figure, stinging against him, as it were, pointing swords toward him irregularly.

From this discussion it becomes clear that the means of expression determine the particular meaning of spatial relationships.

The meaning of light and shadow

Throughout the history of art the meaning of light and shadow has gone through the most interesting and divers phases. If one were to write a history of art, based only upon the changes in the meaning of light and shadow during the different epochs and cultures, he might produce one of the most dramatically written histories of art. The use of light and shadow in art in its different meanings and qualities not only indicates a different creative concept, but allows us, as we shall see, to draw conclusions concerning different attitudes toward life and their psychological implications. A period which has not yet "discovered" the existence of light and shadow must be quite different from one in which light and shadow are accurately

the spiritual forces diminish, the meaning of the substance and surface increases. It is possible, however, that the meaning of substance is so subordinate that light and shadow indicate only the three-dimensional quality of the thing and nothing else. Light and shadow have merely the meaning of characterizing the representations. In such works of art, light and shadow are confined to the objects which are of expressive importance (Fig. 69). The visual experience, which always needs a source of light, in such works is highly subordinate. Therefore, all works of art, in which either expression or the mere abstract characterization of form and substance is predominant, show light and shadow only as means of emphasizing the meaningful parts. If, however, a visual experience is reported— that is, characterized accurately, light and shadow go beyond specific objects and include environment as well. These realistic representations (reports on nature) use light and shadow to characterize nature itself without accentuating our subjective relationship to it. The more the desire grows to give an exact report, as connected with utilitarian purposes, the more light and shadow obey laws related to the laws of perspective. These tendencies are best seen in creative works of individuals who emphasize in their work their realistic or utilitarian relationship to the object. If the experience of light and shadow becomes a dominant experience, if the three-dimensional quality of form becomes the main discovery in a work of art, light and shadow appear exaggerated. This can often be seen in drawings of youths or in periods of art in which the discovery of light and shadow has the quality of a first experience. Such a discovery often leads to the need to find and indicate the source of light. In such works of art, not only light and shadow in their relationship are shown, but also the source from which the light comes (Fig. 70). Paintings of interiors, therefore, deal with this kind of discovery of a special meaning of light.

Epochs and cultures that are dynamic and not content with the mere visible experiences, use light and shadow to give expression to this dramatic quality characteristic of this epoch. In such cultures the work of art is more like a gigantic stage design. Neither life nor atmosphere is real. Both appear in the dramatic illuminations of baroque art in which the fight of earthly with spiritual qualities is deeply symbolized by this specific use of light. When light and shadow lose the quality of dramatic interpretations as well as of realistic representations, they no longer obey the laws of nature. The artist, the Lord as it were, then freely determines lights and shadows. He creates his own laws, which are governed only by the relationship of his intuitive forces to the world outside (Fig. 71). The atmosphere created by these forces is necessarily magically mystic. The best

Fig. 69. Madonna. After a painting by Crivelli. Bache Collection. Metropolitan Museum of Art, N. Y. Light and shadow merely characterize form. (Courtesy Bettmann Archives.)

Fig. 70. Entombment of Christ. After a painting by Caravaggio. Vatican, Rome. Exaggeration of light and shadow. (Courtesy Bettmann Archives.)

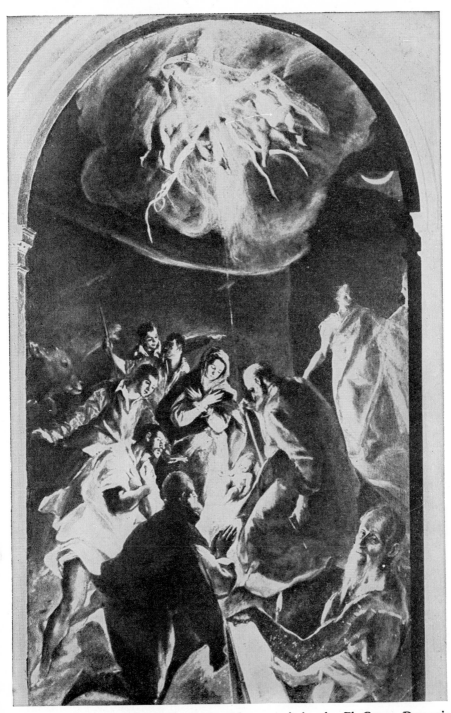

Fig. 71. Adoration of the Shepherds. After a painting by El Greco. Dramatic illumination. (Courtesy Bettmann Archives.)

Fig. 72. Painting by Rembrandt. Magic mystical light.

representative is Rembrandt in his latest works. His greatest strength, and his most precious gift to mankind, is his light vibrating in the darkness and his power of dealing with lights and darks in unlimited and absolute freedom (Fig. 72). The antipode to this most mysterious way of directing lights and shadows intuitively is an art which not only prefers the bright

Fig. 73. Haystack and Sheep. After a painting by C. Pissarro. Light and shadow express atmosphere, surface appearance and distance. (Courtesy Bettmann Archives.)

daylight in which nothing can be hidden, but tries to analyze these daylight impressions with regard to quality of light, shadows, and color (Fig. 73). Visual experiences like atmosphere, the different qualities and intensities of surface appearances, celebrate their triumphs.

Impressionistic art is visual art in its extreme meaning. Light, shadow, and color are no longer means to an end, but ends themselves. In this art the evaluation of lights and darks obeys only the rules of visual perception. Directly opposed to this art we shall find those creations which use lights and darks no longer in connection with visually perceivable appearances. This type of art in which light sometimes is an *expression* of happiness, another time has a mere symbolic meaning, is *purely expressive.* It places light and dark in value relationship to each other, using it *emotionally, expressively,* and *symbolically.* In this art, lights and shadows are neither governed by rules nor do they obey any external laws (Fig. 74a and 74b). How different is the significance of lights and darks if we finally look at

Fig. 74a. Painting by Picasso. Meaning of darks and lights is entirely different from visual impressions. (Courtesy Museum of Modern Art, N. Y.)

the art in which lights and darks seemingly have the purest meaning because in design its significance is not connected with any subject matter. The meaning of light and dark in design is nothing else but their proper distribution.[6]

[6] Compare with Schoen, M., *Art and Beauty*. New York: The Macmillan Co., 1942; Opdyke, George H., *Art and Nature Appreciation*. New York: The Macmillan Co., 1933.

Fig. 74b. Painting by Rouault in which lights and darks are emotionally determined. (Courtesy Museum of Modern Art, N. Y.)

From this discussion it follows that lights and darks must be treated differently according to their special meaning. It would be entirely wrong to stimulate an individual who intends to express his inner relationship to lights and darks by means of visual methods referring to the outside appearance of lights and shadows. It would be just as wrong to stimulate an individual who is mainly interested in the impressionistic qualities of lights and shadows by means of his emotional responses to darks and lights. It is of great significance, therefore, that we know the different meanings of light and shadow as important elements of a composition, because only then will we be able to understand its meaning as a creative force.

Color, an element in composition

Color, as an element of composition, is a means of artistic expression. Therefore, we shall deal with it, in this framework, from this angle only. Thus, we exclude the science of color which is just as remote from our discussion as the teaching of "right measurements" as seen in the "golden mean." [7] Only our subjective relationship to color, the meaning color has to the creator, will be discussed within this chapter.

Color can have as many meanings as line, space, or lights and darks. The simplest is the meaning of mere characterization. Color merely characterizes the object: the grass is green, the sky is blue, the bark of a tree is brown, the foliage is green, and so forth. An artist who uses color merely to characterize objects must put his creative emphasis elsewhere because he must be concerned with other means of expression more than with color. Color has for this artist a subordinate meaning. It is a mere *descriptive* meaning which finds its parallel in the early stages of speech development. The main aim of this descriptive meaning lies in the establishment of a relationship between color and object, or in speech, between word and meaning. The origin of this relationship in art can be visual or haptical— visual when the description is done according to our visual percept, which uses the eyes as the intermediaries; haptical when the description is an outcome of emotional or body reactions. Both relationships can be *general and bold* or *individual and sensitive,* depending upon epoch and culture, and artist personality. The more differentiated these relationships between object and color grow, the more complex becomes the problem of color. The most general and bold visual relationship is the assignment of one local color always related to the same object (see "Objective Stage of Color," p. 157). The visual percept is thus general and undifferentiated, and is satisfied merely by the process of distinguishing objects roughly by

[7] The golden mean is a "most desired proportion" according to the geometrical progression: 8, 13, 21, 34, 55 . . . and so forth or 13/8, 21/13, 34/21 . . . and so forth. This was already known to the Egyptians and Greeks. Hambidge, Jay, *Dynamic Symmetry*. New Haven: Yale University Press, 1923.

relating them to the color to which they pertain. The most general and bold haptic relationship between object and color is the repetition of one and the same color for the same emotional experience. Thus a rigid relationship between emotion and color represents the most primitive haptic color experience. Through such a general validity and repetition, the color becomes a symbol of expression. *Color symbols thus are the most primitive haptic means of color expressions.*

The more differentiated visual color experiences grow, the more we see the need to refrain from using local color tones. With the increased desire *to see* and *observe* color, the quality of color assigned to the objects and the relationships of the colors to one another become more differentiated and complex. Visual relationships of color deal with the optically perceivable influences of one color on another. Red will appear different in a blue or yellow environment. The reflections of colors on one another may, however, assume such importance that local colors cease to exist. In this art, the relationship between object and color has shifted its center of gravity from the importance of the object to the meaning of color. In impressionistic art, the visual percept has attained its highest significance.

The more differentiated haptic color experiences grow, the more we abstain from color symbols of general validity. Color expression becomes a highly subjective experience. Associations with past experiences become fused with emotional reactions to present experiences. Also, with the increasing differentiation of haptic color experiences, color relationships assume major significance. Haptic color relationships are determined by the emotional effects colors have on us. A blue within purple might have a lonely, sad effect, whereas a purple within a bright-yellow environment will create the mood of solemnity. A green close to a shrill yellow might mean "fear," whereas it might calm us down if we place it close to a soft blue. Although much has been written on the emotional meaning and significance of color, color relationship will always be a highly subjective means of expression. Expressionistic art, therefore, is the art in which haptic color experiences receive their highest meaning.

Maitland Graves provides a brief summary of the conclusions on the psychological effects of color "reached by investigators and psychologists as a result of experiments upon thousands of people.[8]

"The warm colors, yellow, orange, and red, are positive and aggressive, restless, or stimulating, as compared to the cool violets, blues, and greens, which are negative, aloof, and retiring, tranquil or serene.

[8] Graves, Maitland, *The Art of Color and Design.* New York: McGraw-Hill Book Company, Inc., 1941, p. 256.

"Color preference is as follows, in the order named (pure colors):
a. Red, b. Blue, c. Violet, d. Green, e. Orange, f. Yellow.

"Pure colors are preferred to shades and tints when used in small areas.

"In large areas, shades and tints are preferred to pure colors." [9]

Although these conclusions are based "on thousands of people," they have no general validity for teaching purposes. That they are based on thousands of people means only that the majority reacted to these colors in the way the summary shows. Since the majority of an average population is visually minded, the haptically minded minority is neglected if we apply the results of this "summary" rigidly. In a classroom situation the haptically minded group may need more attention than the visually minded. In this case, such summaries must be interpreted with great care.

In his *Characteristics and Symbolism of Color,* Maitland Graves refers to historic and present-day symbolisms of colors. He discusses pleasant and unpleasant associations without undue dogmatism. In his analysis of the majority of the colors, he provides interesting and valuable information. But Graves also emphasizes that such information is subjective and is not generally valid. He says, "Yellow, for example, is a sacred color, not only in China but also in European Christianity. On the other hand, it is sometimes used to signify treachery and deceit. This is confusing unless it is remembered that yellow is, and has been, loosely applied to many hues, tints, and shades, ranging from the clear and brilliant cadmium and lemon yellows, to the ochers and bilious greenish yellows. . . . Bright clear yellow is emblematic of the sun and is cheerful, gay, and lively. . . . The darker and the more neutralized yellows and greenish yellows are the most unpopular and disliked of all colors. These yellows are associated with sickness and disease, indecency, cowardice, jealousy, envy, deceit, and treachery. The yellow flag is flown on quarantined ships and sometimes hospitals. In tenth-century France, the doors of the houses of traitors and criminals were painted yellow, and Judas was pictured as clad in yellow garments. . . . Today the terms 'yellow dog' and 'yellow streak' convey the ideas of treachery and cowardice. Nevertheless, these yellows, although unpleasant by themselves, may be satisfactory and even beautiful when properly related with other colors." [10]

Valuable and important as these color associations may be for the proper knowledge and understanding of colors, color itself in art is meaningless unless related to its environment. And, again according to Graves,

[9] *Ibid.*
[10] *Ibid.,* p. 259.

"colors unpleasant by themselves may be satisfactory and even beautiful when properly related with other colors. That shows that there is no general validity or rule in color reactions in art, but that relationships determine their meaning just as they do in space and line."

Instead of discussing the possible meanings of the single colors, we shall, therefore, discuss the meaning of color relationships within a composition. Depending upon period and culture, and artist personality, color relationship can be based on aesthetic or expressive assumptions.

In the visual and decorative arts, color relationships are based mostly on aesthetic functions. Color relationships, therefore, are dependent upon the principles given in color harmony. These principles can best be understood if we compare them with music, especially with tonal music, the music in which the longing for resounding chords is one of the main driving forces. In some of the tonal works of music the interest in the work of art is increased by the dramatic tension under which sounds approach one another under different circumstances, until the longing for the chord is so great, that the chord finally has to resound. Of course, the type of experience underlying this "battle" is different with different works and composers.

In the representative arts we do not deal with different time sequences as we do in listening to music. We can see the whole picture simultaneously. In color, however, we can draw close parallels with music, if we regard the single colors as tones and a color harmony as chord. In a picture, as in music, the resounding of a color harmony can be interrupted by colors which are interpolated in order to increase the tension or interest for the "resounding" color harmony. In the same way that rhythm in music is produced by the principle of repetition, it is also produced in color. In music as well as in color compositions the interest in repetitions is created by varying them, either by different emphasis with regard to the intensity of tones (dynamics) or through different intervals (harmonics).

If the longing for the resounding of a chord is subordinated to the expressive quality, disregarding whether it is produced by discords or chords, we deal with the type of music which can be compared with color compositions in which aesthetic are subordinated to expressive values. In this realm color relationships assume a different significance. Subjective value relationships dominate this type of color composition. There are no absolute bright or poor colors. Everything depends upon the meaning of color with regard to its environment. We may compare this experience with a girl who looks beautifully dressed in her dull environment. As soon as she has to compete with others on the dance floor, she will be submerged in the mass of color and brightness. Bright colors may become dull when overpowered by environmental influences. Bright colors may no more seem bright but monotonous when repeated by equally intensive colors.

The significance attached to color can be apprehended by imagining the feeling of a student who could not graduate but has to sit in her "beautiful" evening dress amongst her graduate colleagues wearing their black baccalaureate gowns. If she would have to paint this picture, the bright colors of her evening dress would not assume the meaning of brightness or significance. Visually bright colors, then, do not necessarily refer to emotional contents of the same meaning. Colors receive their emotional content through the relationships in which they are represented. Since these relationships are an outcome of subjective experiences and associations, color relationships in expressionistic art are highly individual.

Unity, or composition

Unity, or composition, in a work of art we call the integration of all the previously mentioned properties in a sum total in which all compositional elements are interwoven into one consistent pattern. "The purpose of composition is to organize all the physical elements which make up a work of art into a coherent pattern, pleasing to the senses."[11] However, "pleasing to the senses" is a relative value judgment. We all know that many people would oppose our calling Picasso's mural, "Guernica," pleasing to the senses. We have, however, a simple means to prove this "consistent pattern" by attempting to change the unity in a work of art. The greater the work of art, the less is the possibility of making the slightest change in any of its compositional elements. Any attempt to change any one of the compositional properties must subsequently result in a disunity of all other elements. If we would change the arm of "Adam" in the mural by Michelangelo, the whole mural would fall to pieces and would lose its "consistent pattern." The same result would happen if we attempt to raise the line that separates Adam from the Lord. A work of art contains the highest and most complete organization of its elements. In such an organization there is nothing superfluous. It represents the highest form of economy. Every part is related to the whole and the whole is related to every part. The foreground supports the background and the background brings out the foreground. If one can exist without the other, the work of art is incomplete.[12]

[11] Read, Herbert, *op. cit.*
[12] Munro, Thomas, "Powers of Art Appreciation and Evaluation" in *Art in American Life and Education.* Bloomington, Ill.: Public School Publishing Co., 1941.

In recognizing this unity of composition as the highest form of organization and economy in which nothing can be changed without doing harm
to the whole, an important means of criticism is placed in the hands of the
educator. He will no longer look exclusively for balance and rhythm, which
are only some aesthetic properties in a composition, but will become aware
of the integration of all elements and their expressive qualities. He will use
as a criterion the possibility of changes as well as the necessity that each
part is a part of the whole. He will furthermore steer toward this highest
economy in which only the most necessary things are expressed. *Necessary,*
however, also is a relative value judgment. Necessary for a visual work of
art are other properties than for a haptical one. This again is an important
principle of which the educator must be aware. In both realms of art, however, he will not succeed if he does not place the individual above rules, if
he does not consider unity of composition the most *integrated outcome of
personality and creation.*[13]

Fundamental to any aesthetic education is the recognition that the
aesthetic product is only a record of the degree to which the senses have
developed and have been brought into harmonious relationship with the
external world. If the senses have been refined and cultivated it will be
revealed in the aesthetic product.

[13] See also Evans, Joan, *Taste and Temperament.* New York: The Macmillan Co., 1939.

CHAPTER XI   THE CASE OF THE GIFTED CHILD

U<small>NDER THE DEMOCRATIC MOTTO THAT ALL CHILDREN SHOULD BE</small> given equal opportunity to express themselves freely, we might be apt to overlook the child who does not conform with the characteristics generally expected from his classmates. The gifted child definitely belongs to this category and it is with him that we would like to deal in this chapter.

As so often before, the study of extreme cases has magnified problems which might remain unrecognized under normal conditions. I can therefore scarcely think of a better opportunity of discussing certain important educational problems and their implications than by means of two specific cases of specially gifted children.

While every child, regardless of where he stands in his development, should first of all be considered as an individual, the gifted child makes us doubly aware of this responsibility. In fact, his highly developed sensitivity within his special field of interest not only makes him often appear different from others but may also keep him from participating in general activities less important to him. Thus his special problems point with such power at his individuality that we cannot help but consider it as such. To do justice to the gifted child is not only vital to this society, but it is an important educational principle. It is indeed one of the most difficult tasks, for all that ve have learned and studied apparently breaks down

Fig. 75. Bobby, age 7, always engages in much action with a strong feeling for rhythm. For his quick drawings he uses mainly pencil and crayon on small (lined) paper.

under the impact of the power of his individual expression. Developmental characteristics no longer can be validly applied for they are based on the "average." Motivations effective for the "group" might be frustrating to the gifted individual. Media and techniques considered as "thwarting" may become vital parts of expression. Paper sizes considered "restricting" for the average child may become just the ideal area for his particular kind of expression. Quite apart from the aesthetic message, it is this deviation from those things "we have learned and studied" which is the most potent contribution of the gifted child to education, for without it the danger is great of falling into "educational stereotypes" such as: "Draw big"— "Don't use crayons because they are a restricting medium"—"Size of the paper should be at least——etc." All of this advice becomes mere prescription, a type of "academism" which we would not accept elsewhere.

THE INDIVIDUAL CASE

What is it that distinguishes Bobby from the average child? Five major factors stand out among the many to be considered:

1. Fluency of imagination and expression.

2. A highly developed sensibility (in certain areas, especially with regard to movement and space).

3. The intuitive quality of imagination.

4. Directness of expression.

5. The high degree of self-identification with subject matter and medium.

Fluency of imagination and expression

The most obvious characteristic in this specific case appears to be the freedom with which the child adapts his ability to the diverse situation with which he is dealing. This constant change in which one element grows out of the other seems to be not only one of the important factors of the talent of this specific case, but as J. P. Guilford and W. Lambert Brittain, in their independent studies on creativity [1] found, it is a general criterion for creativeness, regardless of where it is applied. In looking at Fig. 75, the eye is almost directed from one event to the other, from one movement to the next. It becomes quite evident that the drawing developed as the imagery "expanded." It was not a preconceived "whole," but went quite fluently from one figure to the other almost as "the fight developed." Such fluency of ideas, or as Guilford calls it, "ideational fluency," is an important part of any creative process. The specially gifted individual has it to a higher degree than is usually found. This spontaneity of expression and the resulting ability to take advantage of the given situation in developing new ones can be seen in all drawings of the gifted. The mind, as it were, never stands still. The imagery expands with the creative process like in a chain reaction. In early childhood this fluency of imagination deals mainly with the continuously developing responses toward subject matter and the flexible use of concepts, called schemas. In the drawing "Indians pursuing a Russian" (Fig. 77), the child obviously started with the fleeing Russian and then, as it were, the pursuit began—the Indian close to him followed— he gave rise to the next Indian using a different motion and "method of pursuit"—and then the fourth swiftly following the third. Had the paper been larger, others would have followed with the same fluency of imagination and the same flexibility in the use of the concepts for horses and Indians. That the sequence was according to "the pursuit" of the Russian can clearly be seen from the overlapping pencil marks of the horses "covering" parts of those who follow. This great inventive power of building up a situation out of continuous chain reactions of stimuli to new

[1] Guilford, J. P., R. C. Wilson and P. R. Christiensen, "A Factor-Analytic Study of Creative Thinking, II. Administration of Tests and Analysis of Results." *Reports from the Psychological Laboratory,* The University of Southern California, No. 8, 1952; Brittain, W. Lambert, "An Experimental Study to Determine a Test on Creativity." Unpublished doctoral dissertation, The Pennsylvania State University.

Fig. 76. Sandra, age 5, never wants to use paint but draws her "Galloping Horses Followed by a Dog" freshly with pencil on newsprint.

and changing responses to subject matter and form is a highly significant criterion of the gifted. As the child grows older the same "chain reaction" also develops in the use of materials and techniques. With the growing awareness toward the art product, he is able to take continuous advantage of accidental or other technical achievements as the artist does. However, it is quite obvious that directing the child's attention to this developing technique at a time when he has no such desires would only interfere with his spontaneous unconscious childish approach.

However unconsciously, the child makes highly sensitive use of the material. It is here where we have to revise some of our preconceived ideas. Both children discussed in this article are using the pencil in its intrinsic quality with such intense self-identification that it can scarcely be substituted by any material more adequately serving their expression. Furthermore, it is the means of expression by their own individual choice. In other words, it is *their* means to express *their* sensibilities. To deprive them of these means or to divert them to others might not only be frustrating to them but deprive them of the most meaningful means of expression. Sandra, in her "Galloping Horses Followed by a Dog," uses the pencil line with such a fluency, sensitivity, and certainty that we would have difficulty in finding such expression on a conscious, artistic level. Bobby, too, never

Fig. 77. Bobby, age 7. "Indians Pursuing a Russian." Rhythm and action in horses and flying arrows were most meaningful to Bobby in this drawing.

seems to have the need of drawing over a line again, so certain is he of his expression and the use of his medium.

The highly developed sensibility

The child's aunt tells us: "When I drove Bobby back to his house, we saw some boats and some trains. To try to increase Bob's scope, I asked him to draw a picture of the boats and the trains and send them to me. He replied, to my astonishment, 'I can't. I only draw things that are moving fast in my pictures.'" This sensibility toward movement and rhythm can readily be seen as one of the outstanding characteristics in Bobby's drawings. But the story of his aunt reveals another important fact. Sensibilities toward various experiences are not always equally developed in the gifted. On the contrary, a certain highly developed area of experience may even characterize the gifted. In the case of Bobby it is first of all movement and to a lesser degree, color. (See Fig. 75.) In Sandra, it is movement only. She never wants to use color. (See Fig. 76.) But both have in common the high degree of sensibility for spatial distribution and "organization." Both Brittain and Guilford regard this "sensitivity for consistency of organization" as an outstanding characteristic of creativeness. The gifted child flexibly adapts this sensitivity for organization to different situations. If he needs the whole area for his battleground or the "story," the organization spreads over the whole sheet. (Compare Fig. 75 with Fig. 78.) However,

Fig. 78. Sandra, age 5. "The Peter Pan Story" necessitates the use of the whole sheet of paper.

if the directional movement is important for expression it determines the organization. (Compare Fig. 76 with Fig. 77.) As we can readily see, movement, rhythm, content, and organization become an inseparable entity. Such integration of thinking, feeling, and perceiving is part and parcel of any creative process. The gifted has it only to a much higher degree. One merely has to look at the "Galloping Horses Followed by a Dog" by Sandra, a five-year-old girl, to realize the degree of sensibility toward motion, rhythm, the almost unrestricted use of the pencil line, the incarnation of movement; or at the beautiful masterly rhythm of the arrows and the tomahawk in the drawing of the "Indians Pursuing a Russian" by Bobby. The meaningful is in such perfect relationship to the meaningless or background area that any change would disturb the harmonious relationship.

The intuitive quality of imagination

Imagination may merely serve the purpose of recalling events either directly or associatively. It may, however, also be used as a vehicle for new adventures into the unknown, bringing into existence constellations or

Fig. 79. Bobby, age 7. "Boat Fight." The schema for his figures is most flexibly used.

events which have not existed before. It is this intuitive quality of imagery which is an important part of every creative act. In the gifted individual it is present to a high degree. It is seen in the great inventive power of Bobby in creating his almost Picasso-like symbols for human expression and movement, particularly in the boat scene, Fig. 79, as well as in the spontaneity and variability of five-year-old Sandra's fleeing horses. It is documented in the great diversity of spatial symbolisms. Both children create the "space" in which their action takes place with such a "lordly" autonomy, as if they were the Creator themselves. One has only to compare the ingenious inventiveness of using base-line symbols in the five reproductions to realize the great intuitive power of the two gifted children. Such intuitive imagery must be expressed; it must be translated into concrete form. This is the main difference between phantasy and art. As soon as phantasy is translated into some form of expression through the intuitive power of the creator it ceases to be mere phantasy. Educationally this is of great significance because it answers the often placed question of how far we should go in stimulating the phantasy of children without "overstimulating" them. We cannot go far enough as long as the child uses it and turns it into "concrete and factual material," such as his creations. It is the intuitive quality of the imagery of the gifted which does not stop without this great fulfillment.

Directness of expression

From the child who expresses his lack of confidence in the often heard phrase, "I can't draw," to the directness seen in the expression of the gifted is a wide range of reactions which constitute the atmospheres of our classrooms. What makes Bobby and Sandra so sure of their expression? The answer to this has important educational implications, for it is quite obvious that it is neither the ability to come close to external reality nor a special skillful dexterity which can be detected in Sandra's or Bobby's work. "I can't draw" is then no indication of a child's lack of skill or his inability to portray external reality. In fact, Bobby has given us the answer in his conversation with his aunt when he said, "I only draw things moving fast in my pictures." With this he indicated that if no basic experience affected him he could not draw it. If, however, an experience is in tune with his desire for expression he draws it with such certainty and directness that we do not doubt for a second the convincing quality of *his* expression. It is the same conviction that we have about a product of nature, or as Malraux says, "Art is, as it were, an independent species." The creator gives it its own life with its independent intrinsic qualities. Bobby and Sandra create with such conviction that no one would ever use any other measure than the one they have set forth themselves. It is this quality of conviction which manifests itself in the directness of expression which is especially highly developed in the creative products of the gifted.

The high degree of self-identification

As has been said before, subject matter and medium become such an inseparable whole in every creative process that they cannot be separated as experiences. Yet, merely for matters of clarification we shall have to discuss them separately. For Bobby as well as for Sandra the subject matter is extremely important. They live in it to such a degree that all the consistency of organization and expression is guided by the intensity of the emotional and physical participation in the experience during the creative process. Indeed we get this vital feeling when looking at every detail Bobby has created. Most of all one can get it from the sequence with which he produced his drawings. He almost went kinetically through the whole action. All this is impossible without an intense identification of the self with the depicted experience. Indeed, without it no creative activity is possible. Yet, it is not only this extreme self-identification with the subject matter, the holding of a dagger, the riding on the horse, the shooting of the arrow, the jumping of a dog, the fleeing of the horses, but also the intense feeling for the medium. The pencil has almost become a continuation of the body of both children. It is no longer a separate means, but a part of them. Bobby and Sandra, as it were, live and breathe through their pencil.

EDUCATIONAL CONCLUSIONS

The question arises, what can the art teacher or the parents contribute to the growth of the gifted child? We have seen that Bobby and Sandra have developed their world of expression on the basis of their high sensibilities and the experiences which were most meaningful to them. Any superficial change of media or subject matter would only—as Bobby's case clearly showed—be rejected or cause confusion. Giving Bobby poster paint might deprive him of the fluency of his lines. It definitely would affect Sandra. Why should they use poster paint as long as their expression satisfies their needs? To have a variety of materials *at their disposal* may eventually lead to other kinds of expression. Yet, as long as the need for other media does not arise, there is absolutely no necessity for *introducing* them. There is some indication that Bobby might enjoy a variation of paper sizes as Sandra does. Pushing him into larger drawings, however, may be discouraging to him if he lacks inner motivation. As soon as Bobby's desire for more details grows, as it is already seen in the drawing of the Indians, which was done after the other drawings, he might welcome a larger sheet of paper. However, such changes only occur as a *result* of an increased sensitivity toward the meaning of details which could not properly be expressed in too small an area. According to his father, Bobby loves to tell interesting stories about his drawings. It could be that such verbalization may lead to more insight with regard to greater concentration and enrichment of areas of interest. It might be that as Sandra grows, in addition to the great movement she will also want more characterization of parts or swifter movements with broader strokes, but all this is purely speculative and shows only too well that motivating the gifted is intensely personal. In fact, it is this demand for completely individual attention which is one of the greatest contributions of the gifted to our classrooms in general, for they make us constantly revise our philosophy and thus prevent us from succumbing to the clichés of the conformities of an academism in art education.

At the end of a discussion on "The Gifted" it should be clearly pointed out that *every child is potentially gifted*. To divide children into "gifted" and "not gifted" would be absurd, for the very foundation of our philosophy is based on the development of all potential creative abilities in *every* child, regardless of where he stands on the continuum from creatively inhibited to gifted children.

THERAPEUTIC ASPECTS OF ART EDUCATION

THE CREATIVE PROCESS AND THE HANDICAPPED

IT IS ONE OF MY DEEPEST INNERMOST CONVICTIONS THAT WHEREVER there is a spark of human spirit—no matter how dim it may be—it is our sacred responsibility as humans, teachers, and educators to fan it into whatever flame it conceivably may develop. I venture to say that the ethical standard of a society can be measured by its relationships to the handicapped. We as human beings have no right whatsoever to determine where to stop in our endeavors to use all our power to develop the uppermost potential abilities in each individual. We all are by nature more or less endowed with intrinsic qualities and no one has the right to draw a demarcation line which divides human beings into those who should receive all possible attention in their development and those who are not worth all our efforts. One of these intrinsic qualities is that every human being is endowed with a creative spirit. Soon after birth he begins to investigate and explore and use this ability for new adventures. New findings in psychology consider this one of the "basic drives," a drive without which we cannot exist; the ability to create is probably what distinguishes man most decisively from the animal. Man creates; the animal does not.

In our discussion of the meaning of art education for the handicapped we shall, then, keep in mind that it is our basic philosophy to develop in every human being his uppermost potential creative ability regardless of the degree of his handicap. This excludes from the very beginning the question as to whether an individual is "good enough" to do creative work. In countless cases I have seen teachers of the handicapped arbitrarily dividing groups into those who can do creative work and those who should merely imitate what others have done for them. They use all kinds of arguments to justify this unethical procedure. The most frequent argument is that handicapped persons need the security and confidence which results from mere imitative occupation, such as copying or tracing. In my many years of experience in teaching physically and mentally handicapped children and adults this by no means has been confirmed. On the contrary, I have found that mere copying and tracing methods increase not only the dependency of handicapped people but also their lack of self-confidence in doing things themselves without a crutch to lean on. Thus, we actually add to their handicap another handicap by not encouraging them to use their own initiative even if there is apparently none.

As I shall later demonstrate, handicapped people not only gain self-confidence through their own creative achievement no matter how primitive it may be, but often derive from it a great deal of the independence and satisfaction so badly needed by them. It should, however, be stated and frankly admitted that copy work and purely imitative methods are most often used only because they are much easier on the teacher, and creative methods in most instances are not known to him. It is difficult to conceive that during an era in which art education—especially in the elementary classroom—is considered as an integral part of the total curriculum, most of the schools for the blind still think of art as a preparatory stage for professional art training and therefore out of the question for the schools of the blind. That creative activities serve as a means for emotional release and adjustment, that they promote independence and flexibility of thinking, that they can be used for group dynamics and social interaction, has not yet penetrated the thick walls of most of our institutions. Happiness apparently is still a luxury which handicapped people cannot afford in a materialistic time in which the education of the handicapped is almost exclusively geared toward preparation for making a living. That one can do this more adequately and efficiently as an adjusted citizen has been greatly neglected.

THERAPY AND ART EDUCATION

Much harm has been done by teachers in using methods of therapy foreign to their own background merely for lack of awareness of a therapy specific to the means of art education. An attempt is made to clarify these means and to distinguish them from other methods.

Every handicap is connected with a greater or lesser detachment from the environment, depending on the degree and kind of handicap. This is true for emotional and mental, as well as physical and social, handicaps. Whether we can—in the individual case—speak of a detachment, depends largely not only on the handicap itself but even more on the individual and his ability to adjust to it. Partial blindness, to give an example of a physical handicap, can mean a serious handicap for one individual, while another might find adequate means of overcoming it. The one partially blind individual, unable to adjust to his inability to see, may always depend on whatever rudiments of sight remain, while the other, completely adjusted to it, never depends on his sight alone but uses his other sensory experiences. While both partially blind individuals have the same degree of visual impairment, their adjustment to it is different. Even the slightest handicap needs some kind of adjustment, which deals mainly with the problem of finding ways of overcoming a detachment from environment imposed by the handicap. Whether one is simply shy, having emotional barriers that do not permit him to communicate easily with the outside world, or whether one is completely emotionally blocked and is entirely cut off from environment, the problem differs only in degree.

Objective and subjective handicap

Therefore, we cannot flatly speak of a handicap without relating the individual to it. Objectively, two individuals may have the same defect or disturbance, but their attitude toward their handicap and their ability to adjust to it may greatly differ. It seems, therefore, of great importance to distinguish between *objective handicap,* the handicap as diagnosed or measured, and subjective handicap, the individual's attitude toward his own handicap. In order to speak adequately of an individual's handicap, both forms of handicap must be taken into consideration. For matters of clarification, a case study is used as an example.

X, who has been an engineer in a chemical plant, has just had a serious accident which caused blindness in both eyes. The initial shock does not allow him to face his handicap, to realize that blindness does not mean complete isolation. To speak in figures, for him blindness means a 100 per cent handicap. This is not surprising, for X has been seeing his whole life, and thus has a certain picture of himself as that of a good-looking person, who likes to play golf and have his fun when going out. All this and more has suddenly to be corrected. Seen objectively, there are people with much greater handicaps. After all, X has his limbs; he can communicate well by speech; his hearing is not impaired; and his mind works properly.

Fortunately—or unfortunately—only few attempts have been made to measure handicaps objectively. To my knowledge, only insurance agencies attach a percentage figure to a handicap. To them, indeed, X would not be 100 per cent handicapped. Merely for getting a better understanding of the status of X and what a therapy could do for him, let us find out what the relationship is between his objective and subjective handicap. X was blinded and his objective handicap, therefore, is that of total blindness. However, his present feeling toward his loss of sight, his subjective handicap, is that of complete isolation. There is, then, a great discrepancy between his objective and his subjective handicap. If we could express blindness arbitrarily in figures, it would help clarify his status and thus could give us a clearer clinical picture of X. Let us arbitrarily say, therefore, that blindness may objectively mean a 50 per cent handicap. X, however, feels subjectively 100 per cent handicapped; that is, the picture he has of himself is one of complete incapability. Any therapy should, then, help X to realize that he has all kinds of possibilities to enjoy his life and become a useful member of society. In other words, a therapy should bring him to the realization that he is only 50 per cent handicapped, and not 100 per cent. The successful outcome of a therapy, then, consists largely of bringing the subjective and objective handicap into harmonious relationship. The following graph may illustrate this.

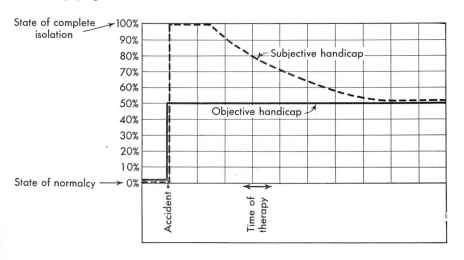

What are the means which art education can offer to make X realize his actual handicap ? for only when he realizes it can he eventually cope with it.

The significance of the body image

Every individual has a mental picture of himself. This mental picture often is in contradiction to how he looks to others. It greatly depends on "the individual's occupation, his own sense of values, and his feeling about his own worth; it may even be culturally influenced." [1] This mental picture may refer to one's own body or any part of it, or it may be a part of one's capabilities, or both. This mental picture is called *body-image*. A violin virtuoso, on the basis of his occupation, may have an exaggerated feeling of the importance of his hands. This has become intimately bound up with his body-image. A person who has had a heart attack may be continually preoccupied with his heart; a member of a minority group may have an exaggerated feeling of his "minority characteristics" when he is among people of the majority group. The body-image is subject to changes according to changes in personality or physical structure of an individual.

The body-image of X, before he had his accident, was that of a forward-looking, normal individual. Suddenly, as a result of his accident, his whole body-image is in a state of confusion. Not only the conception which he had of his own body, but also the sense of his own worth and his relationship to other people, has undergone a drastic change. This psychological change is often far more serious than the physical disability itself. Because the body-image is an integral part of creative expression, art education, in its therapeutical aspects, is concerned mainly with the implications which it has for adjustment.

The specific means of an art education therapy

Even in early childhood the body-image expresses itself in the concepts of children's drawings.[2] Herbert Read has used this fact as the basis for his treatise of children's drawings in his book, *Education Through Art*.[3] If this "flow" of the expression of the body-image is restricted, suppressed or inhibited by emotional or mental forces, motivations have to be used to

---

[1] Menninger, Karl, "Psychological Aspects of Physical Disability." Washington: Office of Vocational Rehabilitation, No. 210.

[2] Lowenfeld, Viktor, *The Nature of Creative Activity*. London: Routledge and Kegan Paul, 1952.

[3] Read, Herbert, *Education Through Art*. London: Faber and Faber, 1943.

release the child from these restrictions and encourage the necessary freedom of expressing it. This indeed is not always easy, but it is the principle
on which an art education therapy functions. It is neither the interpretation
of symbols, nor a diagnosis reached by speculative inferences based on
certain symbols, with which an art education method deals. *Teachers are
neither prepared for this type of diagnosis or therapy nor do they have
the proper background for it.* What they should be prepared for is adequate
motivations which free individuals from their restrictions in expressing
themselves, and that includes the body-image. The question arises as to the
kind of stimulation which is used for therapy. It should be stated here
emphatically that *a motivation used in an art education therapy only differs
from any other art motivation in degree and intensity and not in kind.*

As has been said before, art education does not deal with speculative
inferences in the interpretations of concepts. A nose, in spite of being the
only "protruding body part" (except the phallus), for all practical purposes remains a nose in its *visual* interpretation. Therefore an enlarged
nose, for art teachers, can only be a sign of possible importance attached to
the nose—a part of the child's body-image. Other interpretations should be
left to those who have the proper background. This, however, should by
no means be regarded as a restriction. It is merely a difference in approach
offering its own specific values. Motivations in art education are then only
based on the factual, visually perceivable expression of the child. Mainly
they consist of expanding the child's frame of reference by providing him
with meaningful experiences, as I shall attempt to demonstrate.

If a child cannot identify with his own experience—including his body-
image—he documents this inability by meaningless patterns. Such stereotyped form concepts then must form the basis from which the art teacher
extends the individual's frame of reference, in order to make him finally
"accept" his individual self, for it is the acceptance of the individual self
which ultimately leads to true self-expression. The methods of achieving
this greatly differ with individual cases, and their handicaps. X, for example, might not even want to start to express himself due to his apathy
and also due to his inhibitions to express himself in a "foreign" medium.
After studying his case history and after having established some rapport,
it would be good to acquaint him with his medium, in this case, that of clay.
In the case of a blind individual, this often can best be done by using
both his and the teacher's hand simultaneously, as it were, holding the clay
and kneading it together, simply to overcome his shyness or his feeling
toward the consistency of clay. It is needless to say that this must be done

with great care. Even then, it may sometimes be necessary that the teacher start out with a general rough form and let the individual continue. It was suggested that X model himself "thinking of a chemical experiment" of the kind he used to do. When X did not want to start, the teacher started the general outline form of a head and asked, "Where would the nose be?" When X added the nose an important beginning had been made. This process, called "closure," because he "closes" what has been started, is only legitimate if X could not be brought to express himself without foreign help. Repeated motivation with reference to X may lead to the spontaneous inclusion of the emotional self, and finally, even the ability to face his accident and with it his handicap with all its restrictions and possibilities.

In the case of an emotionally-blocked child who escapes into a repetition of stereotyped patterns, the method would consist of establishing meaningful relationships to his repeated concepts, that is, to make the stereotypes alive and bring them into harmonious relationship to the environment.

In all instances, the principle of an art education therapy is then clear; it always starts on the level of the individual, using visually perceivable documentations—and not their symbolic interpretation—for the extension of the individual's frame of reference until the individual accepts himself, and with it, his own handicap.

GENERAL STEPS IN AN ART EDUCATION THERAPY

Case history

The nature of an art education therapy is to use creative activity as a means of self-realization. Certain general steps evolve out of mere practical experiences. These steps vary from individual to individual depending on the degree and kind of handicap. Severe cases may go through all the stages described in this chapter while borderline cases may skip some of them.

Every therapy should start with a close study of all facts which are available on the individual and his handicap. A detailed knowledge of the *case history* is then the most important understanding which every teacher must have about his case. If he is not informed about the nature of the handicap, it is quite obvious that he has to study it.

Observation

After this initial study of the case and his handicap, *observation* can be done more intelligently. Observation deals with three general criteria:

(1) Criteria related to the kind of handicap.

(2) Criteria related to the degree of handicap of the particular case.

(3) Criteria related to the individual's reaction to his handicap.

The best way to benefit from observations is to write down as many general characteristics as one can observe. To check these characteristics with obtainable data will supply the teacher with an inventory which will give him the important knowledge and understanding of the degree of handicap of his particular case. It is of great significance to get a firsthand experience of the individual's reaction to his own handicap for it will be much easier for the teacher to establish rapport with the individual. It can easily be understood that a handicapped individual who has great difficulty in accepting his handicap must be approached differently from one who "seeks" communication.

Establishment of rapport

The establishment of rapport depends greatly on the teacher's ability to identify himself with his case, to put himself in his place. This feeling of empathy is one of the most important prerequisites for a successful therapy. Depending on the kind and degree of handicap, such self-identification is often very difficult, for it involves (1) a general knowledge of the degree and kind of the handicap itself, that is, of the *Primary Handicap*; (under *Primary Handicap* we understand the defect itself without all its implications for the individual, such as the inability to see, without the accompanying mental, social, or emotional effects); and (2) an understanding of the various handicaps resulting from the *Primary Handicap,* which we shall call the *Secondary Handicap* (under *Secondary Handicap* we understand all the cluster effects of handicaps which accompany the *Primary Handicap* —they usually are of mental, emotional, or social nature). For instance, many other handicaps result from blindness, such as lack of orientation, a greater restriction in freedom, a greater dependency, a restricted imagery, lack of confidence to compete with the normal environment and many others. It also involves (3) an intimate knowledge of the individual's relationship to his handicap.

Even when all of these three points are satisfied it will often be extremely difficult to identify oneself with the individual for the lack of reference of a normal individual is always counteracting a true self-identification. To put oneself into the place of a deaf person would mean that one has to exclude not only hearing, but also all feelings which are connected with it. It is difficult to imagine a complete silence without any background noises —which are probably the most important ones in considering complete silence. But even when we are able to concentrate for a moment on this complete stillness of a deaf person, in the next moment our associative hearing mixes itself into our endeavour and we have failed to realize the endlessness of a complete silence. When we try to identify ourselves with a blind person we can understand how utterly impossible it is to exclude any reference to our optical world. To imagine that the apparent diminishing size of distant objects is non-existent for the blind is almost unthinkable. But it is the ability to identify one's self with the problems of the handicapped individual and a warm and sympathetic feeling for his problems which generally leads to the establishment of rapport.

Acquaintance with the art medium

In many instances becoming acquainted with the art medium is in no way different for the handicapped individual than it is for the normal. This is especially true for situations in which the handicapped individual has previously been exposed to creative activities. For individuals who had no past experiences with art media and for whom such an exposure is entirely new, this first contact may be difficult and if not properly done may be decisive in thwarting the successful use of creative activity as a means of therapy. This can easily be understood, for if early aversions toward the means of expression develop, it is difficult later on to overcome them.

I found this initial acquaintance with art media most important in handicaps which are directly related to a developed greater sensitivity toward the sense of touch. Particularly with deaf-blind or blind persons for whom the sensation of touching clay may create associative experiences with past impressions of consistencies such as dirt, an initial period of getting acquainted is advisable.

Often the mere exposure to the material and trying out "what can be done with it" may be sufficient. In the case of clay, kneading, pounding, pinching, rolling, flattening it out, making indentations, squeezing it in one's hand, may be a good introduction. In some instances, however, I had cases who would not actively engage in such exercises, and needed additional stimulations. The principle of "closure" has been successfully applied by the author. In this case "closure" means the gradual transferring of an experience from the teacher to the subject. The teacher may first hold the clay in his hands. While going through some exercises, he makes the subject "feel" what he is doing by exposing the subject's hands to the activity. This is continued until the subject gradually takes over what the teacher initially started, that is, the subject "closes" the experience. It is needless to say that the successful application of such a procedure greatly depends on the sensitivity of the teacher.

Usually, the acquaintance with art media is a part of the establishment of a meaningful relationship between the subject and his creative activity.

Establishment of relationship to creative process

It will be demonstrated by means of case histories in the following sections (see pages 443–502) that an establishment of a relationship between the creative process and the subject greatly depends on kind and degree of handicap. An emotionally blocked individual may have great difficulty in overcoming the restrictions which are in his way to break through his handicap, that is, his inability to establish more flexible relationships within himself and the outside world. For a schizophrenic individual it may even be an impossibility, depending on the degree of his schizophrenia. For a deaf person this may be a delightful experience for which he has searched for a long time.

In general, it can be said that it is easier to establish such initial relationships by means of stimulations which relate to the subject's body self, especially its function. To start on the level of the individual is indeed an educational principle which should always be kept in mind. Any reaction, body position, or movement of the subject may be used as a starting point. "You are yawning. Are you tired? How is your mouth when you are yawning? Where is your tongue? How does it feel when you are yawning?" Such, or other questions which relate to the individual's own body feelings, may establish an initial relationship to his work. Whether he is merely "sitting" (see page 471) or "riding" (see page 487), the stimulation varies only in degree from a motivation which would establish a more intense self-realization in a normal person. It is, however, through such experiences of heightened sensitivity that initial meaningful relationships to the creative process are established. Whether a meaningless rigid stereotyped repetition has been made "alive" in an emotionally maladjusted individual, whether a schizophrenic person experiences a first organization through his body, or whether a deaf-blind individual "communicates" his presence to the outside world, the initial approach was achieved through the body self.

Establishment of self-identification

The more the individual relates himself to the creative process the greater is the probability of a successful therapy. Ultimately the desired realization of the individual's handicap, his ability, and his dependency greatly depends on the degree of self-identity which the individual establishes in his work. The initial establishment of a relationship between the individual and the creative process based on a greater sensitivity to his body self may soon lead from the emphasis on body functions to an emotional involvement. This emotional involvement may spring from two sources, the working process and the subject matter. Mary may discover herself more and more in her work and as she identifies herself with her concepts and projects herself into them she finds herself increasingly involved in what she is doing. She may, however, also get much satisfaction from the mere fact that she likes "to sit on a swing" or any other self-confrontation. In both instances the increasing satisfaction derived from the final product may become an additional incentive.

The developmental stages through which an individual goes in the establishment of self-identity in his work vary from individual to individual. Generally we can follow four stages. Depending on the kind and degree of the handicap, not every individual would have to go through all the stages.

The first stage is usually marked by a very *"diffuse concept formation."* Under diffuse concept formation we understand a concept which does not at all or only vaguely relates to the individual's experience. It may either consist of a stereotype repetition (see Fig. 96a) or of a concept without any, or having little, coherence (see Fig. 93a). In such a concept, meaningful details are either not present, diffusely expressed, or unrelated to each other.

The second stage usually shows a *greater coherence* in concepts but most often a *rigid adherence to the same symbols* for the same objects. This tendency toward repetition merely expresses the subject's inability to relate himself individually to his experience.

A greater variability in expression usually signifies the third stage. The child has now developed a desire to "characterize" what he expresses by relating himself individually to the things he represents now with specific details. In this stage the individual has developed a greater flexibility toward experience but only when closely motivated (see Fig. 95c). During this stage the individual often finds himself in his own expression, yet this "freedom of expression" is often in marked discrepancy to his still restricted behavior in other areas of living. It appears as if he were two different personalities, one for his creative situation and the other outside of it. Such difference in behavior should not be misleading, for it occurs in almost any therapeutical relationship. It is an outcome of the confidence which the child may have developed within the clinical situation as contrasted to an apparent "hostile" environment.

The fourth stage is usually signified by the *individual's desire to express himself freely* and relate this newly won freedom also to other areas of living and expression. As a result of this attained freedom and flexibility the individual may discover relationships to his past or present experiences. Free from stereotypes, he now projects his body-image unconsciously into his expression (see Fig. 95e).

It is needless to say that these four stages differ from individual to individual. As has been said before, not every individual would even have to go through all these stages, or would be able to attain them. They have been described only for the purpose of giving the teacher some guide to what he may expect in a situation in which art education is used therapeutically.

The development of an attachment

As a therapy becomes more effective it is not only unavoidable but desirable that the individual become attached to his teacher. Sigmund Freud refers to this attachment as "transfer." It always develops with the increased and effective contact between teacher and child in a therapeutical situation. Whenever a situation has been created which releases the individual from his restriction and allows for a more flexible expression of hitherto undiscovered abilities, forms of expression, emotions, or past association, an attachment to the teacher develops as a result of this release. Thus, such an attachment is most often the indication of the effectiveness of a therapy. It is an outcome of a continuous and effective rapport between teacher and child and the "flow" of thoughts and emotions which it produces. It is produced by the awakening process in the individual which may bring about important changes in his personality. Such attachment is similar to the child-mother relationship for indeed in this process of self-discovery, a new personality may be born.

The spontaneous desire for expression

It is then quite obvious that often with the development of greater flexibility, a greater freedom to express intimate relationships leads to a spontaneous desire for expression. Only when this spontaneous desire is reached can a therapy be successful, for it is through this spontaneity that the individual reveals himself and often unravels conflicts which previously were completely dormant (see page 493). Thus the ultimate aim of an art education therapy is to help the individual in his self-discovery because only then can he learn to face his own difficulty. To bring the subjective detachment into balance with the objective handicap, that is, *to make the handicapped individual realize his abilities as well as his restrictions, his freedom as well as the necessary dependency,* is then one of the most important factors in a successful therapy. It is needless to say that the process and kind of this realization not only differ for different handicaps, but also from individual to individual.

The dissolution of the attachment

No therapy can be termed successful unless the individual can master his difficulty on his own without the presence of the teacher or clinician. For this it is necessary to remove the attachment between the subject and the teacher which has developed during the application of an art education therapy. If this is done abruptly the subject often retrogresses into his former stages. Depending on the intensity of the attachment, the dissolution of it has to occur gradually over a longer period of time. Often this dissolution is accompanied with great adjustment difficulties, because the strong affections developed through the mutual participation in all phases of a therapy, often revealing the most inner "sanctuary" of an individual, cannot easily be discarded. Several methods have been developed to make the necessary dissolution of the attachment easier. In the experiences of the author, the method which worked best in a teaching situation is to "distribute the attachment" gradually among several persons by letting them participate in the "art lesson" and in the newly won achievement of the individual. This mere passive participation by others may gradually change into a more active one. The teacher or clinician may now and then ask one of the participants to "take over." The attachment may be "distributed," as it were, and "spread more thinly" over several people until the individual no longer finds the need for the presence of anyone.

SUMMARY

The chart on p. 444 may serve as a *guide* through the stages which may be expected in a therapeutical situation as well as a *clinical record*.

THE PHYSICALLY HANDICAPPED

Creative activity for the visually handicapped

Modeling as a means of self-expression for the blind

It is the aim of good methods of teaching to set free all the abilities in an individual and direct them into the most productive channels. This is true for teaching at all grade levels. It is valid for the normal and the abnormal, for the handicapped as well as for the physically fit. "Setting free" means removing all the inhibitions that stand in the way of the individual's healthy and normal development. An essential part of education consists of removing such inhibitions so that the enrichment of knowledge and experience can be achieved with the least possible effort. This is true for educational methods applied to the normal but it is of even greater importance in teaching those who cannot make full use of their senses and become inhibited mainly though improper contact with those not handicapped. No doubt the blind person feels his inferiority much more when he works with seeing persons who make him aware of his dependency than when working alone. However, this is true only when the activities with seeing persons are mainly designed for the latter. The obvious discrepancy in quality and speed and often the inability of perceiving his own work as a whole have a discouraging effect on the blind.

As we know, the blind individual can perceive objects that are larger than his hand only by moving his hand over the object. Thus, he can only receive partial impressions which he has to unify into a simultaneous whole. The integration of these partial impressions into an impression of the whole object is often achieved only with considerable difficulties. This is one of the peculiar handicaps caused by blindness, which is partly responsible for the blind individual's isolation. It is not only his physical inability to get around, but also his mental incapacity to imagine the

Stages	Characteristics	1st Week	2nd Week	3rd Week, etc.
Dissolvement of Attachment	complete			
	sligh:			
	no			
Spontaneous Desire for Expression	much			
	some			
	none			
Development of Attachment	much			
	some			
	none			
Establishment of Self-Identification	relationship of freedom in expression and other areas			
	greater variability, discrepancy between behaviors			
	generalization of concepts			
	diffuse concepts; stereotypes, vague expressions			
Establishment of Relationship to Creative Process	much involvement			
	some involvement			
	no involvement			
Acquaintance with Art Medium	full acceptance			
	slight acceptance			
	no acceptance			
Establishment of Rapport	much			
	some			
	none			
Remarks				

Name:

Case History:
age: sex: parental data: social and other data:
kind of handicap: degree of handicap:
secondary handicaps:

Observation:
criteria related to kind of handicap:
criteria related to degree of handicap:
criteria related to individual's reactions to his handicap:

world which surrounds him. The space in which the blind individual lives is mainly controlled by his sense of touch. In his world distant objects do not seem to be smaller, as they do for the normally sighted. For the sense of touch, distant objects do not change in size. It has been discussed previously how a blind person who made himself acquainted with a room and became very much interested in a desk lamp modeled it afterward as the outstanding part of the room. In other words, different objects in space receive their proportion by the value the objects have for the blind individual. *The perspective of space is in this world a perspective of value.* When blind children after a ride on a steamship were asked to model the boat, they started with the inside, especially with the place that had made the greatest impression upon them. The captain had showed them around, making a special effort to get them acquainted with the important parts of his boat. So some of the children started with cabins, others with the dining room, and even with the engine room. Some children were able to make a quite detailed model of the inside by adding one part to the other. The outside hull, however, as the imperceivable part, was in many cases left out entirely. Others covered the boat because they knew that it must have a hull, though their main interest remained centered on the inside representation of the boat.

In a Utopia where the blind would only live with the blind it would be possible that the blind with their peculiar space concepts would not feel their handicap at all, just as we do not feel any disadvantage in our inability to see ultraviolet rays. It would, however, be entirely wrong if we should draw from this the conclusion that the blind should avoid any contact with their natural environment. On the contrary, it means we must search for ways that will help them to overcome their detachment by achieving an adjustment to the given environment, which will bring their objective handicap in proper relationship to their subjective. That means that educators of the blind should avoid as much as possible any technique that adds other inhibitions, not necessarily connected with sightlessness, to the restrictions directly resulting from the handicap. This leads us to the realization, that before one can remove inhibitions, it is necessary to recognize them as such. Self-evident as this statement may appear, it is necessary to emphasize it in a discussion about the meaning of modeling in schools for the blind.

It should be observed, for example, that it would be completely wrong to attempt to set free the creative power of a blind individual by trying to remove the inhibitions caused by his lack of sight through an attempt to familiarize him with visual impressions. His haptic experiences are different from visual ones and cannot be "optified." For an instance of this we have only to turn to the many teaching situations where imitative visual likeness is praised as the highest achievement. *Optical characteristics which are our common measurements are by no means applicable to the work of the blind.* One would in fact achieve the exact opposite, just as one would inhibit creative ability by forcing a visually minded, normally sighted person to pay special attention to tactile, or touch impressions, or kinesthetic experiences.

Being unable to see is not always an inhibitory factor. On the contrary, as has been shown in other discussions of this book, it has been proven that blindness may become the basis of a specific and unique creativeness.[4] In it there is not only a distinct difference from visual art expression but also a specific approach to creative art. This specific approach results from the need of building up a whole image from partial perceptions. What the blind individual cannot always, or can only seldom, achieve in life, he can do in art: out of the many partial impressions he builds up a "whole" and arrives thus at a synthesis of his image. What a release of tension when he can contact environment—his sculpture—without interference in his own mode. Through his continuous contact and establishment of relationships between his thinking and his sculpture he increases his ability to integrate his partial impressions, which are touch impressions, into a "whole." This ability surely is not confined only to the field of modeling but reflects upon the whole emotional and mental growth, as I shall later demonstrate.

Since we are aware of this distinct difference in the approach of the blind toward creative activity, why should we not attempt to realize the blind person's Utopia, at least in this single field by leaving him his own realm of creativity? We should use any opportunity to give him back his shaken self-confidence, thereby influencing other fields of work where he often does not dare to assert himself because of the feeling of inferiority resulting from the natural restrictions on his personal and individual freedom.

Attempts have already been made to recognize modeling as a subject in the curricula of a few of the institutes for the blind. But there remains the sad and depressing experience that the "seeing taste" of physically normal "educators" is determining the way of expression and production of the blind. It is time to realize that the most primitive creative work born in the mind of a blind person and produced with his own hands is of greater value than the most effective imitation.

[4] *The Nature of Creative Activity, op. cit.*

The blind child and art education

Children in general are not consciously aware of their own actions and their relationships to their environment.[5] The same is true for the blind child. Most often he is completely unaware of his handicap until, when puberty sets in, he relates himself more consciously to his environment and becomes increasingly aware of the differences between himself and the world of the normal-sighted. Most of the interferences in the education of blind infants, especially when kept at home, occur through an over-sentimental attitude of the normal-sighted adult toward blind children. Since infants usually are completely unaware of their handicap, such an attitude will only result in overprotection and prevent the child from experiences vital to him. The blind or partially blind child should lead as normal a life as possible.

Indeed, the art of the blind and partially blind child differs from the normal-sighted child only in degree and not in kind. As I have demonstrated,[6] both the blind child with his modelings and the partially blind child with his drawings begin with expressions similar in nature to those of the normal-sighted child. The blind child in his modeling begins with a manipulative stage in which he kneads or breaks the clay, while the partially blind child starts with scribbling, just as the normal-sighted child does (see page 86). In my experience, the only difference I found is that the motions of the partially blind child are more restricted in size and kinesthetic freedom. This may be due to the lack of visual control. Both the partially as well as the totally blind child are somewhat behind in their developmental characteristics.

Because the difference between the creative development of the normal-sighted child and the visually handicapped can better be seen in drawings, the drawings of partially blind children are chosen for demonstration.

The drawings of the partially blind child

Partial blindness is usually defined as: "visual acuity between 20/70 and 20/200 [7] in the better eye or in both eyes after all medical and optical help has been provided." It may also refer to cases with "serious, progres-

[5] For an excellent treatise on the general problems concerning the blind child read: Lowenfeld, Berthold, *Our Blind Children, Growing and Learning with Them.* Springfield, Ill.: Charles C Thomas, 1956.

[6] Lowenfeld, Viktor, *The Nature of Creative Activity,* New Edition. Routledge and Kegan Paul: London, 1952.

[7] An object normally perceived at a distance of 200 feet must be brought up to 20 feet in order to be discerned.

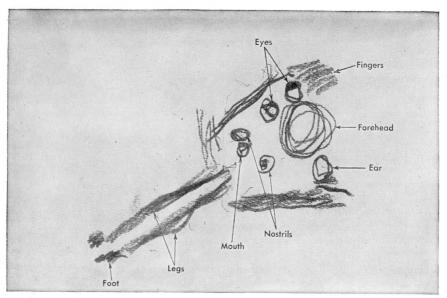

Fig. 80. Unrelated parts in early drawings of seven-year-old partially blind child.

Fig. 81. "I Say 'Hello' to My Friend on the Other Side of the Street." (Children usually waited at the street crossing near the Institute and called each other.) Nine-year-old partially blind boy. (Compare with "folding-over" on p. 147.)

sive eye difficulty" or with "diseases of the eye or of the body that seriously affect vision." [8]

After the partially blind child has engaged in scribblings, he discovers like the normal-sighted child, that he can establish a relationship between the object and his drawings. Since his restricted vision or his touch only allows him to perceive an object in subsequent impressions, the partially and totally blind child, much more frequently than the normal-sighted child, remain with the expression of unrelated parts. (See Fig. 80.) Also his expression begins with what was referred to as "geometric lines." (See page III.) Soon he integrates his partial impressions and after a continuous search for a more definite relationship between what he draws and perceives he finds his concept. Usually the partially blind and totally blind child adhere to a schematic representation quicker than the average normal-sighted child. Most probably there are two reasons for this. One is directly related to their specific handicap. As compared with visual impressions, tactile experiences are much more limited. The other reason refers to the secondary handicap. The greater insecurity and lack of confidence may lead the child sooner to a "fixed representation." (Compare p. 490.)

It is, however, very essential for the teacher of the blind to recognize the vital fact of enriching the blind child's experiences by continuous motivations referring to their tactile recognition. Motivations do not differ in nature from those given to the normal child. (See sections on motivation in the chapters on the "Pre-Schematic" and "Schematic Stage," p. 116 and p. 164.) Figs. 81 to 84 are typical drawings of partially blind children of the "Schematic Stage." In general, it has been found by the author that the schemas of visually handicapped children are less clearly articulated than those of the average normal-sighted child. Yet, the characteristics as well as the means of expression are precisely the same as we find in normal-sighted children. In his space concept the visually handicapped child adheres much longer to the base-line concept. He also uses much more frequently the concept of "folding over." This can easily be understood because his whole world is by necessity much more determined by a self-centered attitude. (See Figs. 83, 84.) Therefore, in his representations also he regards himself as the center and develops his spatial concept accordingly. In Fig. 84 we see a "Girl Picking Flowers." The child picked flowers "to her left" and "to her right" but being in the center made her draw the flowers "to the left" and "to the right" ("folded over") of the base line.

[8] Young, Marjorie, A. C., "The Partially Seeing," from *Psychological Aspects of Physical Disability*. Washington, D. C.: U. S. Government Printing Office.

Fig. 82. Partially blind child (eight years). "A Street Crossing. The Policeman in the Center Guides the Traffic." Notice the lines and the principle of "folding over." (See "Schematic Stage," p. 150.)

Fig. 83. Partially blind child (eight years). "Climbing a Mountain." (Compare with Fig. 16)

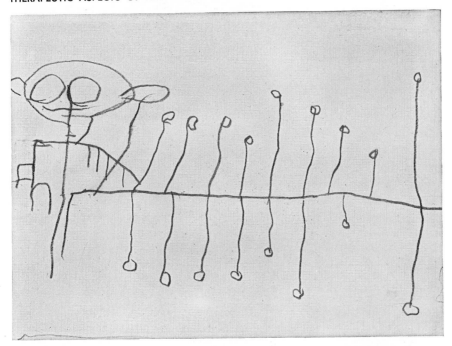

Fig. 84. Partially blind child (nine years). "Girl Picking Flowers." "Flowers Grow to My Left and to My Right."

Fig. 82 shows "A Street Crossing" with houses standing on the base lines in a similar spatial concept.

The congenitally blind and his art

Most blind sculptors do not model in the usual way, with the statue facing them; they stand parallel to the statue or behind it, with the face turned in the same direction as the face of the worker. The reason for this is that the impressions of the outer world do not reach the blind in a mirror-like projection, which is the way these impressions reach the normal eye. The experience of the totally blind is primarily derived from the forms they observe and feel on themselves. Accordingly, the sculpture is formed in the same direction, with the sculptor usually working on the face of his figure as though he were embracing it from behind. This was true of both the individuals, *A* and *B,* whose work we are considering (Figs. 85 and 86). But how extremely different are their approaches.

Sculptor *A* (Fig. 85) starts with the general outline of a head (a). Then he pulls out the nose (c), adds eyes (d) consisting of eyeballs and

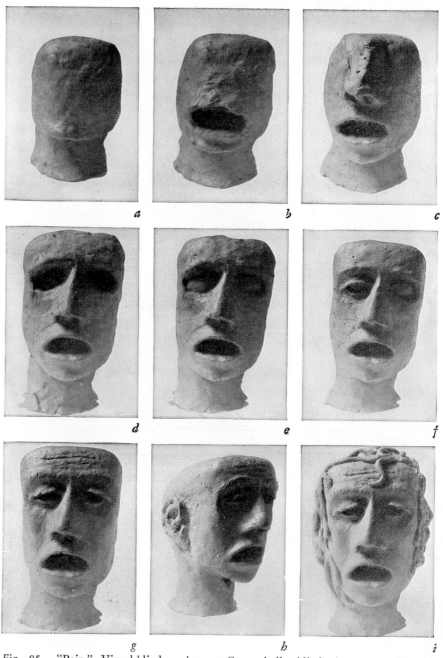

Fig. 85. "Pain." Visual-blind sculpture. Congenitally blind sixteen-year-old girl.

a). General outline

b). Cavity of the mouth is formed

c). Nose is added

d). Eye sockets are hollowed out

e). Eyeballs are put in

f). Lids are pulled over

g). Wrinkles are formed

h). Ears are added

i). The head is finished. All features are incorporated into a unified surface. Typical for the visual type.

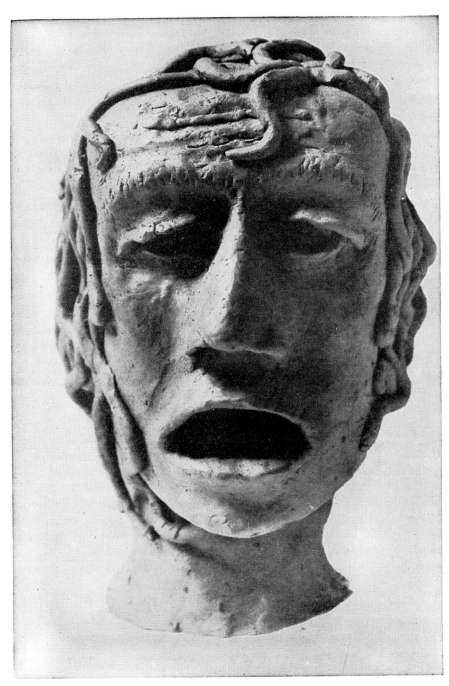

Fig. 85j. Finished product. "Pain."

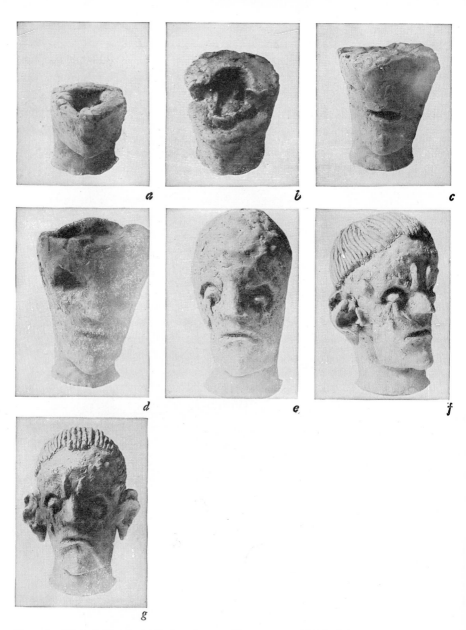

Fig. 86. "Pain." Haptical-blind sculpture. Sixteen-year-old blind **boy.**

a). Start with the chin
b). Teeth, tongue, and so forth are put in
c). Mouth is closed, nothing can be seen of inside features
d). Nose is added, eye sockets made
e). Eyes are put in from inside, head "closed"
f). Features and hair are added
g). Finished head with all features still isolated as partial impressions. Typical for the blind, haptic type.

454

Fig. 86h. All single features, like wrinkles and tears, hair or temples, still remain isolated on the final product.

lids (e, f), mouth, and features (g). Finally he has completed a sculpture in which all single features are fused in a unified and closed surface, very much like a "normal" head (Fig. 85j). Sculptor B (Fig. 86), however, starts with the chin (a), puts in the teeth (and even the tonsils) (b), and prepares the hole for the nose and sticks it on (c, d). Then the eyes are added, from the inside, and the hollow of the head is closed (e). Finally such expressive features as wrinkles and tears (the sculpture represents "Pain") are added (f), but they remain isolated on the finished product (Figure 86g). One feels as if they could easily be removed. They are still partial impressions, isolated from the main form instead of being fused into a "complete" image as in the head in Fig. 85. They are like the many single impressions that we get in looking out of the train, without fusing them into a whole image of the landscape.

I led the two blind sculptors into a room, escorting them along the window side, past the two other walls, and back to the entrance. Then I asked both to point toward the direction of one particular window. A, who made the sculpture with the "smooth" surface, immediately knew the accurate direction, whereas B could not orientate himself at all. B had only the partial impressions in his mind received while moving along a wall. He could not unify these impressions into a whole impression of the room. Since a vital part of orientation consists of the ability to gain this unity, B was completely unable to orientate himself.[9]

These two attitudes may be further observed in two self-portraits, made by two other blind individuals (Figs. 87 and 88). In Fig. 87, all the single features are unified into a "natural vision," whereas in Fig. 88, all partial impressions still remain isolated on the final product. Whereas one was occupied with expressing the unified "appearance" and even "likeness" of his portrait, the other was involved only in the process of adding all the surface features which seemed to him important for his personality. This, in fact, is a manifestation of impressionism and expressionism.

The impressionist world is the world of appearances, the world of our senses. The world of expressionist art is the world of expression, feelings, of subjective processes. In impressionist art, as in "Self-Portrait" (Fig. 87), the *surface structure triumphs,* whereas expressive art, originating from within as in "Self-Portrait" (Fig. 88), places the *self in a value relation-*

[9] Similar experiments on a larger scale are reported by the author in *The Nature of Creative Activity.* Also Révész confirms these observations: Révész, G., *Die Formenwelt des Tastsinnes.* The Hague: Martinus Nijhoff, 1938.

ship to its environment. That which is perceivable in the external universe is contrasted with that which is experienced by the "inward senses." As has been said before, art consists of depicting the relations of the artist to the world of his experiences—that is, depicting his experience with objects, and not the objects themselves. Again, what is of final importance is the *kind of experience;* this is what decisively determines the products of the artist.

If we look in this light at the self-portraits (Figs. 87 and 88), we will understand the different forces at work; we see that it is the psychological attitude of the individual which determines the style of his creative products. The same applies, not only to our creative impulses, but also to our thinking and doing. While one person thinks in details and has difficulty in putting his thoughts together into a whole, another begins with the concept of the whole and finds it difficult to go into details.

The art of the later blinded

We have to distinguish between those who are suddenly blinded by an accident or otherwise and those who gradually lose their sight through some illness, disease, or old age. The adjustment problem of the first is much more serious than the latter. From our previous discussion it can easily be understood that an individual who has been mainly depending on sight as the intermediary for his perception will suffer much more from the changes to blindness than one who never depended much on sight and was haptical to begin with.

In order to understand the effect of an art education therapy on a later blinded individual, let us consider the following case by means of a graph in which we develop the relationship between objective and subjective handicap and the meaning of therapy for both.

A, by profession a chemist, used to paint in his free time with a sensitive appreciation for nature especially in its visual aspects. Through an accident, A lost his sight. This was followed by serious depressions accompanied by a feeling of total disability and worthlessness. After having been hospitalized for some time he was given the feeling that through an operation some of his sight might be restored. While he was never told that he might see again, his hopes were high and his optimism great that he might regain vision. The operation, however, was without the result which A expected, although he could distinguish between light and dark. A went back in his depressive stage until he could gradually discover some

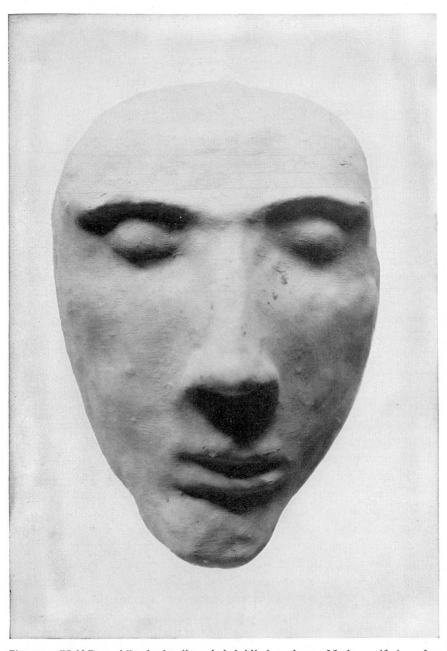

Fig. 87. "Self-Portrait" of visually minded blind sculptor. Notice unified surface appearance.

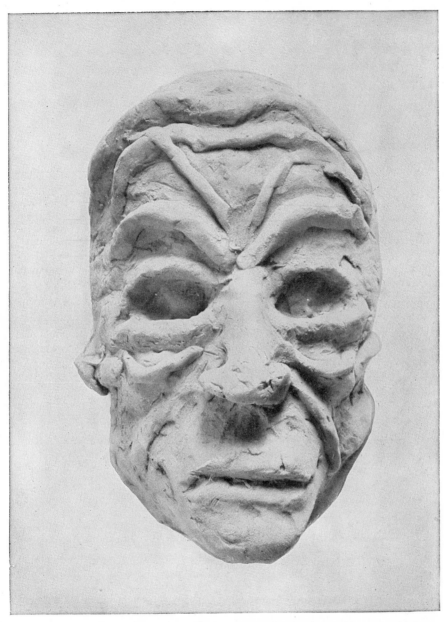

Fig. 88. "Self-Portrait" of haptically minded blind sculptor. Features are very expressive, but remain isolated.

meaning in activities, especially those which helped to relate him to his new life and thus make him realize more objectively his abilities as well as his limitations. For purposes of a clearer graphic presentation let us consider that A was without any handicap before the accident. Let us also arbitrarily set normal blindness as a 50 per cent handicap. (See also p. 433.) As has been previously emphasized, this is indeed an arbitrary figure merely taken when we consider the total function capacity of the human being in this society.

If we interpret the relationship of objective and subjective handicap as expressed in this graph we shall immediately see the ideal effect of a therapy.

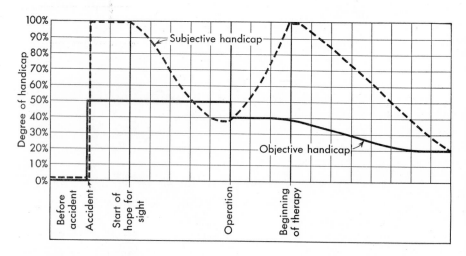

Before the accident the individual was free from handicaps. When the accident occurred the objective handicap, that of blindness, raised the curve of "objective handicap" to 50 per cent (an arbitrarily set figure). The subjective handicap caused by his deep depression and his *total* inability to function, however, raises the curve of "subjective handicap" to 100 per cent. As A was given hope for some sight, his objective handicap, that of blindness, remains the same, while his subjective handicap driven by an over-optimistic attitude toward the success of the operation, falls below the realization of his actual handicap. When the operation proved to be not as successful as he, in his over-optimism hoped for, the subjective handicap caused by his new depression again goes way up high in spite of the improvement of his objective handicap. An ideal therapy brings the patient gradually to the realization of his handicap, his potentialities as well as his limitations. This can be seen in the gradual merging of the two curves. In art education this is done by encouraging the individual's desire to establish a close relationship between the self and his creative product. Through constant reference to the individual's own body-image the subject not only arrives at a better and more accurate concept of himself emotionally, but also physically. Thus he confronts himself with his personality traits as well as with a new concept of space perception, that of integrating partial impressions into a unified whole. By continuously using his sense of touch for the realization of his image, his thinking in terms of concrete images becomes strengthened. This is indeed very important at a time when the patient feels deprived of the many impressions which constantly reach the seeing eye and often withdraws into the world of destructive phantasy. Both of these abilities, the ability to integrate successive partial impressions as well as the ability to increase the scope of the sense of touch, improve the objective handicap. This can be seen in the slight reduction of the curve which stands for the "objective handicap."

To establish rapport with cases such as A, who just went through a serious depression, is not always easy. The following suggestions may be helpful if not rigidly used.

It is needless to say that it is always important to wait with the introduction of the creative medium, in this instance, clay, until the teacher or clinician is well acquainted with the subject. If, in spite of this initial personal contact, the subject refuses to participate in the creative process, a method of *"closure"* is often very helpful. The clinician may begin a rough outline form of a head, or a mask, and by asking, "Where would you model your nose, your mouth, etc.?" the subject may gradually "close" the started image in his own fashion. As topics, it is easier in the beginning to motivate "functions" or "activities" which can be controlled on one's own face or body than emotional interpretations. They are also more remote and "objective" and do not require the immediate breaking down of emotional barriers and inhibitions which is necessary when the subject becomes personally and emotionally involved in his creative interpretation. This breaking down of barriers should be a gradual process and it is for this reason that a start with topics which lend themselves to a more "objective treatment" is suggested. It is, however, always a matter of sensitive relationships between the subject and the teacher which determines the best approach. The more the subject becomes involved in the interpretation of the self, the closer is he to solving his difficulty. As has been said before, it is the goal of an art education therapy to get the individual to realize his potentialities and his limitations through the process of art.

The partially blind

Between those who can see and those who are blind there are cases whose sight is not adequate for visual perception yet whose "blindness" is disturbed because they are not entirely without light. These are the weak-sighted and the partially blind and they are psychologically the most difficult to deal with. The remaining sight may for the one individual be an asset if he has the aptitude to use it, but for the other it can be an irritation, a disturbance in his orientation if he is depending in his aptitude on the mode of perception of the blind. In other words, *a visually minded partially blind individual will be blessed by the remnants of sight left to him, but the haptically minded individual will be disturbed by it.*

Whereas the visually minded partially blind individual, in his work, brings the outside world closer to himself by choosing *environment* as the main subject for his pictorial representation, the haptically minded concentrates on the self. He chooses almost exclusively the expression of the human figure as his subject matter.

The mere physiological question might arise as to whether or not it is harmful to the impaired eyes to put the strain of drawing and painting on them. This is a problem the physician has to solve. For the purely functional possibility of drawing for those cases where there is no medical objection to using the eyes the following points are of importance: (1) The nature of the eye defect and degree of visual acuity must be such that it allows accurate fixation of a point. (2) The training of the eye and the nature of its vision must be such that it is possible to follow the direction and goal of a line.[10]

Among the first visual perceptions are those of color. The visual impressions of the partially blind are at first mostly vague, but unless the organic defect is too severe they can be trained to achieve very fine distinctions.

As has been mentioned before, the blind build up their concepts out of individual elements each of which has been apprehended through the sense of touch. Out of these elements they construct a synthesis of the whole. In the same way, according to the kind of degree of their partial sight, the *partially blind* build their conceptions out of visual or tactual part impressions. This is true, however, only for the reproduction of the form as a whole. Those partially blind subjects whose orientation is visual are helped in achieving their concept of the "whole" by visual impressions, however shadowy and uncertain they may be, whereas those whose orienta-

[10] *The Nature of Creative Activity.*

Fig. 89. "Branch with Blossoms." Several steps in the painting of a partially blind youth, done from nature. This shows clearly the restricting effect of a too-close dependency on nature. Compare with *Fig. 90.*

tion is haptic make no use of such impressions. In both cases the similarity of their creative processes to those of the blind is clear because neither group is able to achieve directly an impression of the whole. In all cases it is constructed out of separate partial impressions. The partially blind who is a visual type assimilates these partial impressions to his visual concept, however indefinite this may be, and in this way gradually develops a structurally more complete image. The partially blind who is a haptic type, on the other hand, will approximate more closely the haptic blind both in regard to his conceptions as a whole and in his creative output. *It is needless to say that also here the two types of expression are on a continuum, and that many individuals have traits of both with a preference for the one or the other.* (See page 263.) The two following cases may clarify these statements of general principles.

S. G., a sixteen-year-old boy, has been partially blind since birth (congenital cataract of both eyes). When he draws, his eyes are approximately

Fig. 90. "Branch with Blossoms." Painted by the same partially blind fourteen-year-old youth from imagination.

1⅛ inches from his work. His field of vision is restricted to 4½ inches. He had the desire to draw a branch with blossoms. Fig. 89 shows several steps of this drawing. First he inspected the blossoms closely with his eye in order to get the *optical* impression demanded by his type (visual). Naturally, since he is mostly concerned with depicting his visual experiences, he relates his subject matter almost exclusively to environment. Having given the blossoms a superficial visual inspection he proceeded to draw Fig. 89a. The one-sided view that his eye acquired had probably led him to believe that there were several petals. He then drew Fig. 89b, but perceived neither the number nor the arrangement of the individual petals. He once again brought the blossom closely to his eye and convinced himself that—because of his high visual defect, which for all practical purposes is equivalent to blindness—he was unable to achieve an impression of the blossom as a whole. He therefore turned the flower and studied the arrangement of the petals. Fig. 89c proves that the act of turning—that is, letting the individual petals pass his eye—resulted in his placing them next to one another in the drawing. This arrangement did not satisfy him, since it did not express the "roundness," an impression of which he had got while turning the blossom. He therefore drew Fig. 89d, in which we can see the influence of the act of turning. Finally, after he had further investigated the flower tactually and by tearing the petals off satisfied himself that there were a number of them, he drew them in the correct circular order in Fig. 89e. After that he studied closely the arrangement of the different blossoms and leaves on the branch. With more certainty and self-confidence he then painted Fig. 89f. After a further visual examination he found that his tactual impression completely corresponded with the optical impression and thereby all further restrictions on his painting were removed. I then took the little branch away from him and he produced Fig. 90, which is, as it were, a mental synthesis of his visual and tactual experiences. It is incomparably more forceful, less concerned with considerations of reality, and altogether a far freer creation.

We see, then, that the optical experience has been constructed out of numerous partial impressions which by a mental act have been fused into a single image.[11]

This is also true to a certain degree for normal-sighted individuals when sketching from nature, only that their partial impressions are much larger. From these observations the following conclusions can be drawn: *For creative production the mental picture is of far greater importance than any realistic representation.*

The partially blind individual has by the process of drawing clarified his vague impression of nature. Through creative expression he has brought environment closer to himself, an act which contributed greatly to help him overcome the feeling of isolation imposed upon him by his impaired sight.

While adding more and more experiences to his imaginative activity, S. G. painted trees and houses in very different settings—in sunshine, at

[11] *The Nature of Creative Activity.*

Fig. 91. "Street Scene." Painted by a fourteen-year-old partially blind youth, visually minded.

night, and in various moods. Fig. 91, one of his later paintings, is one in which he seems to have overcome the greatest obstacles. Through his own experiences and power he arrived at the concept of perspective space. We stand before a miracle when we see S. G. at work. His eyes are extremely close to the paper and he follows bodily even the smallest stroke of his brush because he is not able to see two things next to each other. Nevertheless, he achieves a unified picture. We cannot explain this in any other way than by realizing that the picture as a whole is present in his mind. Only thus can he achieve the astonishing unity of the numerous partial impressions whose synthesis produces the picture he has in mind. The boy in whom the physical ability to see has been restricted to the barest minimum, who is practically blind, achieves this miraculous effect of "natural vision." It is a triumph of the spirit, which has transcended the physical defect and enabled the creator to express without hindrance a sensory experience which nature has denied him. Through the power of his work, he has entered into his birthright.

There is, however, as we said before, another type who experiences

Fig. 92. "The Cry for Help." Painted by a sixteen-year-old partially blind youth, haptically minded.

his remaining sight rather as a disturbing factor than as an asset. He is neither anxious to use his sight nor does he desire to familiarize himself visually with the outside world. He depends far more on his sense of touch and his body experiences.

"The Cry for Help" (Fig. 92) is the product of such a type. H. A., who made the painting, has been partially blind since birth (congenital amblyopia). He is sixteen years old and has far better sight than S. G. In spite of this he does not use his sight either for orientation or for observation. He uses it only when forced to do so. Drawing certainly created in him the desire to use it.

He started his drawing of the head with a simple elliptic outline to which other parts were added in the order of their importance for effecting the intended expression of "The Cry for Help." Thus he begins and continues to work in an entirely *synthetic* way. The drawn-up eyebrows and the widely opened mouth were put in first, for in them the greatest tension is felt. The strong tension between eyes and mouth is probably the most important bodily experience in the act of screaming. This tension, as the drawing clearly shows, starts at the cheekbone just below the eyes and can be felt as a strong pull downward from the nose. This has been depicted with clarity and certainty by the two symbols of expression running from the nose and eyes downward toward the jaw and around the mouth. It is a reasonable analogy to compare the sensation of stretching with that of an elastic band, which in the drawing narrows toward the middle of the cheeks. This forceful experience dominates the whole head. "Tension" in the truest sense of the word is brought into the gesture, and its expressive content is heightened by the eyes squinting with horror. The hollowness of the cheeks is indicated by a dark color as though the artist wished to take something away from the cheeks. This darker shade must not be interpreted as a shadow. It is purely a symbol for "taking away," the symbol for a hollow. The black, wide-open nostrils which have been especially emphasized below the nose, are also important as symbols of expression. The nose has been only partially circumscribed and therefore stands out mainly by contrast with the surrounding shapes, although in accordance with the synthetic mode of procedure it, too, has been "added" as an independent part by means of a darker tone. The wrinkles of the forehead have not been differentiated much and have been treated more as a whole because they do not give rise to clear separate sensations. The ears, which have also been added to the head, clearly show lines that are a result of touch observation. The two ridges are parallel as they would appear to the fingers following the shape of the ear. Again corresponding to the sense of touch, the opening has been placed in the center of the ear. The head is finished by adding the wildly disordered hair. Also of importance are the shoulders, which have been drawn up as in fear. In this painting, quite different from the other, only body feelings and kinesthetic experiences were expressed. During such processes of realizations of the self the individual's thinking constantly goes back and forth, from a conscious awareness of his feelings to the realization of his representation. *This kind of experience is of great educational significance because only through the self and the realization of it will the individual find real contact with the outside world.*

In this kind of creative work the visually minded, partially blind individual pulls his environment closer to himself, whereas the haptically minded individual realizes environment through a more intense awareness of his own ego.

Modeling with the deaf-blind—Case study

Because of the lack of another important sense, hearing, the deaf-blind individual is far more dependent than the blind upon bodily experiences, upon contacts of the self with the outer world. Bodily experiences are the connecting medium between the ego and its surroundings. If they are disturbed or disordered, conscious contact with the outside world is lessened or entirely destroyed. It is therefore most important, in the education of the deaf-blind, to emphasize and stimulate bodily sensations as much as possible. Thus, although the deaf-blind person learns to speak by means of the vibration method, language remains an abstract, sounds without meaning, unless the teacher brings it into relation with reality. This is possible, of course, only through the sense of touch, through bodily feelings which are in close relation to the kinesthetic sensations. But mere acquaintance with various objects does not constitute the whole experience, because the circumstances under which the acquaintance is made determine the nature of the experience.

Experiments have shown that modeling in clay is an excellent means of giving force to these subjective expressions, because it not only allows the teacher to control the circumstances through which experience is attained but permits a plastic representation of touch sensations and bodily feelings. Details that are important in the child's experience are overemphasized in the plastic representation, but meaningless parts are neglected or even omitted. During my investigations it was apparent that these proportions of value as sensed by the deaf-blind and other nonvisual persons, clearly demonstrated the subjective attitude of such individuals toward their surroundings. For a teacher, this development opens new possibilities for understanding and influencing the world of imagery of blind and deaf-blind pupils. An analysis of the results of plastic modeling will not only reveal the lacks and limitations of both the imagination and the bodily feelings, but will serve as a gauge of mental development as the instruction proceeds.

Our purpose here is to show the pedagogical results obtained from employing this method in the very difficult case of a deaf-blind girl at Perkins Institution. This eleven-year-old girl had been totally blind and deaf since birth, and had been exceptionally shut in and restricted in her experiences. She was extremely limited in her expressions, and had much more difficulty than the average deaf-blind person in learning language through vibration. She spoke only when she was forced to do so, and then very poorly. Recognizing that creative activity stimulated by bodily feelings would serve as an excellent medium in the development of language, I encouraged this pupil to begin at once certain experiments in plastic modeling. It is easy to understand the adjusting effect of this kind of work on the mentality of the deaf-blind, because being able to express themselves in any medium not only enlarges their mental scope, but also gives them self-confidence. Through experiencing the self, the handicapped person establishes contact with his surroundings, loses his feeling of isolation, and becomes an integrated member of society. A very important result in this closer association with environment is the stimulation of language development through association of the word and its meaning.

When I began to work with the deaf-blind pupil at Perkins Institution, I let her sit down at the modeling table and, touching her body and placing her finger on my mouth when speaking, I told her, "You are sitting." Again touching her body in order to make her conscious of her position, I said, "You are a sitting girl—a sitting girl." She began to work with the clay, and Fig. 93a, illustrated here, was her first modeling. First she made the body, then the legs, which she placed at the correct angle with the body, showing at once that she wished to indicate the "sitting girl." Then she made the arms, but these, as the illustration shows, were without differentiation, and she was also unaware of their importance in connection with the body. She then made the neck and the head; on the head she fashioned a nose but it was drawn out from the clay rather than added; then she made holes to represent the eyes, and one hole as a mouth.

For the next lesson I brought her an apple in order to make her conscious of the feeling of her hands. Putting it into her hand, I said to her, in the usual manner "Apple in your hand." Then I took the apple away again, and repeated the performance several times, always closing her fingers over the apple. Finally she took up the clay, and made the modeling (Fig. 93b). In this the arms have acquired definite meaning, not only the arm connected with the apple but also the other arm which she modeled associatively. Closer observation will show that the feet are represented in the same manner as the hands. This is obviously an expres-

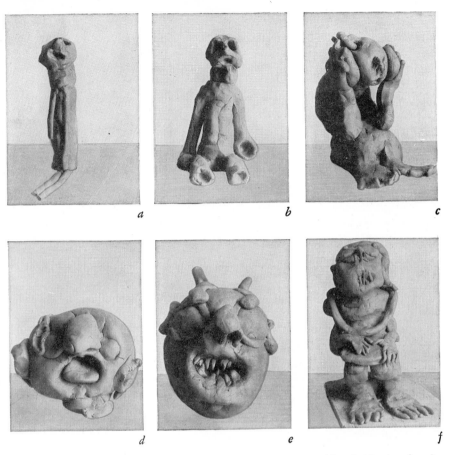

Fig. 93. Modelings by an eleven-year-old deaf-blind girl. (Perkins Institution for the Blind, Watertown, Mass.)

a). "Sitting."

b). "I put an apple in your hands."

c). "I am very tired, sleepy."

d). "I am yawning."

e). "I am eating candy."

f). "I am reading."

sion of the relation between them which probably comes from the sameness of their use in feeling vibrations. This mental progress on the part of the pupil marked her first step in finding her own method of expression: for the first time she indicated in the differentiation of the hands her realization of the close connection between action and representation. This experience also made her conscious of the starting point of the arms, and suddenly she recognized their relation to the body. Step by step we made use of modeling as a means of interpreting in plastic representation her own bodily sensations.

After two weeks she made Fig. 93c representing a very tired girl. Placing her fingers upon my face while speaking, I had said, "You are very tired—sleepy—very tired." She grasped the meaning of my words and leaned forward, relaxing and assuming the position which she later represented in the plastic. Touching her arms, I continued speaking to her. "You are holding your head," I said, "you are holding your head in your hands." Then, suddenly, came my greatest reward, for she repeated spontaneously, "m-y head in m-y hands." The emphatic use of the word *my* indicated that she did more than repeat a sentence, for through her sense of touch she had in one brief experience pushed back the limits of her little world of knowledge.

I cannot convey the sense of gratitude I felt while watching my pupil form this plastic figure. Holding her head in her hands—this heavy, tired head—she became conscious for the first time that she had ears; she grasped them, then added ears to the clay model, overemphasizing them because of their importance to her by exaggerating their size. On this occasion she also found that she had a pin in her hair and this, too, she added to the plastic, as is seen on the left side of the figure. It is obvious, too, that she began at this time to realize the function of fingers in the grasping of objects. The number of fingers is incorrect and they are drawn out from the clay, not modeled as single parts. This indicates that she had become conscious only of their function and her modeling shows only a representative symbol for "hand" and not single fingers. She used a similar technique in forming toes on the feet in this third figure. It is important to note the fact that she drew out fingers and toes. By adding them separately she would have shown her consciousness of them as individual parts, a step not yet achieved in this modeling. But the great step in the development of her imagination and space perception was achieved when she was able to give her model the intended position; she had become aware of the relationship between movement and representation, as well as the differentiation among upper arm, forearm, hand, and fingers. This latter is shown by the position of the elbows resting on the thighs, and the hands holding the head.

I never saw this child more excited than after having finished this plastic. Spontaneously she began to speak to me and to her tutor, who was present. She eagerly started another figure. While she had made rapid progress in her plastic interpretations of the body, there had been very little change in the representation of the face. Therefore, I called her attention to the yawning of a tired girl. "You are yawning—very tired—yawning," I said. I imitated yawning to demonstrate the idea; then she yawned too, and set about forming Fig. 93d. First of all, she abandoned her former technique of drawing features out from the clay; instead, she made the entire head by adding parts to represent ears, eyes, nose and mouth, indicating that she had become conscious of each individual part. Moreover, she modeled a tongue and placed it in the proper position in the open, yawning mouth. This act of adding indicates synthetical process of thinking such as this: "I have a tongue, and form it, and place it in the right place in the mouth." It should be understood that this is a very complicated mental act. Putting on the nose presupposes holding and forming the nose consciously, and placing it properly. The further differentiation of the nostrils shows very clearly the advance from the representative symbol to an actual form of the object. As a single symbol the chin is added and it is significant to note that the ears are no longer exaggerated, indicating that they have now assumed normal importance.

Guiding her attention more and more toward individual experiences, I asked her whether or not she liked candy. "Yes," she answered. I had a piece of candy in my pocket and gave it to her. Then I asked her, "Is this candy hard?" She did not understand until I had given the words meaning by biting something hard myself. Then I asked once more, "Is the candy hard?" "Yes," she replied. "But show me, how hard?" I said, and she bit the candy into pieces, as I did.

At this point I gave her some clay as the traditional signal for starting to interpret the new experience, resulting in Fig. 93e. It can be seen at once how important the representation of the teeth is to her which she has now formed for the first time. But one can also recognize the emphasis of the two eyelids, the action of which accompanies the experience of pressing the teeth together. You can feel this muscular movement on your own face if you reproduce this situation. On this day she had two hairpins of which she was very proud; this may account for their exaggeration and again shows the importance of personal experiences.

After four weeks of work I gave her a braille book. She understood how to read a little. I asked her to read for a while, then I said to her, "Girl reading." She answered by saying, "I *am* reading." I again repeated "reading," handing her the clay. She immediately started to work, modeling the representation of a reading girl (Fig. 93f). Only the day before she had received a necklace as a birthday gift and, as you can imagine, it was of great importance to her. In studying this modeled figure, one should not be misled by the large ring around the neck of the figure. This is supposed to represent her necklace.

If one looks closely at this figure one can find that in it each single part has been added. Therefore we may assume that her consciousness of her own body has undergone a decisive change. Instead of a symbolical lump of clay for a hand, she has made a hand with five single fingers cast in a definite position—that taken when reading a braille book. "One, two, three, four fingers—five, thumb," she said while she worked, and she placed the thumb separately in its proper position as seen on the right side of the picture. She became conscious not only of the fingers but also of their kinesthetic functions in reading. Now every part of the body is emphasized; shoulders, elbows, knees, and so forth. During the last week, while working on Fig. 93f, she talked spontaneously, naming all the details and actions that occupied her attention: "Eyes, lids, finger, reading, book, legs," and so forth. A remarkable improvement in her general attitude took place. She was feeling much happier and freer and started to communicate spontaneously with other children. Her ability to speak developed rapidly with the help of the speech department, since it was carried by a released desire for contact with the environment.

Not only has creative activity relieved the tension which did not permit the individual to communicate freely but it has also contributed to her general growth. The consciousness of body feelings, actions, and kinesthetic experiences brought her in closer contact with the surroundings. But no words can better show the adjusting effect than can the comparison of the first with the last piece of modeling.

The auditory handicapped and art education

Our readiness to sympathize and identify with auditory handicapped individuals is much less than with the visually handicapped, for there are no external signs which lead as directly to the recognition of their handicap as there are in the immediately visible appeal to our sentiments by the sightless. Yet the inability to react properly to the world of sound constitutes a serious handicap which because of its lack of dramatic appeal has been greatly neglected. For the normally endowed person it is almost impossible to identify with the world of stillness which surrounds the deaf. The role which acoustical experiences play in the normal development is difficult to comprehend for it not only means the exclusion from the social intercourse which greatly depends on the use and reactions to the world of words, but also from the psycho-physical participation in an environment constantly filled with a variety of sounds and noises. The world of stillness is a strange world which we can only, to a very slight degree, appreciate if we look at a silent movie, seeing moving lips which don't talk and sweeping trains which don't rattle. Yet in spite of these peculiar absences of coordination between sound and movement, we have the power to associate one mentally with the other. In the world of the deaf such associations are non-existent. In it there is not even the rattling of the movie projector or the occasional coughing in the audience; there is external silence. It is this absolute stillness in which not even background noises enter, which is difficult to imagine for the normal individual. It can then easily be understood how important any form of communication becomes in this world of isolation, especially if this communication releases emotional tensions which have no verbal outlets. It is for this reason that creative activities for the deaf are of great importance.

Usually when we use the term Deaf we mean the whole group of auditory handicapped who cannot effectively use their sense of hearing in their contacts with the environment. We should, however, distinguish three classifications into which the various individuals can be grouped: The Deaf, The Hard of Hearing, and the Deafened.

Creative activity for the deaf

A person is considered Deaf if his sense of hearing is non-functional for the ordinary purposes of life. Inasmuch as there is no direct relationship between an art process and the objective handicap of hearing impairments, an art education therapy may only help to reduce the subjective handicaps resulting from the loss of hearing. This is quite different from the role of a creative therapy for the visually handicapped, for we have seen that the influence of art processes is also on the objective handicap as it helps the blind in his orientation, his sense of touch and in his integration of partial impressions which lead to better recognition. No such relationships can be established in using creative activities for the Deaf. All it can do for them is: help them in overcoming their detachment from their environment; serve them as an outlet for emotional tensions; and bring them in equilibrium with their body-image and thus produce a higher degree of self-realization.

It cannot be stressed enough that perhaps the most important single prerequisite of a successful use of creative activities for the deaf is the ability of the teacher or clinician to identify himself, in all details, with the handicapped individual. In so doing he will soon find out that in addition to the peculiarities intrinsic to deafness there is as wide a range of individual differences as can be found in a normal population. Brunschwig in his research listed a wide range of contrasting opinions on the personality of the deaf which shows that we actually cannot speak of a "deaf-personality." [12] As in other handicaps, the relationship between objective and subjective handicap, that is, the deaf individual's feeling about his deafness, his ability to cope with it mentally, greatly influences his personality.

In any initial period of observation, this relationship will become a vital part of the knowledge of the clinician, for much depends on it in his approach in using art as a therapy. An individual who faces his handicap realistically, who conceives not only of the limitations caused by deafness but also of his potential abilities, may use art merely as a means of expression. His art expression in no way differs from that of the normal individual.

In individuals who cannot cope with their handicap or have difficulty in facing it, art may become a vital release. The first difficulty which every teacher of the deaf faces is that of communication. Art expression can be used successfully even in this initial stage. The deaf individual may go through a simple activity such as "searching for a coin," which the teacher may have dropped on purpose. Having him go through the movement of bending down and searching while encouraging a greater consciousness of the movement by frequently moving the hands over his bent body will stimulate his active knowledge of his action. To model or paint it would immediately create the self-identification necessary for any art education therapy. It is self-evident that through such art activities the deaf individual not only communicates with his environment but also expresses himself emotionally. Particularly in his paintings he can gradually be brought from the realization of the self to a greater appreciation of the world which surrounds him. Even situations which are not possible for him in reality and therefore constitute an external longing, such as participating in a normal social intercourse, seemed to be very rewarding and full of release in my experiences with deaf individuals.

As has been said before, inasmuch as only the subjective handicap can be influenced through art and since this is mainly of an emotional and social nature, the reader is referred to the section which deals with these handicaps.

The hard of hearing and art expression

The hard of hearing have been defined as those in whom the sense of hearing, although defective, is functional with or without a hearing aid. Habbe, Madden, and others have studied whether there is a difference

[12] Brunschwig, L., *A Study of Some Personality Aspects of Deaf Children*. Contributions to Education, No. 687, New York Teachers College, Columbia University, 1936.

between personality traits between the hard of hearing and the normal which are of general validity.[13] None of the investigators has found specific personality characteristics which significantly differentiate the two groups. Personality differences are just as distinct in the hard of hearing as they are in other groups.

Yet there is a distinct problem which must not be overlooked. Since the lack of hearing is not immediately recognizable to the uninformed it can easily be "hidden," especially in initial stages of contacts. If there is one single factor responsible for the emotional or social maladjustment of a hard of hearing person, it is this "opportunity" to hide his handicap. The problem as to why our society has completely adjusted to the wearing of glasses by the visually handicapped as contrasted to the wearing of hearing aids by the hard of hearing may have something to do with this question. Indeed, the difference in degree of efficiency in correcting the handicap is most of all responsible for this difference in attitude. But even with the improving quality of hearing aids this difference in attitude has not changed much. It is, therefore, most often the social and emotional adjustment to the acceptance of a hearing aid which constitutes one of the major problems of the hard of hearing. Inasmuch as this problem is mainly of emotional nature and we can do nothing to improve the primary handicap, the reader is referred to the section on the meaning of art for emotional disturbances. (See pp. 488–494.)

The speech defectives and art education

Among all the speech defects, stuttering is not only the most common one but also the one to which an art education therapy may be most related. Authorities agree with Gifford that stuttering is "purely psychological in origin—a problem of emotional maladjustment involving the total personality." [14] While the cause of stuttering is clearly psychological, there is no doubt that it results in a disturbance of motor coordination, that is, the inability to control those organs responsible for producing speech. Since art expression deals with both emotional factors as well as motor coordination, there may be a common basis of influence. Wright W. Putney in his excellent study [15] provides us with not only a wealth of data regarding stutter-

[13] Habbe, S., *Personality Adjustments of Adolescent Boys with Impaired Hearing.* New York: Columbia University, 1936; Madden, R., *The School Status of the Hard of Hearing Child.* New York: Columbia University, 1931.

[14] Gifford, Mabel F., in *Stuttering, Significant Theories and Therapies,* edited by E. P. Hahn. Stanford University, California, 1943.

[15] Putney, Wright W., *Characteristics of Creative Drawings of Stutterers,* Unpublished doctoral dissertation. The Pennsylvania State University, 1955.

ing, but also with experimental evidence regarding the characteristics found in the drawings of stutterers. While his experiments support the findings that stutterers have significant personality maladjustments, he points out that there is no "stuttering personality" typical of all stutterers. Nevertheless he found significant differences between the drawings of the two groups he tested, the stutterers and non-stutterers. "A lack of details in the drawings by the stuttering group was seen in significantly fewer details used to characterize the self and the environment." He further states, "a lack of movement and gesture" as characteristic for the stutterer group. All this clearly indicates that stutterers, more than non-stutterers, have difficulty in identifying themselves, a fact especially clearly pointed out in the experiment of Putney, in which "stutterers were found to obtain a significantly lower average rank on the self-portrait motivation."

While no controlled experiment was conducted with regard to the therapeutical aspects of art on stutterers, there are clear indications from assembled case histories of positive effects. It was seen that stutterers who improved in their speech handicap showed the same improvement of closer self-identification within the creative process, an improvement of spatial organization, a greater lack of stereotypes, and more flexibility and coordination in movement and the representations of actions.

As has been said before, stuttering long has been considered as basically of a psychological nature and by many investigators even termed as a psychoneurosis,[16] or at least as a symptom which "cannot be isolated from other neurotic manifestations."[17] The therapeutical approach using art education for stutterers will, therefore, in principle be the same as used with neurotic individuals, as will be discussed on pp. 488–494. An additional suggestion is indicated by practices which have shown that a great deal of the initial anxiety of stutterers when contacting environment may be diminished by creating "social situations" through their creative work. The choice of topics as well as group work may be very helpful in promoting this adjusting effect.

Cerebral palsy and creative activity

Generally we understand cerebral palsy to mean any disorder of muscular control due to injury, disease, or malformation of the brain occurring at or near the time of birth. According to type of injury and the resulting

[16] Coriat, Isador H., in *Stuttering, Significant Theories and Therapies,* edited by E. P. Hahn, Stanford University, California, 1943.

[17] Despert, Louise J., "A Therapeutic Approach to the Problem of Stuttering in Children," *Nervous Child,* 1943.

handicap different classifications and types of this disease have been developed. Yet, for the effectiveness of an art education therapy, these classifications have little or no bearing. Therefore, no attempt is made to include them in this treatise or to go further into a discussion of the causes. For our purposes, it is important to keep in mind that in all types of cerebral palsy a disorder of muscular control can be found.

There is scarcely any handicap with as great a variety of cases, both in kind and degree, as cerebral palsy. This great difference makes it difficult to generalize with regard to the effect of cerebral palsy on behavior and especially on intelligence. It is, however, generally agreed that "there is a far higher incidence of borderline and mental deficiency intelligence among the cerebral palsied than is found in the general population." [18] Yet, to use such a generalization for clinical purposes would be harmful indeed. Individual differences in cerebral palsy cases are as great and varied as among a normal population. There are cases of extreme disorder of muscular control with normal or even high intelligence and there are cases which have outwardly relatively little disorder but with extreme mental deficiencies. In identifying oneself with these unfortunate cases one has to consider this relationship of the disorder to the mental ability of the individual. It is needless to say that individuals with high intelligence and much inability for muscular coordination will suffer most. I have known an extremely intelligent individual, a victim of severe cerebral palsy who was unable to use her hands for writing and could only dictate by mustering all her efforts, very slowly, with greatest perseverance and only a few sentences a day. Cerebral palsy is indeed one of the most dreadful handicaps, especially in its severe forms, as it may affect almost any muscular control and thus involve speech, hearing, seeing, one or all extremities and any combination of them.

In addition to the handicap itself, victims of cerebral palsy like those of other handicaps suffer from subjective or secondary forms of handicaps, mainly of an emotional and social nature. Fear and the inability to cope with situations, depressions, emotional instabilities and feelings of inferiority rate among the most common ones.[19] However, authorities by no means agree on an adoption of principles with regard to these most common emotional disorders and how they relate to the different types of cerebral palsies.

As can easily be seen an art education therapy may influence both the

[18] Garrett, James F., *Cerebral Palsy* in Psychological Aspects of Physical Disability. U. S. Government Printing Office, Washington, D. C.

[19] Benda, C. E., *Developmental Disorders of Mentation and Cerebral Palsies*. New York: Grune and Stratton, 1952.

primary handicap of muscular disorder as well as the subjective handicap of the inability to cope with it emotionally. While every individual case must be approached foremost as an individual, it must be kept in mind that in any art process the physical coordination of muscles as well as the emotional involvement are an intrinsic part of it. Depending on the individual case, we shall put the emphasis on either one or both. If we deal with an extreme case of muscular disorder it would be difficult in the beginning to establish any intense self-identification with the creative expression, because the difficulties of controlling the muscles when attempting to coordinate motions and lines are almost insurmountable. But even for these primitive beginnings it should be kept in mind that greater perfection in art always grows from the urge for expression.

Special methods of an art education therapy for cerebral palsy

Even in the very beginning stages in the attempt to establish a better muscle coordination, the meaning which expression plays must not be neglected even if it is through the motor activity itself. Finger painting has been very successfully used in these very beginning stages.[20] Especially children enjoy seeing their motions realized in paint. In painting with a brush the holding of the brush may cause great difficulty. The method of attaching the brush to the hand either with adhesive bandage or with other means has been successfully used in the beginning. However, it should be kept in mind that any independent use should be made an incentive for the child. I have seen a whole group participating in the exciting experience of a single member's independently holding a brush.

Kneading or squeezing soft clay may be another initial stage. To find out who can keep less clay in his hands after squeezing it through the fingers while attempting to make a fist is a little game which has been used with great enjoyment by children. It is, however, necessary for a successful therapy that at some point the individual establish a more intimate relationship to his creative work. The previously discussed method of "closure" (see p. 46) is perhaps the most successful one with cerebral palsy cases. How far the teacher can go in the initial stage greatly depends on the individual case. It must, however, always be used with great restraint. In one case in which the child could not be brought to start, a green base line

[20] The playing of rhythmic music is often an encouragement for the establishment of coordinated motions.

made by the teacher was sufficient for the child to let many flowers "grow out of it" with the greatest emotional participation and involvement (see Fig. 94a). With her greatest efforts for muscular coordination and a perseverance which is difficult to describe, the child "attached" one flower petal after the other to the center, always waiting for the moment when her motions would obey her desires. For another child it was fun merely to "put" a glass on a table, previously drawn by her teacher, add the chairs and "prepare" for a party. Every single item which she added was a great event to her. An adult cerebral palsy case was lacking any initiative or self-confidence to engage in a creative work even when closely motivated. When the teacher started the form of a mask in clay, and put a roughly shaped nose on it by motivating some of the feeling of fear which was present in the subject, he became so involved in adding other forms that he could not leave the mask until he had the feeling that he had related some of the expression to himself. It was clearly the urge for expression which determined the strong desire to overcome the obstacles of a disturbed muscular coordination. Depending on kind and degree of the disturbance and the subjective feeling toward it, closure may be used to a greater or lesser degree, or become entirely unnecessary.

Art education as therapy for the crippled

In discussing the possible effect of an art education therapy on the crippled, a distinction with regard to the kind, cause, and onset of the handicap should be made. In considering the onset of the handicap, we distinguish between those who were born with some kind of crippling disfigurement and those who either through accident or through disease became crippled. If the crippling disease or accident occurred early in life, that is, within the first three years, we can count the afflicted individual psychologically with those who were born crippled. Many researchers do not even find a psychological distinction between those who were born with a crippling disability and those who acquired it before puberty. The major distinction with regard to the onset, however, lies in the individual's ability to adjust to his handicap. This adjustment greatly depends on the acceptance of a changed body-image. Children are far less conscious of themselves than adults and also have a less conscious attitude toward their own body-image. Therefore changes in the body-image during childhood generally affect the individual much less than later on as adults.

The main crippling disease has been poliomyelitis, generally known as infantile paralysis. "About 75 per cent of those reported annually as having

Fig. 94a. Painting by a cerebral palsy child; base line has been painted by teacher.

Fig. 94b. The same child painted this painting without any "help" several weeks later.

polio are between one and fifteen years of age." [21] However, these figures have undergone a radical change in the light of the discoveries of effective methods to combat the disease by Dr. Salk and his staff.

The degree and kind of a crippling disability caused by diseases or accidents is equally varied. The more serious the handicap, the greater are the psychological barriers for the individual. These psychological barriers do not only consist of his own limitations, but also of the reactions of the normal world to the crippled. All this becomes a part of the individual's body-image. Thus, the picture which the crippled individual has of himself not only includes his physical disability and his emotional reactions to it, but also the reactions of the world around him. An individual who was born deformed or became crippled in early youth gradually grows up with his body-image and the reactions of his environment to him, and while the problems of adjustment always differ from individual to individual, they are incomparably greater for the later-crippled who have to adjust to an entirely new body-image.

To identify as closely as possible with the crippled individual and all his problems is indeed essential for the teacher or clinician. To design a check list of those things which the teacher would not be able to do physically or emotionally if he had this particular crippling handicap is very helpful for his ability to identify himself with the particular handicapped person.

Creative activity can become both a great incentive to master a difficult situation physically and an emotional outlet for the many frustrations which the crippled encounter.

The mastery of physical obstacles for doing creative activities is mainly found in those whose upper extremities cannot adequately be used. The story of painters using their feet to hold their brushes and achieving most sensitive coordination is widely known.

It appears to be important that crippled persons should learn to face their handicap in art. In many instances I have found it a great release for crippled individuals to activate those parts of the body which cannot be used. A paraplegic found continuous enjoyment and delight in drawing such actions as "Playing Tennis," "Swimming," or "Hiking," occupations which he loved to do before he was crippled. He "felt good" when motivated in great detail with regard to the actions which he depicted. Indeed he went through them mentally and his muscle tonus became "activated" through his imaginative activity. A girl who was paralyzed through polio loved to draw "Playing Tag," "Jumping Rope," and other actions. In

[21] Seidenfeld, Morton A., *Psychological Problems of Poliomyelitis*. Washington, D. C.: U. S. Government Printing Office.

general I found in my contacts with the crippled that even a mental release of physical energies through creative activity is of great help. It provides for opportunities to do things which are otherwise impossible, but it also serves as a means to release the many frustrations to which the crippled is continuously exposed.

THE MENTALLY HANDICAPPED

Since methods of therapeutical approaches for mentally handicapped so greatly vary, it appears to me important to remind the reader again that methods used in this book are related to the background and materials used in art education. The writer is aware of both the importance of psychoanalytical methods as well as of their frequent misuse by being popularized by incompetently trained workers. Not being adequately trained in this field, he is especially sensitive to the confusion and has refrained from adding to it by using methods which are outside of the realm of art education. Especially in the discussion on the meaning of an "Art Education Therapy for Neurosis and Psychosis" the writer wanted to point out the special contribution of a method growing out of the approaches specific to art education. It is needless to say that if teachers would like to engage more deeply in the use of art as a therapy they would have to study not only the various approaches in order to use the one most adequate for the individual but also the dynamics underlying them.

Mental retardation as expressed in creative activity

A retarded individual usually is one who has not attained the mental capacity of normal individuals of the same age level, and involves no other abnormal condition.[22] Mental retardation indicates only a negative discrepancy between mental and chronological age. In creative activity we might find an eight-year-old child still scribbling and therefore still concerned with his motor activity. Instead, he should already relate his drawings to environment. He might, however, have undergone a perfectly normal development of his scribbling, only he started at a later age and remained in each single stage for a longer period. He might, then, perhaps at nine years, reach his preschematic stage and at twelve years, schematic representations, still using geometric lines. The sequence of his develop-

[22] Gaitskell, Charles, *Art Education for Slow Learners.* New York: Charles Bennet, comp., 1953.

ment might be perfectly normal but the age level at which he reaches the various stages of development does not correspond with the normal average as presented in previous chapters. Retardation, therefore, can be detected by comparing the characteristics found in productions of normal individuals with the creative work of the retarded individual. A discrepancy can be found either in the representation of the human figure or in the concept and representation of space, or in both.

The progress of the development of a human being is very flexible, and rigid criteria of what is normal are not valid. Furthermore, diagnoses ought not to be made merely for their own sake. If we find that there is a distinct discrepancy between what we may expect at the different age levels and what actually exists, we have to do something to find a more forceful stimulation. That only means that we have to increase our efforts or even suggestive power in order to create in the child the desire to increase his active knowledge. The normal child's receptivity for stimulation will be reached much more easily, but the retarded child needs a much greater suggestive power in order to become stimulated. There is, however, no basic difference in the work of the retarded individual and the work of a normal one. Because the retarded child has fewer possibilities of expression, creative activity will also have the effect of releasing emotional tensions.

Abnormal retardation in the Mongoloid type— A case study

The following presentation of an extreme case of retardation, the case of an imbecile, only receives its significance when seen from the broader aspect of the effect of creative activity on human development. But even if we would neglect the general significance that such a case has for normal psychology, the fact still remains that the individual herself was released from a more or less static status of passive mental and emotional existence. Furthermore, her adaptability to institutional life grew remarkably. Although having to be attended to first, she afterwards even took care of her own little apartment which, for therapuetic reasons, was put at her disposal.[23]

A. L. was twenty-seven years old. Her behavior patterns were childish. She loved to play with dolls, loved repetitions, and laughed at the slightest stimulus. Her mental age was that of a five-year-old child. When she was

[23] Experiments made at Lochland School, Geneva, New York, an institute for mentally deficient children. The author would like to use this opportunity to acknowledge gratefully the help and cooperation he received from Miss Florence H. Steward, director of the institute.

asked to draw, she would draw "head-feet" representations only, which is a characteristic representation of a five-year-old child, only that she was repeating them again and again in a stereotyped way. In Fig. 95a she expresses herself going downstairs. Environment was added upon stimulation by the author. At the right she is picking flowers.

Knowing that the next stage should include the "body," all stimulation was directed toward the goal of consciously experiencing the body. Since food meant very much to her, she was given plenty of it that morning, to the extent that she even complained about a stomach-ache. This opportunity was used to ask her to draw herself with her stomach-ache, holding her stomach as she did. Fig. 95b shows that although she first introduced a symbol for the body which she was holding with her arms, she later forgot its meaning and returned to her inflexible "head-feet" representation by drawing the "features" into the symbol first designated as "body."

To the right of this drawing is A. L. wearing her orange Sunday dress (orange line between "legs"). But neither did this experience divert her from her inflexibility, or better, fixation to a definite schema. Since nothing could stimulate her to arrive at a different concept, I gave her clay to work with. Working with another medium such as clay, which she never had used before, diverted her from her inflexible "head-feet" concept. After she was given paper and crayons, she applied the experience gained in her clay work to a new topic. She depicted the body for the first time (Fig. 95c). The significance, however, lies in the fact that she became released from her static inflexibility. The person to the right was spontaneously added by her and represents the author holding his arm around her shoulder. Also, she added the environment spontaneously.

This change from modeling to drawing was continued from now on, since it contributed greatly to making her more flexible in her thinking and concept. It was suggested that she put on her dress and go out for a walk with her doll. Fig. 95d shows her enjoying her "child." Most significant in this drawing is the increased desire to express body actions and also, for the first time, emotions. Whereas in former drawings only an indication of "hand" is given by means of one line, in this drawing the five fingers were represented. She even counted them with great pride. The meaningfulness of the arms, represented by a double line, reminds us of the discussion on emotionally emphasized parts during the schematic stage (seven to nine years of age) of the normal child (see pages 135 and 136).

Approximately one year after making this drawing, she drew Fig. 95e, "Riding Horseback," which she loved to do, probably because of the kinesthetic sensations which, as in rocking or swinging, contribute greatly to

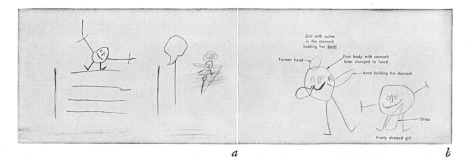

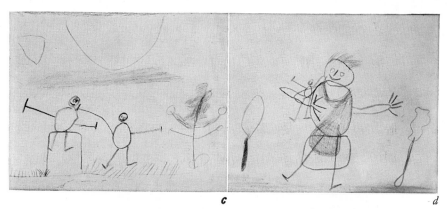

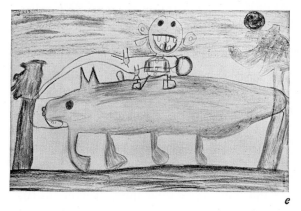

Fig. 95. Drawings by an imbecile (twenty-seven-year-old individual).

a). "Going Downstairs." Five-year-old level of head-feet representation.

b). Stimulation on body creates no deviation of inflexible schema. "Stomach-ache."

c). "Sitting on a Stone." Drawing showing introduction of body.

d). "A and Her Child." Drawing showing greater awareness of the self.

e). "Riding Horseback." Emotional freedom is clearly seen when compared with Fig. a.

her pleasure. This drawing is self-explanatory. Besides the change of the single features, she developed a remarkable freedom in expressing her emotions. She now draws herself laughing loudly, showing her tongue and teeth. She adds her two ears, even the openings in them, and the nose is drawn sideward. The saddle, her suit, even the stirrup into which she puts her feet, are indicated. The galloping horse is represented by the "bent" legs. Environment has become a part of her and her way of drawing.

Compared with her first drawing, this last drawing not only shows the great emotional change and freedom she now enjoys but also a more advanced possibility of mental activity which clearly showed itself in the change of her personality. It further demonstrates how creative activity has actively contributed to bringing her out of the emotional and mental isolation that prevented her from becoming an active member of her group.

Although Mongoloid types cannot be made normal, the great improvement of this case should clearly point out *the general significance of creative activity with regard to developing the potential mental abilities so often neglected and releasing emotional tension and rigidity, thus opening the way to a freer mental development.*

Art education therapy and neurosis— a case study

It shall only be attempted here to show the influence of creative activity on neurotic behavior as described later for the purpose of establishing in a more convincing way the interdependence between creative and mental growth. A neurosis is usually caused by a traumatic experience mostly occurring under certain conditions during early childhood.

A. B. was a very nice eleven-year-old girl who frequently showed "queer" reactions. When unexpectedly asked to do something, she seemed to be blocked entirely. For instance, when somebody asked her, "Anne, bring me a glass of water," or "Blow your nose," she might stiffen her hands, spreading them in a cramp-like position while crying, "Why should I bring a glass of water? Why doesn't John have to bring it? Why . . . ," and so forth. In other words, she could not unexpectedly be brought out of her present state. She could not face a new situation without being blocked. In drawings she could fill pages with the same figures, that of a girl (Fig. 96a), repeating them again and again, an indication that she did not want to be diverted. She felt quite well by assuring herself that she can draw a given pattern. *This repetition of inflexible schemata is characteristic of such emotional inflexibilities.* It always occurs when an individual cannot meet new situations. Unable to react meaningfully to them she escapes into a pattern where she feels secure. Such an inserted escape into meaningless stereotypes represents then an *escape mechanism* which is used when an individual cannot adjust to a given situation.

In the case of Anne we must know that Anne may suffer from her emotional reactions as much as or more than the people around her. So let us approach her with love, sympathy, and a feeling of identifying ourselves with her needs. Apparently Anne was not strong enough to stand all the influences and experiences to which she was exposed. So she built up a world around her, a world of her own, and surrounded herself with a protective wall. She cannot stand any new experiences; she does not want them to reach her. So she draws the same thing again and again, always the same figure—no change. A change would be disturbing. Any change is disturbing for her, because a change needs adjustment. For some people changes are exciting; they look forward to changes, especially pleasant changes. But what is pleasant for one may be upsetting for another, like traveling or moving to another place. It all depends on the flexibility and the state of mind of an individual. For Anne, even small changes are upsetting, like giving her an order. She was not expecting an order. She could not adjust quickly enough to it, so it made her upset. She gets upset easily because she never has time enough to adjust. Let's try to approach Anne more gradually.

Mary also may get upset if you tell her in the middle of her playing with her doll that she has to go to bed. She may also insert an escape mechanism and go into a tantrum, unable to meet the new situation. However, if you *condition* Mary gradually to the necessary change—"Mary, perhaps you should put your doll to bed because you, too, will soon have to go to bed" —Mary will take the order more easily. This is exactly what we try to accomplish through art motivations. We try to start again with an experience on Anne's level.

In the garden of Lochland School, an institute for mentally deficient children where I made these experiments, was a bench on which Anne loved to sit. The bench was in the shade of a tree. When I met Anne there, I asked her to draw herself sitting on the bench under the tree. Of course, I did this only after establishing friendly contact with her. Fig. 96b represents Anne sitting on the bench under the tree. If we examine this drawing closely, we see that the child made merely a schematic representation of a girl. No experience or movement is indicated, although she had the experience of sitting on the bench under a tree. Whenever we asked the child to draw "a girl" she would always draw the same representation,

Fig. 96. Drawings of an emotionally maladjusted eleven-year-old girl.

a). Inflexible schematic repetitions.

b). "Sitting Under a Tree." No spatial correlations.

c). "Picking Strawberries." First correlation with environment.

d). "Picking Strawberries." Second phase of direct connection of arm to berry.

e). "Swinging on Rings." Greater awareness of body action.

f). "Picnic Out of Doors." Profile is introduced.

c

d

g

h

i

k

g). "Family." Freedom of action and spatial correlation show adjustive effect.

h). "Dancing Around a Flagpole." Notice spatial conflict between group and pole.

i). "Our House Burns." Spontaneous expression of oppressed past experience with the effect of final release.

j). "My Best Sunday Dress."

k). "Dancing Around a Tree." Correct spatial correlations of the completely adjusted child.

regardless of any suggested bodily activity or environment. The abnormal child is bound up with its stereotyped representation, repeating it again and again. We can also see from this drawing that no contact with, or relation to, the environment is expressed. Neither is the child sitting on the bench as was suggested, nor is the bench under the tree. The child shows a complete failure to comprehend relations to the environment, and also a trend to draw schematic representations without any consciousness of bodily feelings. A profound change in the emotional response of the child was produced by the stimulation of such bodily feelings. It was easy to arouse her interest in picking strawberries, since eating them was a very pleasurable experience to her.[24] Then she was asked to draw "picking strawberries" (Fig. 96c). She drew the usual schematic representation. When she had finished her drawing I asked her, "Look, did you really pick the berries?" The child, a little confused, connected the line for the arm down to the berry. Having got this reaction, I made her repeat the actual picking movements and also the drawing with the result that this time she drew a direct line from the shoulder to the strawberry (Fig. 96d). This was the first great improvement, consisting, of course, not in the fact that she was able to draw this connection, but that she abandoned her schematic representation. After one month's work with repeated stimulations of her bodily feeling she began to experience connections to things outside of her body, as can be seen in Fig. 96e depicting "swinging on rings," which she loved to do. Gradually she became aware of her muscular sensations, using the joints in her representations, as Fig. 96f shows very clearly. Until this time she had drawn only front views; now we see for the very first time the change to profile representation, which as an original contribution on the part of the child shows her closer connection to her creative work. After two months she finally reached a stage expressed in the drawing of Fig. 96g, where she experienced not only her own bodily movements but also such difficult connections with outside figures as carrying the baby. If her first drawing is compared with this one, it will be clear that her greater consciousness of the self indicated in this drawing represents not only a very great improvement in her creative work but also an expression of her improved general condition.[24] Her emotional reactions were much more normal during her "art classes," although she still withdrew into her "stiffness" outside of them. Such a *dual role* shown by different behaviors during the art education therapy and outside is to be expected because a

---

[24] While she picked the strawberries she was repeatedly encouraged to pay attention to her bodily movements, reported in: Lowenfeld, V., "Self-Adjustment Through Creative Activity." *American Journal of Mental Deficiency*, Vol. XLV, 1941.

certain security and a state of affection have been established in the clinical situation which are not felt outside of it. Such differences in reactions are typical for clinical situations and should resolve in a successful therapy.

Once the children were dancing around a flagpole (Fig. 96h). Most interesting is the conflict in her subjective spatial experience of dancing around the pole in a circle which she represents by the children holding one another, and the placing of the pole on the edge (the base line) of the paper. A few weeks afterward Anne came excitedly into my room asking whether she couldn't make a drawing of "a family and their burning house and how mother saved her best dress" (Fig. 96i). "This am I," she said, pointing at the girl with the dress just catching fire. "My dress just starts burning and mother saved only hers." On the bottom of the drawing are two girls carrying their injured sister. But most significant is the enormously exaggerated representation of mother's dress. Such pathological exaggerations are always indicative of the special significance of an experience.

Regardless of the truth which lies behind the story, the drawing reveals clearly the traumatic experience which caused the neurosis and apparently also the type of behavior of Anne. It also revealed important factors in the relationship between Anne and her mother. Such a relationship of anxiety or jealousy may have been the initial cause for the development of the traumatic experience into a neurosis, for it is *the condition in which Anne was before which made her susceptible to a neurosis*. Thus the drawing made her face an important incident which was brought into her conscious mind by the freedom she acquired in her creative work. Similar to psychoanalysis a connection with the subconscious past had been established. This is one of the most important therapeutic steps for an emotional recovery. Since the dress (psychologically, the dress might be a substitute for something else) played such an important part, I asked her to put on her best Sunday dress. Then she drew Fig. 96j. The suggested larger size of the drawing stimulated her not only to draw a "beautiful dress with a rich design" but made her also draw more details of the self. Her consciousness of the self has rapidly changed. She now draws a neck, lips, eyelids, brows, and so forth, indicating her greater active knowledge of the self.

After the children had been dancing around a tree, a few weeks later, she drew Fig. 96k. At that time she had completely lost her "queer" reactions. She acted entirely normal and could enter public school. If we compare the last drawing with the first one, or even with the drawing "Dancing around the Flagpole," we will understand the relationship between Anne's emotional growth and her creative work. More than that, we can easily realize the adjustive effect it had on Anne.

Art education therapy and psychosis

While one school of thought considers a neurosis a functional disturbance of the brain, and a psychosis of *organic* nature, the other believes that both are on a continuum and differ mainly in severity. Since their cause has not been adequately proven neither psychologists nor psychiatrists completely agree with their definitions. Of the various mental disorders, schizophrenia particularly relates in its various aspects to important attributes of creative processes. In order to understand this relationship it seems important to study the characteristics of this type of mental disorder. Schizophrenia is usually considered as a distintegration of the mind. In this process of disintegration certain symptoms become apparent which will be discussed later. Among them the following relate to our problem:

(1) The inability to distinguish phantasy from reality.

(2) Regression or return to more immature and simpler levels.

(3) A disturbed body-image.

(4) Alteration of motor behavior.

(5) Disturbances of thinking.

(6) A lack of ability to abstract, resulting in a loss of common symbols.

The inability to distinguish phantasy from reality usually results in hallucinations, the tendency to see or perceive things as "real" which are actually non-existent. The problem as to whether the schizophrenic individual subconsciously shuns reality because he "prefers" a life of phantasy or whether he retreats into phantasy because he cannot bear to meet the problems of the world is still unexplained.[25] In the art of schizophrenic individuals this is seen by an apparent *"inconsistent fusion"* of phantasy with reality. Prinzhorn [26] and many others show in numerous illustrations heads growing out of limbs, claws attached to human extremities, bird heads on human bodies, or "organpipes in the sea." Such fusion of items apparently unrelated to one another are often found in schizophrenic art expression. Bruno Bettelheim in an excellent analysis of a case study attempted to explain such relationships in terms of the individual's subconscious feeling.[27] However, symptomatically the schizophrenic child in this respect differs from the adult schizophrenic. The normal child indulges

[25] Bradley, Charles, "Schizophrenia in Childhood," 1944; Bender, Lauretta, "Childhood Schizophrenia," *American Journal of Orthopsychiatry*, 1947.

[26] Prinzhorn, Hans, *Bildnerei der Geisteskranken*, Berlin: Julius Springer, 1923.

[27] Bettelheim, Bruno, "Schizophrenic Art, A Case Study," *Scientific American*, 1952.

in fantastic thinking often unrelated to the surrounding environment. Hallucinations and delusions are often difficult to determine as such under the age of six years and possibly even in older children because they may merely be an outcome of vivid imagery. Lauretta Bender feels that the "schizophrenic child often shows remarkable artistic ability in graphic arts." She feels that the essential psychological problem is the difficulty in recognizing one's self and one's thinking in relation to the rest of the world.[28]

In the process of a disintegration of the mind the individual often *regresses or returns to more immature and simpler levels.* To me, this process of disintegration is like the collapsing of a building in which the parts become completely disorganized, although still existent. "Pieces" of childhood reactions may appear like regressions but actually they exist side by side with other behavior characteristics which are not consistent with a childhood regression. Yet, it is without any doubt that the schizophenic individual loses his inhibitions in expressing himself and often produces drawings not distinguishable from those of children, both in his use of geometric lines to produce a schematic form of representation as well as in the not infrequent use of base lines, of his space schema. In this "return" to more immature and simpler levels not only a tendency toward *childish expression* can be seen but also one toward the use of archaic forms leading back to former and sometimes ancient periods.

Yet also this phenomenon is by no means consistent, because the art of the schizophrenic lacks the coherent quality of child art expression or that of the primitive. One of the factors responsible for this lack of coherence is the *disturbed body-image* of the schizophrenic individual, his inability to recognize the self as one's own self (see Fig. 97a). This not only leads to the inability to identify oneself with his own experiences but also to the total lack of projecting oneself into the needs and feelings of others, and therefore of any social relationships. Schizophrenic individuals often completely lack the capacity for empathy (see Fig. 97b). This documents itself in the creative products of schizophrenics as the *inability to make coherent motions and actions,* and counts for the somewhat "stiff" look of the figures in their drawings.

An excellent experimental study on the *alteration of the motor behavior* of schizophrenic individuals was done by A. Angyal.[29] In it he discusses the differences of motor behavior and kinesthetic experiences between the

[28] *Op. cit.*
[29] Angyal, Andreas, "The Experience of the Body-Self in Schizophrenia." *Archives of Neurology and Psychiatry,* May, 1956.

normal and the schizophrenics. For instance, muscle contractions in antic-
ipation of lifting a weight were not present in schizophrenics, or at least to
a much lesser degree. He says that when a normal person intends to lift a
heavy rock he contracts his muscles, as it were, as a preliminary step in the
process of lifting. This can best be experienced if a person is asked to lift
a cardboard dummy of a rock not knowing that it is not a rock of heavy
weight. His contracted muscles will then contradict the sensation of lifting
the light-weighted "dummy." This coincides approximately with the motor
behavior of schizophrenics. *In the art expression of schizophrenics motor
behavior often deviates* from what is seen in the works of the normal.
Bending down is not always experienced as bending down in the same way
as localization of certain body parts often constitutes great difficulty in
schizophrenic individuals.[30]

Disturbances of thinking in schizophrenic individuals mainly deals with
two factors, the *incoherence* of thinking and the *different kind of reasoning*
often used by schizophrenic individuals. The incoherence of thinking is in
close relationship to the hallucinatory imagery of schizophrenics and their
marked inability to distinguish between the self and non-self. The different
kind of reasoning can best be found in the following example of a schizophrenic individual. He thought he was Switzerland, reasoned on the following basis: I love freedom; Switzerland loves freedom; therefore I am
Switzerland. Von Domarus calls this logic the "paleologic" because it
excludes our present thinking and reasoning based on causal interdepend-
ences and is also used by primitive peoples.[31] However, this kind of reasoning sometimes is also found in children. A child who saw two policemen
together called them twins because he knew that twins often dress alike.

In the art expression of schizophrenic individuals this disturbed thinking,
the confusion of self-identity and the paleologic in reasoning has its own
characteristics. The confusion of self-identity often creates a confusion between "figure and ground." The paleologic thinking allows individuals to
put things together in an extremely incomprehensible way with no apparent
relationship, and devoid of any other relationships than the ones based on
purely "individualistic" associations. A patient when asked to draw a self-
portrait, drew a radiating sun. It was a hot summer day and apparently his
paleologic was: "The sun is hot; I am hot; therefore I am the sun."

With lack of reasoning the schizophrenic individual also *loses the use
of common symbols,* that is, his *ability to abstract.* One of the most impor-

[30] Schilder, P., *Localization of the Body Image.* Research of Nervous and Mental Disorders,
1934.
[31] Kasanin, J. S., *Language and Thought in Schizophrenia.* Berkeley and Los Angeles: University of California Press, 1944.

tant steps in the evolution of man is the use of language. In language common symbols serve man to communicate with each other. In this process of disintegration, the schizophrenic individual often falls back upon the use of "paleosymbols," symbols which have meaning only to him and no one else. In schizophrenic art, *symbols are often not detectable because they have no common meaning.*

Schizophrenia and art education therapy

It should be emphasized in the beginning that there is no "schizophrenic personality," that is, one who possesses all characteristics which are attributed to schizophrenia. On the contrary, there is scarcely any greater diversity of personalities in any other handicap than in schizophrenia. In fact, schizophrenics are all "individuals" with their own peculiarities and they are highly differentiated.

Most of the therapeutic approaches using art are psychoanalytically oriented. They all greatly depend on the Freudian concepts of symbolization pertaining to the subconscious and the analysis of dreams, and the Jungian teaching of the nonpersonal factors of unconscious mechanisms. Margaret Naumburg, somewhat deviating from these concepts, stresses the patient's own reactions to his work. "For it is on the basis of each patient's response to his own symbolic creations that the importance of using spontaneous art projections as a primary mode of therapy can be established." [32] However, whether the therapy described in her book was obtained on the basis of her verbal discourse and analysis, or through art expression, is not quite clear. It is safe to say that both were of great influence. Among all the investigators, only Schaefer-Simmern clearly applied an art education method based on the "visual conceiving" of his cases.[33]

Two case histories

The more an individual is mentally disturbed, the more he becomes bound up with the self, losing contact with his environment. In the more advanced mental disturbances, however, there is not only a lack of connection with the environment but also an entire loss of correlation in bodily actions. There are many intermediate steps.

[32] Naumburg, Margaret, *Schizophrenic Art: Its Meaning in Psychotherapy.* New York: Grune and Stratton, 1950, pp. 33.

[33] Schaefer-Simmern, Henry, *The Unfolding of Artistic Activity.* Berkeley: University of California Press, 1948.

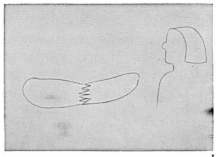

Fig. 97. Drawings by a thirteen-year-old, schizophrenic child.

a). Inflexible fixation on a hallucinatory figure expressed by an imitative schema.

b). "Holding One Another" made her express the "arms" first. No correlation with body could be perceived, because of disturbed body image.

c). Enlarged drawing with partial correlation.

d). Established correlation and change of inflexible fixation on schema indicates better self-identity.

Vera was thirteen years old and considered as a borderline case of schizophrenia. She talked much to herself and to "someone else," going in circles around the same ideas. She neither wanted to be touched bodily, nor did she like any interference with her present state. She loved to draw. In certain periods she always drew the same types of figures, often influenced by picture-book illustrations, although she never did any direct copying. While being in such a state of constant repetition, the following experiment was made. It should be mentioned that Vera was at that time rigidly drawing repetitions of a schematic figure in profile, calling them by names from fairy stories apparently as an escape from reality seemingly strongly influenced by a picture-book illustration (Fig. 97a).

To get her closer to reality Vera was asked to participate in a game with other children. A play "Pulling One Another" was arranged purposely. To incite in her closer relationships to the self, Vera was put in the middle between two other children who tried hard to find out "who is the strongest one" by pulling both arms of Vera. Because Vera only drew "side views" this game was chosen for the purpose of making Vera aware that she has *two* sides which are equally important. These could be drawn only in front view, whereas all her drawings were stiff profile representations. After Fig. 97a was drawn, in which neither pulling nor any other indication of pulling was represented, the game was repeated. This time *holding* one another while pulling was emphasized, by squeezing her hands tightly, not the pulling as such. Fig. 97b shows the attempt to represent this experience.[34] After she had drawn the two hands holding each other, clearly signifying some recognition of the action, she continued again in the usual way with her profile representation. Impatient that she could not attach the "hands" to her rigid profile representation, she got up and complained that the paper was not large enough. After a larger sheet of paper was provided, Vera drew Fig. 97c, quickly calling the figures names from fairy tales. In this drawing she achieved some relation between the two figures to the right by turning them toward each other, but the third figure is still isolated. Although she could not change her profile concept, she was able to turn two profiles toward each other, which indicated at least an initial attempt to establish contact between the figures. Needless to say, no criticism was voiced while Vera was drawing. She was asked to point to herself on the drawing and to show how she feels when she is being pulled. She became excited and asked for another sheet on which she made the final drawing, Fig. 97d. Here, as it can clearly be seen, she comprehended

---

[34] It not only shows her disturbed body image in which she could "feel" the relationships of the hands to herself, but also an apparent lack of relating the motion to herself.

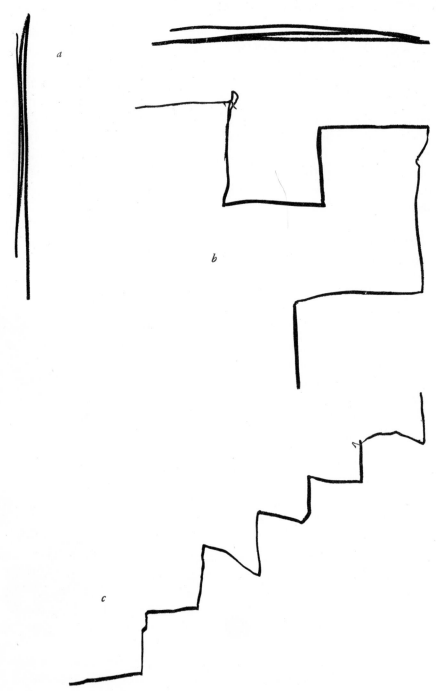

Fig. 98. Drawings of a mentally disturbed fifteen-year-old youth. (Courtesy Lochland School, Geneva, N. Y.)

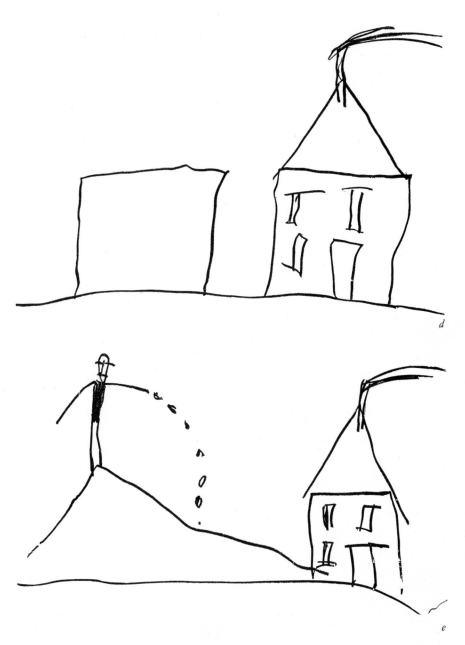

d

e

a). Go "up-down"; "left-right."

b). Go "right-down-right-up-right-down-left-down."

c). Go "up-right-up-right-up-right"; "what is it?" Starting with kinesthetic experiences, ending with a visual concept.

d). Go "up-right-down"; "this is supposed to be a house."

e). "I am throwing stones."

501

the connection among the three figures. Through a close stimulation of body feelings she experienced the significance of both sides of her body. This experience diverted her from her stereotyped profile representations and brought her to a closer realization of her own self. Although the names do not correspond, they were "real" names and not those of fairies.

A much more difficult case was that of a fifteen-year-old boy, also of Lochland School, who was completely incapable of recognizing any connection between the line on the paper and his arm movements. He might have been looking out of the window while making lines on the paper, without recognizing the fact that he had drawn them. Since no control of his motions was established, his drawings looked like disordered scribbling. Movement was not only greatly enjoyed by him, but also relieved him considerably from tensions. Therefore we started a game in which he tried to follow my suggestions for motions. In the beginning I started by moving his hands while saying, "Go up and down." Later I put a crayon into his hand saying, "Go up and down on the paper," which he did (Fig. 98a), recognizing for the first time the connection between the lines on the paper and his motions. In these attempts we find the corresponding steps to the development of scribbling as previously discussed. With close relations between kinesthetic experiences and drawing on the paper established, he became visually interested in the lines, too. After one month I could lead him around on the paper exactly as I wanted to by saying, "Go up, down, left, right, down," and so forth, making the type of broken line shown in Fig. 98b. I also introduced circular movements and their representation. Later he was stimulated to draw first stages of representations related to objects, such as stairs, table, chair, house, ball, and so forth. For example, I said, "Go first up, then right, then up, then right," finally asking him, "What is that?" He answered, "Steps" (Fig. 98c) ; or I said, "Go up, right and down; this is supposed to be a house. Put in the windows and draw the roof on it" (Fig. 98d). The method in these experiments was to start with kinesthetic experiences and finish with a visual concept. Fig. 98e is one of his later drawings, "I Am Throwing Stones," which he loved to do. This was the first drawing that he did on his own account. With it he had discovered a clear relationship between his actions and his representations, and from now on he came often spontaneously to my room, made a few drawings quickly and left with all signs of relief. Although it cannot be claimed that the boy became normal, a mental improvement could clearly be seen. The director and psychiatrist of the School recognized the great change in the condition of this boy.

SUMMARY

In this chapter we have shown that in many instances art education can clarify its problems by means of analyzing extreme cases. The phenomenon of visual and nonvisual or haptic experiences of shape and form, for instance, can best be studied and demonstrated at the borderline of seeing and blindness, where extreme cases of both types reveal themselves fully. The influence and broadening effect of art expression on the development of speech could be impressively demonstrated in the case of a deaf-blind subject who from the very beginning had to struggle for the meaning of every word. The relieving effect of creative activity upon our emotions has been shown by the study of those who suffer from emotional tension or maladjustment. The influence on our mental growth, finally, has been demonstrated by mentally defective subjects, whose rigid patterns were most difficult to change.

We have seen that the common approach to creative work with all handicapped was based upon the recognition of their *isolation from the environment* and that the means of overcoming it depended upon the kind of handicap. In physical handicaps the isolation is mainly caused by the physical defect and the resulting feelings of inferiority. Creative activity can become a means of overcoming this detachment—physically and mentally—through improving those sensory experiences which deal with the establishment of an improved self-concept, and emotionally by relieving tensions and and inhibitions that stand in the way of the development of the potential abilities of the handicapped. In mental defectives, however, isolation from the environment is an effect of their inability to comprehend environmental factors together with a lack of self-identity. The one is indicated by a total absence of spatial correlations in their drawings; the other by a fixation on an inflexible schematic representation. Through stimulating the bodily feelings a closer and more conscious relation with the environment is achieved and rigid patterns are often given up and flexibility may be acquired. Through experience of the self the individual gains contact and connection with the environment, which can bring him out of his isolation and make him a more useful member of society. Nowhere can the integrative effect of the aesthetic experience more clearly be demonstrated than in the realm of the handicapped.

CHAPTER XIII SUMMARY
OF ALL STAGES

IN THE INTRODUCTION TO THIS BOOK THE SUBJECT MATTER OF ART
was discussed and clarified as our subjective relationship to man and
environment. It is this subjective relationship which changes with the age
levels. Therefore, it was our task to analyze, investigate, and study these
changes. Only when these changes in our relationships to man and environment are comprehended do we have an approximate assurance that we
understand the changing quality of our imaginative activity during the
different developmental periods. It is the knowledge of this changing imaginative activity and its expression which is one of the most important
prerequisites for successful art stimulation.

*The following chart has been compiled only for the purpose of sur-
veying these changing conditions with regard to our relationship to man
and environment.* It would be a great misunderstanding if this chart would
be used as an abbreviated prescription for suggested art activities. The
chart has only a dynamic meaning: to show at one glance *horizontally* the
development of the experiences of shape, space, and color, and the adequate stimulation for each age period. *Vertically,* the chart shows the

Stage	Characteristics	Representation of Human Figure	Representation of Space	Representation of Color	Design	Stimulation Topics	Technique
Scribbling (two to four years)	Disordered: no motor control. Longitudinal: motor coordination. Circular: variation of control. Naming: *change of thinking* from kinesthetic to imaginative.	None. / Only imaginatively.	None. / Only imaginatively.	No conscious use. / Color used to distinguished between scribblings.	None.	Through encouragement. In the direction of the child's thinking.	Large black crayon. Smooth paper. Finger paint for maladjusted children. Colored crayons. Poster paint. Clay.
Pre-Schematic (four to seven years)	Discovery of *relationship* between representation and thing represented.	Search for concept. Constant change of symbol.	No "order" in space. Relationships according to *emotional* significance.	Emotional use according to appeal. No relationship to reality.	No conscious approach.	Activating of passive knowledge mainly related to the self. "I" stage.	Crayons. Clay. Poster paint. Large bristle brush. Large sheets of paper.
Schematic Stage (seven to nine years)	Discovery of *concept* through repetition becomes *schema.*	*Definite* concept depending on active knowledge and personality characteristics. Human schemata expressed by means of geometric lines.	First *definite* space concept: base line. Discovery of being a part of environment. Subjective space representation. Space-time concept.	*Definite* relationship between color and object. Through repetition: color, schema.	No conscious approach. Design characteristics received through urge for repetitions.	"We," "Action," "Where," topics in time sequences (stories). Inside and outside.	Colored crayons. Chalks. Poster paint (tempera). Large paper. Bristle brush. Clay.

Stage	*Characteristics*	*Representation of Human Figure*	*Representation of Space*	*Representation of Color*	*Design*	*Stimulation Topics*	*Technique*
Dawning Realism Pre-Adolescent Crisis (nine to eleven years), Gang Age	Greater awareness of the self. Removal from schema. *Removal* from geometric lines. Lack of cooperation. Stage of transition.	Greater stiffness. Emphasis on clothes. Difference between boys and girls. Tendency toward realistic lines. *Removal* from schematic representation.	*Removal* from base-line concept. Overlapping. Discovery of plane. Difficulties in spatial correlation due to egocentric attitude.	*Removal* from objective stage of color. Subjective color experiences with emotionally significant objects.	First conscious approach toward decoration. Use of materials and their function for design.	Cooperation through: (1) Group-work. (2) Working method. (3) Topic. Different professions. Suits, dresses. Overlapping.	*No crayons* because of removal from linear expressions. Poster paint. Clay. Chalk. Linoleum cut. Textiles. Wood. Metal.
Pseudo-Realistic Stage Stage of Reasoning (eleven to thirteen years)	Developed intelligence, yet unawareness. Realistic approach (unconscious). Tendency toward visual- or nonvisual-mindedness. Love for dramatization.	Joints. Visual observation of body actions. Proportions. Emphasis on expression of nonvisually minded.	Urge for three-dimensional expression. Diminishing sizes of distant objects. Horizontal line (visually minded).	Changes of color in nature (visually minded). Emotional reaction to color (nonvisually minded).	First conscious approach to stylizing. Symbols for professions. Function of different materials.	Dramatic actions in environment. Actions from imagination and posing (with meaning, like "Scrubbing"). Proportions through emphasis on content. Color moods. Murals: "from-to." Design in material. Modeling.	Water-color Gouache (water color and tempera). Poster paint. Bristle brush. Hair brush. Clay. Linoleum. Materials for design: textiles, wood, metal, papier-mâché.

Stage	Characteristics	Representation of Human Figure	Representation of Space	Representation of Color	Design	Stimulation Topics	Technique
The Stage of Decision Crisis of Adolescence (thirteen to seventeen years)	Critical awareness toward environment. Three groups: (1) *Visual type* (50 per cent): Intermediaries: eyes. Creative concern: environment, appearance. (2) *Haptic type* (25 per cent): Intermediary: body. Creative concern: self-expression, emotional approach of subjective experiences. (3) In-betweens (25 per cent): Reactions are not definite in either direction. Creative concern: abstract.	*Visual Type:* Emphasis on appearance. Light and shadow. Depiction of momentary impressions. Realistic interpretations of objective validity. *Haptic Type:* Emphasis on inward expressions. Emotional qualities. Proportion of value. Individual interpretations.	*Visual Type:* Perspective representations. Apparent diminution of distant objects. Atmosphere. Appearance. Mood. Three-dimensional qualities. Light and shadow. *Haptic Type:* Perspective of value with relation to the self. Value relationship of objects. Base-line expressions.	*Visual Type:* Appearance of color in nature. Color reflections. Changing qualities of color environment, with regard to distance and mood. Analytic attitude. Impressionistic. *Haptic Type:* Expressive, subjective meaning of color. Local color when insignificant. Color changes with regard to emotional significance. Psychological meaning of color.	*Visual Type:* Aesthetic interpretation of form, balance, and rhythm. Decorative design. Emphasis on harmony. *Haptic Type:* Emotional design of abstract quality. Functional design. Industrial design.	Visual *and* haptical stimulations. Environment *and* figure. Appearance and content. Posing with interpretations. Sketching. Sculpture. Graphics. Design. Painting. Mural.	Sketching in: crayon, oil paint, tempera, water color. *Easel painting. Mural sculpture* in: Plastic media, Casting, Wood, Stone. *Graphics:* Linoleum cut. Etching. Lithography. Silk screen. Stencil. Air-brush. Poster work. Lettering. Design: decorative, functional, industrial.

growth from one stage of development to another again in the different realms of shape, space, color, and design. Thus the chart shows simultaneously what cannot be summarized in text form. However, the chart will be understood only if it is used after the content of the book has been thoroughly understood.

CHAPTER XIV   REFERENCES

BASIC PHILOSOPHY

Alschuler, Rose H. and Hattwick, La Berta W., *A Study of Painting and Personality of Young Children*. Chicago: Univ. of Chicago Press, 1947. 2 vols.

"Art Education Today." *The Teacher*. New York: Bureau of Publications, Teachers College, Columbia University, 1950.

Bartlett, Francis Grant, and Crawford, Claude C., *Art for All*. New York: Harper and Bros., 1942.

Barkan, Manuel, *A Foundation for Art Education*. New York: Ronald Press, 1955.

Bayley, Nancy, "Mental and Emotional Growth and Personality Development." *Mental Hygiene in Modern Education*, Chapter II. New York: Farrar and Rinehart, 1939.

Bland, Jane Cooper. *Art for Children*. Childcraft, Vol. 10. Chicago: Field Enterprises, 1954.

Bowley, Agatha H., *Guiding the Normal Child*. New York: Philosophical Library, 1943.

Cane, Florence, *The Artist in Each of Us*. New York: Pantheon Books, 1951.

Commission on Secondary School Curriculum, *The Visual Art in General Educaton*, New York: Appleton-Century Co. (D), Inc.; 1940.

D'Amico, Victor, *Creative Teaching in Art*. Scranton, Pa.: International Textbook Co., 1953.

D'Amico, Victor and Wilson, Frances. *Art for the Family*. New York: Museum of Modern Art, 1956.

Dewey, John, *Art as Experience*. New York: Minton, Balch, 1934.

Elkisch, Paula, *The Emotional Significance of Children's Art Work*. Childh. Educ., 1947. "Children's Drawings in a Projective Technique." *Psych. Monogr.* No. 1, 1945.

Faulkner, Ray; Ziegfeld, Edwin; and Hill, Gerald, *Art Today*. New York: Henry Holt and Co., 1941.

Gibbs, Evelyn, *The Teaching of Arts in Schools*. New York: Greenberg Inc., Publisher, 1936.

Gregg, Harold, *Art for the Schools of America*. Scranton, Pa.: International Text-book Co., 1941.

Harms, E., "The Psychology of Formal Creativeness." *J. Genet Psychol.* 1946.

Hartman, B. and Shumaker, A., ed., *Creative Expression: The Development of Children in Art, Music, Literature, and Dramatics*. New York: John Day, 1932.

Hurlock, E. B. and J. L. Thomson, "Children's Drawings: An Experimental Study of Perception," *Child Development*, 5, 127–138, 1934.

Kellett, K. R., *"A Gestalt Study of the Function of Unity in Aesthetic Perception."* *Psychological Monograph*, 51, No. 5, 1939.

Kepes, Gyorgy, *The Language of Vision*. Chicago: P. Theobald, 1944.

Koffka, K., "Problems in the Psychology of Art." In *Art: A Bryn-Mawr Symposium*. Bryn Mawr, Pa.: Bryn Mawr, 1940.

——— *Principles of Gestalt Psychology*. New York: Harcourt, Brace and Co., 1935.

Landis, Mildred M., *Meaningful Art Education*. Peoria, Ill.: Chas. A. Bennett Co., Inc. Publishers, 1951.

MacDonald, Rosabell, *Art in Education*. New York: Henry Holt and Co., 1941.

Mitchell, E. L., *Curriculum Experiences for Elementary Schools*. Delaware Curriculum No. 1, 1940.

Rannells, E. W., *Art Education in the Junior High School*. Lexington, Kentucky: University of Kentucky, 1946.

Read, Herbert, *Education Through Art*. London: Faber and Faber, 1943.

——— *Grass Roots of Art*. New York: Wittenborn Co., 1947.

Research Bulletin, Eastern Arts Assoc. Kutztown, Vol. 1, 1950, Vol. 2, 1951.

Schaefer-Simmern, H., *The Unfolding of Artistic Activity*. Berkeley: Univ. of Calif. Press, 1948.

Skinner, Charles E. and Philip Lawrence Harriman, *Child Psychology*. New York: The Macmillan Company, 1941.

Strickler, Fred, *An Art Approach to Education*. New York: A. G. Seiler, 1943.

Winslow, Leon Loyal, *The Integrated School Art Program*. New York: McGraw-Hill Book Co., 1939.

Sherman, Hoyt L., *Drawing by Seeing*. New York: Hinds, Hayden & Eldridge, 1947.

UNESCO. *Education and Art*. Paris: United Nations, 1953.

FIRST STAGES OF SELF-EXPRESSION
(TWO TO SEVEN YEARS)

Alschuler, Rose H., and La Berta W. Hattwick, *"Painting and Personality, A study of Young Children."* Chicago: The University of Chicago Press, 1947.

Bayley, Nancy, *The Development of Motor Abilities during the First Three Years*. Society for Research in Child Development, Monograph 1, 1935.

Blum, Lucille H. and Anna Dragositz, *Finger Painting*. Child Developm., 1947.

Ellsworth, Maud, and Michael F. Andrews, *Growing with Art*, Books 1 and 2. Chicago: Benj. H. Sanborn & Co., 1951.

Eng, Helga K., *The Psychology of Children's Drawings from the First Stroke to the Coloured Drawing*. London: Trench, Trubner, and Co., 1931.

Gaitskell, Charles and Margaret, *Art Education in the Kindergarten*. Toronto: Ryerson Press, 1952.

Gesell, Arnold, *How a Baby Grows*. New York: Harper and Bros., 1945.

Goodenough, F. L., "Studies in the Psychology of Children's Drawings." *Psychol. Bull.*, 25, 1928.

────── "Children's Drawings." *A Handbook of Child Psychology*. Worcester: Clark Univ. Press, 1931.

Line, W., "The Growth of Visual Perception in Children." *Brit. Journal of Psych.*, XV, 1931.

Lowenfeld, Viktor, *The Nature of Creative Activity*. London: Routledge and Kegan Paul, 1952.

────── *Your Child and His Art*. New York: The Macmillan Co., 1954.

McCloy, W., "Passive Creative Imagination." Psychological Monographs, LI, No. 5, 1939.

Mott, S. M., "The Development of Concepts, A Study of Children's Drawings." *Child Development*, 7, 1936.

Read, Herbert, *Education Through Art*. London: Faber and Faber, 1943.

────── "The Art of Children." *Education Through Art*. London: Faber and Faber, 1943.

Wellman, Beth L., "Motor Development from Two Years to Maturity." *Review of Educational Research*, No. 6, 1936.

Wolff, W., *The Personality of the Pre-School Child*. New York: Grune & Stratton, 1946.

THE UNAWARE STAGES OF CREATIVE EXPRESSION
(SEVEN TO TWELVE YEARS)

Alschuler, Rose H. and La Berta W. Hattwick, *Painting and Personality, A Study of Young Children*. Chicago: Univ. of Chicago Press, 1947. 2 vols.

Bannon, Laura, *Mind Your Child's Art*. New York: Pellegrini and Cudahy, 1952.

Bland, Jane Cooper, *Art for Children*. Childcraft, Vol. 10. Chicago: Field Enterprises, 1954.

Browne, Sibyl, Ethel Tyrrell, Gertrude Abbihl, and Clarice Evans, *Art and Materials for the Schools*. New York: Progressive Education Assn., 1943.

Cizek, Franz, *Children's Coloured Paper Work*. New York: G. E. Stechert and Co., 1927.

Cole, Natalie Robinson, *The Arts in the Classroom*. New York: John Day Co., 1940.

D'Amico, Victor. *Creative Teaching in Art,* Rev. Edition. Scranton, Pa.: International Textbook Co., 1953.

Downey, June E., *Creative Imagination*. New York: Harcourt, Brace and Co., 1929.

Ellsworth, Maud, and Michael F. Andrews, *Growing with Art*. Books 3–7. Chicago: Benj. H. Sanborn & Co., 1951.

Erdt, Margaret, *Teaching Art in the Elementary School*. New York: Rinehart and Co., 1953.

Gaitskell, Charles, *Children and their Pictures*. Toronto: The Ryerson Press, 1951.

Groetzinger, Wolfgang, *Scribbling, Drawing, Painting*. New York: Fred. Praeger, Inc., 1955

Harrison, Elizabeth, *Self Expression through Art*. Toronto: W. J. Gage and Co., Ltd., 1951.

Keiler, Manfred L., *Art in the Schoolroom*. Lincoln, Nebr.: Univ. of Nebraska Press, 1951.

Lowenfeld, Viktor, *Your Child and His Art*. New York: The Macmillan Co., 1954.

Mathias, Margaret E., *Art in the Elementary School*. New York: Charles Scribner's Sons, 1929.

———— *The Teaching of Art*. New York: Charles Scribner's Sons, 1932.

McLeisch, Minnie and Ella Moody, *Teaching Art to Children*. New York: Studio Pub., 1953.

Mendelowitz, Daniel, *Teaching Art to Children*. Stanford: Stanford Univ. Press, 1953.

Mitchell, Edith L., and Sallie B. Tannahil, "Art in the Elementary School." *Art in American Life and Education*. Bloomington, Ill.: Public School Publishing Co., 1941.

Munro, T., "Franz Cizek and the Free Expression Method" and "A Constructive Program for Teaching Art." *Art and Education*. Merion, Pa.: Barnes Foundation Press, 1929.

Payant, Felix, *Our Changing Art Education*. Columbus, Ohio: Keramic Studio Publishing Co., 1935.

Pearson, Ralph, *The New Art Education*. New York: Harper and Bros., 1953.

Randall, Arne W., *Murals for Schools*. Worcester: The Davis Press, Inc., 1956.

Schultz, Harold. *Art in the Elementary School*. Univ. of Illinois Press, 1953.

Sobotka, Grace, *Art Instruction in the First Six Grades*. Ann Arbor, Mich.: Edwards Brothers, 1935.

Tomlinson, R. R., *Picture Making by Children*. London: Studio Publications, 1934.

———— *Crafts for Children*. New York: Studio Publications, Inc., 1935.

Viola, Wilhelm, *Child Art and Franz Cizek*. New York: Reynal and Hitchcock, Inc., 1936.

Winslow, L. L., *The Integrated School Art Program*. New York: McGraw-Hill Book Co., 2nd Edition, 1949.

THE CONSCIOUS CREATIVE APPROACHES

General aspects

Arnheim, Rudolph, *Art and Visual Perception:* Univ. of Calif. Press, 1954.

Cole, Luella, *Psychology of Adolescence*. New York: Rinehart and Co., 1942.

D'Amico, V. E. and others, *The Visual Arts in Secondary Education*. New York: Appleton-Century Co. (D.), Inc., 1940.

Faulkner, Ray; Edwin Ziegfeld and Gerald Hill, *Art Today*. New York: Henry Holt and Co., 1941.

Giles, Mary A., *Working Creatively in the Visual Arts with High School Students*. New York: Progressive Assn., 1931.

Hambidge, Jay, *Dynamic Symmetry*. New Haven: Yale Univ. Press, 1936.

Lowenfeld, Viktor, *The Nature of Creative Activity*. Revised Ed. New York: Harcourt, Brace and Co., 1952.

———— "Tests for Visual and Haptical Aptitude." *American Journal of Psychol.,* Vol. 58, 1945.

Meier, N. C., "The Graphic and Allied Arts." *Child Development and the Curriculum.* Bloomington, Ill.: Public School Publishing Co., 1939.

Mumford, Lewis, *Art and Techniques.* New York: Columbia Univ. Press, 1952.

Munro, T., "Adolescence and Art Education." *Methods of Teaching the Fine Arts.* Chapel Hill: Univ. of North Carolina Press, 1935.

———— "Creative Ability in Art, and its Educational Fostering." *Art in American Life and Education.* Bloomington, Ill.: Public School Publishing Co., 1941.

Mursell, J. L., *"The Application of Psychology to the Arts."* New York: *Teachers College Record,* 37, 1936.

Payant, Felix, *Create Something.* Columbus, Ohio: Design Publishing Co., 1943.

Pearson, Ralph, *The New Art Education.* New York: Harper and Bros., 1941.

Poore, H. R., *Art's Place in Education.* New York: G. P. Putnam's Sons, 1937.

Sherman, Hoyt L., *A Manual of Operation with an Emphasis on the Arts.* The Visual Demonstration Center. Columbus: The Ohio State Univ., 1951.

Smith, Janet K., *Design: An Introduction.* Chicago: Ziff-Davis Publishing Co., 1946.

Whittford, W. G. *An Introduction to Art Education.* New York: Appleton-Century (D.) Co., Inc., 1939.

Wiggin, R. G., *Composing in Space.* Dubuque, Iowa: William C. Brown Co., 1949.

Yochim, Louise, *Building Human Relations through Art.* Chicago: L. M. Stein Co., 1954.

Ziegfeld, Ernest, *Art in the College Program.* New York: Columbia Univ. Press, 1953.

Appreciation and history of arts

Baur, John Ireland, *Revolution and Tradition in Modern American Art.* Cambridge: Harvard Univ. Press, 1951.

Boas, Franz, *Primitive Art.* Irvington-on-Hudson: Capitol Publishing Co., Inc., 1950.

Buswell, G. T., *How People Look at Pictures, A Study of the Psychology and Perception of Art.* Chicago: Univ. of Chicago Press, 1935.

Chandler, A. R., *Beauty and Human Nature, Elements of Psychological Aesthetics.* New York: Appleton-Century (D.) Co., Inc., 1934.

Evans, Joan, *Taste and Temperament.* New York: The Macmillan Co., 1939.

Kainz, Luise C. and Olive L. Riley, *Exploring Art.* New York: Harcourt, Brace and Co., 1948.

Leepa, Allen, *The Challenge of Modern Art.* New York: The Beechhurst Press, 1949.

Logan, Frederick M., *Growth of Art in American Schools.* New York: Harper and Bros., 1955.

Lynes, Russell, *The Taste Makers.* New York: Harper and Bros., 1954.

McMahon, A. Philip, *The Art of Enjoying Art.* New York: McGraw-Hill Book Co., 1938.

Munro, T., "Powers of Art Appreciation and Evaluation." *Art in American Life and Education*. Bloomington: Public School Publishing Company, 1942.

Myers, Bernard, *Modern Art in the Making*. New York: McGraw-Hill Book Co., 1950.

Opdyke, George H., *Art and Nature Appreciation*. New York: The Macmillan Co., 1933.

Pearson, Ralph, *The Modern Renaissance in American Art*. New York: Harper and Bros., 1954.

Rathbun, Mary Ch., and Bartlett H. Hayes, Jr., *Layman's Guide to Modern Art*. New York: Oxford Univ. Press, 1949.

Read, Herbert, *Icon and Idea*. Cambridge: Harvard Univ. Press, 1956.

Reid, Louis A., *A Study in Aesthetics*. New York: The Macmillan Co., 1931.

Riley, Olive, *Your Art Heritage*. New York: McGraw-Hill Book Co., 1954.

Schoen, M., *Art and Beauty*. New York: The Macmillan Co., 1932.

Design

Bayer, Herbert, Walter Gropius and Ise Gropius, *Bauhaus, 1919–1928*. New York: Museum of Modern Art, 1939.

Cheney, Sheldon and Martha Candler Cheney, *Art and the Machine*. New York: Whittlesey House, 1936.

Emerson, Sybil. *Design, A Creative Approach*. Scranton: International Textbook Co., 1953.

Frankl, Paul T., *New Dimensions*. New York: Brewer and Warren, Inc., 1928.

Graves, Maitland, *The Art of Color and Design*. New York: McGraw-Hill Book Co., 1941.

Holme, Geoffrey, *Industrial Design and the Future*. London: The Studio, Ltd., 1934.

Kahn, Ely Jacques, *Design in Art and Industry*. New York: Charles Scribner's Sons, 1936.

Kaufmann, Edgar, Jr., *What is Modern Design?* New York: Museum of Modern Art, 1950.

Kepes, Gyorgy, *The Language of Vision*. Chicago: P. Theobald, 1945.

Mangan, James T., *Design, The New Grammar of Advertising*. Chicago: Dartnell Company, 1940.

Moholy-Nagy, Laszlo, *The New Vision*. New York: Wittenborn, Schultz, Inc., 1947.

——— *Vision in Motion*. Chicago: P. Theobald, 1947.

Rasmussen, Henry N., *Art Structure*. New York: McGraw-Hill Book Co., 1950.

Read, Herbert, *Art and Industry*. New York: Harcourt, Brace and Co., 1938.

Smith, Janet, *Design, An Introduction*. Chicago, New York: Ziff-Davis Publishing Co., 1946.

Graphic arts

Biegeleisen, Jacob Israel, *The Silk Screen Printing Process*. New York: McGraw-Hill Book Co., 1941.

Binder, Joseph, *Color in Advertising*. London: The Studio, Ltd., 1934.

Chappell, Warren, *The Anatomy of Lettering*. New York: Loring and Mussey. 1935.

Cooper, Austin, *Making a Poster*. New York: Studio Publishing Co., 1938.

Frankenfield, Henry, *Block Printing with Linoleum*. Camden, N. J.: C. Howard Hunt and Co., 1940.

Friend, Leon and Josephine Hefter, *Graphic Design*. New York: Whittlesey House, 1936.

Holme, Charles G., ed., *Lettering of Today*. London: The Studio, Ltd., 1937.

Pennell, Joseph, *The Graphic Arts*. Chicago: Univ. of Chicago Press, 1921.

Shokler, Harry, *Artists' Manual for Silk Screen Printing*. New York: Amer. Artists Group, 1946.

Sternberg, Harry, *Modern Methods and Materials of Etching*. New York: McGraw-Hill Book Co., 1949.

Summer, Harry, *Handbook of Silk Screen Printing Process*. New York: Creative Crafts Press, 1939.

West, Leon, *Making an Etching*. New York: The Studio Publications, Inc., 1932.

Sculpturing and Modeling

Duncan, Julia H. and Victor D'Amico, *How to make Pottery and Ceramic Sculpture*. Scranton, Pa.: International Textbook Co., 1947.

Glass, Frederick James, *Modeling and Sculpture*. New York: Charles Scribner's Sons, 1929.

Jackson, James, *The Handicraft of Woodcarving*. New York: Pitman Publishing Corp., 1921.

Loland, Charles G., *Woodcarving*. New York: Pitman Publishing Corp., 1931.

Putnam, Brenda, *The Sculpture Way*. New York: Frederick A. Stokes Co., 1939.

Rood, John, *Sculpture in Wood*. Minneapolis: Univ. of Minnesota Press, 1950.

Sowers, J. T., *Woodcarving Made Easy*. New York: Bruce Publishing Co., 1936.

Toft, Albert, *Modeling and Sculpturing*. Philadelphia: J. B. Lippincott Co., 1936.

Wilenski, R. H., *The Meaning of Modern Sculpture*. New York: Frederick A. Stokes Co., 1933.

Architecture and Furniture

Agan, Tessie, *The House*. Philadelphia: J. B. Lippincott Co., 1939.

Goldstein, H. and V., *Art in Everyday Life*. New York: The Macmillan Co., 1940.

Hitchcock, H. R. and Philip Johnson, *The International Style, Architecture since 1922*. New York: W. W. Norton and Co., 1932.

Mumford, Lewis, *Architecture*. New York: American Library Association, 1926.

————— *Sticks and Stones*. New York: W. W. Norton and Co., 1933.

Rogers, Tyler S., *Plan Your House to Suit Yourself*. New York: Charles Scribner's Sons, 1938.

Wright, Frank Lloyd, *Autobiography*. New York: Longmans, Green and Co., 1932.

Crafts

Bayer, Herbert and Walter and Ise Gropius, *Bauhaus*. New York: Museum of Modern Art, 1938.

Butler, J. B., *Problems in Metal Work*. New York: Manual Arts Press, 1929.

Cox, Doris, and Barbara W. Weismann, *Creative Hands*. New York: John Wiley and Sons, Inc., 1945.

Duncan, Hamlin J., and Victor D'Amico, *How to Make Pottery and Ceramic Sculpture*. New York: Museum of Modern Art, 1949.

Flexner, Marion W., *Hand Puppets, A Practical Manual for Teachers*. New York: S. French, Inc., 1935.

Kennard, Joseph S., *Masks and Marionettes*. New York: The Macmillan Co., 1935.

Kenny, John B., *The Complete Book of Pottery Making*. New York: Greenberg Publishers, 1949.

MacIsaac, Frederick J., *The Tony Sarg Marionette Book*. New York: The Viking Press, 1921.

Mansberger, Dale E. and C. W. Pepper, *Plastics, Problems and Processes*. Scranton: International Textbook Co., 1938.

Martin, Charles, and Victor D'Amico, *How to Make Jewelry*. New York: The Museum of Modern Art, 1949.

Perry, Evadna Kraus, *Art Adventures with Discarded Material*. New York: Noble and Noble, Publishers, Inc., 1933.

———— *Crafts for Fun*. New York: William Morrow and Company, Inc., 1940.

Read, Herbert, *Art and Industry*. New York: Harcourt, Brace and Company, 1935.

Robertson, Seonaid. *Creative Crafts in Education*. Boston: Robert Bentley, Inc., 1953.

Wankelman, Willard and Karl Richard and Marietta Wigg, *Arts and Crafts for Teachers*. Dubuque: W. Brown Publ. Co., 1954.

Weinbrenner, Kenneth D., *Jewelry Making as an Art Expression*. Scranton: International Textbook Co., 1952.

Art materials

Clannon, Edward, *Making Your Own Materials*. New York: Museum of Modern Art, Committee on Art in American Education, 1943.

Doerner, Max, *The Materials of the Artist*. New York: Harcourt, Brace and Co., 1934.

Mayer, Ralph, *The Artist's Handbook*. New York: Viking Press, 1940.

ABNORMAL TRENDS IN CREATIVE ACTIVITY

Baker, H. J. and Traphagen, V., *The Diagnosis and Treatment of Behavior Problem Children*. New York: The Macmillan Co., 1935.

Bender, Lauretta, and W. Q. Wolfson, "The Nautical Theme in the Art and Fantasy of Children." *American Journal of Orthopsychiatry*, 13, 1943.

Berrien, F. K., "A Study of the Drawings of Abnormal Children." *J. Educ. Psychol.*, Vol. 26. 143–150, 1935.

Bettelheim, Bruno, Schizophrenic Art, A Case Study. *Scientif. American*, Vol. 186–187, 1952.

Burt, C., *The Young Delinquent*. New York: Appleton-Century Co. (D.), Inc., 1925.

Friedman, I., "Art and Therapy." *Psychoanalytic Review*, 354–361, 1951.

Gaitskell, Charles. *Art Education for Slow Learners*. New York: Charles Bennet, comp., 1953.

Harms, Ernest, "The Arts as Applied to Psychotherapy." *Design,* Vol. 46, No. 6, 1945.

Kris, Ernst, "Psychoanalytic Explorations in Art." *The Psychoanalytic Quarterly,* 1953, Vol. XXII.

Lee, Harry B., "On the Esthetic States of Mind." *Psychiatry: Jour. of the Biology and Pathology of International Relations,* 1947, Vol. 10.

Liss, Edward, "The Graphic Arts." *The American Journal of Orthopsychiatry,* 1938, Vol. VIII, No. I.

Lowenfeld, Berthold, "Psychological Aspects of Blindness." *Encyclopedia of Psychology.* New York: Philosophical Library, 1946.

———— "The Blind Child and His World." *What of the Blind?* New York: American Foundation for the Blind, 1942.

———— "Book Illustrations for Blind Children." *Journal of Exceptional Children,* 1943, Vol. 10, No. 3.

———— *Our Blind Children, Growing and Learning with Them.* Springfield: Charles C Thomas, 1956.

Lowenfeld, Viktor, "Self-Adjustment through Creative Activity." *American Journal of Mental Deficiency,* 1941, Vol. XLV.

———— "Modeling as a Means of Self-Expression in the Schools for the Blind." *The Harvard Educational Review,* 1942. Vol. XII, No. I.

———— *The Nature of Creative Activity.* New York: Harcourt, Brace and Co., 1939.

———— "The Meaning of Creative Activity for the Deaf-Blind." *The Teachers Forum,* American Foundation for the Blind, 1940, Vol. XII.

———— "Therapeutic Aspects of Art" East. Arts Assoc. *Research Bulletin,* 1956, Vol. 5.

Mosse, Eric P., "Painting Analysis in the Therapy of Neuroses." *Psycho-Analytical Review,* 1940.

Naumburg, Margaret, "Studies of the 'Free' Art Expression of Behavior Problem Children and Adolescents as a Means of Diagnosis and Therapy." *Nerv. and Ment. Dis. Monogr.,* New York: Coolidge Foundation, 1947, No. 71.

———— *Schizophrenic Art: Its Meaning in Psychotherapy.* New York: Grune & Stratton, 1950.

Pintner, R., "Artistic Appreciation among Deaf Children." *Amer. Ann. Deaf,* 1941.

Prinzhorn, Hans, *Bildnerei der Geisteskranken.* Berlin: 1923.

Schaefer-Simmern, H., *The Unfolding of Artistic Activity,* Berkeley: Univ. of California Press, 1948.

———— "Color Therapy." *Occupational Therapy,* Feb., 1942.

Schaefer-Simmern, H., and S. B. Sarason, "Therapeutic Implications of Artistic Activity." *American Journal of Mental Deficiency,* 1944, Vol. 49.

Waehner, T. S., "Interpretation of Spontaneous Drawings and Paintings." *Genet. Psychological Monograph,* 1946, Vol. 33.

———— "Formal Criteria for the Analysis of Children's Drawings." *American Journal of Orthopsychiatry,* 1942, Vol. 12.

Woltmann, Adolf, G., "Mud and Clay, Their Function as Developmental Aids." New York: Personality Symposium, 1950.

———— "Plastic Materials as a Psychotherapeutic Medium." *Encyclopedia of Child Guidance.* New York: Philosophical Library, 1943.

INDEX

kinesthetic (?)
personality –

integrity –
stained glass windows